Imagining the Cape Colony

For my mother,
Val Johnson

# Imagining the Cape Colony

History, Literature, and the South African Nation

David Johnson

EDINBURGH
University Press

© David Johnson, 2012, 2013

Edinburgh University Press Ltd
22 George Square, Edinburgh EH8 9LF

First published in hardback by Edinburgh University Press 2012

www.euppublishing.com

Typeset in 10/12pt Goudy Old Style
by, Servis Filmsetting Ltd, Stockport, Cheshire, and
printed and bound in the United States of America

A CIP record for this book is available from the British Library

ISBN 978 0 7486 4308 0 (hardback)
ISBN 978 0 7486 6489 4 (paperback)
ISBN 978 0 7486 5087 3 (webreadyPDF)
ISBN 978 0 7486 5089 7 (epub)

The right of David Johnson
to be identified as author of this work
has been asserted in accordance with
the Copyright, Designs and Patents Act 1988.

# Contents

# Acknowledgments

My first debt is to Jackie Jones at Edinburgh University Press, who contracted the book, and provided wonderful support at every stage of its publication. Eliza Wright and James Dale displayed great professionalism and efficiency in editing the book, and their efforts are much appreciated. It has also been a pleasure to work with Sandy Shepherd of UCT Press, who negotiated and oversaw the details of the co-publication of the book most skilfully and efficiently. Next, I am immensely grateful to three patient and generous friends, who read and commented on drafts of all the chapters in the final six months of re-writing and editing – Emma Barker, Shane Moran and Fiona Wilson. Over a longer period, Shane Moran and Lance Van Sittert read all the earlier drafts, representing 'Literature' and 'History' respectively, and helped me to try and sharpen my arguments. I am indebted to many other people, who gave time and consideration to my work by commenting on individual chapters: Vivian Bickford Smith, Helen Bradford, Richard Brown, Bill Freund, Priya Gopal, Barbara Harlow, Sara Haslam, Stephanie Jones, David Kazanjian, Peter Knox Shaw, Neil Lazarus, Graham MacPhee, Bill Nasson, Anita Pacheco, Nigel Penn, Prem Poddar, Leo Podlashuc, Anita Rupprecht, Kelwyn Sole, Glen Thompson, John Trimbur, Randolph Vigne, Dennis Walder, Linda Waldman and Chris Warnes. Melanie Geustyn and Najwa Hendrickse at the National Library of South Africa in Cape Town were incredibly helpful, as were Sue Ogterop and Sandy Shell at the African Studies Library at the University of Cape Town. I am grateful too for help from several translators: Gerald Groenewald and Alan Marchbank with Dutch texts, Sandrine Legrand with French, Lucia Pradella with German and Anita Pacheco with Portuguese. Aside from translations of Afrikaans passages, the words 'own translation' in the notes refer to their work, not mine. Most of the book was written while working for The Open University, and I am thankful for the unstinting support I have received from my colleagues in the English Department and the Arts Faculty's research committee. Many of the chapters started out as conference or seminar papers, and my arguments have been especially influenced by feedback from History department seminars hosted by Cathy Burns and Keith Breckenridge at the University of KwaZulu-Natal; by

Mohamed Adhikari and Lauren Van Vuuren at the University of Cape Town; by Ciraj Rassool at the University of the Western Cape; and by Bill Nasson at the University of Stellenbosch. Finally, in order to finish the book, I have been helped in various ways by several more people, and would like to record my sincere thanks to them: Gill Clark (who knows what a marathon it's been), Phyl Fenton, Bronwen Findlay, Garth Fourie, Rochelle Kapp, Suvir Kaul, Ania Loomba, Rob Morrell, Clive Van Onselen and Lyn Van Onselen. Substantially shorter versions of some of the chapters have appeared before: Chapter 1 as 'Remembering the Khoikhoi Victory over Dom Francisco Almeida at the Cape in 1510', *Postcolonial Studies* 12, 1 (2009), pp. 107–30; Chapter 2 as 'Representing the Cape "Hottentots", from the French Enlightenment to post-apartheid South Africa' *Eighteenth-Century Studies* 40, 4 (2007), pp. 525–52; and Chapter 5 as 'Historical and Literary Re-iterations of Dutch Settler Republicanism', *South African Historical Journal*, 62, 3 (2010), pp. 463–86.

# Introduction

All nations have an origin, true or fabulous, to which they recur.[1]

On 18 November 2003, South Africa's president Thabo Mbeki delivered a speech to France's National Assembly in which he asserted the connection between eighteenth-century European history and twentieth-century South African politics. According to Mbeki, under apartheid, those struggling against 'racist white minority rule [. . .] would indentify with the French Revolution and draw inspiration', and after the end of apartheid, those struggling for economic justice required 'a realignment of power and what Robespierre called the empire of reason [. . .] our own Age of Enlightenment, with its own Jean-Jacques Rousseau'.[2] As Mbeki was asking for French investment in Southern Africa, his words might be construed as no more than strategic flattery. But his views are shared by many scholars of the eighteenth century, and are expressed concisely in the title of a recent collection of essays, *Postcolonial Enlightenment*, in which the editors declare that 'Postcolonial theory invites us to reconsider the Enlightenment both as an eighteenth century phenomenon and as a concept that bears on modern political formations'.[3]

This book takes up the invitation to reconsider the Enlightenment as both an eighteenth-century phenomenon and a concept bearing on modern political formations by reading the histories and literatures of the Cape Colony during the period 1770–1830 through the critical lenses of the post-apartheid South African nation. The eighteenth-century Cape Colony and post-apartheid South Africa provide a particularly suggestive case study for exploring general questions about the constitution of colonial and postcolonial nationhood. The Cape figured prominently in the writings of several northern hemisphere nations – Portuguese chronicles and epic poems; French travelogues and proto-anthropologies; Scottish Enlightenment theories of political economy, as well as sentimental poems, letters and diaries; and travel narratives by US visitors. There are also significant cases of settlers and indigenes at the Cape 'writing back' to these colonial documents and their normative discourses, with Dutch settler republics declaring independence on the eastern frontier in the 1790s, and the Griqua community of the northern frontier adopting a national constitution in 1813. And as the Cape was a slave economy, the silences and occlusions of these textual constructions of political community at the Cape are at least as interesting and significant. Shifting from the eighteenth to the twentieth century, the post-apartheid South African nation is a useful reference point for exploring how the concept of the Enlightenment bears upon modern political formations. Instancing a unique and historically specific form of the postcolonial nation-state, and at the same time sharing with other developing nations the contradictions of contemporary neo-colonialism, post-apartheid South Africa offers abundant opportunity for examining the continuing dissonances between the democratic idealism of the Enlightenment and the (post)colonial violence and exploitation that have shadowed it.

Two debates structure this study. The first is the historical debate about how northern hemisphere conceptions of nationhood were 'exported' to the colonies. In Benedict Anderson's influential argument, the eighteenth-century revolutions of the 'Creole Pioneers' in the Americas, and then of the Jacobins in France, provided templates for subsequent colonial nationalisms. Anderson contends that 'once [the French Revolution] had occurred, it entered the accumulating memory of print [. . . T]he experience was shaped by millions of printed words into a "concept" on the printed page, and in due course, into a model'.[4] In the same fashion, the American independence movements became 'as soon as they were printed about, "concepts", "models", and indeed "blueprints"'.[5] As a result, 'by the second decade of the nineteenth century, if not earlier, a "model" of "the" independent national state was available for pirating'.[6] Applying Anderson's arguments to Southern Africa, the proposition would be: the 'imagining' of the communities of the Cape Colony, and subsequently of the South African nation, were decisively informed by the models of nationhood generated in the Americas and France.

In assessing whether Anderson's theory of colonial nationalisms fits the Cape Colony and South Africa, two objections are given particular weight. The first is Partha Chatterjee's argument questioning the dependency of anti-colonial nationalisms. For Chatterjee, the agency of those in 'the rest of the world' is diminished in Anderson's formulation:

> If nationalisms in the rest of the world have to choose their imagined community from certain 'modular' forms already made available to them by Europe and the Americas, what do they have left to imagine? History, it would seem, has decreed that we in the postcolonial world shall be perpetual consumers of modernity. Europe and the Americas, the only true subjects of history, have thought out on our behalf not only the script of colonial enlightenment and exploitation, but also that of our anticolonial resistance and postcolonial misery. Even our imaginations must remain forever colonized. I object to this argument not for any sentimental reason. I object because I cannot reconcile it with the evidence of anticolonial nationalism. The most powerful as well as the most creative results of the nationalist imagination in Asia and Africa are posited not on identity but rather on a *difference* with the 'modular' forms of the national society propagated by the modern West.[7]

Chatterjee elaborates his case against Anderson by analysing the distinctive histories of anti-colonial nationalism in West Bengal.[8] Although Chatterjee misrepresents Anderson's arguments in order to stress the agency of Bengal's anti-colonial nationalists,[9] his rhetoric is salutary in drawing attention to how colonial nationalisms have resisted/subverted/even ignored northern hemisphere models of nationhood. Even more so than Anderson's metaphor of colonial nationalisms 'pirating' northern hemisphere models, Chatterjee's formulation demands attention to the political imagination of the colonised.

The second objection is that Anderson's emphasis on the nationalisms of the Americas and France diminishes the formative influence of the period's global superpower – the British Empire. This obvious but important insight has been reiterated recently by Maya Jasanoff:

> The American Revolution marked the [British] empire's single greatest defeat until the era of World War II. Yet in the space of a mere ten years, it bounced back to an astonishing extent. Building on earlier precedents, British power regrouped, expanded, and reshaped itself across the world – in Ireland and India, Canada and the Caribbean, Africa and Australia. All told, the 1780s stand out as the most eventful single decade in British imperial history up to the 1940s. What was more, the events of these years cemented an enduring framework for the principles and practice of British rule. This 'spirit of 1783,' so to speak, animated the British Empire well into the twentieth century – and provided a model of liberal constitutional empire that stood out as a vital alternative to the democratic republics taking shape in the United States, France, and Latin America.[10]

Jasanoff's historical snapshot over-states the significance and status of the American Revolution, but the general point about the influence of Britain's 'model of liberal constitutional empire' as opposed to those of 'the democratic republics' of the United States, France and Latin America has substance, particularly in relation to Southern Africa. With Britain seizing the Cape from the Dutch in 1795, returning it to the Batavian Republic in 1803, reclaiming it in 1806 and then governing the Cape as a British colony until the Union of South Africa in 1910, the British model of nation and colony was hegemonic in Southern Africa. As Robert Ross has argued, English nationalism at the Cape was 'the prime nationalism of South Africa, against which all subsequent ones, whether Afrikaner or African, reacted, either directly or at a remove'.[11]

The second debate is a political one: how does the post-apartheid present inform the reading of South Africa's colonial past? Again, Anderson provides a helpful point of departure. Reflecting upon how his political present informed his writing about the pasts of colonial nationalisms, Anderson has noted how much he was influenced by anti-colonial struggles and their postcolonial denouements:

> [N]ationalist leaders like Nkrumah in Ghana, Sekou Touré in Guinée, Nehru in India, Ho Chi Minh in Vietnam, and Tito in Yugoslavia were still widely

admired in the Bandung Conference spirit. When I returned to the United States [from Indonesia] in 1964, the Vietnam War was looming on the horizon, and the long 1960s were well under way. In the Cold War context, Third World nationalism looked very attractive, and most of my age-mates in academia were very sympathetic. It was thus easy enough for us later on, watching the decay of the Nkrumah, Soekarno, Nehru, Tito, and Touré regimes, to view it in terms of a Fall, given these men's impressive experience in fighting for independence. It has also to be remembered that *Imagined Communities* was written in a polemical spirit, against (especially British) colonialism and imperialism.[12]

Anderson casts the histories of the transition from admiration for Nkrumah's generation of nationalist leaders during their anti-colonial fight for independence to disappointment at their subsequent postcolonial decay as a version of the Old Testament narrative of the Fall, but his reading might more precisely be cast as tragedy: anti-colonial heroes rise to power during the struggle for liberation but are undone by fatal flaw(s) in the postcolonial moment. However, by insisting that *Imagined Communities* was written in a polemical spirit against colonialism and imperialism, he tries to resist the reactionary teleology implicit in the narrative of the Biblical Fall (or indeed the genre of tragedy).

The contradictions Anderson identifies between anti-colonial heroism and postcolonial decay echo in post-apartheid South Africa. But as interesting as the psychologies of the individuals who have travelled from struggle-hero-to-postcolonial-sell-out might be, the more difficult challenge is to understand the structural contradiction in the postcolonial present between national-democratic political discourses on the one hand, and neo-colonial economies on the other. A recent study of the new social movements in South Africa summarises the economic disparities that have increased in the new millennium, notwithstanding the African National Congress (ANC) government's rhetoric:

The net effect of this coupling of economic globalisation and the democratic transition [...] has been devastating. According to the Report of the Committee of Inquiry into a Comprehensive System of Social Security for South Africa, unemployment stands at 36 per cent for the overall population and at 52 per cent for African females. Poverty is pervasive and, according to a recent committee of inquiry for the Department of Social Welfare, stands at an astounding 45 to 55 per cent. About 10 per cent of African people are malnourished and at least 25 per cent of African children are stunted. Evidence suggests that key indicators, such as unemployment and the number of households without a breadwinner, are deteriorating. The level of inequality is also getting worse. South Africa has always been one of the most unequal societies in the world, and the incoming ANC government in 1994 committed itself to addressing this problem. Yet despite the post-apartheid regime's rhetorical commitment to redistribution, the Gini coefficient continued to rise throughout the ANC's first two terms of office. One factor worth noting, however, is that the racial profile of inequality is changing. This is reflected in the fact that the size of the

African component in the richest income decile rose from 9 per cent in 1991 to 22 per cent in 1996. The racial profile of the poorest has, however, remained black, leading many commentators to conclude that the present economic dispensation benefits only a tiny elite within the black population.[13]

These increased economic inequalities co-exist uneasily with the democratic equalities proclaimed in the political discourses of the Mbeki presidencies (June 1999 to September 2008). This contradiction in the present functions as *the* organising problematic for reading the histories and literatures of Cape Colony, 1770–1830. In other words, in studying the forms of political community imagined at the Cape from the late eighteenth century onwards, my inquiries are principally concerned with understanding the relationship between political discourses and modes of economic production.

Juxtaposing the past of Cape Colony history and the present of South African post-apartheid politics requires the negotiation of conflicting pressures. On the one hand, histories of the distant colonial past cannot fully explain the political present without some understanding of the intervening years. The historian Frederick Cooper illustrates the perils of 'leapfrogging legacies'[14] by pointing to two examples: first, to histories in the United States that blame black poverty on the legacy of slavery, but skip over the period of urbanisation and industrialisation between 1863 to 1963, and second, to Mahmood Mamdani's histories that explain authoritarianism and ethnicity in Africa in the 1980s and 1990s as the result of colonial policy of the 1920s and 1930s, but fail to attend to crucial economic and political transitions in the 1950s. On the other hand, obeying the protocols of historical scholarship might suppress connections between the colonial past and the neo-colonial present. This danger is registered in relation to twentieth-century European history by Walter Benjamin, who warned that 'every image of the past that is not recognised by the present as one of its own concerns threatens to disappear irretrievably'; he accordingly enjoined critics to 'seize hold of a memory as it flashes up in a moment of danger'.[15] Without reprising Benjamin's messianic idiom, Suvir Kaul extends the spirit of Benjamin's injunction to the colonial past by arguing that 'postcolonial histories of empire thus diagnose the past with a robust sense of the present, that is, with a clear understanding of the particular form in which the colonial past impinges on, and continues to shape, the politically decolonized present'.[16] Can these competing pressures – to be true to the historical past and to register the political pressures of the present – be reconciled? In relation to the eighteenth-century Cape Colony and post-apartheid South Africa, the objection to leapfrogging the legacies of the nineteenth and twentieth centuries is irrefutable. South Africa's post-apartheid present has clearly been deeply marked by these more recent histories. However, the cost of retaining a professional silence about the continuities from the colonial to the post-colonial is the suppression of the dialectical interconnectedness of past and present.

A second methodological tension to negotiate is the one between the general theories of colonial nationalism by the likes of Anderson, and the specific histories and literatures of the Cape Colony. South African literary criticism and historiography have long been characterised by an intellectual version of 'the cultural cringe', with successive generations of South African critics and historians completing apprenticeships in northern hemisphere universities, and then applying their learnt craft to Southern African materials. Roberto Schwarz identifies the same kind of derivative intellectual culture in Brazil: 'it is a fatal consequence of our cultural dependency that we are always interpreting our reality with conceptual systems created somewhere else, whose basis lies in other social processes'.[17] In South African literary criticism, British and American masters have routinely been copied by their colonial sons (and occasionally daughters), as in the case of F. R. Leavis and his Cambridge journal *Scrutiny* in the 1930s being emulated by Geoffrey Durrant and the Pietermaritzburg journal *Theoria* in the 1950s. South African historiography has followed a similar pattern, with the adoption and adaptation of E. P. Thompson's 1960s practice of social history by the Witwatersrand University's History Workshop in the 1970s an example.[18] Rather than following this established sequence, the aspiration here is to demonstrate that the specifics of Southern African colonial nationalisms demand the rethinking of general theories of colonial nationalism, which themselves were of course forged in relation to specific colonial and postcolonial histories (Anderson on South-East Asia, Chatterjee on West Bengal). In other words, in addition to applying general theories of colonial nationalism to the particulars of the Southern African case, the particulars of the Southern African case function as a questions or challenges to those general theories.

Finally, my discussion of literature and its relation to South Africa's colonial and postcolonial nationalisms also sets out from Anderson's well-known arguments. To recap: borrowing from Benjamin, Anderson argues that with the decline of the religious communities and dynastic realms of the middle ages in the eighteenth century, 'the medieval idea of simultaneity-along-time is [replaced by] an idea of "homogenous, empty time," in which simultaneity is, as it were, transverse, cross-time, marked not by prefiguring and fulfilment, but by temporal coincidence, and measured by clock and calendar'.[19] For Anderson, the novel and newspaper are the two key forms for conveying this new conception of time, and for imagining political community in new ways. Providing an example of a hypothetical novel, he demonstrates how within a novel acts are performed 'at the same clocked, calendrical time, but by actors who may be largely unaware of one another, [thus showing] the novelty of this imagined world conjured up by the author in the readers' minds'.[20] When he turns to actual novels, Anderson argues that narratives of nationhood are homologous with literary narratives. In contributing to the construction of national cultures, novels (and other literary texts) narrate conflicts between characters and their resolution in ways that parallel conflicts within the nation and their hoped-for resolution or containment. Especially instructive are Anderson's examples of novels from the nineteenth-century United States in which 'imaginings of fraternity [emerge] "naturally" in a society fractured by the most violent racial, class and regional antagonisms':[21] in James Fenimore Cooper's *The Pathfinder* (1840), a deep bond unites the white woodsman Natty Bumppo and the Delaware chieftain Chingachgook; in Herman Melville's *Moby Dick* (1851), Ishmael and the Polynesian Queequeg cosily share a bed at the Spouter Inn; and in Mark Twain's *Huckleberry Finn* (1881), the white Huck and black Jim drift companionably on the Mississippi. Neil Larsen acknowledges the impact of Anderson's argument when he notes that it is now a 'perfectly commonsensical idea that "literature" – as a subject of "narrative" – simultaneously "constructs" the national culture or tradition that it had formerly been assumed merely to embody and represent'.[22]

Complementing my engagement with Anderson's theory of nation and novel is a critical dialogue with Fredric Jameson's theory of national allegory, and perhaps as importantly, with the many subsequent challenges to his category of national allegory. Jameson's provocative generalisation that 'all third-world texts are necessarily [. . .] allegorical, and in a very specific way they are to be read as what I will call *national allegories*'[23] has been endlessly criticised, but it has at the same time been applied to many specific nations and their literatures. A recent search of the MLA database lists scholarly contributions on Jameson's national allegory in relation to the literatures and cinema of India, Nigeria, the United States, Vietnam, Mexico, Lithuania, China, the Soviet Union, Egypt, Argentina, Italy, Cuba, Britain, Algeria, North Korea, South Africa, Spain, Japan, Turkey, Malaysia, Kenya, the Philippines and Cameroon. There is a consistency in the structure of these interventions, as they all begin with a gesture to Jameson's argument, and then proceed to establish how the specifics of one selected nation + its literature exceed, complicate or confound Jameson's generalisations. The most frequent objection is summed up in Aijaz Ahmad's polemic, in which he argues that instead of Jameson's 'national allegory', 'we replace the idea of the "nation" with that larger, less restricted idea of "collectivity", and [. . .] start thinking of the process of allegorization not in nationalistic terms but simply as a relation between private and public, personal and communal'.[24] For all the persuasiveness of these replies to Jameson – and I will add to them by examining South African literary works that do not fit the category of national allegory – my own arguments retain a sense of the need to interrogate the nexus between national/political and literary narratives.[25]

With these different concerns in mind, the first four chapters examine how the Cape was imagined by northern hemisphere writers of different nations, with each chapter organised in relation to a contemporary issue or question. Chapter 1 focuses on how Luís de Camões and the Portuguese chroniclers narrated their nation's defeat to the Khoikhoi in Table Bay in 1510, as well as on the reinterpretation of this moment of anti-colonial resistance by British writers like Robert Southey, and South African writers and politicians. Chapter 2 contrasts how French travellers of the early modern period and of the eighteenth century (notably Jean-Jacques Rousseau) produced variable racial identities for the Cape 'Hottentots'. Chapter 3 analyses how Scottish Enlightenment figures like Adam Smith combined political economy and sentiment in scripting a future for the Cape. Chapter 4 uses President John Adams as a point of departure in order to explore how two writers on opposite sides during the American Revolution applied their discourses of land ownership and landscape appreciation in their writings on the Cape. In the final three chapters, the reception, mutation and reformulation of these northern hemisphere concepts of nationhood are analysed in relation to texts both by and about three communities:

the Dutch settler republicans of Graaff-Reinet and Swellendam during the 1790s in Chapter 5; the Cape slaves who rebelled unsuccessfully in 1808 and 1825 in Chapter 6; and the emergent Griqua nation of the early nineteenth century in Chapter 7. As the South African nation has continued to be constituted in forms of writing both historical and literary, in all the chapters the many subsequent histories and literary works which have rewritten the Cape Colony are discussed in detail. Indeed, more than just being 'constituted', the categories of the 'South African nation', 'South African history' and 'South African literature' have always been contested, and remain works-in-progress.

## NOTES

1. Sonnerat, *A Voyage*, p. i.
2. Mbeki, 'Address of the President of South Africa, Thabo Mbeki, at the French National Assembly'.
3. Festa and Carey, 'Introduction', p. 5.
4. Anderson, *Imagined*, p. 80.
5. Ibid. p. 81.
6. Ibid. p. 81.
7. Chatterjee, *The Nation*, p. 5.
8. Anderson does not deal explicitly with Chatterjee's objections in his subsequent book, *The Spectre of Comparisons*, and modifies only slightly the arguments of *Imagined Communities*. The one modification of interest in this context is that the northern hemisphere 'modular forms' described in the earlier book are now conceived as having a haunted subconscious: '[c]olonialism was also nightmare-haunted, because one can plausibly argue, on the evidence, that it dreamed of incipient nationalism before nationalists came into historical existence' (Anderson, *The Spectre*, p. 65).
9. For a defence of Anderson and critique of Chatterjee, see Lazarus, *Nationalism*, pp. 128–33.
10. Jasanoff, *Liberty's Exiles*, pp. 11–12.
11. Ross, *Status*, p. 43.
12. Anderson, 'Responses', p. 231.
13. Ballard et al., 'Introduction', pp. 13–14. These findings are elaborated in Seekings and Nattrass, *Class*, pp. 300–39; and Marais, *South Africa*, pp. 203–37.
14. Cooper, 'Postcolonial', p. 405.
15. Benjamin, *Illuminations*, p. 255.
16. Kaul, 'Coda', p. 306.
17. Schwarz, *Misplaced*, p. 39.
18. This kind of intellectual traffic continues, and this study of course participates in it. With respect to literary criticism, I have discussed the importing of US and British postcolonial theory to South Africa in 'Importing'; and in history-writing, a recent example is Bruno Latour's 1980s network theory providing an analytical vocabulary for post-2000 histories by Alan Lester (*Imperial Networks. Creating Identities in Nineteenth-Century South Africa and Britain* (2001)) and Kerry Ward (*Networks of Empire. Forced Migration in the Dutch East India Company* (2009)).
19. Anderson, *Imagined*, p. 24.
20. Ibid. p. 26.
21. Ibid. p. 203
22. Larsen, *Determinations*, p. 170.

23. Jameson, 'Third-World Literature', p. 69.
24. Ahmad, *In Theory*, p. 110.
25. For a reading of Jameson's theory of national allegory along these lines, see Szeman, 'Who's Afraid'.

# 1 Remembering the Khoikhoi Victory over Dom Francisco de Almeida at the Cape in 1510: Luís de Camões and Robert Southey

In a speech delivered to the South African National Assembly to mark the retirement of Nelson Mandela on 26 March 1999, South African president Thabo Mbeki referred to the victory of the Khoikhoi[1] over the Portuguese Viceroy Dom Francisco de Almeida and his forces in Table Bay on 1 March 1510:

> We are blessed because you [Mandela] have walked along the road of our heroes and heroines. For centuries our own African sky has been dark with suffering and foreboding. But because we have never surrendered, for centuries the menace in our African sky has been brightened by the light of our stars. In the darkness of our night, the victory of the Khoikhoi in 1510 here in Table Bay, when they defeated and killed the belligerent Portuguese admiral and aristocrat, Dom Francisco de Almeida, the first Portuguese viceroy in India, has lit our skies for ever.[2]

Mbeki's tribute to this Khoikhoi victory is unusual, as Almeida's defeat at the Cape has been remembered only sporadically in the last 500 years. I examine three moments when it was remembered – by Portuguese writers in the sixteenth century, by British writers in the period 1770–1830, and by Southern African writers in the nineteenth and twentieth centuries. Literary treatments of the early Portuguese explorers rounding the Cape have largely ignored Almeida's defeat, and have instead repeated versions of the mythic tale of Adamastor, the exiled Titan confined to Table Mountain in eternal punishment by Zeus for threatening to rape the white nymph Thetis. Having reflected on the histories of the Khoikhoi victory and the literary rewritings of Adamastor's defeat, I return in conclusion to the implications of Mbeki's invocation of the Khoikhoi victory over Almeida in post-apartheid South Africa. Mbeki is hardly the first politician to appropriate histories of resistance for post-independence political ends, but the long and complex reception history of this particular event casts his intervention in the postcolonial present in especially clear relief.

## PORTUGUESE ACCOUNTS OF THE SIXTEENTH CENTURY

There were detailed accounts of Almeida's defeat in the Portuguese history chronicles, with versions by João de Barros (1496–1570),[3] Fernão Lopes de Castanheda (1501–59),[4] Damião de Góis (1501–73),[5] and Gaspar Corrêa (d. 1562).[6] They explain that Almeida's fatal journey to the Cape followed the protracted transfer of power in India to his successor Afonso de Albuquerque, and describe how his three ships set sail from Cochin on 19 November 1509, making good progress until setting ashore for water on the south-western tip of Africa.[7] After successful exchanges with the Khoikhoi of calico and iron for cattle, a group of about twelve Portuguese accompanied them to their village inland. What then transpired is unclear. According to Barros, a quarrel arose because the 'negroes took [the Portuguese's daggers], and also other things that pleased them'.[8] In condemning the Khoikhoi, however, Barros is in the minority, as the other accounts blame the Portuguese. Castanheda records the Portuguese leaders recognising that 'very likely their own people were at fault',[9] and Corrêa goes even further, conceding that the Khoikhoi legitimately 'feared we might wish to build a fortress there also and take their watering place, and thus they would lose their cattle'.[10] Describing the conduct of Almeida's sailors, he notes that 'as it is always the character of the Portuguese to endeavour to rob the poor natives of the country of their property, there were some sailors who tried to take a cow without giving what the negroes asked for it'.[11] The Khoikhoi chased the sailors back to their ships, where they at once begged Almeida to exact revenge. Almeida duly conducted a council of war in which (according to De Góis) he acknowledged that 'the fault lay with our people, whose habit it is to be disorderly and ill-conducted in strange countries'.[12] Despite these reservations, a reluctant Almeida and 150 men marched on the village, armed with swords, lances and crossbows. Upon reaching the village, the Portuguese seized a number of children and cattle, when 'the Hottentots, about one hundred and seventy in number, attacked them with stones and assegais of fire hardened wood, against which their weapons proved useless'.[13] The Khoikhoi deployed their cattle as moving shields, hiding behind them, and accurately throwing assegais and stones at the Portuguese. Retreating in disarray to their ships, sixty-five Portuguese were killed, including Almeida and eleven senior officials. Barros stresses the ignominy of their deaths: '[They were] killed by sticks and stones, hurled not by giants or armed men but by bestial negroes, the most brutal of all that coast'.[14]

The story of Almeida's humiliating end in Table Bay interrupted Portugal's sequence of military and naval victories in Africa and Asia, and the uneasy contemplation of its causes by the chroniclers adds weight to Reinhart Koselleck's suggestive hypothesis that 'if history is made in the short run by the victors, historical gains in knowledge stem in the long run from the vanquished'.[15] Barros applauds Almeida's courage and sense of honour, but argues that his fate was meant as a lesson to future generations: 'God allowed this to happen as an example to the living, that they may learn to be more anxious to gain a good name than to acquire wealth'.[16] Barros's judgement is consistent with his life-long commitment to serving Portugal's rulers by his writings, which were produced under the relatively generous patronage of

Dom Manuel I, who reigned from 1495–1521, and Dom João III, who reigned from 1521–57. Educated at the royal court, and then travelling to Guinea in 1522, he settled into secure employment in Lisbon, first as court treasurer from 1525–8, and then for thirty years as factor of the *Casa da India e Mina*. In contrast to Barros, both Corrêa and De Góis were much more critical. Corrêa hints that prior wrong-doing by Almeida caused his death: 'The negroes pursued the viceroy [. . .] And by the misfortune caused by sin, it happened that a stone struck him on the knee and he fell'.[17] Unlike Barros, Corrêa worked most of his life in the East, remote from the European centre of power, and failed to win patronage for his writings, which were never published during his own lifetime. In his biography of Corrêa, Aubrey Bell concludes that 'those in authority [. . .] were too busy enriching themselves to pay attention to [Corrêa's] carping; it was easier to lock up the manuscript, to brush the noisy fly from one's velvet sleeve'.[18] The most explicit condemnation of Almeida is by De Góis:

> [H]ere [the Portuguese] were slain by the hands of unarmed savages with stones and assegais of untempered iron, with so little resolution on their part that it would seem as if God had ordained that they should perish in that place, as a punishment for some cruelties or injustice of which they may have been guilty in their victories which He granted them.[19]

De Góis echoes Corrêa's criticisms, conceding that the Portuguese had a history of being 'disorderly and ill-conducted in strange countries', and attributing the deaths of Almeida and his men to past cruelties and injustices. Like Corrêa, De Góis spent formative years outside Portugal, in his case working in Portugal's diplomatic service in Sweden, Poland, Denmark and Holland, where he was influenced by humanist thinkers like Desiderius Erasmus (1466–1536). He returned to Lisbon in 1546 to work as Keeper of the Archives, and had his *Chronicles* published in 1566. He fell foul of the Inquisition in 1571 for alleged heresy, and died two years later in suspicious circumstances while imprisoned at the monastery of Batalha.

The poet Luís Vas de Camões (1524–80) read the historical accounts of the death of Almeida by Castanheda, Barros, Corrêa (in manuscript form) and De Góis,[20] and refers to it at three points in his epic *The Lusíads* (1572). In Canto One, an ominous note is introduced when Camões-the-poet lists all the Portuguese heroes, including 'the fearsome / Almeidas, whom the Tagus still laments'.[21] In Canto Five, the death of Almeida is predicted in more detail by Adamastor in his angry speech to Da Gama:

> 'As for your first viceroy, whose fame
> Fortune will beacon to the heavens,
> Here will be his far-flung tomb
> By God's inscrutable judgement,
> Here he will surrender the opulent
> Trophies wrung from the Turkish fleet,
> And atone for his bloody crimes, the massacre
> Of Kilwa, the levelling of Mombassa.'[22]

The third account of Almeida's death in Canto Ten is the longest, and is recounted by the sea goddess Tethys to Da Gama. Narrating the deeds of the Portuguese explorers who were to follow Da Gama, Tethys pays tribute to Almeida for his victories in Kilwa, Mombassa and Diu before describing his defeat and death:

> 'The Cape of Storms, which keeps his memory
> Along with his bones, will be unashamed
> In dispatching from the world such a soul
> Not Egypt nor all India could control.
>
> For there, brute savages will achieve
> What eluded more skilled enemies,
> And fire-hardened knobkerries do
> What bows and canon-balls could not;
> God's judgements are inscrutable;
> Pagans, unable to comprehend,
> Attribute to ill fortune or mischance
> What providence ordains and heaven grants.'[23]

The use of the future prophetic voice and of three different narrators (Camões-the-poet, Adamastor and Tethys) to describe Almeida's death might complicate Camões's version, but the repetition of the idea that his death is beyond human comprehension by both Adamastor and Tethys imposes a consistently fatalistic vision. Notwithstanding these three references, the details of Almeida's defeat and more particularly of the character of Portugal's Khoikhoi adversaries remain opaque; as David Quint argues, Camões 'erases the historical natives by turning Adamastor into an image of Portuguese pride and achievement'.[24]

Unlike the disapproving chroniclers, Camões passes no negative judgement on Almeida. Elsewhere in *The Lusíads*, there are passages critical of Portugal's endeavours in Asia – the 'Old Man of the Restelo' berates the Eastward-bound sailors in Canto Four,[25] and Tethys admonishes Da Gama in Canto Nine to 'Keep Avarice under the strictest curb, / And Ambition too'.[26] Looking at the work as a whole, however, it is clear that these occasional criticisms are quibbles over strategic priorities rather than substantial ideological disagreements. In the closing stanzas, the poet-narrator exhorts Portugal to 'Hold your knights in high esteem / For their bloody and intrepid fervour / Extends not only the Holy Faith, / But the boundaries of your great empire',[27] and Islamic centres of power are identified as appropriate prizes – 'destroy by way of Cape Espartel / The ramparts of Morocco or Taroudant'.[28] Politically, Camões therefore appears much closer to Barros than to Corrêa and De Góis, but the personal and social pressures determining his literary choices should be noted. Born into the untitled nobility (*cavalleiro fidalgo*), Camões embarked on a love affair with Caterine de Ataide in 1544, which (it has been speculated) contributed to his exile two years later. Fighting as a common soldier in Morocco, he lost his left eye in 1547, and returned home with reputation restored. This reprieve was short-lived, however, as his return to Lisbon ended following a brawl in 1552, which led to a second exile, this time in India. Serving with distinction on a number of maritime military expeditions, Camões's next brush with authority saw him imprisoned in 1561–2 when Viceroy Francisco Barreto took offence to a satire he had written. After his release from prison, Camões still failed to accumulate wealth, and he left Goa for Lisbon in 1567, spending two years in Mozambique en route in desperate poverty. Having spent at least a decade working on *The Lusíads*, Camões finally saw the work published in 1572. Camões's straitened circumstances were noted by his contemporary, the historian Diogo de Couto, who said the poet was so poor that he depended on his friends for food.[29] Without pondering too deeply the 'poetic intention' in *The Lusíads*, such pressures suggest that Camões had strong motives for writing to win patronage. If the chroniclers were obliged to pander to the prejudices of their patrons during the reigns of Manuel I and João III, the nation's greatest poet worked under even greater duress. Camões was faced with the challenge of writing for the young king Dom Sebastião, who ascended the throne at the age of fourteen in 1568, and who has been justly described as 'one of the least auspicious audiences imaginable'.[30] Educated in an atmosphere of religious zealotry, Sebastião shunned commerce and humanism in favour of reviving the values of medieval chivalry, and Camões tailored his poem to the young monarch's tastes by casting Da Gama's voyage to India in the idiom of crusading patriotism.

Another key to understanding the range of judgements on Almeida's defeat might be located in the different generic imperatives of the historical chronicle and the epic poem. There was an obligation to glorify the powerful in chronicles and epics, but both genres also allowed some space to criticise. The Renaissance historical chronicle was driven by potentially conflicting aims, namely to record for posterity in annalistic order the deeds of the past, and second, to derive from these deeds morally instructive lessons for the present. The moral lessons here were all oriented towards exalting the Portuguese nation. In practice, the narration of facts in annalistic sequence, with little distinction between facts of major and minor importance, had the potential to undermine the ambition to moralise and exalt. The lessons derived by De Góis and Corrêa clearly did not always show Portugal's explorers like Almeida in an exalted light, and the contemporary reception of their work would appear to confirm the disadvantages of the chronicle as a genre for the vulnerable writer. By contrast, both Barros and Camões viewed the epic as more uncomplicatedly suited to glorifying the powerful. Early in his career, Barros had written the romance *Crónica do Imperador Clarimundo* (1520), which concludes with prophecies of Portuguese glory, but he later questioned the value of romances and lyrics and expressed a preference for the epic: 'Of old, at the tables of lords and princes the notable deeds of great men were sung in verse [. . .] If this practice were introduced in Spain and all Europe there would be more profit in such music than in these lovelorn songs and lyrics'.[31] Like Barros, Camões in the early part of his career wrote in a wide variety of poetic and dramatic genres, but ultimately in *The Lusíads* embraced the epic as the genre most likely to win applause. Camões self-consciously followed Virgil's *Aeneid*, but whereas – as Bakhtin explains – the epic characteristically celebrates heroes engaged in feats of arms located 'on an utterly different and inaccessible time-and-value plane',[32] Camões celebrated recent

Portuguese explorers and their relatively peaceful voyages of discovery. According to Richard Helgerson, the epic form predisposed Camões to imagine 'a Portugal that prefers *gloria* to *proveito* [and] Camões aims to bring such a nation into existence by showing it an ideal image of its heroic and nonmercantile self'.[33] Camões excelled in satisfying this requirement, as he claims repeatedly that the achievements of the Portuguese voyagers exceed not only those of earlier historical conquerors like Alexander and Trajan, but also those of classical heroes like Aeneas.

Finally, the contrasting interpretations of Almeida's defeat should be read in the context of the competing ideologies of Portugal's ruling fractions. There was a cleavage within Portugal's ruling class between feudal landowners, who embraced military and chivalric ideals appropriate to the plunder of North Africa's Moorish centres of power, and an emergent merchant class sponsored by the Crown, who were committed to (relatively) peaceful long-distance trade.[34] Recent historians have stressed that the Portuguese language of Christian honour and chivalry concealed a political economy based upon the violent plunder of North and West Africa. Malyn Newitt explains that 'Portuguese expansion was a direct by-product of Portugal's poverty, not wealth [. . .] With the land yielding poor returns, the nobility had always been inclined to seek its fortunes through armed exploits'.[35] These armed exploits involved slavery and kidnapping:

> The voyages of 'discovery' down the coasts of Africa, organised after 1430 by the Infante Dom Henrique and other noblemen, were openly and explicitly a series of raids designed to obtain slaves for sale or important 'Moors' who might be ransomed.[36]

The constant foe for Portugal was Islam, and the function of Portuguese writers was to justify Portugal's military expansion. Robin Blackburn concludes bluntly that 'in a world menaced by Muslim intrigue [Camões] thought Portugal was justified in resorting to what, in another context, would be simple piracy'.[37] These militaristic values were celebrated in Gil Vicente's *The Exhortation to War* (1514), which has Penthesilea, Queen of the Amazons, address King Manuel, and exhort him to 'Gain the fame of fearsomeness, / Not of riches, for that's dangerous', and Hannibal likewise declares that 'No honour can come from gowns, / Nor the richest dresses, / But only from noble deeds'.[38] The same sentiments are expressed in Barros's conviction that it is more important to acquire a good name than wealth, and in Camões's Old Man of the Restelo warning Da Gama that 'You ignore the enemy at the gate / In the search for another so far away'.[39] By contrast, the ideology of peaceful trade was less stridently expressed, although it too 'stood in opposition to a Christian sovereign's purported interest in honor and justice'.[40] Supplemented by an emergent humanist discourse, commercial priorities underlie De Góis and Corrêa's criticisms of the needless aggression of Almeida's sailors at the Cape, and in De Góis's opinion that Almeida and his men had been punished for 'some cruelties or injustice of which they may have been guilty in their victories'. To a substantial extent, however, the military and mercantile factions were compatible, and the occasional criticisms of imperial excesses by the likes of De Góis and Corrêa reflected little more than the views of a minority of Portuguese intellectuals who had been touched by European humanism. As Neil Larsen and Robert Krueger point out, these Portuguese humanists functioned 'as advisors to the nobiliarchical state until such time as their counsel proved more dangerous than useful to the reactionary interests which had hired them'.[41]

## BRITISH ACCOUNTS OF 1770–1830

In the seventeenth and eighteenth centuries, there were occasional references to Almeida's death in Table Bay, and more generally to the Portuguese failures to establish a settlement at the Cape. For example, Thomas Herbert stopped at the Cape in 1627, and recalled Almeida's fate:

> *Almeyda*, one of the bravest Captains the Portugals ever had [. . .] with eleven experienced Captains and other gallants upon a small affront putting some of the savages to death (who grew desperate in revenge) were unexpectedly set upon by these naked Barbarians, who had the *arma antiqua*, i.e. *manu, ungues, dentes*, and slain were every man of them.[42]

The Dutch sea captain Abraham Bogaert, who visited the Cape in 1702, praised the Khoikhoi fulsomely when he referred to Almeida:

> These people [the Khoikhoi] hold freedom very much to heart, and are very jealous of it. They will obey no laws other than those of Nature [. . .] Also they keep the law of Nations so unimpaired, that they can rival the most civilised peoples of Europe. Furthermore, it has been seen that they are brave in battle as was experienced by Franciscus Almeida.[43]

These references, however, were no more than asides in texts which were principally directed towards asserting English or Dutch ascendancy in the colonial world over the increasingly marginal Portuguese.

In late eighteenth-century Britain, however, there was much more sustained interest in Portugal's 'voyages of discovery', and this was reflected in translations of Portuguese literary works,[44] descriptions of Portuguese history and society,[45] accounts of travels through Portugal[46] and English literary works located in Portuguese settings.[47] The longest description of Almeida's defeat was provided by the Scot William Julius Mickle (1734–88)[48] in his 158-page history of Portugal, which introduced his translation of *The Lusíads* (called *The Lusiad* by Mickle). Mickle considers Almeida's record as a whole, and finds it wanting:

> Almeyda [. . .] sailed for Europe, crowned with military laurels. But though thus plumed in the vulgar eye, his establishments were contrary to the spirit of commerce. He fought, indeed conquered; but he left more enemies of the Portuguese in the East than he found there.[49]

And in assessing Almeida's defeat in a footnote, he blames the Portuguese rather than the Khoikhoi for the fatal conflict:

> On his return to Portugal [Almeida] put into the bay of Saldanna, near the Cape of Good Hope, to take in water and provisions. The rudeness of one of his servants produced a quarrel with the Caffres, or Hottentots. His attendants, much against his will, forced him to march against the blacks. 'Ah, whither (he exclaimed) will you carry the infirm man of sixty years'. After plundering a miserable village, on the return to their ships they were attacked by a superior number of Caffres, who fought with such fury in rescue of their children, whom the Portuguese had seized, that the viceroy and fifty of his attendants were slain.[50]

Mickle's description of Almeida's death matches those of the Portuguese chroniclers, but he is more censorious of Almeida. Whereas Barros, for example, praises Almeida's martial spirit and describes him as 'a magnificent captain',[51] Mickle dismisses him as a violent glory-hunter. His hostility towards Almeida in no way derives from any sympathy for the Khoikhoi; indeed, he mocks the Khoikhoi and their supporters like Rousseau – 'the reveries, the fairy dreams of Rousseau, may figure the paradisiacal life of a Hottentot, but it is only in such dreams that the superior happiness of the barbarian exists'.[52] Mickle's criticisms of Almeida derive from his conviction that Almeida betrayed the god of profit, and Mickle dedicated himself to the ideological redefinition of *The Lusíads* from epic of honour and conquest to 'the Epic Poem of Commerce'.[53] This project is even clearer in his later poem *Almada Hill* (1781), where he reinforces his view of Portugal as pioneering commercial nation: the Portuguese 'taught the wondering world the grand design / Of parent heaven, that shore to shore should join / In bands of mutual aid',[54] and further:

> When from the sleep of ages dark and dead,
> Thy Genius, Commerce, rear'd her infant head,
> Her cradle bland on Tago's lap she chose,
> And soon to wandering childhood sprightly rose;
> And when to green and youthful vigour grown
> On Tago's breast she fixt her central throne.[55]

Mickle's emphasis on 'commerce' above 'honour' went beyond poetic generalities, as he also promoted the interests of British chartered companies in the discourse of political economy. In a pamphlet attacking Adam Smith, he stressed the unremitting hostility of the Indians and the Moors towards the European powers in Asia, and derided Smith's optimism regarding Britain's capacity to prevail by peaceful free trade: 'forts and warlike fleets have ever been, and still are, necessary to the very existence of the naval commerce of Europe with India'.[56] Notwithstanding their many mistakes, the Portuguese had at least been right in conducting their trade in the East by means of 'a *regal monopoly*, under the severest restrictions';[57] such regulation of trade along mercantilist principles and supported by military domination set a template which was followed so successfully by the English East India Company.

Although no other British writers of this period discussed Almeida in the same detail as Mickle, there were further sympathetic descriptions of Portugal's imperial past, notably in *An Historical Disquisition concerning the Knowledge which the Ancients had of India* (1791) by William Robertson (1721–93).[58] Robertson praises the pioneering Portuguese voyagers even more lavishly than Mickle: their spirit of enterprise, 'encouraged by success, became more adventurous, despised dangers which formerly appalled it, and surmounted difficulties which once it deemed insuperable'.[59] He describes Da Gama in particularly glowing terms as 'an officer of rank, whose abilities and courage fitted him to conduct the most difficult and arduous enterprises'.[60] Robertson proceeds to locate the different races inhabiting Portugal's imperial world at different stages of development. Africans in the west and south of the continent are located at the earliest stages, described variously as 'the rude inhabitants of the western shore of [Africa]' and 'slender [in] the progress which they have made in the arts of life'.[61] Africans further north up the east coast, however, are more developed – the people of Melinda are 'so advanced in civilization, and acquainted with the various arts of life, that they carried on an active commerce, not only with the nations on their own coast, but with remote countries of Asia'.[62] Although he shares Mickle's Eurocentric assumptions, Robertson therefore represents a liberal variant of Scottish Enlightenment thought, which expresses his conviction that societies in Africa and India can 'progress' to 'the more advanced' stages of commercial civilisation. What Robertson's universalising colonial discourse denies, however, is any room for difference, as Richard Waswo succinctly sums up: '["the primitive"] must develop (fast) or perish; coexistence is precluded'.[63]

Whereas Mickle provided a conservative-mercantilist, Anglocentric version of Portugal's history, and Robertson a liberal-imperial, Scottish Enlightenment version, Robert Southey (1774–1883) in his writings on Portugal set out a third variant. Southey spent two periods in Portugal, in 1795–6, and again in 1800–1.[64] The first visit was an unhappy one, with Southey's youthful radicalism severely challenged by the poverty and corruption of Portugal. He wrote of the Portuguese that 'the higher classes are despicable, and the whole body of people depraved beyond all my ideas of licentiousness'.[65] Southey's writings on Portugal have been interpreted as establishing a binary between rationalist Protestant Britain and superstitious Catholic Portugal, a binary that he applied subsequently to other nations and races confronting Britain's imperial expansion: 'Portugal confirmed Southey in a belief in Englishmen's superiority to the Irish as well as to "Negroes", Indians, Tibetans and the Portuguese themselves'.[66] His disdain extended to Portuguese heroes of the past, including Da Gama, whom he describes as follows:

> Stupid he must have been to mistake a Hindu temple for a Christian church and say his prayers to figures with more arms than Briareus [. . . F]or deliberate cruelty I think him more atrocious than Pizarro. The Portuguese had a physical-European superiority to the people of the East, and plied their guns better, in everything else they were lamentably behind hand.[67]

Southey's opinions moderated in the course of his second visit, as he established himself (in his view) as the leading British authority on Portuguese history and literature, to the extent that he undertook to write the definitive history of Portugal.[68]

Southey elaborated the inadequacies of the Portuguese-as-colonisers (and also of the Spanish and Dutch) in lengthy reviews of the Cape travel writings of John Barrow and Robert Percival. He notes how different European travellers projected their obsessions on to the Cape landscape and its peoples:

> The Cape Good Hope is of importance in many points of view. The poet figures to his mind on the mention of its name the genius of storms, so sublimely described by Camoens: the naturalist regards it as the favourite point, from which he may explore the animal and vegetable pleasures of Africa: the sailor makes to it for refreshments in his voyages from Europe to the East Indies; and the statesman considers the manifold advantages it might afford to any European possessor.[69]

Southey mocks the tendency of travel writers to the Cape to exaggerate, noting in particular that Adamastor's forbidding refuge Table Mountain is in fact not very big:

> arithmetic is a sad leveller, and the Cape must not boast of its Alps nor even enter into a competition with Cader Idris or Snowdon. The height of Table Hill, for this is the name of the mountain, is from the summit to the level of the sea about 4000 feet, and from the outskirts of the town near 3600.[70]

Turning from the landscape to questions of colonial governance, Southey analyses the claims of Britain's European competitors, noting that

> Spain and Portugal have acted cruelly in their colonies heretofore, and all the instances of fervent and disinterested faith, of individual virtue, and of national heroism wherewith their annals abound, have not been sufficient to counteract the painful and indignant feelings which the history of their tyranny excited against them.[71]

He continues that the Portuguese and Spanish have been superseded by the Cape Dutch as the most shameful perpetrators of cruelty against colonised subjects: 'Of all degenerated Dutchmen the African boor is the most thoroughly detestable: the breed, indeed, is the most abominable that can be conceived'.[72] Southey declared his sympathy for the indigenes of the Cape, endorsing Barrow's view of the 'Hottentots' – 'a more gentle or docile race [. . .] does not exist, nor any class of men, savage or civilized, in whom the moral sense seems to be less degraded'.[73] Summarising one of Barrow's accounts of a fatal encounter between Dutch villainy and 'Hottentot' honour, Southey describes the 'Hottentots' as 'insurgents', and explains that 'when that name is applied to men struggling against oppression, be it in Switzerland, or St. Domingo, or Caffraria, it is a most honourable appellation', and then concludes his summary of the encounter by noting, '[h]ad this fact occurred in Grecian history,

how often would it have been quoted for admiration'.[74] Southey sets out his ultimate ideal for the disparate groups at the Cape. The Dutch should first be subdued
by violence, the 'Kaffers' and the 'Hottentots' would then feel secure and eager to
trade, and their new-found security would encourage new settlements based upon
peaceful exchange:

> At these meeting-places villages would immediately grow, and towns at no
> distant period; and here schools should be established. In a few generations
> English might be made the language of the settlement, and the African boor
> might be reduced to the shape of man, and exalted to the character of a civi-
> lized being and a Christian.[75]

Although Southey engages with the specificities of the indigenes and settlers of the
Cape to a greater degree than Mickle and Robertson, for all his promises of civilising the 'African boor' and bringing honest trade to the 'Hottentots' and 'Kaffers',
his bucolic communities in the wilds of the Cape Colony remain a resolutely British
projection, constituted for securing British trading profits and backed by British
military violence.[76]

In much the same way that the sixteenth-century Portuguese chronicles of
Almeida's death and Portugal's 'age of discovery' were adapted in histories by
Mickle, Robertson and Southey to suit Britain's imperial project, Camões's epic
poem was reworked to serve the same ends. Mickle's translation of *The Lusíads*
followed the approach set out by William Tytler, who argued that in the act of
translation 'the subtle spirit of poesy evaporates' unless the translator infuses the
work with 'a new, or an original spirit'.[77] Confidently inhabiting the role of 'an
original spirit' in translating *The Lusíads*, Mickle inserted 300 extra lines. In addition to elevating the benefits of trade above the glories of conquest wherever
possible, Mickle also followed the example of Alexander Pope's translations of
Homer in muting the violence of the original, 'harmonising a stormy and often
savage text with gentler, enlightened tastes'.[78] His translation of Almeida's death
as described by Adamastor is typical, as Almeida is cast as the passive victim of
Africa:

> 'With trophies plumed behold an Hero come,
> Ye dreary wilds, prepare his yawning tomb.
> Though smiling fortune blest his youthful morn,
> Though glory's rays his laurel'd bows adorn,
> Full oft though he beheld with sparkling eye
> The Turkish moons in wild confusion fly,
> While he, proud victor, thunder'd in the rear,
> All, all his mighty fame shall vanish here.
> Quiloa's sons, and thine Mombaze, shall see
> Their conqueror bend his laurel'd head to me;
> While proudly mingling with the tempest's sound,
> Their shouts of joy from every cliff rebound.'[79]

Rose Macaulay contrasts Mickle's translation unfavourably with Sir Richard Fanshawe's – '[c]ertainly, Mickle reads more smoothly; bland and moralizing eighteenth-century pompousness has taken the place of naïf, colloquial seventeenth-century charm'.[80] Macaulay's dismissal of Mickle's language can be supplemented by Lynn Festa's more historicised explanation for the decline of the epic and its gradual replacement by the sentimental novel in the late eighteenth century. Festa argues:

> The transition from an aristocratic model of conquest to one grounded in commerce meant that the epic was of diminished service to eighteenth-century discussions of colonialism [. . .] As the terms used to justify empire shifted from the acquisition of specie to commerce, from evangelization to enlightenment, from notions of barbaric others to a shared and potentially civilized humanity, sentimentality comes to the fore.[81]

Festa's snapshot here of Britain's imperial history in the years 1770–1830 understates the extent to which violent military plunder continued to alternate with commercial forms of colonial engagement into the nineteenth century,[82] but her generalisation about the generic shift away from the epic does explain the awkwardness of Mickle's translation of *The Lusíads*. In Festa's terms, 'an epic of commerce' is an oxymoron; Mickle would have been more in tune with the zeitgeist had he written a sentimental novel encouraging trade.

Like Mickle, Southey wrote both histories and literary works, but unlike Mickle, he theorised the relationship between literature, history and politics, thus providing an explicit basis for his opinions on Camões and the Portuguese past. Southey endorsed the Romantic ideal of the poet as guiding spirit of the nation, but his position shifted during the course of his writing life. During his early radical phase, Southey set out the relation between nations and their poetic geniuses as follows:

> Individual genius will be found then to have flourished most when the community shall have been most flourishing; Athens was most glorious when Sophocles and Euripides succeeded the aged Aeschylus; and Ovid, Horace, and Virgil wrote at the time when Augustus sent forth his decree, that all the world should be taxed. Uniform experience will attest the truth of the observation; why this sympathy should exist, I know not; but poetical genius is certainly a barometer that rises or falls according to the state of the political atmosphere.[83]

In identifying a connection between historical moments 'when the community shall have been most flourishing' and works of individual literary genius, Southey historicises literature in much the same way that Romantic writers began to historicise human personality more generally. James Chandler argues that from the 1790s, it was no longer possible 'to assume the possibility of moral exemplification across period boundaries [and that there emerged] a strong sense of epochal constitution of human personality'.[84] In Southey's case, however, this appreciation of 'the spirit of the age' was overdetermined by an idealist faith in the capacity of poets of genius to communicate within an international fellowship that transcends time and space:

'The poet is indeed a citizen of the world; in every country and in every age, he meets with some congenial spirit; to him, time is annihilated, and he converses with Homer and with Ossian'.[85] Twenty-five years later, Southey retained a residual faith in the productive synergy between poet-genius and healthy nation, but perceived a dire threat to the relationship posed by what he termed the 'Satanic school' of poets. In *The Vision of Judgement* (1821), he describes the positive contribution of English literature to society: 'For more than half a century English literature had been distinguished by its oral purity, the effect, and in its turn, the cause of an improvement in national manners [. . .] This was particularly the case with regard to our poetry'.[86] Unfortunately, Southey continues, this happy reciprocity has been undermined by subversive literary works (pre-eminently Byron's), which threaten the survival of society:

> The publication of a lascivious book is one of the worst offences that can be committed against the well-being of society [. . .] There is no maxim more frequently enforced by Machiavelli, than that where the manners of a people are generally corrupted, there the government cannot long subsist [. . .] a truth which all history exemplifies; and there is no means whereby that corruption can be so surely and rapidly diffused, as by poisoning the waters of literature.[87]

These anxieties mark Southey's comments on Camões, notably in his 1822 review of Adamson's study of the poet, where he pronounces disapprovingly upon Camões's 1561 satire against Viceroy Francisco Barreto. To libel any person, declares Southey, is

> to be a pest to society – a man who perverts literature to the annoyance and injury of mankind [. . .] Personal satire [. . .] is not to be justified; no man is entitled to hold up another to ridicule for his private defects or errors.[88]

Unlike Mickle, Southey therefore refuses to venerate Camões as a great poet:

> [Mickle] raises [Camões] to a profound equality with Homer, and Virgil, and Milton; but Camoens must not be lifted up so high, neither must Homer, and Virgil, and Milton, be degraded into such company: though Camoens may, perhaps, come the next to Tasso.[89]

He singles out the Adamastor episode for particular ridicule: 'when Gama interrupts [Adamastor], demanding who he is, a tale follows which would only be tolerable in a school-boy's imitation of Ovid'.[90] Southey never tried to translate *The Lusíads* himself, but believed that the translations of Camões's poetry by Mickle, Strangford and Adamson substantially improved Camões's original:

> [Camões's] poetical character can neither be estimated by [Strangford's] volume, nor by [Mickle's] English *Lusiad*: the merits of the one must be assigned to Mickle, and the other to Lord Strangford [. . .] Being acquainted with the

Portugueze poet, we were well pleased to discover originals where we only expected translations.[91]

Southey's irritation with The Lusíads is in part based upon his impatience with its epic elements, as when he notes Camões's addition of Venus and Bacchus to Da Gama's history, and asks in exasperation: 'What can be more puerile?'[92] Against these epic intrusions, Southey defends the primacy of history, arguing that

> there is no incident in modern history more impressive than the voyage of Vasco da Gama; but to feel and comprehend it, it must be read with all its details in Castanheda or Barros, where it comes to us with the deep and abiding interest of truth. The slightest admixture of fiction debases it like an alloy.[93]

Southey's metaphor here echoes that of William Jones, who had argued that '[t]he poetical fables of the old Persians [. . .] ought not to be mixed, like glittering drops, with the pure ore of true History'.[94] In other words, whatever the value of combining fragments of history and fiction in the writing of epics, the unalloyed ore of True History must be uncontaminated by any admixture of fiction. Southey's disparaging of the epic qualities of The Lusíads was not an isolated attack, as he also criticised exemplary heroic epics like Virgil's Aeneid, and praised as alternative models Lucan's Pharsalia, Milton's Paradise Lost, and the romance epics of Ariosto, Tasso and Spenser.[95] However, Southey's antipathy towards Camões and the epic genre was complicated by the constant shifting and blurring of the demarcation between history and epic in his own output, as he produced both major epics like Thalaba the Destroyer (1801), Madoc (1805) and The Curse of Kehama (1810), and lengthy works of history like his three-volume History of Brazil (1810–19).

It should be noted, however, that Southey's confidence in his ability to sift history from fiction in his own epic poems was not shared by all his readers. Thomas Love Peacock, for example, argues that

> Mr. Southey wades through ponderous volumes of travels and old chronicles, from which he carefully selects all that is false, useless, and absurd as being essentially poetical; and when he has a commonplace book full of monstrosities, he strings them into an epic.[96]

Byron's contempt for Southey's epics went even further. In Don Juan (1819–24) he mocks his 'epic brethren gone before [because] they so embellish, that 'tis quite a bore', but unlike Southey, Byron treats the competing truth claims of history with equal irreverence, as he appeals ironically in the next stanza 'to history, tradition, and to facts'[97] to confirm the transparently fictional tale of Juan's elopement with the Devil. For all their differences, Southey and Byron attest to the difficulties of negotiating the inherited laws of genre theory in the early nineteenth century.

Jacques Derrida has observed how the history of genre-theory 'is strewn with these fascinating outlines that inform and deform reality, a reality often heterogeneous to the literary field',[98] and the contortions of the epic genre in the period 1770–1830 exemplify how 'reality' pressurised the received genre theory, precipitating the emergence of new genres and new theories of genre. Byron's sense of the mortality of the epic as a genre was indeed prescient – according to Hayden White, after the Enlightenment, 'the Epic form, it was generally agreed, was not suited to the representation of historical events',[99] and most of the subsequent Southern African reiterations of Almeida's death and Portugal's 'voyages of discovery' turned to the genres of the novel, the lyric poem and the satire.

## SOUTHERN AFRICAN ACCOUNTS OF THE NINETEENTH AND TWENTIETH CENTURIES

There were a couple of brief descriptions of Almeida's death in nineteenth-century writings at the Cape. In an unpublished history of the Cape written in 1806–7, Samuel Eusebius Hudson provided the following inaccurate summary:

> [Dom Manuel I] determined to plant a Colony at the Cape of Good Hope. The Portuguese, naturally pusillanimous, had conceived that the natives of this new found land were Cannibals, resisted for some time the order of their sovereign [. . .] However, a more formidable body of adventurers under the Command of Francis d'Almeijda, who was at that time Viceroy of Brazil, effected three landings under some difficulties from the natives who took every opportunity to annoy them with their spears and Missile weapons. After some skirmishing they were shameful defeated, their Viceroy and fifty of his Men killed in the engagement.[100]

A shorter but much more widely read description was provided in John Philip's *Researches in Africa* (1828). Philip uses the Khoikhoi confrontation with Almeida to establish the defining opposition in his work between virtuous indigenes and rapacious colonisers:

> When the Portuguese first visited the Cape of Good Hope, they found the inhabitants rich in cattle, living in a happy and comfortable manner, and possessed of sufficient spirit to repel aggression and to resent unjust treatment [. . .] It was said, that they were remarkable for the excellence of their morals, that they kept the law of nations better than the most civilized peoples, and that they were valiant in arms. Of this latter quality, they gave a memorable proof in the year 1510, when Francisco Almeida, the first viceroy of the Portuguese India, was defeated and killed in an obstinate engagement with the Hottentots, near the Salt River, in the neighbourhood of where Cape Town now stands.[101]

Aside from these two references, there are no signs of interest on the part of white settler writers in the Khoikhoi victory over Almeida. There are, however, any number of reworkings of the Adamastor myth, with poems by John Wheatley (1830) and D. F. C. Moodie (1887) explicitly invoking Da Gama and Adamastor,[102] and an

1859 magazine essay in praise of Camões's mythic creation.[103] In the years preceding the Union of South Africa in 1910, the historian George McCall Theal wrote short a summary of Almeida's death, presenting it as the result of a misunderstanding – 'unfortunately a quarrel arose between the two parties, and two of the white men were severely beaten'.[104] His view on the fate of the Portuguese-as-colonisers was elaborated in more detail in his ten-volume *Records of South-Eastern Africa* (1898–1904), where he attributes their decline to miscegenation with African slaves in the fifteenth century:

> The slaves, on embracing Christianity, had various privileges conferred upon them, and their blood became mixed with that of the least energetic of the peasantry, until a new and degenerate stock, frivolous, inconstant, incapable of improvement, was formed. In the northern provinces [. . .] a pure European race remained, fit not only to conquer, but to hold dominion in distant lands, though too small in proportion to the entire population of the country to control its destinies.[105]

According to Theal, the consequences of such racial mixing were devastating for the Portuguese: 'long before the end of the sixteenth century they had ceased to be participants in the great progressive movement of the Caucasian race'.[106] Their replacement in India by first the Dutch and ultimately the British was therefore inevitable. This historian's view of the Portuguese was repeated in other genres, notably in novels like John Buchan's *Prester John* (1910). Buchan's representation of Africans in the novel has rightly been criticised, but it is arguable that the hero Richard Hannay's Portuguese adversary Henriques is an even more negative stereotype. Hannay describes Henriques on the first encounter as 'the most atrocious villain I have ever clapped eyes on [. . .] whose skin spoke of the tar-brush',[107] and later contrasts him unfavourably with the African Adamastor/Prester John figure Laputa: 'I was consumed with a passion of fury against that murdering yellow devil. With Laputa I was not angry; he was an open enemy, playing a fair game. But my fingers itched to get at the Portugoose – that double-dyed traitor to his race'.[108] A part of the explanation for the intensification of this racialised discourse in British writings on the Portuguese lies in the escalating tensions between the Britain and Portugal over the land between Mozambique and Angola.[109]

Camões experienced a rather different fate to the Portuguese nation in South African writing, with the most extended endorsement provided in two 1909 articles by literature professor John Purves. Purves argues that *The Lusíads* is a 'demonstration of the life of a nation';[110] Camões is to Portugal what Shakespeare is to England and what Dante is to Italy and '[i]t is the alliance of these two elements – national spirit and feeling for the past – which gives equilibrium to the genius of Camoens, making him superior to the best exclusive spirits of the Renaissance'.[111] Purves is concerned to rescue Camões from Mickle's identification of *The Lusíads* with commerce; for him, the true heart of Camões's epic lies in its celebration of nationalism. Purves argues that the inspiration of Camoens was a deliberate reaction against the depressing influence of "mercantilism" [. . .] He saw nationalism being strangled by self-interest [. . .] and he wished to recall his countrymen to the earlier and more heroic example of the fifteenth century.[112]

Purves concludes his argument by claiming *The Lusíads* for the about-to-be-constituted Union of South Africa: 'The Lusíads is then [. . .] not only the first but also the greatest of South African poems. It is our portion of the Renaissance'.[113]

Purves's sense of a firm bond between Portugal and South Africa was endorsed in Lucio Lupi's report on Portuguese President Craveiro Lopes's 1956 tour of African colonies. According to Lupi, critics of Portuguese colonialism foolishly

persist in following the teachings of the 'Old Man of Restelo'. They are the unfortunate people, the ever-indignant ones, still-born creatures who continue to wander among the living like ghosts – souls in pain who hate the past and fear the future.[114]

Lopes's tour of Africa culminated in Pretoria, where the South African Governor-General Ernest George Jansen endorsed Lupi's arguments:

Must the European powers in Africa relinquish a civilizing mission which is creating roads, railways, new sources of power, industries, schools, hospitals and homes for the people of this Continent? [. . .] You, Sir, [Lopes] in your determination to maintain and develop your ancient Empire, and we in our equal determination to build a lasting civilization in our part of Africa, can give only one answer. It was indeed a happy accident of history that made us neighbours in Southern Africa. I believe that together, in the fullness of time, we shall enjoy the vindication of history.[115]

Such sentiments were not restricted to apartheid ministers; other South African writers of the period were similarly well disposed to Portugal's heroes. Both Sidney R. Welch's history *South Africa under King Manuel, 1495–1521* (1946) and the poems of Roy Campbell represent the Portuguese in a positive light. Welch recounts Almeida's death in detail, and provides a sympathetic interpretation of Portuguese conduct, explaining that the conflict 'arose out of the guileless friendliness of the Portuguese sailors'.[116] Welch's account is even more generous to them than Barros had been in the sixteenth century, and although he does not register the possibility of a competing Khoikhoi version of the battle, he is sensitive to triumphalist British historiography. In a footnote, he approves of the fact that 'Portuguese historians applied the same moral law to allies and enemies [whereas British history] has one law for the "fierce avarice" of Portuguese and Spaniards, but another law for similar deeds of the Anglo-Saxons'.[117] Like Welch, Campbell displayed a keen sympathy for the Portuguese in general, and with Camões in particular. In the poems 'Rounding the Cape' and 'Tristan da Cunha' in the collection *Adamastor* (1930), Campbell expressed his great pleasure in *The Lusíads* and especially the figure of Adamastor, and in the poem 'Luís de Camões' in *Talking Bronco* (1946), he claims to share with Camões the Romantic formula of transmuting isolation and suffering into poetry: 'I find a comrade where I sought a master / [. . .] / [He] Wrestled his hardships into forms of beauty, / And taught his gorgon destinies to sing'.[118]

In the final years of apartheid, South Africa's historical connections with Portugal were again the focus of attention, most elaborately in the 1988 Dias Festival,[119] but also in several Southern African publications: Ungulani Ba Ka Khosa's novel *Ualalapi* (1987), Malvern Van Wyk Smith's anthology *Shades of Adamastor* (1988), André Brink's novel *The First Life of Adamastor* (1993), Anthony Fleischer's novel set in Mozambique, *Children of Adamastor* (1994), and poems by James Greene (1987) and Kelwyn Sole (1992 and 2006). There was also a major artwork entitled *T'kama-Adamastor* by Cyril Coetzee, which was commissioned for the Cullen Library at the University of the Witwatersrand and accompanied by a collection of essays in 2000.[120] Van Wyk Smith's anthology has the Adamastor myth as its organising principle, and makes no reference at all to Almeida's defeat. The introduction outlines early modern European images of Africa, there is an unreliable summary of *The Lusíads* (with Thetis of Canto Five conflated with Tethys of Canto Ten),[121] and the anthology includes Guy Butler's translation of Canto Five of *The Lusíads* (the Adamastor section) as well as a number of South African poetic reworkings of the Adamastor theme. In many of the poems, the connection with Adamastor is extremely tenuous, and in the final section, which includes poems by black South African poets, it is all but impossible to discern even the faintest shade of Adamastor. Van Wyk Smith concedes as much – 'throughout Africa black poets seem to have paid little attention to the exploits of the Portuguese, but where they have the fall-out has been sulphurous'[122] – so that the anthology ultimately stands as testimony to the decline of a resilient but solipsistic settler myth. A similar trajectory is to be found in André Brink's relationship with Adamastor. Like Van Wyk Smith, Brink neglects Almeida's defeat in favour of a protracted engagement with Adamastor, a choice consistent with Brink's theoretical elevation of Literature above History.[123] Brink identifies Adamastor as the key European image to be redefined in contemporary South Africa:

> In the case of Adamastor, Camões set the example by offering a mythopoetic response to an historical challenge [. . .] The time is now ripe to look again at that watershed event in our history [. . .] and to reimagine that event from inside our African experience. Redefining that moment, redefining and reacknowledging Adamastor, is part of the demand that we redefine ourselves.[124]

As a contribution to redefining South African identity in the 1990s, Brink produced *The First Life of Adamastor*, which was 'intended originally as only the first part of a novel which would trace, through thirteen avatars, the continuing hold of Adamastor on the southernmost tip of Africa'.[125] Attempting to retell from an African point of view the first encounters between the indigenes of the Cape and European explorers, Brink adopts as narrator an Adamastor figure called T'kama. Like Brink's novels with contemporary settings, *The Rights of Desire* (2000) and

*Before I Forget* (2004), the plot in *The First Life of Adamastor* is as much concerned with sex between an older man and a younger woman as it is with interrogating Eurocentric history. T'kama worries about his ability to have sex with the white woman castaway character, asking 'But how to cleave her cleft with that enormous tree of mine?'[126] Brink has written seven novels since *The First Life of Adamastor*, many of them engaged with South Africa's past, but the stories of the subsequent twelve avatars of Adamastor remain uncompleted. Like Van Wyk Smith, Brink has struggled to find a continuing relevance for Adamastor as white settler authority has declined in the post-apartheid dispensation.

It is arguable that although Camões remains (like Shakespeare) an entrenched institution, satire and pastiche have been the literary genres employed most frequently in Southern African reworkings of the Adamastor story, lending weight to Fredric Jameson's argument that 'the older generic categories do not, for all that, die out, but persist in the half-life of the subliterary genres of mass culture'.[127] Douglas Livingstone's 1964 radio play 'The Sea My Winding Sheet' includes 'a debased twentieth-century Adamastor',[128] and James Greene's 1987 poem 'Camões's Birthday' declares: 'These elderly or middle-aged [Portuguese] children / Display their wounds like medals / and in their Camões, imperialism's flunkey, recognise themselves'.[129] A different angle is provided in Khosa's novel *Ualalapi*, which implicitly rejects Adamastor as any kind of model for African anti-colonial resistance, and instead uses the Adamastor myth obliquely in order to reflect critically upon the nineteenth-century Mozambican nationalist icon Ngungunhane.[130] In his short poem 'A White South African Poet Rounds the Cape', Kelwyn Sole satirises the portentousness of Campbell's original poem: 'On this page / between two tinctured, smoking seas / at last / I grant myself / a glimpse of what I long to be / the mythopoeic – / and inspired/ begin to adamastor / bate'.[131] Fourteen years later, Sole assumes the voice of a demoralised game reserve guide in 'The Dream of the Big Five', and explains 'so when Adamastor Tours expanded and offered me a bit more pay to guide people around the Kruger I thought it might make sense'.[132] Sole's sense of Adamastor's decline from Myth of Africa to marketing brand is confirmed by O. J. O. Ferreira, who points out that the *Adamastor Trading Company* sells plants in the Cape Town Company Gardens, and that *Adamastor Atelier* in Northcliff, Johannesburg makes television commercials.[133]


## ANC ANTI-COLONIAL HISTORY

The decline of the Adamastor myth coincided with Mbeki's reference to Almeida's defeat in his 1999 speech. By recounting the history of the Khoikhoi victory over Almeida rather than the literary tale of the encounter between Adamastor and Da Gama, Mbeki replaces a white settler myth of the first colonial encounter in Southern Africa with the indigenous history of the first moment of black anti-colonial struggle. Mbeki's reference to the Khoikhoi victory is not an incidental remark; it is an element in a much broader political narrative which underwrote his ideological project of the African Renaissance.[134] Officially launched in August

1998 at a made-for-television banquet,[135] Mbeki's African Renaissance strove to reverse the destruction wrought by colonialism and apartheid by recovering and revaluing Africa's cultural riches and histories of resistance.[136] Mbeki explains that 'an essential and necessary element of the African renaissance is that we must all take it as our task to encourage her [. . .] to rebel, to assert the principality of her humanity – the fact that she, in the first instance, is not a beast of burden, but a human and African being'.[137] The Khoikhoi victory of 1510 exemplifies this impulse to rebel, and Mbeki goes on to invoke many other South African and African anti-colonial struggles. For example, he recalls that 'African armies at Omdurman in the Sudan and Isandhlwana in South Africa out-generalled, out-soldiered and defeated the powerful and arrogant British Empire in the '70s of the last century'.[138] And in an important initiative to recover histories of anti-colonial struggle, Mbeki opened the ANC archive at the University of Fort Hare by declaring that the archive speaks in 'the language of the reinforcement of the pride and identity of the formerly oppressed and despised, because in it will be found much which says that, after all, indeed, we were never conquered'.[139]

Mbeki's anti-colonial historiography of the sixteenth to the twentieth centuries was complemented by approving quotations from the works of more recent anti-colonial intellectuals, as his speeches are punctuated with quotations from Frantz Fanon, Kwame Nkrumah, Amílcar Cabral, Ngũgĩ wa Thiong'o, Marcus Garvey, Walter Rodney, W. E. B. du Bois, and Malcolm X. Nor has Mbeki been alone in his predilection for citing such iconic figures; the South African Government Information website reveals (via its search engine) how frequently ANC ministers quote anti-colonial and anti-capitalist intellectuals. On my last count, since 1994 there have been 54 quotations of Frantz Fanon, 44 of Ngũgĩ wa Thiong'o, and 49 of Karl Marx. But as with Mbeki's invocation of the Khoikhoi victory over Almeida, so too with these quotations of anti-colonial thinkers, the filiations with post-apartheid economic policies are complicated. For example, Mandisi Mpahlwa, Minister of Trade and Industry, delivering a speech at the Black Management Forum Annual Achievement Awards on 12 October 2007, quotes Fanon 'the anti-colonialist writer, [who] once said that "in the world through which I travel, I am endlessly creating myself",[140] and then turns to an inspirational example from India to give content to Fanon's words:

Ladies and gentlemen, how we create ourselves is determined by us. No amount of transactions will by itself bring about self-reliance and boldness. The boldness and self-reliance I am talking about is the boldness and self-reliance of the founder of Tata Enterprises, Jamsetjie Tata, who in the early 1900's upon arriving by invitation at the best hotel in India was turned away at the door, because he was Indian. His response? To build the Taj Mahal Hotel, a bigger and better hotel than anywhere in India and one from which no-one could turn him away.[141]

In another example, Michael Mabuyakhulu, the Member of the Executive Council (MEC) for Economic Development and Tourism, in an address delivered at the

KwaZulu-Natal Youth Chamber of Commerce and Industry on 26 August 2010, looked not to India but to the United States for inspiration, and applauded the achievements of 'Mark Elliot Zuckerberg (born May 14, 1984) [. . .] the youngest billionaire in the world, with a net worth of United States $4 billion in 2010 due to his 24 percent share of Facebook', before asking, 'why can KwaZulu-Natal not produce its own Mark Zuckerberg?'[142] Mabuyakhulu acknowledges that there are good arguments explaining the shortage of dotcom billionaires in KwaZulu-Natal, but then concludes:

> Most of the arguments that you advance will be true and factual but if we are to change the world and develop a cadre of young business people to take our province forward, then we will need to heed the words of Karl Marx who said: 'The philosophers have only interpreted the world, in various ways; the point, however, is to change it'.[143]

What these examples demonstrate is that references to heroic moments of anti-colonial struggle (the Khoikhoi in Table Bay, the 'African armies at Omdurman', the Zulu at Isandhlwana), together with the inspirational words of Fanon et al., are mobilised in order to promote role models like Tata and Zuckerberg, and more generally, to legitimise economic policies that have prioritised free markets, privatisation, deregulation of exchange controls and limited public expenditure. Consequently, some of the most zealous supporters of Mbeki's African Renaissance were South Africa's moneyed elites of all races, who interpreted his words as a clear endorsement of their profiteering in sub-Saharan Africa, so that between 1998 and 2000, South Africa's trade with the rest of the continent increased by 36 per cent, earning an estimated cumulative surplus of R60 billion (£4 billion).[144] For the poor of Southern Africa, the African Renaissance has had less appeal, for as Njabulo Ndebele points out, 'the call for black roots has less effect than the provision of water and sanitation, electricity, telephones, houses, clinics, transport, schools, and jobs'.[145] In other words, remembering victories over European invaders from previous centuries, or listening to the inspirational words of iconic anti-colonial intellectuals, offers limited consolation to those living in poverty and confronting a state with maladministered public welfare provision.

## CONCLUSION

In the last five centuries, the lessons drawn from the Khoikhoi victory over Almeida in 1510 have mutated remarkably – that the Portuguese failure to value honour above money caused their deaths at the hands of 'bestial negroes' (Barros, Camões); that the Portuguese pursuit of military glory rather than commercial profit resulted in them being killed by 'barbarians' (Mickle); that the Khoikhoi were noble 'insurgents' justified in resisting Portuguese tyranny, but ultimately best served by accepting benevolent British rule (Southey, Philip); that the 'guileless friendliness' of the Portuguese enabled uncivilised indigenes to murder them (Welch); and that the heroic Khoikhoi overcame great odds to defeat 'belligerent' Portuguese aggressors and inaugurate South Africa's tradition of anti-colonial resistance (Mbeki). And at least as significantly, that for two centuries the key lessons of the colonial encounter were learnt not from the history of the Khoikhoi victory, but from the European myth of Adamastor's defeat (Wheatley, Campbell, Brink). Rather than add to this long list of lessons, I would suggest finally that the task now is to understand how Mbeki's post-apartheid appropriation of this polysemic event functions ideologically – like the conjunction of Fanon and Tata, and of Marx and Zuckerberg – to obscure the dissonance between the inclusive ideals of his African Renaissance and the structural exclusions generated by South Africa's economy and the ANC's commitment to capitalism.

## NOTES

1. In the racist nomenclature of the Cape Colony, the Khoikhoi were referred to as 'Hottentots', and the San as 'Bushmen'. The distinction between the Khoikhoi and the San has always been vague, but in the seventeenth and eighteenth centuries the Khoikhoi were pastoralists, whereas the San were hunter-gatherers. The two groups are now referred to collectively as the Khoisan. I have used quotation marks when using the terms 'Hottentots' and 'Bushmen' to register their racist etymology.
2. Mbeki, 'A Farewell'.
3. Barros, Da Asia, pp. 298–306. For Barros's biography, see Boxer, João de Barros.
4. Castanheda, History, pp. 466–9. For Castanheda's biography, see Avelar, Fernão Lopes de Castanheda.
5. De Góis, Chronicle, pp. 134–40. For De Góis's biography, see Hirsch, Damião de Gois.
6. Corrêa, Legends, pp. 45–7. For Corrêa's biography, see Kriegel and Subrahmanyam, 'The Unity'.
7. Castanheda identifies their landing place as Table Bay; Barros as Saldanha Bay. Karel Schoeman explains the apparent confusion – the watering place in Table Bay for much of the sixteenth century was known as Aguada de Saldanha (at the intersection of the present-day Adderley and Strand Streets in central Cape Town). See Schoeman, Armosyn, p. 15.
8. Barros, Da Asia, p. 298.
9. Castanheda, History, p. 468.
10. Corrêa, Legends, p. 46.
11. Corrêa, Legends, p. 46.
12. De Góis, Chronicle, p. 136.
13. Castanheda, History, p. 468.
14. Barros, Da Asia, p. 302.
15. Koselleck, The Practice, p. 76.
16. Barros, Da Asia, p. 306.
17. Corrêa, Legends, pp. 46–7.
18. Bell, Gaspar Corrêa, pp. 62–3.
19. De Góis, Chronicle, p. 139.
20. For discussion of Camões's sources, see Catz, 'Consequences'.
21. Camões, The Lusíads, p. 5. Of the many available translations of The Lusíads, I have used White's one for its determination to 'err on the side of plainness' (p. xxii).
22. Camões, The Lusíads, p. 107.

23. Camões, *The Lusíads*, p. 204.
24. Quint, 'Voices', p. 134.
25. For a survey of how the Old Man's speech has been interpreted over the centuries, see Moser, 'What did'.
26. Camões, *The Lusíads*, p. 195.
27. Camões, *The Lusíads*, p. 227.
28. Camões, *The Lusíads*, p. 228.
29. For this episode, see Bell, *Luis de Camões*, pp. 132–7. For a sample of recent scholarship, see the Special Issue on Camões of *Portuguese Literary and Cultural Studies*.
30. Silva, 'Moving', p. 739.
31. Quoted in Figueiredo, 'Camões', p. 218.
32. Bakhtin, *The Dialogic*, p. 14.
33. Helgerson, *Forms*, p. 158.
34. On the contending factions in Portugal's ruling class of the fifteenth and sixteenth centuries, see Thomaz, 'Factions', pp. 97–109; Subrahmanyam, *The Career*, pp. 38–57; and Raman, *Framing 'India'*, pp. 55–60.
35. Newitt, *A History of Mozambique*, p. 14. On Portugal's ostensible motives for their 'voyages of discovery', see Boxer, *The Portuguese*, pp. 17–18; and Scammell, *The First*, pp. 51–70.
36. Newitt, *A History of Portuguese Overseas Expansion*, p. 15.
37. Blackburn, *The Making*, p. 119.
38. Vicente, *Three Discovery*, pp. 203, 209.
39. Camões, *The Lusíads*, p. 97.
40. Bennett, '"Sons"', p. 26.
41. Larsen and Krueger, 'Camões", p. 70.
42. Herbert, *Some Years*, p. 19.
43. Translated and reprinted in Raven-Hart, *Cape*, pp. 490–1.
44. See, for example, Lord Viscount Strangford, *Poems from the Portuguese of Luis de Camoens* (1804); and John Adamson, *Memoirs of the Life and Writings of Luis de Camoens* (1820).
45. See, for example, Arthur Costigan, *Sketches of Society and Manners in Portugal* (1778).
46. See, for example, Richard Cumberland, *Memoirs of Richard Cumberland. Written By Himself* (1806); and William Beckford, *Italy, with Sketches of Spain and Portugal* (1834).
47. See, for example, Byron, *Childe Harold* (1809).
48. For biographical details, see Caudle, 'Mickle'.
49. Mickle, *The Lusiad*, p. lxx.
50. Ibid. p. 208.
51. Barros, *Da Asia*, pp. 304–5
52. Mickle, *The Lusiad*, p. ii.
53. Ibid. p. i.
54. Mickle, *Almada*, p. 20.
55. Ibid. p. 30.
56. Mickle, *A Candid*, p. 17.
57. Ibid. p. 20.
58. For sympathetic accounts of Robertson, see Brown, *William Robertson*; and O'Brien, *Narratives*, pp. 163–70.
59. Robertson, *An Historical*, p. 133.
60. Ibid. p. 134.
61. Ibid. pp. 134, 145.
62. Ibid. p. 134.
63. Waswo, *The Founding*, p. 216.
64. See Speck, *Robert Southey*, pp. 62–5, 83–7; and Storey, *Robert Southey*, pp. 81–5.
65. Southey, *Selections*, p. 21.

66. Fulford, 'Heroic', p. 49.
67. Southey, *New Letters*, p. 337.
68. See Humphreys, *Robert Southey*.
69. Southey, 'Review of Robert Percival', p. 375.
70. Ibid. p. 376.
71. Southey, 'Review of John Barrow', p. 24.
72. Ibid. p. 24.
73. Ibid. p. 27.
74. Ibid. p. 28.
75. Ibid. p. 33.
76. There are useful accounts of Southey on empire in Bolton, *Writing*, and Craig, *Robert Southey*, but neither of them discusses Southey's writings on the Cape.
77. Tytler, *Principles*, p. 36.
78. Lipking, 'The View', p. 166.
79. Mickle, *The Lusiad*, pp. 208–9.
80. Macaulay, *They Came*, p. 97.
81. Festa, *Sentimental*, pp. 57–8. See too Dentith, *Epic*.
82. On Britain's many colonial wars throughout this period, see Farwell, *Queen Victoria's*.
83. Southey, 'On the Poetry of Spain', pp. 451–2.
84. Chandler, 'History', p. 355. Chandler elaborates these arguments in *England*, pp. 94–114.
85. Southey, 'On the Poetry of Spain', p. 453
86. Southey, 'A Vision', p. 10.
87. Ibid. pp. 11–13.
88. Southey, 'Review of Memoirs', p. 5.
89. Southey, 'Observations', p. 787.
90. Southey, 'Review of Memoirs', p. 25.
91. Southey, 'Review of Poems', p. 577.
92. Southey, 'Review of Memoirs', p. 21.
93. Ibid. p. 20.
94. Quoted in Javed Majeed, *Ungoverned*, p. 61.
95. For more on this point, see Leask, 'Southey's *Madoc*', p. 135.
96. Hart-Davis, *Thomas Love Peacock*, p. 128.
97. Byron, *The Major Works*, p. 428.
98. Derrida, 'La Loi', p. 207.
99. White, *Metahistory*, p. 54.
100. Shell et al., *Out of Livery*, p. 221.
101. Philip, *Researches*, p. 3.
102. See Van Wyk Smith, *Shades*, pp. 73–7.
103. 'Adamastor', pp. 310–17.
104. Theal, *The Portuguese*, p. 113. Theal's views were shared by the major English historian of Portugal, Whiteway, *The Rise*, p. 25.
105. Theal, *Records of South-Eastern Africa*, Vol. 8, p. 387.
106. Ibid. p. 408.
107. Buchan, *Prester John*, pp. 27–9.
108. Ibid. p. 95.
109. On the context of Theal and Buchan, see Henshaw, 'The "Key"'.
110. Purves, 'Camoens and the Epic of Africa, Part 1', p. 544.
111. Ibid. p. 550.
112. Purves, 'Camoens and the Epic of Africa, Part 2', p. 744.
113. Ibid. p. 745.
114. Lupi, *Portugal*, p. 13.

115. Ibid. p. 36.
116. Welch, *South Africa*, p. 153.
117. Ibid. p. 479.
118. Van Wyk Smith, *Shades*, p. 112. A number of critics have analysed Campbell's poetry, with most praising his poetry and regretting his politics. See Gray, *Camoens*; Cronin, 'Turning Around'; Chapman, 'Roy Campbell'; Crewe, 'The Spectre'; Monteiro, *The Presence* (pp. 120–31); and Meihuizen, *Ordering Empire* (pp. 163–246). Of these critics, Cronin is exceptional in antipathy towards Campbell's poetry *and* his politics.
119. See Witz, 'Eventless History'. The main historian of the Portuguese in Southern Africa after Welch was Eric Axelson, who provides a neutral description of Almeida's death in *Portuguese*, pp. 111–13.
120. This artwork is discussed in sympathetic detail in Vladislavic, *T'kama-Adamastor*.
121. See Van Wyk Smith, *Shades*, p. 14
122. Ibid. p. 35.
123. Brink mentions Almeida's death briefly in his essay 'A Myth', p. 41, but moves swiftly to a lengthy discussion of Adamastor. For Brink on the relation between History and Literature, see his *Reinventing*, p. 191.
124. Brink with Nethersole, 'Reimagining', p. 57.
125. Brink, 'A Myth', p. 46.
126. Brink, *The First Life*, p. 102. Brink was a finalist in the 2004 *Literary Review* Bad Sex Award. For details, see 'The Bad Sex Award'.
127. Jameson, *The Political Unconscious*, p. 107.
128. Van Wyk Smith, *Shades*, p. 162
129. Greene, 'Camões' Birthday', p. 199.
130. See Banks, 'Adamastorying'.
131. Sole, *Projections*, p. 41.
132. Sole, *Land*, p. 75.
133. Ferreira, 'Adamastor', p. 40.
134. Mbeki's ideas on the African Renaissance are set out in two collections of his speeches: Mbeki, *Africa: The Time* and *Africa: Define*.
135. For a longer-term perspective on Mbeki's African Renaissance, see Gevisser, *The Dream*, pp. 322–6, and for the immediate political context of its launch, see Gumede, *Thabo Mbeki*, pp. 202–4.
136. For sympathetic commentaries on Mbeki's project of the African Renaissance, see Makgoba, *African Renaissance*; and Mulemfo, *Thabo Mbeki*. For critical accounts, see Moloka and le Roux, *Problematising*; and Vale and Maseko, 'Thabo Mbeki'.
137. Mbeki, *Africa: The Time*, p. 242.
138. Ibid. p. 243. Mbeki's rhetorical references and the consensus of historical scholarship are not always in agreement. Most historians believe that the Battle of Omdurman (1898) ended in a victory for Kitchener's British Army.
139. Mbeki, *Africa: The Time*, p. 287.
140. Mpahlwa, 'Speech'.
141. Ibid.
142. Mabuyakhulu, 'Address'.
143. Ibid. These are extreme examples of what Patrick Bond designates the ANC's strategy of 'Talking Left, Acting Right' (see Bond, *Elite*, pp. 192–5), and what Hein Marais describes as 'the melange of neoliberal tropes and African nationalist liberation ideology, a discourse aimed at reconciling idealism and expediency' (Marais, *South Africa*, p. 421).
144. Gumede, *Thabo Mbeki*, p. 204.
145. Quoted in Vale and Maseko, p. 129.

## 2 French Representations of the Cape 'Hottentots': Jean Tavernier, Jean-Jacques Rousseau and François Levaillant

Mbeki's 2003 address to France's National Assembly quoted in the Introduction in fact reveals but one side of his contradictory attitude to France's legacy in Southern Africa. But before examining the second and contrary side, Mbeki's effusive words in Paris warrant more detailed exposition. He opened his address by quoting at length from a speech Maximilien Robespierre made in February 1794. Mbeki repeats Robespierre's bold claims for the new French nation: "'[That France may] become a model to nations, a terror to oppressors, a consolation to the oppressed, an ornament of the universe and that, by sealing the work with our blood, we may at least witness the dawn of the bright day of universal happiness'".[1] For Mbeki, France's revolutionary aspirations speak directly to the new South Africa:

> like the people of France in the eighteenth century, we too had to engage in struggle to free ourselves from another tyranny [. . .] We, the victims of a pernicious system of racist white minority rule, which considered and treated us as sub-human, would identify with the French Revolution and draw inspiration from what was done in this country which led to the solemn declaration that 'Men are born free and remain free and equal in rights', which proclaimed the vision of Equality, Liberty, Fraternity![2]

Mbeki moves from these tributes to describe key moments in the history of France's relationship with South Africa – the sinking of the *Mendi* battleship in the English Channel in 1917, and the deaths of 616 black South African auxiliaries on board; the exploitation and death of the Khoisan woman Sarah Bartmann, who died in France in 1816, and whose remains were returned in 2002 for reburial in South Africa; and the settlement of French Huguenot refugees at the Cape in the seventeenth century – before reaching the essential part of his speech: an appeal for financial aid from

France. Mbeki describes African poverty, summarises France's contribution in the years 1994–9 to enriching the poorer nations in the European Union, and outlines how South Africa (as a relatively wealthy African country) might with France's support enrich its poorer African neighbours. In his closing remarks (quoted in my Introduction), he clinches this appeal by referring to French eighteenth-century ideals, declaring that 'for this [economic plan] to happen, is going to require that globally we achieve a realignment of power and what Robespierre called the empire of reason [. . .] Perhaps all this calls for our own Age of Enlightenment, with its own Jean-Jacques Rousseau'.[3]

Mbeki's enthusiasm for the French Enlightenment, however, was substantially qualified by his critique of French colonialism. In a speech delivered at the funeral of Sarah Bartmann[4] at Hankey in the Eastern Cape on 19 August 2002, he denounced French eighteenth-century racism, and quoted the racist words of a number of the *philosophes*. He quotes Baron Georges Cuvier, who dissected Sarah Bartmann's body: "'These [Negro] races with depressed and compressed skulls are condemned to never-ending inferiority [. . .] Her moves had something that reminded one of the monkey and her external genitalia recalled those of the orang-utang'".[5] He quotes Montesquieu: "'You will find in the climates of the north, peoples with few vices, many virtues, sincerity and truthfulness. Approach the south, you are leaving morality itself, the passions become more vivacious and multiply crimes'".[6] He quotes Voltaire: "'[Africans] are not capable of any great application or association of ideas, and seem formed neither in the advantages nor the abuses of our philosophy'".[7] And he quotes Diderot's words that "'[Africans are] always vicious [. . .] mostly inclined to lasciviousness, vengeance, theft and lies'".[8] Mbeki makes it clear that these ideas were a necessary condition for the humiliation, exploitation and death of Sarah Bartmann, and he then argues that her fate was emblematic of the fate of all African people:

> The story of Sarah Bartmann is the story of the African people of our country in all their echelons. It is a story of the loss of our ancient freedom. It is a story of our dispossession of the land and the means that gave us an independent livelihood.[9]

Mbeki resolves the contradiction between the democratic France he celebrates in the 2003 address to the French Assembly and the racist France he criticises in his 2002 Hankey speech by arguing that in the two centuries since the Revolution and Sarah Bartmann's death, the former France has prevailed over the latter. As proof, he quotes with warm approval the French Minister of Research Roger-Gérard Schwartzenberg's rhetorical question – "'This young woman was treated as if she was something monstrous. But where in this affair is the monstrosity?'"[10] – and a second unnamed French parliamentarian's commitment to anti-racism:

> 'Saartjie Baartman's fate does not solicit our repentance. This would be too easy. It must be viewed as an incentive to continue the critical re-examination of our own history. This work is necessary if we want to eradicate racism, xenophobia and the contempt of some for other people.'[11]

Mbeki's interpretation of French eighteenth-century history and his understanding of its meaning for post-apartheid South Africa deserve closer scrutiny, and to this end I analyse the writings of French travellers to the Cape Colony in the years 1648–91 and the years 1748–92. In looking at these two generations of French travellers, I pose two questions: how did these writers represent the Khoisan? And, how did they understand France's economic and political expansion at the Cape? In addressing these questions, I hope to elaborate a more complex reading than Mbeki's of French Enlightenment thought in relation both to the eighteenth-century Cape Colony and to post-apartheid South Africa. In relation to the eighteenth century, it appears that as the French travellers to the Cape were representing the Khoisan in an increasingly positive light in their writings, so the Khoisan themselves were suffering a deterioration in their economic circumstances. This asymmetry between the cultural representations of the Khoisan and their economic plight prompts uncomfortable questions about Mbeki's optimistic teleology of the French Age of Reason spreading its light to Africa: do the more positive representations of the Khoisan serve a compensatory ideological function? Do such representations offset the economic devastation inflicted upon them by the expanding capitalist economy of the settlers? Crucially, for Mbeki, has this eighteenth-century contradiction between cultural representation[12] and economic impoverishment been transcended in post-apartheid South Africa? Scholarly versions of Mbeki's political arguments about Khoisan history and politics have also fixed overwhelmingly on the cultural and political representations of the Khoisan, and have failed to address the relationship between their cultural/political representation and their economic exploitation consistently and directly.[13]

## 1648–91: 'A SORT OF HUMAN BEASTS'

In the first fifty years after the Dutch established a settlement at the Cape in 1652, there were a number of French travellers to the Cape. During this period, the official policy of the Dutch East India Company (VOC) was to treat the Khoisan as an independent people and as trading partners, to be neither conquered nor enslaved. The VOC's escalating demand for cattle and farming land, however, soon precipitated tensions, and the Khoikhoi were defeated in three wars: in 1659–60, an attack by the Khoikhoi under the leadership of Doman was ruthlessly quelled; in 1673–7, the Khoikhoi under Gonnema suffered a more protracted and damaging defeat; and in 1693, the former interpreter and ally Dohra (known as Klaas to the Dutch) and his followers were humiliated and subdued. Assessing these encounters, historian Richard Elphick concludes '[a]ll responses to the Dutch had failed: the open resistance of Doman, the cautious withdrawal of Gonnema, the eager co-operation of Klaas'.[14] These military reverses enforced the political subordination of the Khoikhoi chiefs, which was accompanied by the incorporation of increasing numbers of landless and impoverished Khoikhoi into the settler economy as labourers.

Seventeenth-century French travellers who left written accounts of their impressions of the Cape include: Étienne de Flacourt (1607–60), who visited the Cape en-route to Madagascar in 1648; Jean Tavernier (1605–89), who visited the Cape in 1648; Guy Tachard (1651–1712), the Abbé François-Timoléon de Choisy (1644–1724), the Chevalier Alexandre de Chaumont (1640–1710), and the Comte Claude de Forbin (1656–1733), members of King Louis XIV's delegation en route to Siam in 1685; Simon de La Loubère (1642–1729), leader of the second delegation to Siam in 1687; Guillaume Chenu de Chalezac (1672–1731), the Huguenot 'French Boy' who was shipwrecked and lived amongst the Xhosa of the Eastern Cape in 1687–8; and François Leguat (1637–1735), who stopped on his way to France's Indian Ocean islands in 1691.[15] There were important differences between these writers, most notably over their religious allegiances – Tavernier, Chalezac and Leguat were Protestants, whereas Tachard, Choisy, Chaumont, Forbin and La Loubère were Catholics – but their negative descriptions of the Khoisan were substantially the same.

In describing the 'Hottentot' physiognomy and way of life, these writers identify them repeatedly as 'beasts' and 'brutes'. Tavernier declared:

> I never saw any so hideous nor so brutish as the Comoukes [. . .] and those of the Cape of Good Hope, whom they call Cafres, or Hosentotes [. . .] Neither men nor women are asham'd to shew their nakedness, for indeed they are but a sort of human Beasts.[16]

Both Chaumont and Forbin contrast their relative physical attractiveness with what they see as repulsive qualities: for Chaumont, 'the inhabitants of the country have a fine physiognomy, but herein deceitful, for they are mere brutes',[17] and for Forbin, they are 'well made of body, very amiable, but otherwise the most uncivilised and brutish people in the world [. . . and] they sleep all together pell-mell without distinction of sex, in miserable huts, and couple like beasts with no regard for relationship'.[18] Tachard concedes that the 'Hottentots' have certain redeeming qualities, but ultimately concludes that 'whatever good Opinion they may have of themselves, they lead a wretched life. They are nasty even to excess, and it would seem they study to make themselves hideous'.[19] Leguat's summary of the Cape's local inhabitants repeats these kinds of images; he writes: 'the Cafre Hottentots are extreamly ugly and loathsome, if one may give the name of Men to such Animals'.[20] The identification of 'Hottentots' with animals is extended in Leguat's description of communal life: 'They feed, lie, and live together like a Herd of Oxen and Cows, doing like them the ordinary functions of Nature with all manner of simplicity'.[21] Finally, on the few occasions when distinctions are drawn between the sexes, the 'Hottentot' women are described as even more bestial than the men. For example, Leguat alleges that '[t]he wives have somewhat yet more ugly and forbidding Phyz's than their Husbands',[22] and proceeds to list unappealing customs unique to 'Hottentot' women. Tavernier makes the bizarre claim that

> [t]he women are of so hot a constitution of Body, that at the times that their monthly customs are upon 'em, they happen to make water, and that a

European chances to set his feet upon it, it causes an immediate Head-ach and Feaver, which many times turns to Plague.[23]

The cumulative impression of these descriptions is that the 'Hottentots' were being inscribed in the great chain of being as intermediaries between man and beast, with 'beast-like' qualities repeatedly attributed to them.

These negative remarks about the 'Hottentots' were moderated very slightly by occasional words of praise, mostly in relation to their physical prowess. Tavernier declares that 'there are some that will catch a Roe-buck running', and that they are skilled in medicines, 'which they know to apply to several Diseases, which the Hollanders have several times exprienc'd'.[24] In the writings of the Catholic emissaries to Siam in the 1680s, comments on physical appearance and capabilities are also prominent: Choisy writes 'they appear to be good people; have a fine allure, open countenance';[25] Forbin observes 'they run very fast';[26] La Loubère enthuses 'many of them can outrun a horse [and] there is no torrent they cannot outswim'.[27] Only Tachard goes beyond the physical, and describes positive moral qualities, which he believes makes them potential converts to Catholicism: 'they have more Charity and Fidelity toward another than is to be found commonly among Christians', and further, 'Barbarity has not so totally effaced all Traces of Humanity in those People, but that there remains still some footsteps of Virtue'.[28] Leguat's racist discourse too concedes certain positive moral qualities to the 'Hottentots': 'They mutually assist each other in their Necessities, to the degree that they may properly be said to have nothing of their own', and as a community, 'they have divers other usages founded upon natural Equity, which they make use of for conservation of their Kind, and the Republick'.[29] However, these minor concessions do not threaten the collective sense of European superiority, as they all generate a sequence of discursive binaries that position the 'Hottentots' in every respect as the negative term. The only French traveller of this generation who challenges the received opposition between Europe and Africa is Chalezac, whose more protracted and precarious existence among the Xhosa[30] appears to have produced in him more complicated responses. He acknowledges the received French wisdoms about race, but in the light of his own experiences with the Xhosa, calls them into question: 'All Caffres in general are held to be gross and brutish people: those with whom I stayed, however, were much less so than others'.[31] He writes with particular affection of the kindness shown by his Xhosa 'foster-father', 'who received me with a tenderness not of a barbarian', and who upon finally parting 'rent the air with his cries, and I in turn could not refuse the love of a man to whom I owed so much'.[32] Further, Chalezac describes the encounter between Europe and Africa as detrimental to the latter: 'At one time the blacks here were trustworthy and good to deal with, but the busy trade they had with the Portuguese made rogues of them'.[33]

One thread that runs through all these writings is a preoccupation with the 'Hottentots'' potential as trading partners or as servants. Arriving at an early stage of Europe's penetration of the Cape, Tavernier focuses on the 'Hottentots' as traders. His descriptions of the early encounters between Europeans and the Cape's inhabitants reflect poorly on the former, but they register the strategic utility of 'Hottentot' trade for Europeans:

> So soon as the Ship arrives, they bring their Beeves to the shore, with what other commodities they have, to barter for strong water and Tobacco, Crystal or Agat Beads; or any sort of old Iron work. If they are not satisfi'd with what you offer them, away they fly; and then giving a whistle al their Cattel follow 'em; nor shall you ever see them again. Some, when they saw 'em fly, would shoot and kill their Cattel; but after that for some years they would never bring any more. 'Tis a very great convenience for the Vessels that touch there, to take in fresh Victuals; and the Hollanders did well to build a fort there.[34]

Flacourt also describes bartering with tobacco for cattle and sheep, but complains that the indigenes of the Cape 'are Nature's frankest vagabonds, and never cease from begging'.[35] The later seventeenth-century travellers comment less on the 'Hottentots' as trading partners than on their potential as servants. The consensus is that 'Hottentot' laziness is a major obstacle. Tachard complains that 'the Hotentots [sic] being persuaded that there is no other life after this, labour at little and take as much ease as they can in the World'.[36] This laziness, combined with the fact that 'they are excessively jealous of their Liberty', makes them avoid working as servants for the Dutch, as they choose rather to 'follow no other rules than what Nature taught them'.[37] Choisy declares that 'they are very lazy; they prefer not to eat rather than work',[38] and La Loubère observes that they 'have a pleasing build [and] are always gay', but their apparent lack of interest in money is ascribed to extreme laziness: 'they sometimes even commit murder in order to rob, showing that their contempt for riches is in reality nothing but their hatred for work'.[39] Leguat initially repeats the complaint that '[t]hey are extreamly lazy, and had rather undergo almost famine, than apply themselves to any Labour, contenting themselves with what Nature has produc'd her self', but later in his discussion offers advice on how to transform the lazy 'Hottentots' into good servants: 'for a bit of Bread and Tobacco, [they] may be made to work a whole Day', but to achieve this result, 'by no means abridge their Liberty [and do not] give them any thing to eat till after their Work is done'.[40] What underlies these remarks is the European colonisers' concern as to whether the 'Hottentots' could be incorporated into the emerging colonial economy as cheap labour.[41]

As regards how French colonial expansion is described in these writings, it is clear that at this stage religious allegiances continue to undermine emergent national aspirations.[42] The most vivid example is Chalezac's hostility towards French Catholics. While in Madeira, at an early stage of his flight from France, Chalezac escaped two Jesuits determined to return him to France by joining an English ship headed for the East Indies, and he asked rhetorically, 'Who was happier than I, who had escaped [. . .] the hands of the Jesuits, for whom I had a special loathing?'[43] Chalezac's anti-Jesuit sentiments are affirmed by his English benefactors, and during the journey to the East Indies, he appears to absorb (at least temporarily) their national identity too. When they have to fight off an attack by French pirates, Chalezac stoutly declares during the preliminaries to the battle that 'it was not the custom of us Englishmen to follow the wishes of the scum of the sea'.[44] The priority of religion over nationality in defining identity evident in Chalezac's writings is repeated in the comments of his contemporaries. Leguat expresses hostility towards his Catholic countrymen, and praises lavishly both 'this vast Powerful and Glorious Island of Great Britain, where the charity of the Generous Inhabitants has held out its Hand to me',[45] and the Dutch at the Cape: 'the poor French Protestants [. . .] peaceably enjoy their Happiness and live in good Correspondence with the Hollanders, who, as everyone knows, are of a frank and downright Humour'.[46] Unlike Chalezac and Leguat, the French Catholic travel writers do not appeal explicitly to co-religionists of other European nations, but they do foreground religious differences in their criticisms of the Dutch Empire. Tachard regrets the absence of Catholic priests at the Cape, and argues that they should be introduced as a matter of priority to 'be assistant to the Catholics at the Cape, who are many years without Masses and Sacraments, for want of Priests [and to] instruct the Hottentots'.[47] Choisy too notes the oppression of Catholics at the Cape, and is especially critical of the Dutch Protestant hegemony in the East:

> it is impossible to establish or maintain the Christian [Catholic] religion in the Orient as long as the Dutch are the most powerful here. They are its greatest enemies and have expelled it from Japan, the Moluccas, Malacca, Ceylon, Cochin and generally all places where they are strongest.[48]

In other words, European competition over access to colonial trade was conceived as much as a struggle to extend religious empires as conflicting attempts to consolidate national interests in distant lands.

What is also evident is that these seventeenth-century French travellers focus on the 'Dutch East India Company (VOC)' rather than 'the Dutch nation', or in other words, on the economic trading body rather than the political state. Tavernier's publication *Recueil de plusieurs relations et traitez* (1679), which contains a blistering attack on the VOC, is exemplary in this respect. Tavernier's uncompromising hostility, however, was slightly unusual, as French commentaries more characteristically combined envy with the recognition that Dutch merchants had the flexibility and initiative to establish lucrative foreign trade links in ways their European competitors had yet to emulate. Fernand Braudel notes that '[c]ompared to France, Holland with her trade networks and credit machinery could change policy at will',[49] and Giovanni Arrighi summarises:

> All variants of mercantilism had one thing in common: they were more or less conscious attempts on the part of territorialist rulers to *imitate* the Dutch, to become themselves capitalist in orientation as the most effective way of attaining their own power objectives.[50]

The French writings on the Cape therefore invariably praise the VOC for organising its colonial economies so successfully along mercantile principles. For example,

Tachard declares the Company's agents at the Cape to be 'men of Worth, and it was a happy Encounter for us, that we had such Men to treat with',[51] and in a private memorandum written in 1686, Choisy sets out clearly what makes the VOC successful in the East:

> To see what has to be done in establishing a post in the Indies, one should look at what the Dutch do. They are the masters there. They have ruined the Portuguese and the English, and looking at the situation of their affairs, it can be concluded that their procedure is not bad. Their fortresses are well supplied, their cities handsome, military discipline is well observed, the hospitals good, the temples beautiful, externally religion is well satisfied, justice is exact, there is magnificence in the senior people (the court of the Governor-General of Batavia is ostentatious), there is no familiarity with the natives [. . .] One rises in the ranks through merit, and one does not grow old in the Company's service without being promoted. An upstart from Europe is never given an important position in the Indies.[52]

Notwithstanding these laudable practices and impressive achievements, Choisy argues that a French chartered company run along similar lines under the patronage of Louis XIV would have the potential to supersede the VOC, as he detects cracks in its system. In the first place, the VOC has failed to win the support of the East Indies, as 'all the kings of the Indies are afraid of them and seek but to attack them', and second, the VOC's huge profits are substantially diminished by 'the thieving of its junior officials [who] steal regularly thirty percent'.[53]

To summarise. In the second half of the seventeenth century, French travellers to the Cape represented-as-portraits the Khoisan in a profoundly negative fashion, identifying them as 'beasts' and 'brutes'. At the same time, they were for the most part rejected as pliable cheap labour for the colonial economy on account of their laziness and 'love of Liberty'. Second, at this stage 'nation' had yet to replace 'religion' conclusively as the primary marker of identity for French travellers to Southern Africa, as the opposition between Catholic and Protestant (Huguenot) continued to complicate and at times even precede allegiance to the French nation. Finally, colonial expansion was conceived along mercantilist lines, with the hegemonic economic model being that of chartered companies (like the VOC) establishing trade monopolies in Africa, the Americas and the East.

# 1748–92

## Children of nature

Before moving on to the French travellers of the second half of the eighteenth century, it is necessary to register at least schematically the changed historical contexts of both France and the Cape Colony. France's absolutist state and its associated court capitalism came under increasing pressure from 'growing numbers of bourgeois *parvenus* who inevitably sought advancement through the structures of the *ancien régime*, and the growing economic and military supremacy of Britain over France'.[54] The first of these pressures was expressed in the gradual realignment of commerce along free trade lines. A key work was the Abbé G.-F. Coyer's *La noblesse commerçante* (1756), which attacked the traditional aristocratic disdain for commerce, and contributed to the general shift in French economic thought away from mercantile principles, and towards an embrace of free-trade capitalism.[55] The second pressure was expressed in the reconfiguration of France's political self-definition. Liah Greenfeld has argued convincingly that '[t]he idea of the nation took root in France around 1750. It became an integral, if not the central, part of the elite discourse and affected a profound change in mentality'.[56] The content of this idea of 'nation' was contested in the next fifty years, and came to include the ideals (if not the corresponding social reality) of equality, individual liberty and fraternity. Metropolitan ideas about distant 'savage nations' had also undergone a major change since the seventeenth century. The most influential work in this context was Jean-Jacques Rousseau's (1712–78) *Discourse on the Origin of Inequality* (1755). Rousseau's ideas about man-in-a-state-of-nature were derived from the works of travel writers,[57] and he draws inter alia upon descriptions of the Cape 'Hottentots' to explain how man's faculties develop in the state of nature:

> Because the savage's self-preservation is almost his sole concern, his best-developed faculties must be those devoted mainly to attack or defence: to overpower a prey or to avoid becoming the prey of another animal [. . .] What is true of animals in general is, according to the reports of explorers, true of most savage peoples as well. Thus we should not be surprised that the Hottentots of the Cape of Good Hope sight with the naked eye ships on the high seas at as great a distance as the Dutch see with their telescopes.[58]

There are three further references to the 'Hottentots' in Rousseau's Notes. In the first, he cites travellers' reports that 'the Hottentots [. . .] being very neglectful of their children, let them walk on their hands for so long that later it is hard for them to straighten up'.[59] In the second, he expands upon how much more developed the 'Hottentots' are than Europeans with respect to physical abilities, quoting Peter Kolb's[60] descriptions of their swimming prowess, fleet-footedness, and hunting skills – '"They have such quick sight and a hand so unerring that Europeans do not even come close to them"'.[61] And in the third reference, Rousseau quotes Kolb's story of a converted 'Hottentot' rejecting Christian civilisation, informing the disappointed Dutch Governor Van der Stel, '"My resolution is to live and die in the religion, customs, and usages of my ancestors"'.[62] Although Rousseau claims to know that 'it would be most simple-minded [. . .] to accept the authority of uncultured travellers',[63] he himself drew heavily on travel writers of questionable reliability in order to assemble his own influential impression of 'savage nations'. This impression was then recycled and decisively influenced subsequent travellers to the Cape.

At the Cape in the eighteenth century, there were also many changes. The gradual disappearance of mercantilism in France was paralleled in the Cape with the decline of the VOC, which finally went bankrupt in 1795 and ceded its assets to the Dutch state. In the early part of the century, settlers moved in significant numbers for the first time into the Tulbagh basin; the VOC relinquished its exclusive right to trade in cattle with the Khoisan, with the free burghers swift to take full advantage; there was a devastating smallpox epidemic in 1713, which barely one in ten of the Khoikhoi in the south-western Cape survived; and the 'Bushman War' of 1739–40 saw unprecedented levels of theft and slaughter perpetrated against Khoikhoi of the interior. Historians paint a bleak picture: Nigel Penn argues that

> [t]o a large extent the history of the period 1700–1740 is simply an account of the processes whereby the Khoi were stripped of their livestock and denied access to grazing and water resources – unless they were prepared to work for the colonists.[64]

And in a similar vein, Elphick concludes that

> [b]y 1720 the transformation of the Western Cape Khoikhoi into 'colonial Hottentots' was almost complete. The Khoikhoi had been reduced to a small fraction of their former population, their ancient economic and political institutions had virtually disappeared, and even their traditional culture was showing signs of erosion.[65]

Subsequent encounters between Europeans and independent Khoisan peoples as a consequence could only take place on the eastern and northern frontiers of the Colony, and such encounters were over-determined by the prior history of unequal trade, dispossession of land and cattle, and ongoing efforts to transform 'Hottentots' into 'good servants'. The mid-century decades following the 1739–40 war were relatively quieter, but the Khoisan's status as an independent people continued to decline, and settlers consolidated their control over all economic resources. In the latter part of the century, increasing pressure for land and livestock saw the deterioration of colonial relations and renewed outbreaks of violence, and the raising of the General Commando in 1774 proceeded with the dual aims of crushing all Khoisan opposition to settler advance and acquiring obedient Khoisan labour. The end of the VOC enabled unfettered free trade, but this effectively meant freedom for the *trek-boers* to murder and to exploit the Khoisan with greater impunity than ever before. Penn concludes that '[t]he situation of the Khoi at the end of the eighteenth century was therefore substantially worse than it had been before 1770'.[66]

The French visitors to the Cape for this period included: Pierre Poivre (1718–86), who visited in 1748–9; the Abbé Nicolas Louis de La Caille (1713–63) in 1751–3; Jacques Thomas Perrot and François Rubion in 1752; Bernardin de Saint-Pierre (1737–1814) in 1771; Pierre Marie François Pagès (1748–93) in 1773; Pierre Sonnerat (1748–1814) in 1774; François Levaillant (1753–1824) in 1781–4; Louis O'Hier de Grandpré (1761–1846) in 1786–7; and Jacques Julien Houten de Labillardière (1755–1834) in 1792. As was the case with the seventeenth-century French visitors to the Cape, so too these later travellers brought to bear a wide range of metropolitan perspectives upon the indigenes of the Cape. For our purposes, however, perhaps the most significant distinction to note is between the very few travellers who had direct contact with the indigenous peoples beyond the borders of the Colony (Perrot and Rubion in 1752, and Levaillant in 1781–4), and the rest of them, who were reliant on the oral and written testimony of other colonial reporters.

Three years before the publication of the Rousseau's *Discourse on the Origin of Inequality*, two illiterate French sailors recounted their positive impressions of the Khoisan and Xhosa of the Southern Cape. In 1752, Jacques Thomas Perrot and François Rubion were the only two of nine sailors from the French ship *Le Nécessaire* who survived being abandoned near Algoa Bay, and who then walked the 500 miles to the Cape. In their statement to the Secretary of the Political Council at the Cape (recorded in the third person), they describe their encounters with local inhabitants in a generous light:

> After five days walking they were still surrounded by Cafres who however did them no harm [. . .] They encountered Hottentots who treated them well and gave them a buck killed in the hunt [. . .] He was always treated well by the Hottentots, who gave him abundant sustenance.[67]

The statement records one instance of their being attacked by 'Hottentots', but like Chalezac sixty-five years before them, they do not draw from isolated incidents of hostility any general conclusions about 'African savagery', but instead emphasise repeatedly the kindnesses shown towards them.

Rousseau's influence is very marked in all the subsequent writers. In a passage in his *Journey to Mauritius*, Bernardin de Saint-Pierre reflects on his time at the Cape in 1771, and contrasts European animals to those of the Cape:

> Cape wolves are far less dangerous than ours. I could add to that observation that this superiority spreads to the people of our continent. We have more spirit and courage than the Asiatics and the blacks; but it would be worthier praise if I could say we surpass them in justice, goodness and social virtues.[68]

In a later note, Bernardin retracted this claim, attributing it to 'European prejudice and Montesquieu's opinion',[69] and argued instead that all nations should be respected equally, and that any differences between them are to be understood as the consequence of 'government that shapes human beings and [. . .] education that prepares them'.[70] There are brief and sympathetic descriptions of the 'Hottentots' in *Journey to Mauritius*, but in truth it is the Dutch settlers at the Cape that Bernardin extols as exemplifying the advantages of a life close to nature. His hostess's brother is described as 'over six feet tall and strong like a man who had been brought up in nature', and his killing of a lion bare-handed helps to convince Bernardin 'that nature has given man the ability to naturally tame all animals'.[71] There are also echoes of Rousseau's attack on the Arts in the *First Discourse* in Bernardin's approving description of the taciturn Dutch settlers, whose hearts and minds are excited by 'the sweet emotions of nature [and are] neither stimulated by artifice nor constrained by false decencies'.[72]

Much like Bernardin, Pierre Marie François Pagès[73] viewed the Cape's inhabitants through the philosophical lenses provided by Rousseau:

> At the Cape I expected likewise to obtain proper information respecting the route and best mode of travelling to the country of the Savage, or to speak more properly, the independent tribes of the Hottentots, who, constantly adverse to a foreign yoke, live to this day in the quiet and innocent enjoyments of pastoral life. To inquire into the manners of men, in a simple and unrefined state, was an object always uppermost in my thoughts, and had entered as a principle into the plan of my travels round the world.[74]

As his efforts to travel inland and establish to what extent the 'Hottentots' of the Cape conformed to Rousseau's 'savage nations' living in a state of nature were frustrated by practical obstacles, Pagès was obliged to rely on a brief encounter with two 'Hottentot' leaders in Cape Town and the reports of other travellers in order to confirm the veracity of Rousseau's ideas. He assembles a lengthy and sympathetic description of 'Hottentot' physiognomy, economy and customs, and concludes with a determined rejection of negative European stereotypes: 'the vivacity of [their] eyes seems to indicate something lively and intelligent [. . . We] cannot, without being chargeable with ignorance or injustice, impute to them a turn of mind peculiarly stupid and insensible'.[75] Also like Bernardin, Pagès sees the positive benefits of proximity to nature reflected in the virtuous character of the Dutch settlers. He recounts two anecdotes of settler heroism, and attributes them to 'how naturally the mind is disposed to imbibe great and intrepid sentiments, when removed from the pernicious influence of luxury, and placed in the ease and freedom of rural life'.[76] Like Bernardin and Pagès before them, both Louis O'Hier de Grandpré in 1786–7 and Jacques Julien Houten de Labillardière in 1792 struggled to observe 'savage Hottentots' first hand, and their descriptions are heavily reliant on a combination of earlier accounts and Rousseau. Grandpré draws on Anders Sparrman (1748–1820) and Levaillant for his description of the 'Hottentots' as 'destitute people who have the gentlest and most patient nature, faithful to a fault'.[77] Labillardière failed to meet any sufficiently wild 'Hottentots', and his search for the 'savage-man-in-a-state-of-nature' only culminated much later when he observed aborigines in Van Diemen's Land, whom he described accordingly: 'These people seemed so nearly in a state of nature, that their smallest actions appeared to me to merit observation'.[78]

Levaillant is the most interesting of these writers, as he produced lengthy accounts of his travels in the Cape Colony between 1781 and 1784.[79] During his two lengthy trips to the eastern and northern interiors of Southern Africa, Levaillant had extensive contact with the 'Hottentots' of the Cape, and applied Rousseau's ideas to the people he encountered. Rousseau's opposition between European civilisation's worship of luxury and complacent acceptance of inequality, and man-in-a-state-of-nature's practical egalitarianism, is faithfully echoed in Levaillant's writings.

Levaillant contends that the 'savage Hottentots'' proximity to nature guarantees equalities long since lost in Europe:

> In a country [the Cape] where there is no difference in birth or rank, every inhabitant is necessarily on an equality. Luxury and vanity (which in more polished countries consume the largest fortunes) create a thousand unhappy distinctions, entirely unknown to these savages; their desires are bounded by real wants, nor are they excluded from the means of gratifying them; and means may be, and are effectually pursued by all: thus, the various combinations of pride for the aggrandisement of families, all the schemes for heaping fortune in the same coffer, being utterly unknown, no intrigues are created, no oppressions practised, in fine, no crimes instigated.[80]

He returns to this theme repeatedly, and shifts between recounting the specifics of his Cape experiences, and proclaiming general Laws of Nature. He declares that 'the painful comparison of riches mounted on a car of gold, while poverty is training her tatters in the dust, never wrings [the 'Hottentot's'] heart; it is, indeed, an idea that never entered his imagination'.[81] The 'savage Hottentots'' lack of individual greed and their lived equality is then explained in general terms as a result of their conditions of existence; these are qualities necessary for their collective survival:

> Such is the general disposition of mankind in a state of incultivation; indeed, nature herself seems to inculcate the lesson, and declare it unreasonable that anyone should monopolize for his own particular purposes, what is the general birth-right of all; and any glaring instance of inequality, may bring on the most alarming consequences.[82]

These natural egalitarian habits, however, are disrupted with the intrusion of European ways, and Levaillant asserts that as soon as the 'savage Hottentot' is westernised, all these qualities are immediately lost. Levaillant contrasts the inadequacies of the 'Hottentots' employed at the Cape to the virtues of 'savage Hottentots' beyond the Colony's borders. Indeed, those groups like the Gonaquais who live furthest from the Cape earn his highest praise:

> [The Gonaquais] were not here degenerate and miserable Hottentots like those who languish in the neighbourhood of the Cape, despising and despised, remembering of their origin nothing but the empty name; and enjoying, at the price of their liberty, a little peace bought dearly at the expence of excessive labour. But here I could contemplate a people brave and free, possessing only independence, yielding to the impulse of their natures, which is truly philanthropic and magnanimous.[83]

There are many inconsistencies in Levaillant's descriptions of the 'Hottentots'. For example, he praises his guide Klaas (a westernised 'Hottentot') in extravagant terms which flout his distinction elsewhere between 'savage' and Cape-based

'Hottentots',[84] and on his second journey to the Orange River, following a rebellion by his 'Hottentot' servants, his bitter complaints about their unreliability contradict his earlier tributes to their natural virtues.[85]

There are many objections that might be raised against such representations of the 'Hottentots-as-children-of-nature'. Of direct relevance, for example, is Jacques Derrida's critique of Claude Lévi-Strauss's representation of non-western, pre-modern communities. Responding to Lévi-Strauss's embrace of Rousseau in *Tristes Tropiques* as the true guide to modern anthropology,[86] Derrida observes that:

> Non-European peoples were not only studied as the index to a hidden good Nature, as a native soil recovered, of a 'zero degree' with reference to which one could outline the structure, the growth, and above all the degradation of our society and or culture. As always, this archaeology is also a teleology and an eschatology; the dream of a full and immediate presence closing history, the transparence and indivision of a parousia, the suppression of contradiction and difference.[87]

By reading Lévi-Strauss's descriptions of the Nambikwara against the grain, Derrida discovers that far from being a society of natural innocents, 'we are dealing here not only with a strongly hierarchized society, but with a society where relation-ships are marked with spectacular violence'.[88] Levaillant's observations of the Cape 'Hottentots' precede Lévi-Strauss's studies of the Nambikwara by nearly two centuries, but a similar objection might be raised: by universalising Rousseau's state of nature, and projecting it onto the 'Hottentots', Levaillant both misreads the specificities of 'Hottentot' societies, and prescribes a teleological narrative of their fate as a people. Such criticisms notwithstanding, it remains important to register that the descriptions of the 'Hottentots' in these eighteenth-century writ-ings are some distance from the 'beasts' vilified a century earlier. Furthermore, these relatively positive representations never displaced the earlier racist inscriptions. Walter B. Cohen has pointed out that '[w]hereas the Noble Savage enjoyed a liter-ary vogue, he never really conquered eighteenth-century French thought.'[89] As a consequence, the trope of 'Hottentots-as-children-of-nature' receded with the rise of racial science in the nineteenth century, and the 'Hottentots' were redefined as sub-human in the pseudo-scientific discourses which updated seventeenth-century prejudices.

### Useful citizens

In the writings of Pagès and Levaillant, the image of the 'Hottentots-as-children-of-nature' alternates with a second image of the 'Hottentots-as-potential-citizens'. This image is developed in more detail by Pagès, who argues for a model of colonial rule based on assimilation and equality:

> Foreign settlements, in my opinion, are only so far desirable as they are the means of increasing the number of useful and active citizens, who may co-

operate at home and abroad in promoting the riches, stability, and splendour of the parent state [. . .] The number of useful citizens may be increased by incorporating the natives with the colonial settlement. The Indians, though little advanced in the arts of civilization, are in general tractable; and were they to find themselves emancipated from the rigorous yoke of their own domineering aristocracy, and admitted to the full participation of a mild and equitable government, they would be naturally engaged to respect and imitate the character and genius of their masters.[90]

Pagès argues further that in constituting a colonial citizenry immigrants from Europe should be added to the emerging body of assimilated natives, and that the process of integration should be accelerated further by promoting the inter-marriage of natives and immigrant settlers. Their relations should be governed by principles of equality:

Equality, as far as is consistent with the difference of talents and property, ought to subsist between the natives of the new country and the descendants of the parent state. Rewards, honours, and employments, at least of a subordinate nature, should lie open to merit, in whatever order of men it may be found [. . . I]n general, whatever may contribute to unite the people in one liberal society, appears to me rationally practicable, in instilling into the minds of aliens and foreigners the true principles of fidelity and allegiance.[91]

He restricts his proposals for inter-marriage to the colonies, for he believes such a policy in the French nation itself 'might bastardize the native character and genius of the people at large'.[92] In other words: racial purity for the nation; racial integration for the colony. Despite this considerable limitation, Pagès's proposals for French colonial governance are clearly some distance from the views of his predecessors, and although they do not refer explicitly to the 'Hottentots' of the Cape in Volume 1, his subsequent sympathetic discussions of both the 'Hottentots' and of the slaves at the Cape suggest that his commitment to assimilation and political equality would have extended to all the peoples of the Cape Colony. In arguing that 'natives of the new country' might become 'useful citizens', Pagès is the first French writer to raise the possibility (however remotely) that indigenes might be represented in the political sense, as opposed to being confined to being represented-as-portraits in the writings and sketches of French travellers.

Levaillant does not entertain the possibility of colonial subjects graduating to citizenship in anything like the detail of Pagès, but in a passage attacking the violent Spanish and Dutch practices of colonial governance, he proposes a more humane approach that he hopes the French might follow:

I conceived that, by gradually introducing milder institutions among these people, an important and interesting revolution might be effected; which could not fail to take place, the moment their tranquility and safety, which ignorance, which the terror of their name had for so many years disturbed, should, by equitable laws, be secured to them.[93]

In common with Pagès's inclusive blueprint for French colonial expansion, Levaillant in passages like these tentatively imagines the non-violent constitution of new communities in the colonies made up of an equal citizenry of settler and indigene united in sympathy to France's national interest. In other words, like Pagès, Levaillant departs from exclusively aesthetic representations of the 'Hottentots' to consider the political representation of 'Hottentots' within a common citizenry.

It might be tempting to interpret Pagès and Levaillant's arguments for the inclusion of 'natives' into a 'useful citizenry' as an unequivocal improvement upon the explicit and obvious racism of the seventeenth century. However, read in context, their formulations constitute an early and incomplete formulation of what came to be known as 'direct rule'. The discourse of direct rule approved formal political equality for all colonial citizens, but such equality was strictly limited, as Mahmood Mamdani explains: 'There would be a single legal order, defined by the "civilised" laws of Europe. No "native" institutions would be recognized. Although "natives" would have to conform to European laws, only those "civilized" would have access to European rights'.[94] In other words, Pagès and Levaillant's proposed admission of indigenes into the body of the colony's 'useful citizens' prefigures the system of colonial governance based upon the inclusion of a small minority (who satisfy a certain standard of 'civilization') and the exclusion of a majority consigned to function as cheap labour. That such a system was falling into place at the Cape is confirmed by historian Robert Ross's observation that 'the Khoi had, by the end of the eighteenth century, been reduced to the level of unfree servants. Rights they might have retained, but they could no longer exercise them'.[95] In other words, these positive discursive representations of the 'Hottentots' in the late eighteenth century were of ambiguous consolation; the new egalitarian political discourse imagining a common colonial citizenry was the emergent ideology of direct rule, and for the majority of 'Hottentots' who were excluded from colonial civilisation, their fate was further exploitation and dispossession.

## Servants

In one key respect, the representations of the 'Hottentots' in the second half of the eighteenth century repeated those of the seventeenth, namely with regard to their continuing concern with the capacity of the 'Hottentots' to function in the Cape economy as servants. Following his visit to the Cape in 1748–9, Pierre Poivre does not mention the indigenes of the Cape explicitly, but in praising the Dutch, he denigrates their ability as farmers:

> The countries around the Cape were condemned to the same sterility before the Dutch took possession of them [. . .] The abundance this colony enjoys, compared to the barrenness of the surrounding countries, evidently demonstrates that the earth only denies her favors to the tyrant and the slave.[96]

Although Poivre attacked the Europeans' short-sighted plunder of the colonies' natural resources, the ill-treatment of indigenous populations and the institution of slavery, his vision of self-sustaining rural economies of small-scale farmers managed along physiocratic principles consigned the indigenes to a subordinate labouring function. The Abbé Nicolas Louis de La Caille, a visitor to Cape Town in 1751–3 comments on the 'Hottentots' in the context of his extensive criticisms of an earlier publication – Peter Kolb's *The Present State of the Cape of Good Hope* (1719).[97] In correcting Kolb, La Caille repeats many of the earlier myths of 'Hottentot' inferiority. For example, he declares that they lack religious belief, and he flatly rejects Kolb's claim that the 'Hottentots' make good servants,[98] arguing that those

> in European employ conspire at times with [the Bushmen] to rob the colonists [and that] their great laziness has made them forget the traditions of their ancestors as regards this, since the supreme good for a Hottentot is to do nothing, and even to think of nothing.[99]

Pierre Sonnerat, who was the nephew of Poivre, also only spent only a short time at the Cape in 1774, and his descriptions of the 'Hottentots' repeat entrenched clichés about their lack of religion and reluctance to work as servants. He explains that

> [a]ccustomed to independence, they cannot bear servitude. If a Hottentot enters into the service of the Dutch, in the station of a domestic, as soon as he has gained any thing he quits his employment, and returns to his family.[100]

Sonnerat does at least concede that 'these people are yet but little known',[101] and he looks forward to the explorer Robert Jacob Gordon[102] (1743–95) publishing his discoveries to address this lack of knowledge.

Levaillant, despite his frequent celebrations of the 'Hottentots' as children of nature, and even as potential citizens, also displays in certain passages a keen concern with their capacity to work as servants for European settlers. Levaillant assesses the capacity of the 'Hottentots' to function as productive servants of the colonists in much the same terms as he discusses the economic potential of the land. This underlying economic pragmatism is nowhere more evident than in his arguments for promoting miscegenation. In paragraphs that anticipate the racism of the nineteenth century, Levaillant argues that the children of unions between European men and 'Hottentot' women produce superior offspring – 'they have more courage and energy [. . .] and are not so averse to labour'[103] – and then encourages yet more varieties of miscegenation:

> [T]he race produced by the Hottentot women and negroes is far superior than the others [. . . T]hey are in general request for labour; but what renders them still more estimable, is, that to great activity without turbulence, they join the merit of fidelity which may be depended on. Unhappily this kind is scarce, owing to the disdain with which the Hottentots look on the negroes. It would long since have been of public utility, and a particular advantage to the colonists, had administration encouraged the propagation of this sort of people;

the expence would not have been burthensome, and in the end would have returned an hundredfold.[104]

For Levaillant, there is no contradiction between this conception of the 'Hottentots' as human stock for breeding reliable servants, and his view of the 'Hottentots' as children of nature or as potential citizens. In common with his contemporaries, the concern over securing a colonial labour force shadows his writings about the 'Hottentots', and an awareness of their potential economic value never disappears entirely from his effusive celebrations of their natural virtues.

### Emulating the VOC

At least two of the eighteenth-century French travellers continued to praise the VOC's achievements at the Cape. Poivre contrasts the VOC's agricultural achievements at the Cape with the destructive greed of their European competitors, and singles out the Company Gardens in Cape Town for particular praise: 'the India Company have caused to lay out two or three gardens, extensive and magnificent, which they support with an expense worthy of a sovereign Company'.[105] For Bernardin, the Dutch at the Cape represent a salutary contrast to the brutal French-controlled slave society of Mauritius, and as such provide an exemplary model of European expansion into Africa. For French writers to criticise Dutch achievements at the Cape would be bad manners: 'those Frenchmen who had travelled in the [Dutch] Company's ships had published hostile accounts. Such actions showed a lack of gratitude towards hospitality, and this consideration has stopped me from publishing my thoughts on how this colony might be attacked'.[106] Instead Bernardin promises to 'write something that would increase its prosperity' as a gesture of thanks to 'such a quiet society of happy people in a land rich in all sorts of provisions'.[107]

Poivre and Bernardin, however, are exceptions, and all the other French travellers are uncompromising in their criticism of the Dutch at the Cape. La Caille's comments on the quality of the agricultural products from the Cape are withering:

> the inhabitants of the Cape do not know yet how to get good results from the produce of their land [. . . They] make very bad bread from the best grain in the world [. . . They] do not take the trouble to make their butter as is done in Europe [. . .] Very bad beer is brewed at the Cape.[108]

His outrage at the poor quality of these products is exacerbated by how expensive they are – '[it] is difficult to believe that, in a country whose herds are its principal riches, butter and milk should be so dear'[109] – and he attributes these iniquities in the Cape's agricultural economy to the monopoly on all trade enjoyed by the VOC. Pagès's comments on the Dutch at the Cape are relatively neutral (he praises their 'industry and perseverance'[110] in establishing the settlement at Simonstown), but in looking at their empire more broadly, his comments are scathing:

The conduct of the Dutch in the administration of their distant settlements
is at least equally exceptionable with that of the Spaniards. The miserable
state of the natives who have the misfortune to live immediately under their
authority, and their inhuman massacre of Indians and Chinese for venturing to
oppose the torrent of Batavian oppression, are striking examples of the tyrannical maxims which actuate the tools of this mercantile government. During
my short residence at Batavia the Dutch beheaded one Indian, and impaled
another in circumstances of such savage barbarity, as I believe are scarcely to
be paralleled in the annals of Turkey.[111]

In their extreme cruelty towards their colonial subjects and in their single-minded
pursuit of wealth, the Dutch, like the Turks and the Spanish, represent for Pagès
a clear example of how not to manage an empire. Pagès moderates his complaints
about the inflated prices and monopolistic practices of the VOC by acknowledging
the Cape's capacity to supply necessary provisions for passing ships:

From the fertility of the soil, and numerous herds of cattle, the Dutch at the
Cape, as well as the planters in the remote parts of the settlement, live at a very
moderate expence; an advantage, however, but little felt by Europeans, government having arrogated to itself a monopoly, not only of supplying ships with
stores, but even daily subsistence to strangers. Provisions are sold at a very high
price; and hence the profits of purveyance constitute a very considerable part of
the colonial revenue. Still, however, it is a matter of agreeable surprise to find
at the extreme point of the African continent, plenty of every thing necessary
or convenient for a long voyage.[112]

As in La Caille's criticisms of the VOC twenty years earlier, so too here in Pagès's
writings, injustices arising from the protectionist policies of the mercantile system
are identified, but no elaborated argument for an alternative based on competition
and free trade is made.

Much like Pagès, Levaillant argues that when the 'Hottentots' were confronted
by rapacious Dutch settlers greedy for their land, their way of life was destroyed
by the colonisers' strategies of dishonest trade and violence. Levaillant suggests
that '[b]efore the arrival of Europeans at the Cape, commerce was unknown to the
Hottentots; perhaps they had not even the idea of exchange'.[113] With their tobacco,
alcohol and trinkets, the Dutch corrupted these pastoral innocents, who epitomised
'human nature in its infancy'.[114] The impact of this trade is described by Levaillant
in terms which echo the Fall of Adam, with the Dutch cast as the serpent: the
Dutch prevail 'by offering to the Hottentots two highly seductive lures: tobacco, and
brandy. From this moment on, no more liberty, no more pride, no more nature, no
more Hottentots, no more men'.[115] This sense of a tragic fall is expressed in a further
passage where the westernised 'Hottentot' is described as 'no longer the acknowledged child of nature'.[116] When trade failed to wrest sought-after goods and resources
from the 'Hottentots', the Dutch turned to violence to achieve their ends, and in
all his descriptions of the initial encounters between Europeans and 'Hottentots',

Levaillant lays the blame for the descent into murderous conflict on the colonists. He defends the 'Hottentots' against Dutch-settler accusations of cruelty, and reflects upon how Europeans might themselves have responded to being colonised:

> In a state of nature man is essentially good; why should the Hottentot be an exception to this rule? It is without reason that he is accused of being cruel [. . . C]an anything be more sensible than to repel force by force? It is ridiculous to expect from these children of nature the practice of our refined humanity, whose rules, indeed, we are more ready to expect that to perform [. . .] Suppose the savages of Africa and America [. . .] should assemble from all parts, armed with destructive weapons, invade Europe, and endeavour to chase us from our possessions? [. . .] Yet such has been our practice with respect to them [. . .] Wherever we have sought fit to establish ourselves, we have reduced the unhappy nations to slavery or flight; we have appropriated to our own use, without scruple, whatever appeared to answer our purpose.[117]

Two further passages are of particular interest. The first occurs in his journey along the east coast, where he praises the agricultural potential of the Eastern Cape in comparison with that of the Western Cape. He writes of how he 'talked to myself as I walked up the hill, forming vain wishes for the conquest of this beautiful country',[118] and of how he imagined establishing shipyards and warehouses for timber, and exploiting the highly fertile soil to grow 'better crops and attract more intelligent colonists'.[119] He breaks off his happy fantasies with the recognition that his plans are likely to be sabotaged by the fact that the Cape is a colony where 'the general good is subordinated to the private advantages of a few united entrepreneurs, interested in stifling any conception that might tend to diminish their profits'.[120] The second passage occurs in his second journey to the north-east, when he writes with a similar enthusiasm about the area of Twenty-four Rivers, describing it as '[t]his fertile country, so highly favoured by nature'.[121] He attributes its lack of (European) agricultural development in the first instance to 'the inferior agents [the Government] is obliged to employ',[122] but goes on to locate responsibility for its underdevelopment more broadly with the policies of chartered companies like the VOC: 'has the commercial policy of privileged companies ever been known to unite their private interest to the interest of the public?'.[123] Condemning the Company and its agents' 'ardent thirst of gold, [. . .] mistaken selfish motives [and] greedy avarice', Levaillant concludes that because of their vices the Cape will 'remain almost a desert [and] lose the benefit of every thing that nature has done for its fecundity'.[124]

If anything, Grandpré's attack on the Dutch at the Cape is even more vehement than that of Levaillant. Like Pagès and Levaillant, Grandpré raises the negative example of the Spanish Empire, and compares the Dutch treatment of the 'Hottentots' at the Cape to the Spanish slaughter of the native peoples of Latin America:

> [T]he Dutch will always be to blame for the ruin of the Hottentot nation in the eyes of sensitive men; they have repeated at the tip of Africa the same bloodied

scenes as the Spaniards first enacted in America. Perhaps they only lacked a Las Casas to make a formal complaint against them before the tribunal of the whole of Europe. When they did not slit the throats of these people by the thousand, they wiped them out one at a time. If they did not train their dogs to hunt them down initially, they did so in due course [. . .] The Dutch government failed its obligations to these destitute people [. . .] There remain some eight thousand of them; but what can be done for them? Half of them are slaves and, as for the others, such is the barbarity of their oppressors, they wouldn't dream of civilizing these wretched remains of a nation whom they have abandoned, and whom they have left to sink into abject ignorance, in a savage state resembling, in part if not completely, that in which they lived before Europe sent them gun powder and chains.[125]

Grandpré's description of the colonial encounter moves on to describe the geno-cide of the 'Bushmen', arguing that the Dutch exceeded the cruelties of Cortés and Pizarro in the Americas, as 'they have hunted the Boschis as one would hunt hares; their dogs have been trained for it. Hunting packs of dogs, horses, slaves, children, women, men; all are put to this dreadful purpose'.[126] Labillardière's criticisms of the Dutch at the Cape focus less on offences of the past than on their continuing reli-ance on slavery – he notes that at the Cape slave traders get 'two or three negroes for one fine dog'[127] – and upon the greed and despotism of the VOC officials. A recent biographer of Labillardière has suggested that considering the help he and his crew received at the Cape, Labillardière 'was somewhat ungracious'[128] towards his Dutch hosts. However, read alongside the similar comments of his French contemporaries, Labillardière's anti-Dutch sentiments appear to coincide with other French travel-lers of the period committing themselves more zealously than ever before to the French nation, particularly in relation to European imperial competitors.

La Caille, Pagès and Levaillant appear more concerned to mount a strong case against the mercantilist economic system of the Dutch at the Cape than to argue the case for a reconfigured colonial economy based on centralised political governance and free trade. Grandpré and Labillardière, however, go beyond simply criticising the VOC, and make a strong case for an alternative model of colonial governance. For Grandpré, the Company's officials are 'second-hand traders with no education, no training, very vain, and they regard themselves as filling the most important position in the world'.[129] Their 'narrow-mindedness [and] petty avarice'[130] have prevented them from seeing the wider potential of the Cape, and have made the colony vulnerable to being taken over by imperial competitors with greater vision, like the British. Grandpré believes the British lost their North American colonies as a consequence of their protectionist trade policies, and that they can only succeed in the Cape if they relinquish such policies in favour of free trade:

If the British crown wants this colony to prosper, it has to be very careful to avoid conferring exclusive privileges. If the goal is to serve the Company's interests exclusively, it will only languish as it has done so until now. It needs to trade with the whole universe.[131]

Labillardière too rails against the 'despotic power'[132] and corrupt ways of the VOC's Cape officials, and accuses them of profiteering on an outrageous scale:

> The mercantile spirit of the Dutch East India Company has often induced them to feign a great scarcity at the Cape, in order to enhance the price of provisions. The cultivators are not allowed to contract directly with foreigners [. . .] but are obliged to dispose of them to the Company, who often give them not a fourth of the price.[133]

Over time, such practices had generated resentment towards the VOC, which according to Labillardière would ultimately lead to its collapse. His criticisms proved prescient, as the VOC went bankrupt and transferred its assets to the Dutch state in 1795.

## CONCLUSION

An exclusive focus on the representations of the Cape 'Hottentots' in French writings of the seventeenth and eighteenth centuries might lead to the conclusion that by 1800 a distinctively modern sensibility had emerged at the Cape, based on a positive representation of the Khoisan, an increased emphasis on national-democratic (as opposed to religious) definitions of community, and a rejection of mercantile trading practices in favour of free trade. The evidence to support such a view is substantial. First, from the mid-seventeenth century to the late eighteenth century, the representation of the Cape 'Hottentots' changed from their being described as 'beasts' and 'brutes' in the decades 1648–91 to their being described as 'children of nature' and as potential 'useful citizens' in the decades 1748–92. Indeed, writers like Pagès and Levaillant even broke with the dominant tradition of conceiving the 'Hottentots' exclusively as objects of literary/artistic/philosophical representation by European observers, and contemplated their capacity for political representation within a common polity. Second, the religious discourses of the seventeenth century were superseded by the egalitarian political discourses of nationhood in the eighteenth century. This transition is perhaps best conveyed by recalling Choisy's approving remarks in 1686 on how the Dutch in the East indulged 'no familiarity with the natives', and contrasting it with Pagès's argument in 1782 that 'the number of useful citizens may be increased by incorporating the natives with the colonial settlement'. Third, there was a general shift in French views on the Cape's economy through this period, from praise for the mercantile domination of trade, production and distribution by the VOC in the seventeenth century, to fierce criticisms of the corruption and protectionism of the VOC, and arguments for an economy based upon free trade by the late eighteenth century. The scale of the shift in French attitudes is expressed in the contrast between Tachard's recollections of his 'happy Encounter' with the VOC's 'men of Worth' at the Cape in 1688, and Grandpré's scathing description of the Company's officials as 'second-hand traders with no education' in 1801. More substantial than these kinds of *ad hominem* remarks, however, was the gathering consensus in the late eighteenth century that the era of exclusive privileges for state-sponsored companies had passed, and that – in Grandpré's words – a successful nation needs to pursue 'trade with the whole universe'.

However, looking beyond the writings of these French travellers to the histories of the Khoisan of the Cape in the years 1650–1800, it is clear that a more complicated reading is required. Over the same period that the aesthetic representations of the Cape 'Hottentots' improved from 'beasts' to 'children of nature', and even extended to considering their political identity as 'useful citizens', their material existences deteriorated dramatically, as they declined from being significant independent communities in 1650 to being scattered handfuls of impoverished servants in 1800. This history suggests that there is no inevitable or necessary correlation between being represented-as-portrait in positive terms (as, for example, as a 'child of nature'), and an improvement in material living conditions. Indeed, if anything, it might be argued that there is an asymmetry between the improving aesthetic representations of the 'Hottentots' in the eighteenth century and their material dispossession and impoverishment.

The question as to whether the inclusive political representation of the 'Hottentots' contemplated by Pagès and Levaillant in the 1770s and 1780s – and only ultimately enacted with South Africa's first democratic elections in 1994 – has a more direct correlation with the Khoisan's material security is the one I want to conclude with by looking at two recent documents produced by the ANC government. The first document is the address by Mbeki at the unveiling of the new coat of arms at Kwaggafontein on 27 April 2000. Mbeki explains the choice on the new coat of arms of two Khoisan figures and a motto in the Khoisan language /Xam – !ke e: /xarra //ke ('Diverse peoples unite') – as follows:

> Those depicted, who were the very first inhabitants of our land, the Khoisan people, speak to our commitment to celebrate humanity and to advance the cause of the fulfilment of all human beings in our country and throughout the world [. . .] They are depicted in an attitude of greeting, demonstrating the transformation of the individual into a social being who belongs to a collective and interdependent humanity [. . .] We have chosen an ancient language of our people. This language is now extinct as no one lives who speaks it as his or her mother tongue. This emphasises the tragedy of the millions of human beings who, through the ages, have perished and even ceased to exist as peoples, because of people's inhumanity to others [. . .] By inscribing these words on our Coat of Arms – !ke e: /xarra //ke – we make a commitment to value life, to respect all languages and cultures, to oppose racism, sexism, chauvinism and genocide.[134]

The prominence accorded the Khoisan in South Africa's new coat of arms has been widely applauded as an appropriate gesture that simultaneously registers the value of pre-colonial African societies, and seeks to compensate, at least symbolically, for the genocidal destruction of the Khoisan by European settlers from the seventeenth to the nineteenth centuries.[135] There is a consensus that in post-apartheid South

Africa the Khoisan should be represented – both in the aesthetic and the political sense of 'represent' – in positive terms.

As to the question of whether the improved representation of the Khoisan has seen a corresponding improvement in their material existences, some indication is provided in a more obscure government document – the Ministry of Welfare and Social Development report, *Mothers and Fathers of the Nation: The Forgotten People – Report of the Ministerial Committee on Abuse, Neglect and Ill-Treatment of Older Persons*. Triggered by a public outcry following a television exposé on the treatment of the elderly, the report includes a summary of the living conditions for the older members of the Khoisan community living in the small Northern Cape town of Smitsdrift:

> 65 persons presented the plight of the 300 older persons from Smitsdrift. Their main problems were.

* Housing: Persons still live in tents after 10 years, most tents are torn
* Inadequate supply of water: Persons walk over 2 km for water
* Healthcare is inadequate with only one clinic, a doctor once a month and hardly any medicines
* Forty residents still do not have identity documents and cannot get social grants. Attempts to resolve this with Home Affairs and the Department of Welfare have failed.[136]

How to explain the contradiction between these two documents, between the symbolic elevation of the Khoisan of the past on the coat of arms, and the material neglect of surviving Khoisan peoples in Smitsdrift in the Ministry of Welfare report? One local explanation is that the state's tardiness in addressing the current plight of the Smitsdrift Khoisan is due to the fact that they worked as trackers for the South African Defence Force during the apartheid years. But the contradiction points more generally once again to the difficulties of connecting positive racial representation (as in the coat of arms) and inclusive political representation (as 'South African citizens') to survival in an economy generating vast disparities of wealth and opportunity.

## NOTES

1. Mbeki, 'Address of the President of South Africa, Thabo Mbeki, at the French National Assembly'.
2. Ibid.
3. Ibid.
4. There is extensive scholarship on Sarah Bartmann, with two recent books – Rachel Holmes's *The Hottentot*, and Clifton Crais and Pamela Scully's *Sara*. For a critical overview of the scholarship, see Abrahams, 'Colonialism'.
5. Mbeki, 'Speech at the Funeral'.
6. Ibid.

7. Ibid.
8. Ibid.
9. Ibid.
10. Ibid.
11. Ibid.
12. See Spivak on the dangers of conflating the two meanings of 'represent' – represent-as-portrait in art, literature or philosophy (*darstellen*) and represent-as-proxy in politics (*vertreten*) – in 'Can the Subaltern', pp. 275–7. Also useful, and more wide-ranging, is Prendergast's discussion of the terms used for 'representation' in languages other than English in *The Triangle*, pp. 1–16.
13. As my concern here is to analyse the primary sources, I have not engaged with the vast detail of recent research on the Khoisan in particular, and on eighteenth- and nineteenth-century European racisms in general. As examples of the former, see Bassani and Tedeschi, 'The Image'; Van Wyk Smith, '"The Most Wretched"'; Smith, 'Different Facets'; Skotnes, *Miscast*; Merians, *Envisioning the Worst*; Hudson, '"Hottentots"'; and the sections on the changing definitions of 'Hottentots' in Wahrman, *The Making*. As examples of the latter, I have in mind Foucault, '*Society Must Be Defended*'; Pratt, *Travel Writing*; and Wheeler, *The Complexion*. I have learnt much from this work, but question its limited interrogation of the relation between racism and capitalism.
14. Elphick and Malherbe, 'The Khoisan', p. 16. The standard work on the history of this period remains Elphick, *Kraal and Castle*. For variations on Elphick's reading of this period, see Ross, *Beyond*, pp. 166–80; and Keegan, *Colonial*, pp. 15–36.
15. There are useful introductions to all these travellers in Strangman, *Early*.
16. Tavernier, *The Six*, pp. 204–5. Tavernier was the most popular of these seventeenth-century writers, and by the middle of the eighteenth century twenty-one editions of his *Travels* had been published in several European translations. See York, 'Travels in India', p. 142.
17. Smithies, *The Chevalier*, p. 24.
18. Extract in Raven-Hart, *Cape*, p. 264.
19. Tachard, *Relation*, pp. 69–70. Tachard's editor Michael Smithies suspects Tachard of inserting his own views in the account by the Siamese delegate Ok-Khun Chamnan of his encounters with Hottentots after being shipwrecked at Cape Agulhas in 1686 and walking for thirty-one days to Cape Town. Chamnan (as transcribed by Tachard) expresses the delegation's fear of becoming slaves to the 'Hottentots' as follows: 'Our vexation was increased by the sad thought that we were going to serve under and be dependent on the most repulsive and barbarian people in the universe' (Smithies, *A Siamese*, p. 43).
20. Leguat, *A New*, Vol. 2, p. 287. There is a long-running debate over whether Leguat wrote this account himself, or whether it was copied and embellished from Tavernier and others by Maximilien Misson. The case against Leguat as author was made originally by Georges-Louis Leclerc Comte de Buffon (1707–88) and Georges Cuvier (1769–1832), and was elaborated in the twentieth century by Geoffrey Atkinson in *The Extraordinary Voyage*. Leguat's status as the original author is stoutly defended by North-Coombe in *The Vindication*.
21. Leguat, *A New*, Vol. 2, p. 296.
22. Leguat, *A New*, Vol. 2, p. 291. Leguat's disdain for 'Hottentot' women needs to be read alongside his eroticised descriptions of black women in Batavia: 'I met at Batavia, divers very pretty Negro-women, with faces much like ours of Europe, large brilliant eyes, wonderful white Teeth, fine Shapes, beautiful and soft Breasts, as were likewise all the other parts of their Bodies, tho' black as Jett [. . .] If we moreover remember that the Black Colour has its Lustre and Value, as well as any other, we must cease to wonder at their

Taste who love a fine Negro-woman as much, or rather more than a White one' (Leguat, *A New*, Vol. 2, p. 270).

23. Tavernier, *The Six*, pp. 206–7.
24. Ibid. pp. 204, 205.
25. Choisy, *Journal*, pp. 84–5.
26. Extract in Raven-Hart, *Cape*, p. 264.
27. Extract in Raven-Hart, *Cape*, p. 319.
28. Tachard, *Relation*, pp. 67, 71.
29. Leguat, *A New*, Vol. 2, pp. 293, 295.
30. In the seventeenth century, the Nguni-speaking communities like the Xhosa, who lived further east from the Cape Colony, were identified by Europeans as 'Caffres' (with variations on the spelling). Like the terms 'Hottentot' and 'Bushmen', the term 'Caffre' has been widely rejected as racist.
31. Vigne, *Guillaume*, p. 35.
32. Ibid. pp. 34, 44.
33. Ibid. p. 45.
34. Tavernier, *The Six*, p. 205.
35. Extract in Raven-Hart, *Before*, p. 175.
36. Tachard, *Relation*, p. 69.
37. Ibid. pp. 71, 72.
38. Choisy, *Journal*, p. 85
39. Extract in Raven-Hart, *Cape*, pp. 319, 321.
40. Leguat, *A New*, Vol. 2, pp. 287, 290.
41. The Dutch writer Johannes Willem de Grevenbroek, who settled at the Cape, and therefore had extensive direct experience of the Khoikhoi as servants, was more enthusiastic: 'They are apt in applying their hands to unfamiliar tasks [. . .] They make faithful and efficient herds [. . .] They make trusty bearers, porters, carriers, postboys and couriers' (Schapera, *The Early*, pp. 271–3).
42. For a discussion of Protestant consciousness at the Cape in the late seventeenth century, see Romero, 'Encounter'.
43. Vigne, *Guillaume*, p. 21.
44. Ibid. p. 24.
45. Leguat, *A New*, Vol. 1, p. lxxxviii.
46. Leguat, *A New*, Vol. 2, p. 287.
47. Tachard, *Relation*, p. 78.
48. Smithies, *The Chevalier*, p. 176.
49. Braudel, *The Perspective*, p. 258.
50. Arrighi, *The Long*, p. 140.
51. Tachard, *Relation*, p. 46.
52. Smithies, *The Chevalier*, pp. 182–3.
53. Ibid. pp. 172–3.
54. Mooers, *The Making*, p. 61.
55. See Greenfeld, *The Spirit*, pp. 132–53; Faccarello, 'Galiani', pp. 120–95; and Fox-Genovese, *The Origins*.
56. Greenfeld, *Nationalism*, p. 177. See too Bell, *The Cult*.
57. For a summary of the travel writers Rousseau relied upon, see Muthu, *Enlightenment*, pp. 31–46.
58. Rousseau, *Discourse*, p. 32.
59. Ibid. p. 87.
60. Kolb (1625–1726) had *The Present State of the Cape of Good Hope* first published in German in 1719, with translated editions following soon after in Dutch (1727), English (1731) and

French (1741). Immanuel Kant also drew heavily on Kolb, but unlike Rousseau, suppressed the positive qualities Kolb ascribed to the 'Hottentots'. On Kolb, see Penn, 'The Voyage'; Raum, 'Reflections', pp. 30–40; and Pratt, *Imperial*, pp. 41–9.

61. Kolb, *The Present*, p. 92.

62. Ibid. p. 118.

63. Ibid. p. 109.

64. Penn, 'Labour', p. 4.

65. Elphick, *Kraal*, p. 235. For the history of the Khoisan on the frontiers of the Cape Colony, see the complementary studies by Newton-King, *Masters*; and Penn, *The Forgotten*.

66. Penn, 'Labour', p. 19.

67. Sienaert-van Reenen, *Die Franse*, pp. 154–5 (own translation).

68. Bernardin de Saint-Pierre, *Journey*, p. 200. In a subsequent passage, Bernardin reverts to older explanations of racial difference: 'Strong animals have [. . .] thick blood, and the more docile ones have thin blood. To this cause I willingly attribute the superiority of the whites over the blacks' (pp. 203–4).

69. Ibid. p. 245.

70. Ibid. p. 246.

71. Ibid. p. 200.

72. Ibid. p. 205.

73. The son of Toulouse nobility, Pagès was an intrepid traveller, whose journeys around the world took him to North America, the Far East, and on expeditions to both the South and North Poles. He fought with distinction in the Seven Years War and with the French navy in the American War of Independence, and retired finally to Santo Domingo, where he was killed in 1793 at the start of the slave uprising.

74. Pagès, *Travels*, Vol. 3, p. 10.

75. Ibid. p. 28.

76. Ibid. p. 34.

77. O'Hier de Grandpré, *Voyage*, p. 180 (own translation). Grandpré's compassion for the colonised and the enslaved, and his radical-sounding criticisms of Dutch imperialism should however be read with caution, as the details of his life at the Cape suggest some distance between his theories and practices. He was a slave-trader who had disembarked in Mauritius carrying slaves infected with smallpox. The resulting epidemic on the island killed 4,000 people, and with a price on his head, Grandpré fled, spending ten months at the Cape in 1793. In later years, he translated John Barrow's travel writings on the Cape into French. These events are described in a recent biography of Grandpré by Romain, *Mes ennemis*.

78. Labillardière, *An Account*, Vol. 2, p. 41.

79. Levaillant was by some distance the most popular of this generation of French travel writers to Africa, and translations of his works soon appeared German (1792), Russian (1793) and Swedish (1795). The English translations of Levaillant I have quoted from are: Glenn's modern translation of *Travels*, Vol. 1; the eighteenth-century translations of *Travels*, Vol. 2, and *New Travels*, Vols 1–3. Many of Levaillant's contemporaries questioned the truthfulness of his accounts, pointing out many inconsistencies and exaggerations in his tales. For examples, see Barnard, *The Cape Journals*, p. 413; Barrow, *An Account*, Vol. 1, p. 360; Lichtenstein, *Travels*, Vol. 1, pp. 29–30; Campbell, *Travels*, Vol. 2, p. 330; and Latrobe, *Journal*, p. 295. An entertaining fictional attack on Levaillant's ideas and his influence in Europe is contained in Elizabeth Hamilton's satirical novel *Memoirs of Modern Philosophers*, pp. 141–4. In recent years, Levaillant's travels have been extensively researched. For generally sympathetic discussions of his life and times, see J. C. Quinton et al., *François le Vaillant*; L. C. Rookmaaker et al., *François Levaillant*; and Meiring, *The Truth*. For more critical analyses of his writings, particularly with regard to his representations of

'Hottentot' women, see Schiebinger, *Nature's Body*, pp. 159–62; and Strother, 'Display', pp. 17–22.

80. Levaillant, *Travels*, Vol. 2, pp. 67–8.
81. Ibid. pp. 160–1.
82. Ibid. p. 213.
83. Levaillant, *New Travels*, Vol. 1, pp. 14–15.
84. See Levaillant, *Travels*, Vol. 1, pp. 103–4.
85. See Levaillant, *New Travels*, Vol. 2, pp. 298–305.
86. See Claude Lévi-Strauss, who describes how 'I had gone to the ends of the earth to look for what Rousseau calls "the most imperceptible stages of man's beginnings" [. . .] I believed that, having been luckier than Rousseau, I had discovered such a state in a moribund society [the Nambikwara]' (*Tristes*, p. 316). He concludes, following Rousseau, that '[n]atural man did not precede society, nor is he outside it. Our task is to rediscover his form as it is immanent in the social state, mankind being inconceivable outside society; this means working out a programme of the experiments which "would be necessary in order to arrive at a knowledge of natural man" and determining "the means whereby these experiments can be made within society". But the model – this is Rousseau's solution – is eternal and universal' (p. 392).
87. Derrida, *Of Grammatology*, pp. 114–15.
88. Ibid. p. 135.
89. Cohen, *The French*, p. 72. For Cohen's discussion of the limits of Levaillant's influence in France, see pp. 91–2.
90. Pagès, Vol. 1, pp. 257–8.
91. Ibid. Vol. 1, pp. 260–1.
92. Ibid. Vol. 1, p. 261.
93. Levaillant, *New Travels*, Vol. 1, p. 72.
94. See Mamdani, *Citizen*, pp. 16–17, 65–7.
95. Ross, *Beyond*, p. 180.
96. Poivre, *Travels*, pp. 9–10. This US edition is the English translation of a speech made by Poivre in Lyons in 1763. Poivre integrated these positive impressions of Dutch farming at the Cape into his own version of physiocratic ideology, which he applied in pursuing conservationist policies of reforestation as a colonial official in Mauritius from 1767–72. For a discussion of Poivre, see Grove, *Green*, pp. 168–263.
97. La Caille's criticisms are directed at the unreliable 1741 French translation of Kolb published by Jean Catuffe. It is hard to find a subsequent travel writer to the Cape who does *not* try to correct Kolb's descriptions of the Cape's indigenous population: for an especially comprehensive attack, see O. F. Mentzel's, *A Geographical and Topographical Description of the Cape of Good Hope* (1785–7). Mentzel is even more outraged by Kolb's descriptions of the fauna of the Cape (see, for example, Vol. 3, pp. 224, 237).
98. Kolb wrote '[The Hottentots] make excellent Servants, and perhaps the faithfullest in the world,' *The Present*, p. 38.
99. La Caille, *Travels*, p. 41. La Caille's time at the Cape was dedicated principally to mapping the stars of the southern hemisphere, and his ad hoc remarks on Cape society were first published in 1763.
100. Sonnerat, *A Voyage*, p. 89.
101. Ibid. p. 89.
102. Although not French himself, Gordon is of interest in the context of how the French Enlightenment influenced thinking at the Cape, as he met and discussed ideas about man in a 'state of nature' with the *philosophe* Denis Diderot (1713–84). For a description of their encounter, see Cullinan, *Robert*, pp. 22–4.
103. Levaillant, *Travels*, Vol. 2, p. 164.

104. Ibid. pp. 165–6.
105. Poivre, *Travels*, p. 14.
106. Bernardin de Saint Pierre, *Journey*, p. 191.
107. Ibid. p. 191.
108. La Caille, *Travels*, pp. 30–4.
109. Ibid. p. 30.
110. Pagès, *Travels*, Vol. 3, p. 10.
111. Pagès, *Travels*, Vol. 1, p. 294.
112. Pagès, *Travels*, Vol. 3, p. 19.
113. Levaillant, *Travels*, Vol. 2, p. 144.
114. Ibid. p. 145.
115. Levaillant, *Travels*, Vol. 1, p. 122.
116. Levaillant, *Travels*, Vol. 2, p. 161.
117. Ibid. pp. 149–51.
118. Levaillant, *Travels*, Vol. 1, p. 92.
119. Ibid. p. 96.
120. Ibid. p. 97.
121. Levaillant, *New Travels*, Vol. 1, p. 193.
122. Ibid. p. 192.
123. Ibid. p. 194.
124. Ibid. p. 194.
125. O'Hier de Grandpré, *Voyage*, pp. 179–81 (own translation).
126. Ibid. p. 182.
127. Labillardière, *An Account*, p. 85.
128. Duyker, *Citizen*, p. 92.
129. O'Hier de Grandpré, *Voyage*, p. 155 (own translation).
130. Ibid. p. 200.
131. Ibid. pp. 198–9.
132. Labillardière, *An Account*, p. 85.
133. Ibid. p. 106.
134. Mbeki, 'Address by President Thabo Mbeki at the unveiling'. There was some debate
     subsequently over the precise meaning of the motto, with Petrus Vaalbooi of the Khomani
     San Association of the Northern Cape claiming that it meant 'going to take a leak
     [urinate].' See Le May, 'Wee'.
135. See, for example, Lewis-Williams and Pearce, *San*, pp. 231–4.
136. Republic of South Africa, Ministry of Welfare and Social Development, *Report*, Section G.
     1. 1. 5. The more recent circumstances of the Khoisan community at Smitsdrift (also spelt
     Schmidtsdrift) – including their move to the farm Platfontein – are described in newspaper
     articles by Smith, 'New'; and Weidlich, 'Southern'.

# 3    The Scottish Enlightenment and Colonial Governance: Adam Smith, John Bruce and Lady Anne Barnard

## INTRODUCTION

The seizure of the Cape Colony by Britain in 1795 introduced new ideas as to how the relation between nation and colony in Southern Africa should be articulated. After first surveying British writings on the Cape in the seventeenth and eighteenth centuries, this chapter examines the contrasting models of colonial governance produced for the Cape Colony by two eighteenth-century Scottish Enlightenment thinkers – Adam Smith (1723–90) and John Bruce (1744–1826). There is no explicit debate between Smith and Bruce to record – Smith wrote in the 1770s and Bruce in the 1790s – but they both range between the general question as to how Britain's colonial policy should proceed, and the particular question of how Britain should reconfigure the political economy of the Cape. Although the primary material analysed here is narrowly focused, Smith and Bruce's writings on the Cape not only reveal the variety of British models of colonial governance for the empire as a whole, but they also provoke theoretical questions about the articulation of the economic and the political in emergent colonial nationalisms. I focus upon three issues. The first is how in political terms the relation between nation and colony should be constituted, or more specifically, whether Britain should govern through indigenous proxy rulers (indirect rule) or whether it should develop its own colonial administration (direct rule). The second issue is how the economics of colonial trade should be regulated, or more specifically, whether trade protectionism or free trade should be the guiding principle. The third issue is how the indigenes of new colonies should be represented within and integrated into Britain's political economy. Are the indigenes potential citizens in a common British polity, or are they tribal subjects to be governed by a paternalist British authority? Are they equal trading partners, or a cheap source of labour? The chapter concludes by examining the reception of Smith and Bruce's ideas at the Cape, considering first how their ideas on political economy were applied, and second, how the Scottish Enlightenment discourse of sentiment was extended to the Khoisan and Cape slaves in the writings of the Scottish diarist, Lady Anne Barnard (1750–1825).

## BRITAIN AT THE CAPE: JOHN CROSS (1615) TO HENRY PEMBERTON (1785)

Although there is some evidence that the English East India Company Directors considered establishing a halfway station to India at Saldanha Bay in 1613, the first British attempt to establish a base at the Cape itself took place two years later. Edward Terry explains the background to this initiative:

> Ten English men having received the sentence of death for their several crimes at the sessions house in the Old Baily at London, had their execution respited by the intreaty of the East-India Merchants, upon condition that they should be all banished to [the Cape], to the end (if they should find any peaceable abode there) they might discover something advantageous to their trade; and this was accordingly done.[1]

The ten men were transported from London in February 1615, and upon being deposited in Table Bay, were obliged to sign two documents thanking both King James I and the Honourable East India Company for saving their lives, and for giving them the opportunity of redemption through hard work by swelling Company profits. Following a skirmish with the local inhabitants during which one of them was killed, the survivors under the leadership of John Cross borrowed a longboat and rowed to Robben Island, where they barely survived by eating penguins. Several months later, when another English ship passed by Table Bay, three of the group were drowned trying to reach the ship; three more returned to England to be hanged rather than remain at the Cape; and the final three stayed on the island, and were (it has been assumed) rescued and taken to the East by a non-English ship. There was another attempt to people the Cape with three more convicts in 1616, but this too was short-lived and ended in comprehensive failure. In 1620 at Saldanha Bay, admirals Andrew Shilling and Humphrey Fitzherbert 'concluded to intitle his Majeste King [James I] supreme head and governor of the continent not yet inhabited by any Christian prince'[2] by raising a small mount of stones and delivering a flag to the native inhabitants. However, no permanent British settlement followed this symbolic occupation, and with the Dutch installing themselves in Table Bay in 1652, there were no further British attempts to settle at the Cape for over 150 years. British ambitions in the region receded, and Saint Helena was used as a refreshment station en route to the East instead.

Notwithstanding the Dutch presence at the Cape, a number of British travellers passing through commented on the commercial viability of the Cape. These travellers expressed different views on chartered companies in general and on the VOC in particular. For example, reporting on his visit to the Cape in 1689, John Ovington praised the 'indefatigable Diligence and Industry of the *Dutch*', describing them as 'remarkable for Improvements, for their commendable Pains and Cares wherever they Inhabit'.[3] Ovington's praise was qualified, however, by words of criticism for the profiteering of the VOC at the expense of the Cape's independent farmers: 'The Governour and Council agree with the Countryman for his Goods and Cattle at a very low rate, and sell them to the Ships that put in there as dear as they please'.[4] Visiting the Cape a decade later, Woodes Rogers expresses similar views, arguing that

> [the Dutch] Form and Government, their Industry and Neatness abroad, is justly to be admir'd, and worthy to be imitated. I saw nothing I could blame, unless it be their Severity, for which they no doubt have a very good Reason, tho' it seem'd harsh to me, who was born with English Liberty.[5]

Rogers notes that VOC regulations 'enable the People to pay a great Excise for their Commodities',[6] but he does not identify this form of taxation as an injustice. By contrast, William Symson, another Englishman who visited the Cape at the time, is much more sympathetic to the settlers than to the VOC:

> Notwithstanding this Encouragement [for new settlers], they have a great Hardship upon them, which is, that they must sell their goods to the Governor, and at his Price; so that he runs away with most of the Profit arising by their Labour and Industry; for the Governor buys at very low rates, and sells to Ships that come in as dear as he pleases; and no Man can sell any thing to Strangers without the Council's leave.[7]

These kinds of criticisms of the VOC at the Cape were repeated intermittently by English writers travelling past the Cape in the second half of the eighteenth century, although several still continued to express admiration for the Dutch system of governance. Jemima Kindersley (1741–1809), for example, a visitor to the Cape in 1764, is full of praise: 'the Dutch policy is admirable! Oeconomy, regularity, and decency, are the effects of it'.[8] The Dutch settlers enjoy an envious lifestyle: 'they are blessed with a moderate government, and a delightful climate. I was never in a place where people seemed to enjoy so much comfort'.[9] Like Rogers, Kindersley describes the VOC's trading restrictions in neutral terms, and her only criticism also relates to Dutch forms of punishment. The suffering inflicted upon slave convicts, she declares, 'was the most cruel that could be invented by the art of man'.[10] In a similar vein, the botanist William Paterson (1755–1810) a decade later describes uncritically the VOC exercising its trade monopoly, and he attributes the hardships experienced by the Dutch farmers not to the misrule of the VOC, but to the farmers' own laziness:

> But the generality of those people are of so indolent a disposition, that they seldom trouble themselves either to build houses or to cultivate the ground. Those of them who chuse to be industrious, and to make the most of their advantages, are enabled to live in a very comfortable manner.[11]

Both Kindersley and Paterson had strong ties to the status quo, Kindersley as the wife of an East India Company officer, and Paterson as a botanist heavily dependant upon the help of the Dutch official and explorer, Robert Jacob Gordon, so their views on the Dutch at the Cape are perhaps unsurprising. Another botanist, Francis Masson (1741–1805), initially shared Paterson's sympathetic views on VOC rule in his Cape travels of 1772–4, but later, at the end of his second and longer sojourn at the Cape (1786–95), confided in a letter to the Swedish botanist Carl Peter Thunberg (1743–1828) that 'the whole colony has for some years been falling in decadence and at last almost General State Bankruptsy, having nothing but wretched paper money'.[12]

Although these observations by British passers-by suggest how Britain might have tried to improve upon Dutch rule at the Cape, they do not quite amount to models of colonial governance. However, in 1785 two senior British officers, William Dalrymple and Henry Pemberton, did produce more detailed plans for a British settlement in Southern Africa. Both were on board the *Pigot*, which had sailed for England from Madras on 12 February 1785, and had anchored at the Krom River mouth for repairs on 2 May 1785. In separate letters to Prime Minister William Pitt, Dalrymple and Pemberton appealed to him to establish a British settlement on the southern Cape coast. They argued that rather than following the dangerous and costly path of deploying British troops to drive the VOC out of Cape Town, Britain should establish a settlement at 'Croeme Rivier Bay', which is the site of the modern town of Cape St Francis.[13] Dalrymple argues that carrying through such a plan 'would be of the most important consequences to Britain and the India Company',[14] and Pemberton echoes his enthusiasm, declaring 'that a post on the South East Coast of Africa would be of the utmost benefit to this Nation in general and to the Honourable East India Company in particular'.[15] Both of them thus identify Britain's national interest with the East India Company, and argue that the southern Cape can both replace the North American colonies within Britain's colonial economy, and secure the trade route to the Indies. Indeed, the southern Cape meets all of Britain's needs, as Dalrymple declares,

> We have lost America, and an half way house would secure us India, and an Empire to Britain. We are at a loss where to send our Convicts – to send them to this Country would indeed be a Paradise to them, and Settlers would crowd here.[16]

Local conditions strongly favour the British, as the inept Dutch officials have few friends in the Cape – according to Dalrymple, '[the Dutch and "Caffres"] are inveterate enemies to each other', and the settlers are 'ready to revolt from Holland if England would establish a port in the Province'.[17] Pemberton echoes Dalrymple's confident view that the local inhabitants would be well disposed towards the British, and argues further that they would be readily transformed into willing labourers: the 'aboriginal inhabitants, the Hottentots, are of peaceable, mild and laborious dispositions, making excellent household and farm servants'.[18] Dalrymple and Pemberton's proposals do little more than repeat the fundamentals of Britain's mercantilist colonial model, and transpose them to the southern Cape. The political administration of the Krom River settlement would be managed by the East Indian Company; the economic benefits would accrue in the first instance to the Company, and only in the longer term (via the taxes paid by the Company) to the British nation in general; and the indigenes of the Cape would be incorporated as docile labourers. That this model had failed in the North American colonies did not prompt any rethinking by Dalrymple and Pemberton; for Adam Smith, however, the American Revolution demonstrated that a new model of colonial governance was required.

## SMITH'S NORTH AMERICAN MODEL: RESISTING THE OPPRESSIVE GENIUS OF AN EXCLUSIVE COMPANY

Smith's comments on the governance of colonial settlements are dominated by an uncompromising hostility towards chartered companies. Comparing the different European colonies in the Americas, Smith concludes that '[t]he government of an exclusive company of merchants is, perhaps, the worst of all governments for any country whatever'.[19] Smith argues further that not only colonies, but all political systems should strive to banish exclusive companies. The national sovereign must 'open the most extensive market for the produce of his country, to allow the most perfect freedom of commerce, in order to increase as much as possible the number and competition of buyers'.[20] David McNally paraphrases Smith as prescribing that 'the state must construct an institutional setting in which merchants and manufacturers are denied access to situations in which they can monopolize their trade'.[21] Smith's favoured models of colonial governance are those of Greece and its colonies, and of Britain and its North American colonies. According to Smith, the Greek

> mother city, though she considered the colony as a child, at all times entitled to great favour and assistance, and owing in turn much gratitude and respect, yet considered it as an emancipated child over whom she pretended to claim no direct authority or jurisdiction.[22]

Giving new colonies substantial liberties benefited the Greek 'mother city' because within a short space of time, these colonies emerged as self-sufficient entities: 'the progress of many of the ancient Greek colonies towards wealth and greatness seems accordingly to have been very rapid'.[23] Of the colonial enterprises of his own age, Smith argues that the British in North America have come closest to replicating the Greek model in that the colonists have enjoyed '[p]lenty of land, and liberty to manage their own affairs their own way', and that as a result 'there are no colonies of which the progress has been more rapid than that of the English in North America'.[24] What impresses Smith about Britain's North American colonies is how cheaply they are governed – he notes that '[a]ll the different civil establishments in North America [except Maryland and North Carolina . . .] cost the inhabitants above £64,700 a year; an ever-memorable example at how small an expense three million people may not only be governed, but well governed'.[25] Furthermore, the colonial assemblies come much closer than Britain's own House of Commons to providing an equal representation of the people, and as a consequence citizens of the North American colonies enjoy 'more equality, [. . .] their manners are more republican [. . .] and their governments [. . .] have hitherto been more republican too'.[26]

Smith's antipathy towards exclusive companies is not confined to their role as political institutions; he is even more vehement in condemning their economic effects. He describes the mercantile trading system both as a malfunctioning machine, and as an unhealthy body. Free trade is described as 'one of the great springs which puts into motion the great part of the business of mankind', and the 'exclusive trade of the mother countries' by contrast is described variously as a 'dead weight' and 'a clog', which 'cramps', 'encumbers', 'excludes' and 'confines' free trade.[27] Shifting metaphors, the 'monopoly of the colony trade'[28] is compared to a 'small stop in that great blood vessel, which has been artificially swelled beyond its natural dimensions, and through which an unnatural proportion of the industry and commerce of the country has been forced to circulate'.[29] Smith expands upon this grim diagnosis of mercantile trading systems by examining the history of colonialism. He locates the roots of mercantilist forms of colonialism in the Roman Empire, an authoritarian model of colonial rule which assigned all conquered land to Roman citizens and relied upon slave labour. Unlike the Greek colonies, the Roman colonies stagnated, and Smith bemoans the fact the Roman model of colonisation has been the more common one, as he sees the authoritarian structures of the modern European colonies copying the Roman model. Smith records that in the early stages of commerce with the East, the Portuguese established a trading monopoly, and there was no improvement when they were superseded by the Dutch, English, French, Swedes and Danes, who also enabled small groups of merchants to acquire exclusive trading charters and monopolise trade; as a consequence, 'no great nation in Europe has ever yet had the benefit of a free commerce to the Indies'.[30] The impact on these European nations was that '[m]erchants and manufacturers [. . .] derived the greatest advantage from this monopoly of the home market';[31] for the vast majority of the 'home' population, the monopolies inflated prices and thus exacerbated poverty and hardship. Although the monopolies claim to represent Britain's collective national interest, Smith rejects such arguments as instances of 'national prejudice and animosity, prompted by the private interest of particular traders'.[32] The pre-eminent example of such monopolies is the English East India Company, which has impoverished most inhabitants of England on account of 'the extraordinary waste which the fraud and abuse inseparable from the management of the affairs of so great a company, must necessarily have occasioned'.[33]

Smith's reflections on the impact of colonialism on the indigenes are framed by the four-stage teleology of human development accepted by Scottish Enlightenment thinkers. In Chapter 1, we noted Robertson's application of this teleology to different African communities, from Southern Africa to the northern reaches of the East coast of Africa. Like Robertson, Smith identified Britons as the fortunate heirs of the final stage of traders and manufacturers prospering in a commercial society, but in *The Theory of Moral Sentiments*, he registers some uneasiness with this model of uncomplicated progress.[34] He contrasts how the qualities of 'self-denial and command of the passions' are valued in 'civilised' and 'barbarous nations', and concludes that in the case of the 'savages in North America '[t]heir magnanimity and self-command [. . .] are almost beyond the conception of Europeans'.[35] Smith praises the 'savage's' courage in the face of torture and death, and extends his discussion to Africa, where he observes that '[t]here is not a negro from the coast of Africa who does not [. . .] possess a degree of magnanimity which the soul of his sordid master is too often scarce capable of conceiving'.[36] He concludes from these two examples that '[t]his heroic and unconquerable firmness, which the custom and education of his country demand of every savage, is not required of those who are brought up to live in civilised societies'.[37] Smith was not alone among his contemporaries in expressing grave doubts about this model of progress. Adam Ferguson (1723–1816) in *An Essay on the History of Civilisation* (1767) questioned the axiomatic tie between 'progress' and 'empire', arguing that the greed of 'ambitious men' sabotaged the interests of 'the citizen': 'Hence the ruinous progress of empire, and hence free nations, under the shew of acquiring dominion, suffer themselves, in the end, to be yoked with the slaves they had conquered'.[38] And John Millar (1735–1801) in *The Origin of the Distinction of Ranks* (1771) refers with approval to Kolb on the 'Hottentots', and concludes that 'a savage' is always reluctant 'to abandon his family and friends [. . .] to be banished from them is accounted the greatest of all misfortunes. His cottage, his fields, the faces and conversation of his kindred and companions, recur incessantly to his memory'.[39]

Smith reiterates his doubts about the superiority of commercial societies in *The Wealth of Nations*, as he assesses the impact of colonialism on indigenous peoples. Of the Spanish occupation of South America, he writes with regret that '[t]he savage injustice of the Europeans rendered an event, which ought to have been beneficial to all, ruinous and destructive to several of those unfortunate countries'.[40] Focusing on the shepherd economies of Peru and Mexico, Smith is critical of how 'the [Spaniards'] pious purpose of converting [the indigenes] to Christianity sanctified the injustice of the project', and notes further their 'injustice in coveting the possession of a country whose harmless natives, far from having ever injured the people of Europe, had received the first adventurers with every mark of kindness and hospitality'.[41] However, these compassionate sentiments are undermined by Smith's conviction that notwithstanding these cruelties, the native Americans benefited from the European presence:

> it seems impossible that either [the Peruvian or Mexican] empires could have been so much improved or so much cultivated as at present, when they are plentifully furnished with European cattle, and when the use of the iron, of the plough, and of the many arts of Europe, has been introduced among them.[42]

Furthermore, Smith continues, miscegenation has also brought progress, since 'we must acknowledge, I apprehend, that the Spanish creoles are in many respects superior to the ancient Indians'.[43] Summarising the effects of European colonialism on the colonised, Smith declares that the 'discovery of America, and that of the passage to the East Indies by the Cape of Good Hope, are the two greatest and most important events recorded in the history of mankind',[44] but then moves on to a more complicated assessment of their significance:

To the natives, however, both of the East and West Indies, all the commercial benefits which can have resulted from those events have been sunk and lost in the dreadful misfortunes which they have occasioned. These misfortunes, however, seem to have arisen rather from accident than from anything in the nature of these events themselves.[45]

In other words, violence is an accidental and not a natural component of colonialism; correctly conceived, colonialism should bring commercial benefits to 'the natives'.

How did Smith apply these general principles on politics, economics and the fate of the colonised in his brief discussion on the Cape? The Dutch exclusive company at the Cape (the VOC) presents a potential anomaly for Smith because the Cape was – as he himself concedes – in many respects a successful colony.[46] However, Smith explains the success of the VOC's settlements both at the Cape and Batavia as entirely due to the fact that 'both these settlements are peculiarly fortunate in their situation'.[47] The Cape's strategic position equidistant between Europe and the East Indies guarantees that all trading ships stop there for fresh provisions, and Batavia's location as the central marketplace for Far Eastern trade too ensures a constant traffic in ships. These unusual advantages have helped the Cape and Batavia to overcome the negative effects of being governed by a merchant company: 'such advantageous situations have enabled those two colonies to surmount all obstacles which the oppressive genius of an exclusive company may have occasionally opposed to their growth'.[48] Smith concludes his short discussion of the Cape by repeating this dictum: 'such exclusive companies, therefore, are nuisances in every respect; always more or less inconvenient to the countries in which they are established, and destructive to those which have the misfortune to fall under their government'.[49] Smith is similarly sympathetic in describing the indigenes of North America and the Cape: 'the Cape of Good Hope was inhabited by a race of people almost as barbarous and quite as incapable of defending themselves as the natives of North America'.[50] Combining these brief comments and his positive account of the North American colonies, Smith's model of colonial governance for the Cape would require: a cheaply administered colonial assembly, republican in nature, and dedicated to the equal representation of all citizens; the banishment of the VOC (notwithstanding its success to date) and its replacement with a system of free trade; and the sympathetic incorporation of the previously wronged indigenes within the political economy of the Cape.

## BRUCE'S EAST-INDIES MODEL: REFUTING THE SPECIOUS REASONING OF THE PRIVATE ADVENTURER

Some explanation for selecting the relatively minor figure of Bruce as Smith's antagonist is required.[51] Smith and Bruce knew each other quite well in Edinburgh in the 1780s. On two occasions Smith wrote letters of introduction on behalf of the younger man. When Bruce was taking Robert Dundas (1771–1851), the son of

Henry Dundas (1742–1811), on the grand tour of Europe, Smith wrote to the Abbé André Morellet (1727–1819) in Paris on 1 May 1786, and described him as 'my particular friend, Mr John Bruce, Professor of Logic in the University of Edinburgh'.[52] A few days later, Smith wrote a more substantial letter of introduction to his London publisher, Thomas Cadell, in which he set out Bruce's virtues in greater detail:

> This letter will be delivered to you by my very intimate and particular friend Mr John Bruce. He has a work upon Moral Philosophy which, though he and I differ a little, as David Hume and I used to do, I expect will do him very great honour.[53]

Smith's patronage would appear to have worked, as a London edition of Bruce's *Elements of the Science of Ethics, on the Principles of Natural Philosophy* was published later in that same year by William Strahan and Cadell. Smith's support for Bruce ended with his death in 1790, and he therefore did not live to see Bruce's subsequent career unfold. In the 1790s, Bruce's intellectual interests shifted, much as Smith's had done, from moral philosophy to political economy, but whereas their respective views in the former discipline might merely have 'differed a little' in 1786, their ideas about political economy were much further apart.

Bruce's claims on our attention, however, rest neither on this acquaintanceship with Smith, nor on the originality of his mind, but on his proximity to power in the 1790s. After Bruce left his job as Professor of Logic at Edinburgh University in 1792, he acquired as patron the powerful figure of Henry Dundas, home secretary (and from July 1794 secretary of state for war) to prime minister William Pitt (1759–1806). Bruce's employment under Dundas involved initially working as tutor to his son Robert; from 5 July 1792 as Keeper of the State papers; and then from 10 July 1793 as Historiographer to the East India Company. These official appointments were in the first instance to enable Bruce to elaborate Dundas's case for renewing the exclusive trading charter of the East India Company, which was up for consideration in 1793. Dundas made his own arguments for extending the charter in a famous parliamentary speech on 23 April 1793,[54] and Bruce in the same year provided a 632-page report[55] in support. Bruce and Dundas's views were in every respect identical, as James Mill observed in his assessment of Dundas's Indian interventions: '[Bruce] is '[t]he friend of Mr. Dundas, and, as well from intellect, as from office, the advocate of his schemes, the historiographer of the Company'.[56] Dundas's victory in having the Company's charter extended until 1813 did not conclude Bruce's duties, as Dundas then commissioned him to write a succession of historical reports on both the European and colonial dimensions of Britain's economic and political system.[57] In each case, Bruce's historical scholarship addressed the political challenges of the 1790s, as he vigorously promoted the interests of his political master. Following his contribution to the debate on the East India Company, Bruce accordingly produced: in 1795, a report on the United Netherlands and its colonies, with particular attention to the weaknesses of the Dutch East India Company;[58] in 1796, first, a detailed history of the trade agreements between the major European powers,[59] and second, a history of the Cape Colony, including a set of proposals on how it might be governed following the transfer of the Cape to the British in 1795;[60] in 1798, a history of how British military assaults on foreign ports had protected Britain itself from foreign invasion;[61] and in 1799, a sympathetic history of the union of England and Scotland, with an eye to promoting a similar such union with Ireland.[62] Betty Joseph has observed '[the East India Company's] official record was never deemed to be a repository for public scrutiny; it remained throughout this period an instrument of governance',[63] and Bruce's mammoth output conformed to this pattern in that it circulated exclusively amongst carefully selected figures in government and commerce who were potential recruits to Dundas's political causes.

Bruce's writings of the 1790s were dominated by the fear that the recent revolutions in North America and France might inflict permanent damage on Britain's autonomy and prosperity. As a back-room ideologue of Britain's ruling class, Bruce's Burkean interpretation of history counterpoised wise patrician governance and varieties of utopian mob rule.[64] He extended this dichotomy to colonial rule, with the East India Company cast as the guarantors of prosperous stability. In his *Historical View of Plans for the Government of British India* (1793), Bruce reproduced a version of Montesquieu's argument that each nation must have a legal system true to its own unique spirit, arguing that 'there is a kind of government which is adapted to the particular character of a people'.[65] He then observes that '[u]topian schemes uniformly have produced anarchy, and, in no instance, could they be more dangerously attempted, than in forming a plan of government for the dominions of Great Britain in Hindoostan'.[66] The reason why utopian schemes are so inappropriate, Bruce continues, is because

> from the earliest times, the natives of Hindoostan have been habituated to a government, less or more absolute, and that an institution, of any other description, would be repugnant to their notions of subordination, and to the kinds of religion in which they believe, so that, relatively to them, it would be foreign and unintelligible.[67]

Bruce thus presents a benevolent variety of the theory of Oriental Despotism, which rewrites Indian pre-British history in close accord with 'the political and ideological interests of Europe'.[68] According to Bruce, the genius of the Company in India has been to '[engraft] only the portion of the British Government, which had been delegated to them, within their limits, upon the Mogul system'.[69] In other words, indigenous absolutist governance has been respected by the Company in order to maintain stability: 'proceeding upon something like their ancient system of government, we can only expect to preserve the allegiance of the natives, or to hold the balance of power in India'.[70] The result is a form of indirect rule, with Indian rulers securing existing social hierarchies and thus guaranteeing stability.[71] In so doing, they function as proxies for British economic interests in exchange for a percentage of trading profits, an arrangement justified by Bruce as consistent with Indian history and society.

Bruce's commitment to the cause of the East India Company was unwavering, as he repeated the arguments in his *Historical View of Plans for the Government of British India* some eighteen years later in his *Report on the Negociation between the Honourable East-India Company and the Public, respecting the Renewal of the Company's Exclusive Privileges of Trade, for Twenty Years from March, 1794* (1811). In both works, Bruce relies upon three arguments: he cites the Company's history of profit-making; he raises the spectre of Britain being superseded by its national rivals should the Company be sidelined; and he attacks the motives and arguments of adversaries who promote free trade. As to the history, Bruce provides a chronological summary of the Company's successive charters, starting from the grant of the first charter by Elizabeth I in December 1600, and concluding with the payment of £400,000 by the Company in March 1791 for a three-year extension of their charter. In all periods, the Company has been Britain's best option for successful foreign trade. Bruce then sets the Company's record against alternative dispensations: 'If any plan should be adopted, originating in speculative schemes of commerce, the permanency of our present Asiatic commerce might be endangered, and the balance of profit, arising from it [. . .] might pass into the hands of rival European Companies'.[72] Bruce acknowledges that in the 1790s the arguments for free trade had initially enjoyed popular appeal, but suggests that over time 'speculation began to give way to experience',[73] and that the true value of the East India Company to Britain was recognised: 'the East-India Company were, in fact, the agents of the British Nation, trading to Asia, under public regulations, and acting [. . .] under the control of the Executive Power and of Parliament'.[74] Viewed in this light, he concludes that 'the East-India Company were not a private Corporation trading exclusively to the East, but the British Nation trading [. . .] to that part of the world [. . .] exclusively of other Nations'.[75] Bruce's final rhetorical strategy is simply to abuse those he regards as the Company's enemies – 'men who wish to become adventurers in Eastern trade; men who are to draw their fortunes from stock-jobbing; [. . .] men who may wish to speculate in our manufactures, and the emissaries of foreign Companies' – who seek to manipulate the British public with their 'specious propositions'.[76] Although these men might contend (in terms that echo Adam Smith) that the fresh energy of private merchants 'would become a new spring to the industry of the European and Asiatic subjects of Great Britain', Bruce rejects their arguments as 'the specious reasoning of the private adventurer'.[77] Bruce's efforts on the Company's behalf contributed to its successful negotiation of the difficult war years up to 1815; the historian H. V. Bowen points out that

> [Company officials] kept an eye on the balance sheet and they sought financial compensation for most of the Company's contributions to the national war effort. As a result [. . .] the government [paid] a large amount of money [. . .] for armaments, goods and stores supplied by the Company.[78]

As regards the indigenes of new colonies, both Bruce and Dundas regard Britain's presence in India as entirely beneficial. Bruce is peremptory on the topic of how East India Company rule benefits India itself, but Dundas compensates with expansive descriptions:

India [. . .] is in a state of prosperity unknown to it under the most wise and politic of its ancient sovereigns. The British possessions, compared with those of the neighbouring states in the peninsula, are like a cultivated garden compared with the field of the sluggard; the revenues of India have been increased, and the trade connected with them is in a state of progressive improvement.[79]

Dundas echoes Bruce in emphasising the advantages of grafting Company rule onto existing systems of government, explaining that

[the Natives] had been long habituated to look up to, and to rest upon the protection of the Company. The Natives of India look back to the ancient sovereignty of the Moguls, and their confidence in the Company has its source in the country governments, exercising power as a branch of that subordination to which their forefathers were subjected.[80]

He argues further that ancient indigenous hierarchies had been observed by the Company, and notes that the rewards have been a successful and stable trading relationship. The image of the indigenes of India constructed by Bruce and Dundas is therefore a combination of shrewd rulers eager to do business with the Company, and conservative labourers anxious to continue working within the existing social hierarchies, with both classes united in their enthusiasm for the progress brought by the British.

How did Bruce apply his general principles of colonial governance to the Cape? The Cape was seized by Britain in September 1795 following the defeat of the House of Orange and the creation of the Batavian Republic as an appendage of France. In occupying the Cape, the British War Office and Admiralty were supported by the East India Company – in May 1795, seven East Indiamen had captured a fleet of nine Dutch ships near St Helena, and three more of the Company's vessels were sent from India to the Cape to aid the invasion. Accompanying Britain's capture of the Cape, there were a number of proposals wrestling with how the relationship between the East India Company and the British colonial administration should articulate. Bruce followed much the same approach in setting out the Cape's future as he had for the East Indies in 1793 in his *Sketches of the Political and Commercial History of the Cape of Good Hope* – Dundas laid down the policy, and he provided the historical support. In his introductory comments, Bruce acknowledges his substantial debt to a number of earlier writers on the Cape,[81] and then produces 443 pages on the Cape's geography, economy, legal system and military institutions, followed by a 220-page outline of how the English should govern the Cape. In exploring how to regulate the political governance of the Cape, Bruce begins by examining the existing Dutch system, and notes that 'the Dutch have always formed and conducted their Foreign Dependencies merely as Commercial and Military Stations, <u>not as Colonies</u>'.[82] Under such a system, the settlers enjoyed no autonomy; instead,

the Founders of the Settlement at the Cape proceeded upon the plan of peopling the Country from Europe, but without vesting in the inhabitants any

Legislative powers, subjecting them on the contrary to the Civil and Criminal Laws of Holland, and to the Financial and Commercial Bye Laws of the Dutch East India Company.[83]

Although this system is very similar to the one followed by the English East India Company in the East Indies (of which Bruce warmly approves), in the case of the VOC at the Cape, Bruce criticises the Dutch Company's misrule. The VOC's minimal political structures failed to check the corruption and profiteering of its own officials. The settlers at the Cape as a result had been alienated, and had turned to dangerous alternatives:

> The Usages and Manners of the Settlers have been formed upon the prevailing Maxims of the Dutch East India Company, but only a small number of the Colonists retain a prejudice in favour of the System of Government which obtained in their ancient Country; the greater part of them are infected with the new French principles, under the idea of forming the Cape into an independent Republic that shall command the Eastern and the European World.[84]

Bruce returns repeatedly to this danger – that the Dutch settlers at the Cape 'are almost all Converts to the French Revolutionary Principles'[85] – and argues that if Britain fails to check their enthusiasm, the Cape could easily be lost. Britain's acquisition of the Cape occurs at a particularly sensitive moment, as Bruce envisages that with the political connection between the Cape and Batavia severed, 'a new Motive will be held out to the settlers at the Cape to foster and to attempt the becoming of an independent power'.[86] Such ambitions will be fanned further by 'the existing Anarchy in Europe, if improvident encouragement shall be given to Adventurers'.[87] To check any such revolutionary scenario unfolding at the Cape, Bruce proposes that the most glaring injustices of VOC rule be swiftly addressed, but that major procedural and institutional changes to the existing political system be cautiously introduced: 'it may be expedient to proceed on experiment only, in all these points, leaving it to practice to discover that System on which shall be equally calculated for the interest of the Empire and of the East India Company'.[88] He dismisses those who 'thought it would be easy to lay down a better theoretical System of Government at the Cape', and suggests that there would be distinct advantages in retaining where possible the existing forms of government 'which the new Subjects of Britain at the Cape understand and in which they have confidence'.[89]

In considering the economic challenges facing the British at the Cape, Bruce is again sensitive to the hardships suffered by the settlers under VOC rule. He notes the specifics of settler grievances like the 'heavy Quit rents paid by the landholders [and] arbitrary and excessive prices paid to the Company by the Cultivators of the Soil',[90] and argues that these repressive measures imposed by the VOC were ultimately counterproductive, as they prevented the Dutch from exploiting to the full the Cape's commercial potential. In reflecting upon how Britain might overcome these failings, Bruce notes that 'little aid, in forming a system, can be derived from the practice of the Dutch'.[91] Echoing one of Smith's favourite pejorative metaphors, Bruce contrasts the great possibilities afforded by the Cape – 'the Cape Country can furnish Provisions for its Inhabitants, and an indefinite quantity for Export' – and the retarding influence of the VOC – 'the Regulations, with which this Export has been clogged, have been adverse to the Plan of raising the Settlement to Commercial prosperity'.[92] Bruce's flexibility in this regard was at odds with more conservative contemporaries, who continued to see free trade as the end of British prosperity.[93] He also sees the Cape playing a vital role in relation to Britain's colonies in both the Americas and the East Indies. As regards the economies of the West Indies, Bruce argues that the Cape can fill the void left by the North American colonies following the American War of Independence: 'the Situation of the Cape, relative to the West Indies, would, if the Country was properly cultivated, enable it to supply our Islands with provisions of the same kind which they now draw from the United States of America'.[94] By taking full advantage of its natural advantages, 'the Cape may be put upon the same footing as our remaining American colonies'.[95] Looking to the East, Bruce notes the strategic importance of the Cape – 'the Cape, in the hands of the English, would become equally a check upon the French and the Dutch, the only Nations likely to disturb the peace of India'.[96] Bruce's cautiousness nonetheless tempered his support for an open trading system at the post-VOC Cape. Specifically, he insists upon regulations at the Cape to protect the English East India Company's interests within the existing designated limits, in effect therefore conceding freedom-to-trade to Cape merchants only in those zones beyond the limits of the Company.

As regards the indigenes of the Cape, Bruce repeats the standard European stereotype of the Khoisan as inferior beings subsisting at an early stage of human development. The VOC had failed to incorporate them into the economy in a productive fashion:

> [T]he Natives have advanced by very slow degrees from the State of Barbarity in which the Dutch originally found them, and no attempts have been made to induce them into habits of Industry by creating in them new wants, or an interest in the labours which they performed.[97]

However, Bruce argues that with the appropriate encouragement, the 'Natives' could ultimately benefit from the colonial encounter quite as much as the British: 'if the Natives shall have encouragement to Industry given to them, and full protection in that property which this industry may create, they may become useful subjects of Britain'.[98]

## SMITH V. BRUCE?

Before considering the reception of Smith and Bruce's ideas at the Cape, it will be useful to summarise the differences and similarities between them on the three key issues identified at the outset, namely the relation in political terms between nation and colony, the economic transition from mercantilism to free trade, and the integration of colonised indigenes into Britain's political economy.

As regards the political question, their views on nationalism are fundamentally opposed. For Smith, the competitive nationalisms of Europe are anachronistic, destructive and function in the interests of Britain's mercantile elite, not of the general populace; the merchants' claims to be acting in Britain's national interest are but 'national prejudice and animosity, prompted by the private interest of particular traders'. Bruce takes the opposite view, arguing that there is a correspondence between the interests of the East India Company and the British nation. Bruce's mantra is that 'the East-India Company were in fact the agents of the British Nation', or more succinctly, 'the British nation trading'. Further, whereas Smith sympathised with the American Revolution, and was initially claimed by supporters of the French Revolution, Bruce loathed both revolutions, and viewed them as inimical to Britain's interests. Bruce's vehemence is in part due to the fact that he was writing in the 1790s, but his fear that Britain's allies and dependencies might be 'infected with the new French principles' haunted him for the rest of his life. As regards their respective understandings of 'colony', again they hold quite different views. Smith's Greek model of colonisation aims to 'develop' the colonies by extensive European settlement, and to encourage them to emerge ultimately as independent nations. Based upon the example of Britain's North American colonies, Smith argues that with free trade established, nation and colony would be bound in a reciprocally beneficial relationship of 'parental affection' and 'filial respect'. In his paragraphs on the Cape, Smith suggests that such a regime of efficient colonial governance and free trade should replace VOC rule. By contrast, Bruce's model of colonial rule discourages European settlement in the colonies, and sees Britain governing through the indigenous elites of colonised societies and maintaining colonies in a continuous state of dependency. Based upon the example of the East India Company in India, Bruce argues that as far as possible indigenous power structures should be preserved so as not to disrupt the 'natives' notions of subordination'. In writing about the Cape, Bruce's identification of British and East India Company interests is moderated. He concedes that the VOC model of governance at the Cape is unsustainable, and admits the need for an efficient British colonial administration (not East India Company rule) to 'unclog' the VOC system and restore commercial viability. Although an explicit line of influence might be difficult to trace, it is arguable that Smith's model of governance for North America and the Cape anticipates nineteenth-century direct rule, whereas Bruce's model of governance for India (but not the Cape) approves indirect rule.

Second, as regards the issue of the transition from mercantilism to free trade, there are again obvious differences between Smith and Bruce; indeed, they might legitimately be read as representative spokesmen for free trade and mercantilism, respectively. Smith argues that the freedom-to-trade for *all* merchants, including the merchants of Britain's European competitors, produces ultimately a dispensation beneficial to all. Conversely, by impoverishing European trading competitors and by keeping colonies in a state of dependency (as per the Roman model of colonisation), Britain's own national interest must ultimately suffer. Bruce by contrast sees protectionist measures guaranteeing the profits of Britain's chartered companies as essential to Britain's national economy, and as ultimately enriching all British subjects through the companies' payment of taxes. The main corollary of Bruce's view is that any shift from mercantilism to free trade jeopardises Britain's economic interests.

Third, there are differences in their views on the indigenes of Britain's colonies, with Smith's ambivalent expressions of regret over the violent destruction of non-western societies contrasting with Bruce's uncomplicated teleology of indigenes lifted from barbarity to civilisation as a result of European colonialism.

These are important differences, but at least as significant are the similarities between Smith and Bruce. Crucially, as many subsequent critics have pointed out, the opposition between Smith's free trade and Bruce's protectionism disguised how the two ideologies in fact complemented each other during the formation of national-imperial states from the late eighteenth century onwards. Marx, for example, describes the ideas of the protectionist Henry Carey and the free-trade propagandist Fréderic Bastiat as mirror images, as 'antipodes' of each other.[99] That the freedom of 'free trade' benefited Britain and effectively sabotaged competing national economies was an argument elaborated by Alexander Hamilton, Friedrich List and Carey, as they justified the adoption of protectionist measures by Britain's competitors, notably the USA, Germany and France.[100] Under a free-trade regime, Britain as the pre-eminent trading power was guaranteed the major share of the profits, a point Bruce indirectly acknowledged by allowing a space for free trade at the Cape in 1796. Second, Smith and Bruce are also alike in the priority they accord economic over political concerns. For both of them, questions of political governance, including questions of nationhood, arise only insofar as they influence the profits of European traders. Smith's antipathy to nationalism is grounded in the view that it frustrates free trade and therefore ultimately retards human progress, and Bruce's advocacy of Britain's national interest was modified when it interfered with commerce, as his qualified concession to free trade at the Cape demonstrates. Indeed, the vigour of their emphasis on matters economic calls into question Anderson's idea of how northern-hemisphere models of the nation were replicated in the colonies. At least in the case of Britain at the Cape in the late eighteenth century, securing the profits of British merchants preceded and dictated the forms of political governance.[101] Third, their views on the colonised indigenes are ultimately similar. Although Bruce's silences contrast with Smith's express sympathy for the colonised of non-western societies, they both approve of Europe's colonial expansion. Smith's sympathy for pre-commercial communities (including African societies) in *The Theory of Moral Sentiments* and his criticisms of Spanish imperial plunder in *The Wealth of Nations* are undermined by his conclusion that violence is not axiomatic to European colonialism; rather, violence against the indigenes arose 'from accident'. Further, they both accept the four-stage teleology of human development that consigns the indigenes to a position inferior to Europeans: Smith describes the Cape's inhabitants as 'almost as barbarous [. . .] as the natives of North America', and Bruce complains that the Dutch have done little to lift them from 'the State of Barbarity'. Their readings of the Cape's inhabitants as potential labourers working to produce profits for Europeans traders (whether for chartered companies or competing merchants) marks them both as theorists of what Marx called 'primitive accumulation'.[102] For Smith and Bruce alike, progress for the barbarous indigenes of the Cape lay in selling their skins to European settlers.

## THE SCOTTISH ENLIGHTENMENT AT THE CAPE

### Political economy

A frequently repeated anecdote has Prime Minister William Pitt telling Adam Smith at a dinner party hosted by Henry Dundas that 'We are all your scholars'.[103] Careful study of the immediate reception of Smith's work, however, suggests that Pitt's tribute was exaggerated, as the ideas in *The Wealth of Nations* had a mixed reception among British policy-makers in the years following its publication. In 1779, his arguments for freeing up the restrictions governing trade with Ireland were partially conceded by Dundas, who acknowledged that 'the bearing down of Ireland, was in truth bearing down a substantial part of the Naval and Military strength of our own country'.[104] In 1783, however, Smith's support for the India Bill, which sought to establish parliamentary control over the East India Company, was entirely ineffectual. Smith's biographer Ian Simpson Ross records that 'Smith was woefully wrong in predicting that this Bill would go through the Upper House [. . .]t was defeated [. . .] at the instigation of the King, who correctly judged that the country was opposed to the terms of the Bill'.[105] The French Revolution further undermined Smith's influence: in the 1780s, some ground had been conceded to the argument that a profitable imperial economy did *not* depend upon restrictive trade practices, but after 1789 trade reform was halted and British economic nationalism reasserted.[106] In more general terms, the 1790s saw Smith's ideas reinterpreted by Pitt and his acolytes to serve their own more conservative political agendas. Emma Rothschild summarises the shift as follows: '[Smith] was remembered, until the mid-1790s, as a subversive and as a friend of French philosophy; by the end of the century, he had been rediscovered as a theorist of established institutions'.[107]

At the Cape, it is clear that Smith's ideas actually had very little influence on British policy after 1795. Whatever metropolitan acclaim Smith's *Wealth of Nations* might have enjoyed in the 1780s, at the Cape a decade later it was certainly Bruce's arguments which had the more direct impact on policy. Bruce handed over his *Sketches of the Political and Commercial History of the Cape* to the new governor of the Cape, Lord George Macartney (1737–1806), on 17 December 1796, shortly before he departed for his post. Macartney ruled at the Cape from 4 May 1797 until his departure on 21 November 1798, and he read Bruce's *Sketches* with great care, annotating the margins of his copy liberally with his own first-hand impressions of the Cape. When he left the Cape, Macartney also attached an eight-page commentary on Bruce's *Sketches* for his successor. Most of Macartney's comments focus on specific details in Bruce's text. For example, alongside Bruce's claim that '[farmers] paid a large Quit Rent to the Company', Macartney notes 'No tithe or tenth is paid for what is consumed in the interior of the country altho it was originally meant to be levied'.[108] At other times, Macartney provides up-to-date statistics to correct Bruce's general descriptions, as in the section on the settlements of the interior, where Macartney writes of Bruce's report, 'This is not an exact statement. To descend a little closer to particulars by way of explaining the poverty of the inhabitants, let us take the district of Graaf Reinet which was the one so greatly in arrears',[109] and then provides a lengthy list of the relevant data. Besides correcting such factual details, Macartney more than once dismisses Bruce's more general judgements of the Cape's inhabitants. Responding to Bruce's claim that 'These Boschmen every Spring made incursions for plunder of Cattle, Sheep, etc.', Macartney notes that 'The accounts given of the Boschmen by the Dutch have always been much exaggerated'.[110] Bruce's reliance on out-of-date authorities made such errors of detail inevitable, and Macartney soon abandoned Bruce as his guide, and deferred instead to his own energetic secretary, John Barrow, whose first-hand account of the Cape was more influential in the longer term.[111]

These particular corrections aside, Macartney's approach to governing the Cape was in close accord with the priorities of Bruce and Dundas. Although there was a loosening of restrictions on internal trade to meet pressing domestic needs immediately after Britain seized the Cape in 1795, the advent of Macartney saw the introduction of an authoritarian regime that was more efficient than the VOC, but in most key respects shored up existing institutions and practices.[112] In particular, Macartney passed regulations to take effect in May 1797 that the English East India Company retain its exclusive monopoly of all trade east of the Cape, and he tried to keep a close check on contraband trade at the Cape which threatened the Company's profits.[113] Macartney was in favour of treating the Cape as a political as well as an economic appendage of the Indian Empire, and in memoranda to both Dundas and the Company Directors, encouraged the East India Company to acquire the Cape.[114] The Company Directors themselves displayed rather less enthusiasm for the Cape, and responded half-heartedly to Macartney's appeals, choosing instead to view the Cape's function as restricted to securing their interests in the East, and to pay desultory attention to the needs of the Cape's internal market. Macartney's successor, Sir George Yonge (1731–1812), was less sympathetic to the East India Company, arguing that '[i]t is desirable to knit and tye this Colony to the Mother Country as much as possible, and to make it look no more to the East',[115] but during his short tenure as governor (1799–1801) did little to undo the Company's monopoly. In the next two decades, the Company's preferential trading status at the Cape weakened as a consequence of competition from independent merchants and its own inefficiency, and in 1814 it eventually lost its Eastern trade monopoly (excluding tea) at the Cape. Summing up the gradual transitions in the economy of the Cape after the British occupation, W. M. Freund concludes that by 1815 '[t]he Cape was not yet transformed from an entrepot, essentially dependent on its marginal role in the Europe-Asia trade, to a colonial export economy [but] it was moving in that direction'.[116] In the next two decades, the break-up of mercantilist modes of governance accelerated as the Cape government provided further troops to protect white farmers, undertook new public works and encouraged private enterprise. This process culminated in an 1834 Act which rescinded the remaining privileges of the

East India Company.[117] In the terms of these eighteenth-century British models of colonial governance, the Cape therefore initially followed Bruce's mercantilist model, but from the second decade of the nineteenth century (and roughly contemporaneous with the early stages of the free trade movement in Britain[118]), Smith's ideas exerted an increasing influence at the Cape.

## Sentiment

That the application of the Scottish Enlightenment laws of political economy prescribing a journey for colonised indigenes 'from Savages to Scotsmen'[119] came at some cost was registered. Smith – as we have seen – condemned the 'ruinous and destructive' impact of colonial intrusions, and he attributed to societies beyond Europe the qualities of 'magnanimity', 'self-command', 'heroic and unconquerable firmness', 'kindness' and 'hospitality'. But although Smith acknowledged the virtues of the victims of colonial expansion, he expressed doubts as to how deeply British readers might be moved by (fictional or factual) accounts of colonial suffering. Smith's general formulation of the workings of sentiment – 'though our brother is on the rack, as long as we ourselves are at ease, our sense will never inform us of what he suffers'[120] – is applied to colonial contexts in his sceptical appraisal of how reading news of a catastrophic earthquake in China might affect a British reader: 'If he was to lose his little finger to-morrow, he would not sleep tonight; but, provided he never saw them, he will snore with the most profound security over the ruin of a hundred millions of his brethren'.[121] However, Smith's doubts about humanity's capacity to sympathise with distant suffering in no way retarded the increase of sentimental representations and narratives in British writing. On the contrary, as the eighteenth century wore on, Peter Hulme argues, 'sentimental sympathy began to flow out along the arteries of European commerce in search of its victims'.[122]

With Britain seizing the Cape in 1795, one of the 'arteries of European commerce' was re-routed from Holland to Britain, and for British writers, there were new 'victims' to serve as objects of 'sentimental sympathy', namely the Khoisan and the Cape slaves. The first significant figure to visit the Cape and to write within the same intellectual tradition as Smith and Bruce was the minor Scottish aristocrat, Lady Anne Barnard. Like Bruce, Barnard was closely tied to Dundas, having rejected a proposal of marriage from him, and having successfully petitioned him on her husband Andrew's behalf for employment under Macartney at the Cape. Despite her subordinate position as a woman within the colonial community, Barnard's writings display a shrewd political sense,[123] as she repeatedly proclaims the economic improvements brought to the Cape by British rule. For example, in her journal entry for 21 May 1798, she notes,

> I believe the farmers are far better contented with the English Government than the people of the Town, yet all benefit by it a few excepted who have lost good places, and whose wings are fledged respecting *monopolys*, and who cannot when the fancy strikes them encroach on the rights of the weak.[124]

Of the weak whose rights can no longer be encroached, the Khoisan are the most frequent objects of Barnard's sympathetic but contradictory gaze. She represents the Khoisan as victims, first, by describing how they lost their land as a result of the Dutch colonists' deceptions – she repeats an account of how 'Mr. Cloete of Constantia [. . .] had tricked [fertile land] away from the Hottentots, the Original possessors, by getting one of them for a trifle to give him up a bit of cultivated land'[125] – and second, by pointing out how badly they are paid by many of the farmers, who 'entrap the poor Hottentots as completely as a Soldier is entrapped who gets drink and is persuaded to pocket a shilling'.[126] To evoke sympathy for the Khoisan in her readers, Barnard on more than one occasion compares individual Khoisan women to friends and acquaintances in Scotland: 'a right Boshe woman' is likened to Lady Abercorn,[127] and a 'a gallant looking [Hottentot] girl [. . .] resembled a good deal my old and kind friend Mrs. Lawson when she was about that age'.[128] The common humanity of Khoisan and Briton is more explicitly announced in Barnard's description of her encounter with a jealous Khoikhoi wife and her younger rival. The two women's behaviour proves for Barnard that

> real and true love [. . .] when it takes place in true hearts, whether clothed in a dark Skin or a fair, whether under Satin or sheep skin . . . whether in Man or Woman will always be ready to sacrifice any thing for its object, its own comforts . . . its Pride . . . All . . . all except (in Educated life) its worth and virtue.[129]

In this instance of Khoisan behaviour, Barnard sees similarities not with people she knew in Britain, but with fictional characters, namely the unhappy wife Emma and her beautiful rival in *Henry and Emma* by Matthew Prior (1664–1721). Barnard was so struck with the comparison that she drafted a poem, relocating the scenario in Prior's poem to Baviaans Kloof, and translating Henry to 'Omar' and Emma to 'Mona'. Adopting the voice of Omar, Barnard writes, 'I'll oil her person, and braid her hair / Her Calabash with purest water fill, . . . Pluck the wild Peacock, dress wate'er you kill'.[130] Running contrary to Barnard's sentimental identification with the Khoikhoi in this poem, however, is a second aesthetic impulse that simultaneously endorses the stadial theory of development, and regrets the loss of Khoikhoi innocence. Much preoccupied with completing accurate sketches of the Khoisan, Barnard (like many other European travellers) complains about how difficult it is to find the 'original savage': at a mission station, she observes, '[a]ll barbarous customs having been civilized away here by the Fathers I saw nothing of the sort here'; indeed, she continues, 'the [early travellers'] description of the Hottentot ceremonies [. . .] applies now only to those at a greater distance'.[131] The artist in Barnard thus requires an exotic other for 'picturesque'[132] aesthetic transcription, a requirement directly at odds with the British 'civilising' project she otherwise uncritically approves.

Similar contradictions characterise Barnard's sentimental representation of the Cape slaves. Anecdotes about cruelties suffered by the slaves are all located in the past under the justice system of the VOC. For example, Barnard repeats the story of a slave cheated out of manumission, who in desperation killed another slave because 'he knew his Master loved his money *better* than his *life*, that by stabbing a slave worth *1,000 dollars*, and by being hanged for it, he should be doubly revenged'.[133] In a longer anecdote, Barnard recounts the torture 'by thumb screws and other abominable modes'[134] of the slave Gasper, who had been falsely accused of theft. Aside from backdating such cruelties to the bad old days of the Dutch, the capacity of these anecdotes to provoke sympathy in British readers is further diminished by Barnard's reassurances that the slaves at the Cape are in fact quite happy. Soon after her arrival at the Cape, Barnard reflected,

> I could not help feeling more pity for [the poor Slaves] than I thought perhaps that I was justified for afterwards, when I saw the kind manner in which the *Stromboms* and some of my acquaintances treated theirs [. . .] so much the reverse of what I have heard of the hardships shown to those in the West Indies.[135]

And a few months later, Barnard expands upon her judgement:

> I must own that Slaves are but rarely ill used at the Cape – their being the property of the persons who superintend them is one reason why they are more cherished than in the West Indies where the task Master has no interest in their comfort, and as to their being unhappy, when one sees that lightness of heart in them which can sing and dance all day long and be ready to sleep sweetly and soundly at every spare moment one cannot think their sense of hardship is deep. If this disposition attend complexion, who would wish to be white?[136]

Barnard shifts from slavery as social landscape to slavery as metaphor when she changes the subject to 'talk of a different Species of Slavery [. . .] the Bonds which are forged by the gay God of Love'.[137] As in the case of the Henry/Omar and Emma/Mona, Barnard finds an appealing topic for a sentimental poem in another tale of unrequited love – in this case, the tale of a slave, his young lover and a goat. Titled 'The Slave of Africa', Barnard's eight-stanza draft poem tells the story of a slave called Urbain, who was banished to the mountains for making love to a young woman named Meechie. Alone in the mountains, Urbain played his flute to his goats, and fell in love with a particular goat he named Meechie after his lost love (he declares, 'Like thee she was tender and meek'[138]). When Meechie was carried off by a wolf, Gasper threw a stone at the wolf, who turned on him and killed him. The poem concludes with the consoling thought that death has liberated Urbain: 'O rest poor Urbain / Freed from Bonds . . . and Earths Controul'.[139]

The tensions within Barnard's writings on the Khoisan and the slaves are symptomatic of tensions in late eighteenth-century sentimental discourse more broadly. With the masculine discourse of political economy requiring the 'progressive' transformation of pre-capitalist societies, the feminised discourse of sentiment provided a means of registering those on the receiving end of such economic 'progress'. Lynn Festa has argued that imaginative sympathy could give a voice and human face to the victims of British and French imperialism, but that there were always strict limits to such sympathy. European colonisers and settlers were the principal objects of sentimental discourse; by contrast, 'unfettered sympathy'[140] for indigenes or slaves posed a threat to the European colonial project. What Festa's formulation suggests is that the discourse of 'sentiment' has radical possibilities – if sympathy for the colonised is unfettered – but that it can as easily serve a compensatory ideological function for primitive accumulation. In Barnard's case, her sympathy for the Khoisan and the slaves is contained in the first instance by her assertions that the plight of the Khoisan and the slaves is not actually that bad. At the end of the third volume of her journal, she draws the two constituencies together, and concludes:

> The Slaves and Hottentots [. . .] seem happy too upon the whole, from knowing no other State than that which they are in, the idea of drawing a comparison between themselves and their Masters is one belonging to the first step of cultivation, and they have not reached to it, as far as I can judge.[141]

Applying the stadial theory of civilisation, with the slaves and Khoikhoi consigned to the earliest stage, Barnard explains the happiness of the 'Slaves and Hottentots' as the result of their undeveloped state. Once they ascend through the stages of civilisation, they will acquire self-consciousness, and in the process, the capacity to be unhappy. The second way in which Barnard's sympathy for the Khoisan and slaves is 'fettered' is by the translation of their experiences into aesthetic form – either 'picturesque' sketches of Khoisan in their 'uncivilised state', or sentimental narrative poems about unrequited or doomed love. In this context, the aesthetic functions as an anaesthetic for British readers by numbing the impact of colonial violence.

## CONCLUSION

Smith, Bruce and Barnard imagine the Cape Colony in distinctive ways. Smith provides a model of colonial governance premised upon free trade, an efficient colonial administration, and the humane treatment of the indigenes; Bruce scripts a future for the Cape based upon the East India Company's continued domination of the Colony's political economy; and Barnard repeats Bruce's model of colonial governance, and extends Smith's discourse of sentiment to the Khoisan and Cape slaves. However, their interest rests less upon their individual readings of the Cape than upon how they cumulatively imagined the community at the Cape. Read together, Smith, Bruce and Barnard apply the Scottish Enlightenment discourses of political economy and sentiment to the Cape Colony and, by example, to the British colonial project more broadly. For all their differences, whether writing in the discourses of political economy or sentiment, they agree that British rule guarantees for the indigenes of the Cape a progressive/developmental journey from 'Savages to Scotsmen'. But perhaps the more striking congruence is their evasiveness on the subject of colonial violence, as they employ a variety of rhetorical strategies, from silence (in Bruce's case), to characterising such violence as accidental (in Smith's case), to attributing such violence to the Dutch, or casting it in aesthetic form (in Barnard's case).

## NOTES

1. Terry, *A Voyage*, p. 25. Another early account is provided in Hamilton, *New Account*. For a detailed description of this ill-fated episode, see Mackenzie, 'Captain Cross'.
2. Letter by Eustace Man to the East India Company from Jakarta Roads on 13 October 1620. Reprinted in Raven-Hart, *Before Van Riebeeck*, p. 106.
3. Ovington, *A Voyage*, p. 283.
4. Ibid. p. 290.
5. Rogers, *A Cruising Voyage*, pp. 418–19. Rogers is remembered for having rescued Alexander Selkirk, the principal source for Daniel Defoe's *Robinson Crusoe* (1717). Selkirk was with Rogers on this trip, and spent four months at the Cape.
6. Ibid. p. 417.
7. Symson, *A New Voyage*, p. 218.
8. Kindersley, *Letters*, p. 62.
9. Ibid. p. 63.
10. Ibid. p. 67.
11. Paterson, *A Narrative*, p. 84.
12. Bradlow, *Francis Masson's Account*, p. 77.
13. The longitudinal measurements and the distances from Cape Town in nautical miles provided by Dalrymple and Pemberton correspond to Cape St Francis, not far to the west of Algoa Bay (Port Elizabeth).
14. Dalrymple, 'Proposal', p. 53.
15. Pemberton, 'Desirability', p. 21.
16. Dalrymple, 'Proposal', p. 53.
17. Ibid. pp. 53, 68.
18. Pemberton, 'Desirability', p. 20.
19. Smith, *The Wealth*, p. 151.
20. Ibid. p. 222.
21. McNally, *Political Economy*, p. 225.
22. Smith, *The Wealth*, p. 136.
23. Ibid. p. 147.
24. Ibid. p. 153.
25. Ibid. p. 155.
26. Ibid. p. 167.
27. Ibid. p. 174.
28. Ibid. p. 187.
29. Ibid. pp. 187, 187–8.
30. Ibid. p. 26.
31. Ibid. p. 35.
32. Ibid. p. 52. Smith expands here on his criticisms of nationalism in *The Theory of Moral Sentiments* (see pp. 228–30).
33. Smith, *The Wealth*, p. 215.
34. For a sympathetic account of Smith on colonialism, see Harkin, 'Adam Smith's Missing'.
35. Smith, *The Theory*, p. 205.
36. Ibid. p. 206.
37. Ibid. p. 207.

38. Ferguson, *An Essay*, p. 62.

39. Millar, *The Origin*, p. 178.

40. Smith, *The Wealth*, p. 26.

41. Ibid. pp. 142, 170.

42. Ibid. p. 149.

43. Ibid. p. 149.

44. Ibid. p. 209.

45. Ibid. p. 209.

46. Smith understates the expansion of the Cape's economy in the eighteenth century under the VOC. For a corrective to the conventional wisdom that the VOC stifled the Cape economy, see Van Duin and Ross, *The Economy*, who argue that 'it has been far too generally accepted that the presence and policies of the VOC necessarily impeded the internal economic development of the colony' (p. 5).

47. Ibid. p. 219.

48. Ibid. p. 220.

49. Ibid. p. 226.

50. Ibid. pp. 219–20.

51. For biographical details on Bruce, see 'Obituary: John Bruce'; T. C. 'Bruce, John'; Foster, 'John Bruce'; and Fry, 'Bruce, John'.

52. Smith, *The Correspondence*, p. 295.

53. Ibid. p. 296.

54. When the East India Company's charter came up for renewal again in 1813, Dundas's speech was republished. It is from this later version I quote below.

55. John Bruce, *Historical View of Plans for the Government of British India, and Regulation of Trade to the East Indies and Outlines of a Plan of Foreign Government, of Commercial Economy, and of Domestic Administration, for the Asiatic Interests of Great Britain* (1793).

56. Mill, *The History*, p. 4. Mill's critical views on Bruce and Dundas are set out in more detail in 'Publications', pp. 127–57. Notwithstanding these criticisms, Mill relied heavily on Bruce's best-known work, *Annals of the Honourable East India Company, from their Establishment by the Charter of Queen Elizabeth, 1600, to the Union of the London and English East-India Companies, 1707–8*, 3 vols (1810).

57. Bruce's wide-ranging writings provide scope for exploring Michel Foucault's observation that 'while colonization, with its techniques and its political and juridical weapons, obviously transported European models to other continents, it also had a considerable boomerang effect on the mechanisms of power in the West, and on the apparatuses, institutions, and techniques of power' (Foucault, 'Society', p. 103). In Bruce's work, there is no evidence at this stage in Britain's colonial history of any 'boomerang effect'; Britain was exclusively an exporter of models of governance.

58. *Notes on the History of the United Netherlands, Compiled During a Residence at the Universities of that Country, and Intended as an Introduction to its History* (1795).

59. *Review of the Events and Treaties which Established the Balance of Power in Europe and the Balance of Trade in Favour of Great Britain* (1796).

60. *Sketches of the Political and Commercial History of the Cape of Good Hope* (1796).

61. *Report on the Arrangements which Have Been Adopted in Former Periods, when France Threatened Invasion of Britain or Ireland, to Frustrate the Designs of the Enemy, by Attacks on His Foreign Possessions, or European Ports, by Annoying Coasts and by Destroying His Equipments* (1798).

62. *Report on the Events and Circumstances, which Produced the Union of the Kingdoms of England and Scotland; on the Effects of this Great National Event on the Reciprocal Interests of Both Kingdoms; and on the Political and Commercial Influence of Great Britain in the Balance of Power in Europe* (1799).

63. Joseph, *Reading*, p. 6.
64. Despite Britain's success in frustrating the political ambitions of both France and the United States, Bruce ultimately felt pessimistic. In his final public utterance, a speech to the British Parliament in 1813 in support of the (unsuccessful) bill for the renewal of the East India Company charter, Bruce closed with the gloomy words: 'It would [. . .] be a melancholy reflection indeed, to have lived to see one political and financial error lose to the country its American colonies, and to be convinced, that the proposed Resolutions, if passed into a law, in opposition to a most full and complete body of evidence, would, in a short time, probably lose its Indian empire to Great Britain' ('Speech', p. 437).
65. Bruce, *Historical View*, p. 335.
66. Ibid. p. 335.
67. Ibid. p. 339.
68. Thapar, *Cultural Pasts*, p. 3.
69. Bruce, *Historical View*, p. 342.
70. Ibid. p. 344.
71. Bruce's defence of indirect rule in India contrasts sharply with the contemporaneous shift in western European states from indirect to direct forms of governance. Charles Tilly notes that '[a]fter 1750 [. . .] states began moving aggressively from a nearly universal system of indirect rule to a new system of direct rule' (*Coercion*, p. 103), and James C. Scott argues that much of the 'statecraft of the late eighteenth and nineteenth centuries was devoted to the project of [reducing] the chaotic, disorderly, constantly changing social reality beneath it to something more closely resembling the administrative grid of its observations' (*Seeing*, p. 82).
72. Bruce, *Historical View*, p. 291.
73. Bruce, *Report on the Negociation*, p. 24.
74. Ibid. p. 24.
75. Ibid. p. 49.
76. Bruce, *Historical View*, p. 532.
77. Ibid. pp. 533, 537.
78. Bowen, *The Business*, pp. 51–2.
79. Dundas, *Substance*, p. 5.
80. Ibid. p. 9–10.
81. Bruce demonstrates his extensive research in quoting from the writings of François Valentyn (1666–1727), Peter Kolb, François Levaillant, Anders Sparrman and Carl Peter Thunberg, as well as from the documents on the Cape collected by Sir Joseph Banks (1743–1820) of the Royal Society, and the official dispatches of VOC officials.
82. Bruce, *Sketches*, p. 278.
83. Ibid. pp. 279–80.
84. Ibid. pp. 280–1.
85. Ibid. p. 383.
86. Ibid. p. 385.
87. Ibid. p. 385.
88. Ibid. pp. 375–6.
89. Ibid. pp. 378, 378–9.
90. Ibid. p. 283.
91. Ibid. p. 312.
92. Ibid. pp. 312, 313.
93. In relation to the Cape, see Charles Grant, *Observations Respecting Commerce of the Cape of Good Hope* (1796). On economic policy for the colonies more generally, see the anonymous pamphlet *A Short Conversation on the Present Crisis on the Important Trade with the Indies* (1813). The pamphlet dismisses Adam Smith as 'most wonderfully deficient in

the knowledge of the East-India trade' (p. 23). On Grant's role in the East India Company, see Bearce, *British Attitudes*, pp. 51–60.

94.  Bruce, *Sketches*, pp. 316–17.
95.  Ibid. p. 332.
96.  Ibid. p. 350.
97.  Ibid. pp. 283–4.
98.  Ibid. p. 285.
99.  See Marx, *The Grundrisse*, pp. 883–9. For a persuasive analysis of these passages, see Kazanjian, *The Colonizing*, pp. 213–23.
100. See Bernard Semmel's books *The Liberal Ideal* and *The Rise*.
101. The insistence on the priority of economic interests above questions of political governance in Smith and Bruce's writings challenges not only Anderson's theory of colonial nationalism, but also Michel Foucault's elevation of issues of governance in his explanation for the decline of mercantilism. Foucault describes mercantilism as 'the first sanctioned efforts to apply this art of government [as an exercise of sovereignty] at the level of political practices and knowledge of the state', and sees its failure at the end of the eighteenth century as due to the fact that 'the art of government [. . .] was trapped within the inordinately vast, abstract, rigid framework of the problem and institution of sovereignty' (*The Foucault*, pp. 97–8).
102. See Marx, *Capital, Volume 1*, pp. 873–940. On Marx's critique of Adam Smith, see Harvey, *The Limits*, pp. 413–17; and Postone, *Time*, pp. 130–8. On the continuing significance 'primitive accumulation', see Harvey, *The New Imperialism*, pp. 229–53.
103. For accounts of this episode, see Rae, *Life*, p. 405; and Furber, *Henry Dundas*, p. 296.
104. Quoted in Ross, *The Life*, p. 322.
105. Ibid. p. 352
106. See Semmel, *The Liberal*, pp. 61–2.
107. Rothschild, *Economic*, p. 52. See too Perelman, *The Invention*, pp. 241–52, which summarises the lukewarm reception of Smith's ideas in post-independence America.
108. Bruce, *Sketches*, p. 64.
109. Ibid. p. 190.
110. Ibid. p. 210.
111. Barrow's views on the Cape were published as *An Account of Travels into the Interior of Southern Africa in the Years 1797 and 1798*, 2 vols (1801, 1804). Barrow claims that during his time under Macartney at the Cape, '[t]he interests of the Company [. . .] were secured and promoted in every respect' (Vol. 2, pp. 273–4). For an account of Barrow, see Penn, 'Mapping', pp. 20–43.
112. See the studies of the British occupation of 1795 by Boucher and Penn, *Britain*, and Giliomee, *Die Kaap*.
113. Arkin, 'John Company', pp. 199–203; and Boucher and Penn, *Britain*, pp. 225–8.
114. See Arkin, 'John Company', pp. 195–7; and Penn, 'Mapping', pp. 20–2.
115. Quoted in Arkin, 'John Company', p. 203.
116. See Freund, 'The Cape', p. 333.
117. On the Cape's economy in the early nineteenth century, see Müller, 'The state', pp. 58–76.
118. Three recent publications that reprint the relevant primary texts, and chart the rise of free trade after the Napoleonic period are Cain, *The Wellesley Series*; Schonhardt-Bailey, *The Rise*; and Overbeek, *Free Trade*.
119. A phrase attributed to Walter Bagehot. See Leask, 'Romanticism', p. 278.
120. Smith, *A Theory*, p. 9.
121. Ibid. p. 136.
122. Hulme, *Colonial*, p. 229.
123. I have discussed Barnard as a political commentator in Johnson, 'Talking'.

124.  Barnard, *The Cape*, pp. 375–6.
125.  Ibid. p. 340.
126.  Ibid. p. 378.
127.  Ibid. p. 374.
128.  Ibid. p. 381.
129.  Ibid. pp. 337–8.
130.  Ibid. p. 338.
131.  Ibid. p. 339.
132.  Ibid. pp. 326, 380.
133.  Ibid. p. 300.
134.  Ibid. p. 393.
135.  Ibid. pp. 157–8.
136.  Ibid. pp. 215–16.
137.  Ibid. p. 216.
138.  Ibid. p. 215.
139.  Ibid. p. 215.
140.  Festa, *Sentimental*, p. 223.
141.  Barnard, *The Cape*, p. 424.

African Land for the American
Empire: John Adams, Benjamin
Stout and Robert Semple

---

## INTRODUCTION

In the decades following the American War of Independence, the United States was a significant presence at the Cape Colony.[1] This chapter traces the writings of two US visitors to the Cape: Benjamin Stout and Robert Semple (1766–1816). Stout, a patriot and ship's captain, was shipwrecked in the Eastern Cape, and undertook an overland journey to Cape Town from June to November 1796. Very little is known about him other than that he was an American sea-captain plying his trade in the Indian Ocean.[2] He was transporting rice from Bengal to Britain under charter to the English East India Company, when his ship *Hercules* ran aground on 16 June 1796 between the Begha and Keiskamma rivers on the Eastern Cape coast. Washed up with most of the crew intact, the survivors walked the 500-mile journey to Cape Town, helped along the way by sympathetic native inhabitants and Dutch settlers. When Stout returned to England in November 1796, he wrote an enthusiastic 112-page account of his journey, which was published in 1798, together with a 58-page Dedication to American president John Adams (1735–1826), exhorting Adams to colonise the Eastern Cape for America. There is no evidence that Adams read Stout's *Narrative*,[3] but the general reading public enjoyed his tale, with edited versions appearing in many different compilations and one further full-length edition in 1820.[4]

Semple was a loyalist and merchant, who travelled on horseback from Cape Town to Plettenberg Bay and back in August and September 1801. He was born in Boston, Massachusetts to Scottish parents, who were imprisoned for siding with the British during the American War of Independence. From 1798 to 1803, Semple was a successful merchant at the Cape, and he published his impressions of the Colony in a short book, *Walks and Sketches at the Cape of Good Hope, to which is subjoined a journey from Cape Town to Blettenberg Bay* in London in 1803.[5] After departing the Cape, he wrote a novel, *Charles Ellis; or, The Friends* (1806), and four more books on his various travels. In 1815, he was appointed governor of the territories controlled by the Hudson's Bay Company in Canada, but was killed a year later in a skirmish with the rival North-West Fur Company of Montreal. The experiences of Semple's youth – and particularly his parents' imprisonment – coloured his attitude towards the new nations of the United States and France, as he repeatedly declared his firm attachment to Britain and its empire. Semple's trajectory was typical of the 60,000 loyalists who at the end of the American War of Independence decided to leave North America with the British and seek futures elsewhere in the British Empire. As Maya Jasanoff explains, for these loyalists, post-independence America 'seemed less "an Assylum (sic) to the persecuted" than a potential persecutor [and] it was the British Empire that would be their asylum'.[6] For the peripatetic Semple, the Cape would be one of a number of asylums from his persecutor, the United States.

Both Stout's dreams and Semple's fears of US colonial expansion are expressed in simplified forms of the aesthetic vocabulary of landscape appreciation, with both of them relying particularly on the adjective 'romantic' to describe a variety of Cape landscapes. At the same time, both of them also use the language of political economy in assessing how the land of the Cape Colony might be transformed by capitalist agriculture into profit-bearing farms. In relation to landscape painting, W. J. T. Mitchell has suggested that 'we need to explore the possibility that the representation of landscape is not only a matter of internal politics and national or class ideology but also an international, global phenomenon, intimately bound up with the discourses of imperialism'.[7] In this chapter, Mitchell's challenge is taken up and extended to written representations of landscape, as I examine the differences and similarities in how Stout and Semple express their respective preoccupations with the land, landscapes and peoples of the Cape. The key questions are: how does writing about the economic appropriation of land under colonialism articulate with the aesthetic appreciation of colonial landscapes? And: how are the inhabitants of colonial landscapes represented?

## INVITING PRESIDENT JOHN ADAMS TO THE CAPE

Stout's Dedication to Adams appeals to America's revolutionary nationalism, which was anchored in an ideological project dedicated to transforming the rebellion of the Thirteen Colonies into the consolidation of a unified nation state by means of generating 'a mythology of national signs'.[8] One key element in this project was the popular press. In the same year that Stout ran aground on the Cape coast, Adams defeated Thomas Jefferson (1743–1826) by 71 electoral votes 68 to succeed George Washington (1732–99) as president of the United States, and the American press wrote up this close-fought contest with an emphasis on what united the two adversaries. The Philadelphia *General Advertiser* (better known as the *Aurora*) concluded, 'Upon the whole, America has a right to rejoice in the prospect she has of a wise and virtuous administration under two such distinguished patriots as Adams and Jefferson', and the *New York Journal* agreed: 'That [Adams's] administration may be propitious to the spirit and intention of our late revolution, and to the true dignity, peace and happiness of the people of our empire, is the sincere wish of every good citizen'.[9] The cumulative effect of the press's extensive political reporting post-1776 is summed up by the historian William Earl Weeks: 'The construction of a national-ist/imperialist mythology and its dissemination via national print media point to the way in which American nationalism conforms to Benedict Anderson's definition of nationalism as an "imagined community"'.[10] The efforts of the press were sup-plemented by literary contributions, with the expansion of 'our empire' a promi-nent theme. The poems of the Connecticut Wits like Joel Barlow (1754–1812) and David Humphreys (1752–1818) imagined exporting the American revolution to distant shores: Barlow wrote, 'Soon shall our [American] sails, in commerce unconfin'd, / Whiten each sea and swell every wind', and even more extravagantly, Humphreys rhymed:

> Bid from the [American] shore a philanthropic band,
> The torch of science glowing in their hand,
> O'er trackless waves extend their daring toils,
> To find and bless a thousand peopled isles . . .
> Bid them to wilder'd men new lights impart,
> Heav'n's noblest gifts, with every useful art.[11]

Stout's address to Adams should be read in this context – as a practical attempt 'to wilder'd men new lights impart', or more specifically, to Southern Africa the United States' nationalist/proto-imperialist project extend.

The years of Adams's presidency (1797–1801) were busy ones, and it is unsur-prising that he failed to find the time to colonise the Southern Cape, or to respond to Stout's appeal.[12] Stout constructs Adams as an American president opposed to slavery and in sympathy with Native Americans, a champion of democracy and an enemy of economic protectionism. In all but one of these respects, the historical figure of Adams differed from Stout's idealised presidential reader. First, Adams might have voiced his opposition to slavery, but under pressure bowed to the slave-owning politicians of the South. In 1821, for example, after the Missouri Compromise allowed the extension of slavery in the western states, Adams declared, 'I have been so terrified of the Phenomenon [of slavery] that I constantly said in former times to the Southern Gentlemen, I cannot comprehend the object; I must leave it to you. I will vote for forcing no measure against your judgments'.[13] Second, his commitment to democracy was always qualified. For example, he was critical of Tom Paine's *Common Sense* (1776), arguing that the proposals were 'so demo-cratical, without any restraint or even an attempt at any equilibrium or counter-poise, that it must produce confusion and every evil work'.[14] Third, as regards US foreign policy, Adams opposed involvement in anti-Spanish struggles in the South American colonies, and was especially determined never to repeat the belligerent maritime empire-building pursued by Britain, declaring, 'God forbid that American naval power should ever be such a scourge to the human race as that of Great Britain has been!'[15] Only with respect to his love of free trade was Stout accurate in his construction of Adams. In a recent study of Adams and Adam Smith, John E. Hill concludes that although the historical evidence suggests Adams never read *The Wealth of Nations*, his ideas on free trade accorded with those of Smith:

Adams's free trade views were the result of his experiences as a patriot, one of many Americans chafing at British mercantilist restrictions on the colonies' trade. His free trade views paralleled Smith's, but he owed Smith no intellectual debt for these ideas.[16]

## STOUT'S AFRICAN LANDSCAPES

Stout's Dedication to Adams begins by explaining the history of the changes in land ownership on Southern Africa's colonial frontier:

> As these colonists advance, they hunt the unfortunate natives as they do the lion and the panther, dispossess them of their lands by force, rob them of their cattle, and, by every possible means, endeavour to effect a total extirpation of the original and unoffending inhabitants. This inhuman conduct must surely meet the execration of every man not totally lost to the feelings of humanity; but still it may be alledged [sic], that, having once possession of these lands, no matter how obtained, their right is established, and they cannot be dispossessed by a foreigner, as such conduct is not warranted by the law of nations. I will admit (but for the purpose only of elucidating the matter in question), that successful violence gives a title to the possessor, and that the colonists, as far as they have penetrated, are lawfully entitled to these estates; still this argument does not apply so as to exclude an American, or any other foreigner, who settles at a distance (suppose a 100 miles) from the most advanced colony belonging to the government of the Cape.[17]

In summary, successful violence against Africans, however inhuman, gives legal tenure to European colonial (dis)possessors, and the law of nations prescribes that subsequent European colonists are obliged to observe such tenure. On this basis, Africans might qualify as objects of pity, but they can never qualify as legitimate claimants for land restitution. Only land owned as private property by citizens of European nations enjoys legal protection. Stout introduces a further proviso when he suggests that 'the people of any nation have an unquestionable right, provided the natives give their assent, to settle on such parts of the southern continent of Africa, as do not interpose with the lands already in possession of the colonists'.[18] Stout is not entirely clear here as to which carries the greater weight: the law of nations, which endorses the colonial acquisition of African land by successful violence, or the moral consideration that allows the colonial acquisition of land on condition that the natives give their assent. The implication is that the latter route to land acquisition might be preferable, but that native assent was not a legal prerequisite for Americans to acquire African land as yet unclaimed by other colonial possessors.

Stout's logic repeats in simplified form the legal explanation of land acquisition and property ownership inscribed in the US Declaration of Independence. The opening paragraph of the Declaration invokes 'the Laws of Nature and God's Nature', and the list of charges against King George III includes that he had constrained the 'population of these States [by] raising the conditions of new Appropriation of Lands', and that he had 'endeavoured to bring on the inhabitants of our frontiers, the merciless Indian Savages'.[19] These charges establish private land ownership as a core element of the new nation – white settlers must have an unrestricted right to the 'new appropriations of land', and the competing land claims of 'merciless Indian Savages', which Britain had 'endeavoured to bring on', must be rejected. Underwriting the Declaration's version of land conflict on the North American frontier was the seventeenth-century British law of nature as expounded by John Locke (1632–1704).

In Chapter Five of his *Second Treatise of Government* (1689), Locke starts with the observation that 'God, who hath given the world to men in common, hath also given them reason to make the best use of it to the best advantage of life, and convenience'.[20] As individuals labour on the commonly held property, however, they acquire private ownership of particular properties: 'His labour hath taken it out of the hands of nature, where it was common, and belonged equally to all her children, and hath thereby appropriated it to himself'.[21] As to who should and who should not acquire property, Locke is emphatic: '[God] gave it to the use of the industrious and rational, (and labour was to be his title to it;) not to the fancy or covetousness of the quarrelsome and contentious'.[22] Locke sets down a clear map of where different nations stand on the journey from common ownership to private property, referring twice to North America. First, he notes that while European nations have long since emerged from the state of nature, there are many other communities that still live in the state of nature, specifically in 'some inland, vacant places of America'.[23] Second, he asks rhetorically,

> whether in the wild woods and uncultivated waste of America left to nature, without any improvement, tillage or husbandry, a thousand acres will yield the needy and wretched inhabitants as many conveniences of life as ten acres of equally fertile land do in Devonshire where they are well cultivated?[24]

Roughly a century later, America's founding fathers argued for their rights to land on the same basis, with Pennsylvania replacing Devonshire as the implicit reference point for disparaging 'Indian' land ownership further west. And Locke's argument, mediated via the documents of the new American nation, serves Stout equally well in legitimising the potential American occupation of African land in the Cape Colony.

Stout's descriptions of the Cape are marked by a tension between the economics of land production and the aesthetics of landscape appreciation. The tension is nicely captured in a passage Stout lifts from Levaillant (mentioned in Chapter 2), in which the latter contrasts views of the Eastern Cape and of Cape Town:

> [In the Eastern Cape] nature appeared in all her majesty; the lofty mountains offering from every side the most delightful and romantic views I have ever seen. This prospect, contrasted with the idea of the parched and barren lands about the Cape, made me think myself at a thousand miles distance [. . .] What

a being is the sordid speculator, whose views, bounded by commerce, port fees and customs, can prefer the storms and dangers of Table-Bay, to the safe riding, or natural and charming ports, that are so common on the oriental coasts of Africa.[25]

Stout initially endorses Levaillant's opposition between the 'romantic views' of the Eastern Cape, and the views of the Western Cape 'bounded by commerce', but he then proceeds to insist that the Eastern Cape is not only pleasing to the eye, but *also* has immense potential for economic exploitation. Stout emphasises that the land of the Eastern Cape 'abounds in timber of the best quality; possesses many excellent harbours; is blessed with the richest pasturage that feeds innumerable heads of the finest cattle; [. . .] and their shores are frequented by fish of every quality'.[26]

Stout's descriptions of the landscape where the *Hercules* ran aground also range between the economic and aesthetic attractions:

> During our miserable abode under the sand-hills, we frequently contemplated the scene before us. Nearly as far as the eye could travel, we beheld a country finely wooded, and considering the season, which was their winter, producing a most bountiful vegetation. Their cattle appear in such prodigious numbers as to baffle calculation; and their condition, which was equal to the best fed oxen in Great Britain, clearly demonstrated the richness of their pasturage. Sheep were not to be discovered, nor could we perceive the most distant traces of agricultural labour. The country in our view was of an immense extent, yet surrounded by a chain of hills that appeared to contain the fountains of those numerous rivulets which glided through the plain in a variety of directions. The *mimosa tree* appeared native to the soil, and the woods were so beautifully interspersed, as to give the lands all the appearance of a plantation originally defined by art, and afterwards perfected by the hand of elegance. In my opinion, the whole wanted nothing but villages, corn and inhabitants, to render this spot an enviable abode for the most enlightened and luxurious of our countrymen.[27]

The sequence of Stout's description of the landscape here develops from images of bounty ('finely wooded' with 'bountiful vegetation', 'prodigious numbers' of cattle and 'numerous rivulets'); to an appreciation of the land's aesthetic qualities (trees and woods 'beautifully interspersed' and lands 'defined by art'); and culminates in a concrete vision of the land transformed into profitable farmland (the addition of 'corn and inhabitants' will make the land into an 'enviable abode'). These compelling attractions, in combination with an absence of any 'traces of agricultural labour', make Stout's case for the colonisation of this land by US settlers.

In claiming that the landscapes of the Eastern Cape are pleasing to the sensibilities of the European or North American viewer, Stout (like Levaillant) relies upon the capacious adjective 'romantic' to describe the aesthetic appeal of the landscape. In each of the two instances Stout uses the term, however, he refers to different kinds of landscape. In the first instance, Stout declares:

The countries through which we passed were alternatively hill and dale, and often afforded the most romantic prospects. We frequently perceived vast quantities of wolves, and often such droves of that species of deer which the farmers call *spring buck*, that we supposed one flock alone could not contain less than from *twelve* to *fourteen thousand*.[28]

What Stout stresses in this description is the wildness of the landscape, with the sheer numbers of wild animals attesting to the absence of human agency. In the second instance, the term 'romantic' has slightly different connotations:

It is called by the settlers *Long Cluff*, and affords, perhaps, as many romantic scenes as can be found in any spot of the same extent on the face of the earth. The hills for seventy or eighty miles run parallel to each other. The lands between are wonderfully rich, and produce vast quantities of a plant similar in its smell and taste to our thyme. On this fragrant herb are fed immense quantities of sheep and cattle; they devour it with great eagerness, and it gives the mutton a flavour like our venison, that an epicure might be deceived in the taste.[29]

'Romantic' here *is* associated with human cultivation, as it is not the numbers of wild animals but the numbers of sheep and cattle that are emphasised. However, what the descriptions of the two landscapes have in common is that neither acknowledges human agency in the landscape, and second, both passages describe vistas of great natural abundance from an elevated viewpoint.[30] These aspects require further elaboration.

Stout emphasises repeatedly the emptiness of the land.[31] Shortly after leaving the site of the shipwreck, he notes that 'in the course we pursued, not a human footstep could be traced; no cattle, no sign of cultivation could be observed'.[32] A couple of weeks further into the journey to Cape Town, Stout still encounters vacant land: '[w]e likewise travelled this day through delightful country [. . .] but not a sign of *agriculture* was to be observed'.[33] Only as Stout and his fellow travellers near the Western Cape are there signs of human habitation. In a sequence with Biblical echoes,[34] they pass first with trepidation through 'a dismal valley of about three miles in length [. . .] called *Boshisman's path*', where they anxiously anticipate a Bushman attack, before entering 'upon a champaign country'[35] populated with increasing numbers of Dutch farmsteads. Stout proclaims how successfully the settler farmers have taken advantage of the bountiful landscape:

The country, as we advanced, increased in population; and the farm-houses were, in several places, not more than two hours distant from each other. Many of them were beautifully situated, and their land produced grain, oranges, figs and lemons in abundance.[36]

Stout's enthusiasm both for the unpopulated landscapes of the Eastern Cape *and* for the inhabited and cultivated farmlands of the Western Cape challenges the contemporaneous conventions of the picturesque. Malcolm Andrews explains that for writers like William Gilpin (1724–1804), '[t]he appraisal of landscape, principally in terms of its formal and affective qualities, excluded appraisal of its economic or political terms'.[37] The contrast with Stout is striking, as he rejects the separation of the aesthetic from the economic by reading the latter as an enhancement or development of the former – from romantic landscape to capitalist farmland. The energy and logic of Stout's descriptions of the landscape demand once again the conclusion that the addition of American settlers to the vacant land of the Eastern Cape will emulate the agricultural achievements of the Dutch settlers in the Western Cape.

In addition to descriptions proclaiming the romantic aspect of the landscape and its potential for cultivation, Stout also provides passages that emphasise its dangers and terrors. For example, soon after crossing the Fish River, a spectacular view greets Stout and his party:

> We had scarcely put ourselves in motion, when a scene of the most extensive and luxuriant beauties burst in a moment on our view. The danger we had just escaped, engaged our attention entirely, when we gained the summit, that we did not immediately perceive the world of beauties that now lay spread before us. All stood for some time in a state of rapture and amazement. The country was mostly a level, yet pleasingly diversified with gentle elevations, on the tops of which we could perceive clumps of the *mimosa tree*, and the sides clothed with shrubs of various denominations. A thousand rivulets seemed to meander though this *second Eden*; frequently skirting or appearing to encircle a plantation of wood [. . .] As we stood gazing on this sylvan scene, we perceived innumerable herds of animals, particularly of the species of the gazelle, scouring over the plains; some darting through the woods, others feeding, or drinking at the rivulets. As far as the eye travelled in pursuit of new beauties, it was most amply gratified, until at length the whole gradually faded on the view, and became lost in the horizon. We were so wrapt in extacy [*sic*] at this landscape, that we forgot our danger, and remained too long upon the mountain. We at length descended, and proceeded on our journey.[38]

Such descriptions of the vast and intimidating landscapes of the Eastern Cape satisfy the requirements of Edmund Burke's 'sublime'. According to Burke, '[a]stonishment [. . .] is the effect of the sublime in its highest degree; the inferior effects are admiration, reverence and respect'.[39] The expansive views that leave Stout and his party 'wrapt in extacy' certainly provoke astonishment, and the impact is enhanced by the fact of their own vulnerability within the landscape.

Stout's various descriptions of the landscape – those he terms 'romantic', those he describes as ripe for economic development, and those we might designate 'sublime' – are all viewed from above.[40] John Barrell has argued that in Britain in the late eighteenth century, the capacity to appreciate panoramic landscapes in art was tied to both a facility with abstract thought and a mastery of the public sphere.[41]

According to Barrell, an opposition tying landscape appreciation to politics is constructed during this period:

> Those who can comprehend the order of society and nature are observers of a prospect, in which others are merely objects. Some comprehend, others are comprehended; some are fit to survey the extensive panorama, some are confined within one or other of the micro-prospects which, to the comprehensive observer, are parts of a wider landscape, but which, to those confined within them, are all they see.[42]

The geographer Denis Cosgrove makes the point in slightly different terms. He argues that the rise of the concept of landscape is coterminous with early modern capitalism, as it consigns those working the land to the position of 'insiders', who can never see their land as landscape: 'The insider does not enjoy the privilege of being able to walk away from a scene as we can walk away from a framed picture or from a tourist viewpoint'.[43] In Stout's descriptions of the colonial landscape, he is the one who observes and comprehends the extensive panoramas of the Cape; the inhabitants themselves are either absent or bounded by the landscape, in that they are incapable of seeing its full (economic) potential – they are 'insiders'. As an American observer of African landscapes, Stout's assumption of this observer-position has an added resonance. By demonstrating his capacity to appreciate panoramic perspectives, Stout lays claim to the related political status of citizen (Barrell) and economic mastery (Cosgrove), a claim invigorated by the separation from Britain. The power associated with the capacity to appreciate panoramic landscapes, located in eighteenth-century Britain with 'the lords or the meritocratic bourgeoisie',[44] is thus claimed by a confident New World adventurer competing with recently defeated colonial masters for imperial land. The crucial continuity, of course, is that those who work the land, in Britain and the colonies alike, are denied this panoramic perspective, and the elevated outside viewer diminishes, and often effaces, their labour from the landscape.

### Inhabiting Stout's landscape

What of the people inhabiting the landscapes of the Cape? Stout declares over and again that the native inhabitants of Southern Africa have been misrepresented in settler writings. In concluding his address to Adams, he argues:

> I have been encouraged to publish [this narrative . . .] from a belief that some useful information may be derived from a genuine description of the natives and their country [. . .] To remove, therefore, such prejudices as have arisen from the extravagant and deceptive tales of those travellers who have represented the natives as monsters, that delight only in human slaughter, becomes a duty, as it may encourage future adventurers in their pursuits, and relieve the unfortunate from unnecessary apprehensions.[45]

In the narrative itself, he notes that descriptions of the Tambouchis (a Xhosa clan) as 'the most *ferocious*, *vindictive* and *detestable* class of beings that inhabit the vast and fertile territory of Cafraria' amount to 'a calumny so undeserved, so atrocious, and possibly so mischievous in its tendency, I can not suffer to pass without censure and contradiction'.[46] Stout cites the great kindnesses shown to him and his men by the native inhabitants, describing them as 'possessed of all those compassionate feelings, that alone give a lustre to, and adorn humanity', and further, that they are 'people of great natural sagacity, and of an active and enterprising disposition'.[47] Any perceived deficiencies on their part he ascribes to climate and lack of educational opportunities: 'To say, therefore, that any race of mortals are *naturally savage*, and of course not capable of enjoying the blessings of civilisation, is a dogma arising from ignorance, or a want of due consideration'.[48] To reinforce this cultural relativism, Stout juxtaposes examples of the alleged 'savagery' of the Africans and the 'civilisation' of Europeans. Right at the outset, for example, he contrasts the hospitality and protection afforded by the natives with the unfriendliness he had encountered in the 'polished nations of Europe'.[49]

However, there are two exceptions to Stout's generous descriptions of the native inhabitants. The first relates to a particular Xhosa clan 'distinguished, by their countrymen, as a *bad tribe*'.[50] Stout's encounter with this 'bad tribe' concludes with the following image of one of their number:

> At the moment he stood in this attitude, a more finished picture of horror, or what we understand of the *infernals*, was perhaps never seen before. The savage wore a leopard's skin; his black countenance bedaubed with red ochre; his eyes, inflamed with rage, appeared as if starting from their sockets; his mouth expanded, and his teeth *gnashing* and *grinning* with all the fury of an exasperated demon. At this instant, the *tout-en-semble* of the figure would have been a subject highly deserving the pencil of *Raphael*.[51]

By declaring 'the savage' to be a fit subject for High European art, Stout summons an Italian Renaissance visual aesthetic in order to inflate the terror of his colonial encounter. The effect, however, is to wrench the particular Xhosa tribesman from his context, and to inscribe him within a typology of European demonic iconography.

The second exception is Stout's descriptions of the 'Bushmen', which alternate between acknowledging their potential for improvement and compassion for their cruel treatment, to the uncritical repetition of settler tales of Bushmen savagery. In the address to Adams, he introduces the Bushmen as terrifying – they 'wage perpetual war with every horde, and plunder wherever they come'[52] – and reinforces this impression when he describes settler relations with the Bushmen in the narrative itself. Given his earlier criticisms of settler hostility towards the native inhabitants, Stout is uncharacteristically silent about the treatment of the Bushmen:

> The *Bushmen*, when they are sufficiently strong in number, attack and kill the *Hottentots* and *Caffrees* wherever they find them; and the *colonists* hunt the

*Bushmen* as they do the *lion* and the *tiger* – A farmer never thinks of giving quarter to these people; but slay[s] them the very instant they are in their power.[53]

After describing further experiences of settler hospitality, and the dangers posed by Bushmen arrows to travellers on a particular mountain pass, Stout tacitly endorses the genocidal behaviour of the settlers towards the Bushmen: 'The farmers told us, they frequently assemble to the number of *forty* or *fifty*, and then go in quest of the *Bushmen*, whom they destroy without mercy if they come upon them'.[54] These lines suggest the Bushmen, integral to the pre-colonial landscape, should be violently purged in order that the land might be transformed for commercial agriculture.

It is instructive to compare Stout's proposals for the 'Bushmen' with contemporaneous American plans for the Native Americans. The historian Edward Countryman has argued that the significance of the American Revolution for Native Americans was that they were subjected to a relentless new form of colonial rule, with 'a shift from external colonialism under the British to "internal colonialism" within the United States'.[55] As regards land ownership, Walter LeFeber notes that from 1782, 'the Indians were to be "civilised" and made to act like white farmers', and he cites as exemplary Jefferson's instructions to a group of Indians that they should become small capitalist landowners: '"you will mix with us by marriage. Your blood will run in our veins and will spread with us over this great land"'.[56] Should they fail to observe this American version of the Scottish Enlightenment road to 'civilisation', they face a fate not unlike the one Stout anticipates for the Southern African 'Bushmen'. In Jefferson's words, '[The Indians] will relapse into barbarism and misery [. . .] and we shall be obliged to drive them, with the beasts of the forests into the Stony [Rocky] Mountains'.[57]

In addition to providing extensive descriptions of the terrain and its native inhabitants, Stout's concern is to assess Kaffraria's potential as a colonial enterprise. To this end, he gives attention to the different nations who have colonised Africa, with the ultimate aim of setting out the best means for American settlement of the region to proceed. Of the Dutch, Stout is contemptuous for two reasons. Their treatment of the native inhabitants is barbarous, and Stout refers to them with heavy irony as 'those *enlightened savages*, who, under the appellations of *Christians* and *Dutchmen*, settled themselves by violence on the southern promontory'.[58] He describes their seizing of the Cape in critical terms:

> The Dutch [. . .] and their people have, within this century, proceeded into the interior, cultivated land and formed settlements 400 miles distant from the Cape [. . . B]y every possible means, [they] endeavour to effect a total extirpation of the original and unoffending inhabitants.[59]

At least as offensive to Stout as the Dutch treatment of the native inhabitants is their ineptitude as colonial administrators. Given the remarkable natural resources at their disposal, their failure to pursue a vigorous policy of free trade appals Stout. He quotes with approval the angry complaints of an unnamed settler, who describes the punitive protectionist policies of the VOC, and appeals for more enlightened colonial governance:

> We are, (said these people) although living on the confines of the deserts, so barbarously treated by our rulers, that we are unable to proceed [. . .] We live in the hope however, (continued these colonists) that some nation more liberal than ours, will form a settlement on the eastern or western coast, that we may get supplied with such articles as are necessary to our situation, and will trade with us on principles of mutual advantage.[60]

The only glimmer of hope for the Dutch Empire, according to Stout, lies in the impact of the 'late revolution [. . .] on the national character', as it might have the effect of 'expanding their minds, teach them to found their commerce on the principles of *humanity* and *justice*'.[61]

As regards the English, Stout's views are more forgiving.[62] In the address to Adams, he concedes that 'the inhabitants of the Cape, and the colonists in general, entertain a strong predilection in favour of the British, and the sagacity of the English government will soon point out the means of perpetuating their friendships'.[63] Both in terms of their treatment of the native inhabitants, and in their sympathy for promoting free trade, the British exceed the Dutch handsomely. Aware that England's struggle with France remains in the balance, Stout declares his sympathies for the English in the conclusion of his address to Adams: 'as I have been apprehensive that you would consider a settlement of this description as a measure which American policy forbids, I have likewise directed my observations to the *English nation*, whose prosperity has ever had a second place in my affections'.[64] He emphasises the enormous benefits that would accrue to Britain should it develop the Cape along the lines he suggests, and on the final page of the travelogue concludes that 'if in the present work I have furnished a single hint that eventually may be found useful to the BRITISH NATION, I shall not hereafter repine at the calamities I have suffered'.[65]

Having identified the failings of the Dutch and English, Stout concludes by extolling the Americans, as he imagines the relation between America and Africa to be mediated in a non-coercive fashion by the means of free trade. In promoting the humane treatment of the native inhabitants and policies of free trade, Stout casts America in a benign role. He appeals in the first instance to what he assumes to be the humane sensibilities of John Adams:

> The untutored tribes of America have already experienced the beneficence of your nature, and I am desirous to arrest your attention and interest your feelings, on behalf of those wandering children of nature, who are scattered over the deserts of the African world.[66]

However, he is swift to emphasise the economic benefits for America: 'I shall now endeavour to draw your attention to those commercial benefits which I conceive may be obtained by establishing a colony from America, on that part of the coast where the ship I commanded was unfortunately wrecked'.[67] Given the harsh treatment both native inhabitants and settlers have suffered at the hands of Dutch rulers, the Americans are likely to receive a warm welcome: 'they would hail the American, when they were convinced of his justice, as their friend, their protector, and deliverer'.[68] As to the appropriate strategy for containing any remote possibility of native resistance, Stout recommends free (if unequal) trade and liberal governance: 'their acquiescence could be soon obtained, by gifts of little value to the donor, and their allegiance secured by a kind and liberal treatment in the course of their negotiations'.[69] With all these advantages, Stout has little difficulty in imagining a happy future for American colonists settling and farming cash crops on the fertile land of the Southern Cape: 'An American well acquainted with the growth and manufacture of [tobacco], must, in a few years, if settled in these parts, become not only independent, but opulent'.[70]

Stout's *Narrative* combines a number of distinct elements into a powerful case for American imperial intervention in Southern Africa: (1) prime land, principally for commercial agriculture, but also as romantic vista and sublime spectacle; (2) friendly (or absent) local inhabitants, made up of indigenous African communities and Dutch settlers, with both groups amenable to integration into an American economy; (3) weakened imperial rivals, with the Dutch mired in antiquated forms of mercantile protectionism, and the English preoccupied with France; and (4) an ideology of free trade, guaranteed to invigorate the economies of America and Africa alike.

## SEMPLE'S AFRICAN LANDSCAPES

As a loyalist in the American Revolution, Semple arguably belongs more properly in the tradition of British writers on the Cape. There are close similarities, for example, between his judgements and those of Lady Anne Barnard. But by focusing on his antipathy towards the American Revolution, I hope to draw out here the distinctiveness of US imperial discourse as applied to the Cape. Semple's political allegiances are captured in an inflated reverie prompted by his climbing Table Mountain with his fictional companion Charles.[71] He begins with the rhetorical questions, 'Whence arises this pleasure in my breast [and] Why does the current of my blood glide so swiftly through my heart?', and promptly provides the answer: 'I have enjoyed an extensive prospect from a lofty mountain'.[72] The view from the top of Table Mountain provokes his imagination to range well beyond the Cape:

> In looking towards the mountains of Hottentot Holland, by means of that intellectual power which God has bestowed on man, we winged our way to their highest summits, and thence discovered with astonishment, in the inmost recess of Africa, hordes of undiscovered and undescribed savages, prostrate before the light of a new-born day. Beyond the waves of the Indian Ocean, the nations of Asia with their pagodas, their white-robed bramins, their inoffensive manners, and their antique superstitions. In the distant bosom of the southern

ocean, we beheld clusters of peaceful islands, defended by reefs of coral, over which the waves slowly broke, and the friendly inhabitants asleep under the shade of their cocoa nut trees. With rapid thought we passed the shores of the Brazils and Spanish America, stained with innocent blood, and where the murmur of the waves upon the shore was mingled with the crack of the task-master's lash – the cries of the feeble Indian – and the noise of his mattock as he dug for gold. On the banks of the majestic rivers and lakes, and in the bosom of the forests of the western world, we beheld, with pardonable pride, English laws and institutions, English manners and men, firmly rooted; and pleased ourselves with the thought, that our language would thereby one day become the most extended that has perhaps ever been spoken upon the face of the globe. Then reverting towards the north, we lingered amidst the various cities, the polished arts, and the domineering policy of enlightened Europe; and fixing upon our own happy island, we forgot, for a short moment, all ideas of grandeur and sublimity, and melted at the recollection of the ties by which we felt con-nected with it. With hearts thus attuned, and in the midst of a scene so inter-esting and so magnificent, we long remained in silent wonder and gratitude.[73]

Semple has by no means been the last white hiker to reach the summit of Table Mountain and hyperventilate on splendours geographical and profundities philo-sophical,[74] but the reach of his mountain-top epiphany is exceptional. The elevated perspective propels his imperial fantasy, as his imagination circles the globe – from Africa, to India, to the Indian and Pacific islands, to South America, to North America and finally, to northern Europe – before ending 'upon our own happy island'. Semple and Charles appreciate the 'grandeur and sublimity' of the wider world Britain graces with its presence, but they melt with 'hearts attuned' at the thought of their own ties with Britain. Of particular interest in this context is how Semple rewrites the American Revolution: rather than instancing Britain's loss of a colonial possession, North America has been implanted with 'English laws and institutions, English manners and men', and the English language.

An interesting sequel to this passage is provided in Semple's novel published three years after these reflections from Table Mountain. In *Charles Ellis*, the epony-mous protagonist finds himself detained in Rio de Janeiro, and like Semple in Cape Town, he climbs the highest peak to look down on the colonial settlement. From the ruins of an old Portuguese fort, he speculates on the future of Britain's empire:

Seating himself on the edge of the parapet, [Charles] thought of the renowned warriors of Portugal, when Portugal was still great in arms; and reflecting that as they only conquered to extend their commerce, and acquire riches, he saw that their wealth had increased, but that their battlements were falling to decay.—'Such may one day be the fate of my own country,' said he to himself, 'a foreigner may sit on the ruined fortifications of one of her distant colonies, and trace with cool precision the causes that led to the gradual extinction of her military spirit, though to the increase of her commercial greatness. But that period can be but short and transitory. When England ceases to be great in arms, she will soon cease to be great in science and commerce – and like this rich country, which I now behold, await her doom from a more warlike though less opulent nation.'[75]

Whereas Cape Town's prospect for Semple and Charles inspires happy thoughts of Britain's global dominion, the view over Rio for the fictional Charles triggers gloomy musings about the decline and fall of the British Empire. The shift from the optimism of Semple's 1803 travelogue to the fatalism of his 1806 novel might be attributed to the immediate context of Cape history, with Britain having handed the Cape back to the Batavian Republic in 1803. But given Semple's direct experience of Britain's defeat at the hands of a 'more warlike though less opulent nation' in North America in 1776–81, a more likely cause was his fear that the United States would replace Britain as supreme imperial power.

Semple's euphoria on top of Table Mountain did not survive for long even in Cape Town; he explains that his journey along the Colony's east coast was motivated in part by his desire to help a fellow merchant refloat a vessel run aground in Plettenberg Bay, but also in part 'by the hopes of chasing away the melancholy ideas which had began to take possession of my mind'.[76] This mindset predisposes Semple to seek out landscapes that appeal to his sensitive spirit, and he designates those that have such an effect on him 'romantic'. As with Stout, so too with Semple, viewing a romantic spectacle by definition requires climbing a mountain: near Swellendam, '[b]y degrees we began to ascend, and soon had a view of the hills above Zwellendam, through a romantic opening on our left, where the river Sonder End seems to have cut its way through the hill';[77] near the Great Brak River, '[w]e had to climb a high and very steep hill, keeping under our view, during the whole of our ascent, a most romantic and deep valley on our left, the sides of which, though seemingly almost perpendicular, were covered with lofty trees';[78] on the return journey, at a farm near Riversonderend, 'I therefore went up towards the mountains to look for deer. After a romantic ride, and scrambling across several torrents running down from the hills, I got within gun shot of a herd of deer';[79] and finally, from Paarl, 'I ascended alone the steep hill, at whose foot the Pearl lies, and in about three quarters of an hour, reached its stony and romantic summit. Thence I had a fine view of the whole range of the Cape Hills'.[80] These romantic views never recreate for Semple the intensity of his Table Mountain moment, but they still function as muted versions of the same spiritual experience.

As regards the other key terms of landscape appreciation, Semple refers to the 'sublime' fleetingly. He mentions the sublime in contrasting the landscapes of Africa and North America, observing that '[t]o an admirer of the sublime in Nature, few spots on the surface of the globe present such scenes as the Cape of Good Hope'.[81] He notes further that Africa provides a different variety of sublime landscape to that of North America: whereas 'America abounds in immense forests, in majestic rivers, and inland seas of fresh water', the African landscapes offer 'chains of lofty and craggy mountains [. . .] deep beds of torrents rather than of rivers [. . . and] great deserts of sand'.[82] But aside from the early reference to the 'sublimity and grandeur' of the Table Mountain vista, Semple's only African experience of 'some degree of horror'[83] arises not from an instance of viewing a sublime landscape, but rather from an instance of failing to achieve the elevation required to view *any* landscape:

> [A]fter wandering about till sun down, I found myself alone in a wild country with no house in view. Apprehensive that if I remained in the bushes, I stood some chance of being devoured by the Hyenas before morning, I determined to make the best use of the little day light that remained, and accordingly ascended the nearest rising ground, and looking all round to my great joy saw the house of P. Duprés on a small eminence on the right.[84]

In Cosgrove's terms, Semple the 'outsider' to the landscape temporarily loses his way to become an 'insider' within the landscape, and experiences feelings of acute vulnerability.

Unlike Stout, Semple pays only limited attention to the capacity of the Cape landscapes to be transformed into productive farmland. Indeed, he conforms quite closely to Gilpin's aesthetic as summed up by Andrews: 'Aesthetic valuation was substituted for valuation in terms of real estate or farming potential'.[85] Semple does provide one description on his return journey in which the economic is a consideration: 'The road continued flat for several miles, through a country seemingly very fertile though almost totally uncultivated, one or two farms at a distance on our right being all that we saw'.[86] However, for Semple it is the Romantic communion between the elevated and sensitive individual and the supine landscape that supersedes all other modes of engaging with the Cape's land and landscapes.

### Inhabiting Semple's landscape

To appreciate the filter through which Semple viewed the inhabitants at the Cape, it is helpful to return once again to his novel *Charles Ellis*, and to note a key chapter in which Charles describes post-independence America in a letter to the Reverend Williamson in England. His judgements on the citizens of the new nation are entirely negative. He encounters in the conversation of Americans 'a woeful deficiency compared with that which I had been accustomed [to in England]'.[87] Specifically, they are obsessed with making money, and '[t]he sole topic in the towns is trade, and in the country, the price of grain and spirits'.[88] He discerns in the 'well-informed men of this country [. . .] a very dictatorial air', and in their mode of expression, 'a kind of polite insolence of manners and address'; indeed, they display 'a great deal of that spirit which we find too frequently in our neighbours the Irish – that false honor, which [. . .] is always prompting a man to superciliousness'.[89] What particularly irks Charles is their hostility to literary attainments: 'it may be said that there is no such thing as polite literature amongst them. The builder of an improved saw-mill would be treated with more attention than a poet of the first order'.[90] Moving from literature to politics, Charles complains of the precocious imperial ambitions of the American, who 'grasps in idea all the continent to the northward of the Isthmus of Darien; and tells you with great self-complacency, that the time is not very distant when the United States shall rule the destinies of the globe'.[91] Charles notes how much of their political vocabulary they have borrowed from 'their friends the French', and accordingly, how 'they are very fond of talking of their liberties, and their detestation of slavery', but he points out their hypocrisy on this score: 'their mouths are foaming with the word "Liberty," and their houses and plantations are stocked with negro slaves'.[92] The language of politics and of familial duty blur in Charles's recriminations against America for its coldness and lack of gratitude to England for providing 'their origin, their language, their manners, their laws, their religion, and their love of liberty'.[93] Charles suggests that the 'rancor' Americans feel towards Britain 'forms the greatest blot in their character', and he concludes his letter first by repeating the metaphor of the severed filial bond, and then by returning to the (ultimately prescient) fear that Britain's empire will be overtaken by America's:

> Perhaps they are like an untoward youth, who cannot conceive himself man enough while his father lives, without he shews to all the world how much he can disregard or despise him. In the course of ages, when the temples, the palaces, and still more, the liberties and laws of Great Britain shall have fallen into decay, all animosity then being extinct, the American traveller may visit our island, and sigh over their ruins.[94]

The same values and standards expressed in Charles's letter from America are applied in judging the inhabitants of the Cape Colony. Of Cape Town's settler populace, for example, Semple finds them (like the North Americans) obsessed with money: '[t]heir ideas are almost entirely commercial; their general conversation is of buying and selling'.[95] But he finds that they constitute a less coherent community than their North American counterparts:

> As yet the people of the Cape are only about to assume a character. They are neither English, nor French, nor Dutch. Nor do they form an original class as Africans, but a singular mixture of all together, which has not yet acquired a consistence, and is therefore almost impossible to be exactly represented.[96]

Semple's sense of the unformed nature of the Cape settler community had been also noted a few years before by Lady Anne Barnard. But whereas Barnard aimed 'to effect [. . .] if possible to *bring the Nations together* on terms of good will',[97] Semple is haunted by the memory of the liberated North American colonies, and for the Cape Colony he accordingly insists upon 'the importance of forming a white population, a colony of Englishmen speaking our language, and bound to us by every tie, on this great angle of Africa'.[98] To the white farmers encountered on his travels beyond Cape Town, Semple continues to apply the same standards, criticising the Dutch settlers' ignorance, although he sees some hope for them with the spread of the spirit of religion: 'Wide may this spirit spread, and happy may its influence be! [. . . L]et us hail it as the dawning of a brighter day, and rejoice at any ray of light piercing through so thick a gloom as the gross and uncultivated mind of a Cape boor'.[99] There is some complexity in Semple's descriptions of the Colony's Dutch settlers – he concedes their hospitality, honesty, peaceable nature and sobriety[100] – but his observations remain superficial, and perhaps most substantially, fail to mention the Graaff-Reinet and Swellendam rebellions of the late 1790s, which were inspired by the American and French Revolutions, and would surely have invited his strongest censure (see Chapter 5).

Semple's tendency to impressionistic cliché extends to his descriptions of the slaves at the Cape and the 'Hottentots'. In terms that repeat Barnard's sentimental discourse, Semple condemns slavery in general, 'which depraves the mind, and debases human nature', but in the particular case of the Cape Colony, he declares, 'the slaves of the Cape are not ill treated, are well clothed, and well fed'.[101] Semple counsels sympathy for slaves, especially dead slaves:

> Even the slave must not be committed to dust without a tear; and perhaps were we to find that he too had a wife, and a brother, and a friend, and behold them weeping over his grave, we might not be ashamed to sit down with them, and pay our tribute likewise to his memory.[102]

In the very next chapter, Semple gets an opportunity to display his compassion when he and Charles come upon a woman slave weeping at the grave of a loved one on 'Lion's Hill': 'we stood with tears in our eyes to look at the female slave mourner [. . . H]er whole figure was rendered doubly interesting by the mingled ideas of sorrow and oppression, for she was a female, a mourner, and a slave'.[103] After a description of a slave auction, at which Semple's friend Charles intervenes to ensure a slave woman and her child are sold to 'a mild master', Semple lists the different varieties of slaves at the Cape. Unusually, he includes in his list of slave types the colonial-born slave, or 'Hottentot', but suggests that they make the worst slaves: they 'labour only through absolute necessity, and would quickly sink into profound indolence', and he claims further to have seen 'many instances of cold ingratitude among those of this nation'.[104] In a separate chapter on the 'Hottentots' added in the second edition, Semple attempts a more sympathetic portrait, starting with Charles declaring, '"this ancient soil [of the Cape] – these venerable mountains and wide spread plains are his, and all the motley crew that now inhabits here with us Europeans at their head, are but usurpers of his undoubted rights"'.[105] Semple replies to Charles, explaining that 'the Hottentot' is full of contradictions: 'He is simple, credulous, and easily imposed upon, yet withal, at times shrewd and cunning [. . . H]e is indolent, yet capable of violent exertions; mild, and timid, yet displaying at times great resolution'.[106] Semple continues that English (but not Dutch) masters appreciate their qualities as servants – they are 'faithful and affectionate in a high degree' – and concludes by rejecting the French idea that they are the lowest link 'that connects man with the brutes': Britain will 'be the first to rescue the character of this unfortunate race from such calumnies, and in time to assign them that rank in the scale of man which they ought justly to hold'.[107]

Contrary pressures determine Semple's compassionate declarations about the slaves and 'Hottentots'. On the one hand, Semple's demonstrations of tender feelings distinguish him from the anti-sentimental rationalism of the American Revolutionary leaders. Hannah Arendt observes:

> [T]he passion of compassion was singularly absent from the minds and hearts of the men who made the American Revolution. Who would doubt that John Adams was right when he wrote: 'The envy and rancor of the multitude against the rich is universal and restrained only by fear or necessity. A beggar can never comprehend the reason why another should ride in a coach while he has no bread', and still no one familiar with misery can fail to be shocked by the peculiar coldness and indifferent 'objectivity' of his judgement.[108]

For Adams, relations between rich and poor are governed by envy, rancor, fear and necessity, whereas for Semple, relations between master and slave provoke tears of sympathy. On the other hand, Semple did not want to be thought too much at the mercy of his compassionate feelings. His reaction to critical reviews of the first edition of *Walks and Sketches* reveals that he was anxious not to overdo the sympathy. In the Advertisement to the 1805 edition, he discloses that critics had accused him of an excess of sentiment, a charge that particularly troubled him: 'Amongst others, the cant of sentiment has been attributed to me, a cant which, notwithstanding the authority of Sterne, is to me still more tedious than that of criticism'.[109] His prickliness suggests that the discourse of sentiment – deployed successfully by Sterne in *A Sentimental Journey Through France and Italy* in 1768 – had by the start of the nineteenth century become increasingly feminised, and therefore fine for Lady Anne Barnard, but an embarrassment for Robert Semple.

Semple might have tried to disavow sentimentalism, but like the hero of *Charles Ellis*, his identity was anchored in his capacity as a solitary individual to feel emotions, to appreciate landscapes and to discern truths beyond the reach of lesser mortals – standard markers of Romantic ideology. But within the colonial landscape, Semple's capacity to feel has very definite limits, which are apparent in a passage towards the end of *Walks and Sketches* in which Romantic subjectivity and colonial discourse converge. After descending the mountain outside Paarl, Semple returned to his Dutch settler hosts:

> At the house I found my companions [. . .] engaged with a party of young female visitors, who danced and sung and laughed away all care. They formed a circle round a little woolly-headed Boshies boy, and obliged him to go through all antics – climbing like a monkey, bounding on all fours like a deer. He frequently attempted to make his escape through the circle, but was always brought back, with great shouts of laughter. Thus passed the evening away, and in something like this passes life itself away.[110]

Fresh from the romantic view from the Paarl mountain-top, Semple is isolated from the party, and does not join in the game with the 'little woolly-headed Boshies boy', but he also does not criticise the cruelty of his hosts. Indeed, the spectacle provokes no specific comment or judgement, but rather some maudlin philosophising – 'in something like this passes life itself away'.

CONCLUSION

There are differences between Stout and Semple's descriptions of the lands and landscapes of the Cape, most notably in the prominence of Stout's economic arguments for capitalist land appropriation as opposed to Semple's aesthetic appreciation of romantic landscapes. But the differences are matters of emphasis, and they ultimately agree on certain fundamentals: the land of the Cape is ready to be transformed by capitalist agriculture; the landscapes of the Cape provide many romantic and occasional sublime vistas; and the peoples of the Cape can serve either as farm workers (the 'Hottentots' and slaves), or as farmers, traders and citizens (the Dutch settlers). There is no doubt that in the short term the loyalist Semple's vision for the Cape prevailed. After a brief boom at the beginning of the nineteenth century, American trade with the Cape slumped under pressure from, first, the American Embargo Act of 1807, and then from strictly enforced British trade protection policies. From a high of US$473,345 worth of American exports to the Cape in 1806, American trade to the Cape diminished to US$13,495 in 1822,[111] and Britain dominated the Cape economy for the rest of the century. However, since the mid-twentieth century, the patriot Stout's ambition and the loyalist Semple's fear that US influence should increase in Southern Africa have been realised. For example, after South Africa left the British Commonwealth in 1961, US businessmen 'richly capitalised on the loosening of Britain's hold on the South African economy and on growing anti-British feelings among important Afrikaner figures'.[112]

Since the end of apartheid, and for reasons other than anti-British sentiment, economic ties between the two nations have strengthened further. Declarations celebrating these ties by leaders on both sides of the Atlantic abound. In 1997, Thabo Mbeki, then deputy president of South Africa, proclaimed, 'We would like to see the number of US companies operating in South Africa increase from the current 700 to more than double, with a concomitant increase in sales as well as their asset base'.[113] A year later, US President Bill Clinton reciprocated when he addressed the South African Parliament:

> We share the same basic values: a commitment to democracy, a commitment to open markets, a commitment to give our people all they need to succeed in the modern world [. . .] As Africa grows strong, America grows stronger through prosperous consumers in the continent and new African products brought to our markets.[114]

And in 2001, Mbeki and George W. Bush continued in the same spirit, issuing a joint statement pledging *inter alia* to 'work together to support [. . .] the growth of agricultural trade and [to build upon] expanded trade and investment between the two countries'.[115]

If these optimistic statements are interpreted as the realisation of Stout's eighteenth-century dreams and of Semple's nightmares, we might conclude by remembering the eighteenth-century casualties of Stout's dream, and reflect upon the prospects for their twenty-first century descendants. Recall the eighteenth-century American solution for those indigenes resistant to working the land in accordance with the imperatives of capitalist agriculture: for Jefferson in 1782, those 'Indians' would be driven 'with the beasts of the forests' into the Rockies, and for Stout in 1798, those 'Bushmen' would be destroyed 'without mercy' by Dutch settler commandos. What prospect for the landless poor of post-apartheid South Africa? Rhetorically at least, their interests have been at the core of South Africa's land reform programme, but the results of the programme have been modest, as a recent study concludes:

> [D]espite the high hopes vested the programme, and the hard work of many to see it through, the achievements of land restitution have fallen far short of what its various proponents in 1993 had hoped. The discontinuities of land reform have become a source of disappointment or anger, even fear in some cases.[116]

In seeking the causes for such disappointments, certain development economists have criticised the application of principles dear to Jefferson and Stout – private property and the free market. For example, Harald Winkler argues that the vast majority of the rural poor will remain impoverished, as they simply will not be able to raise the credit necessary to buy land:

> '"the willing buyer/willing seller" principle [. . .] seeks to entrench free market principles, which *at this point* will simply continue to dispossess black people [. . .] This restricted vision of land reform will fail to meet the needs of most black South Africans.[117]

A corollary of the argument that the black rural majority will remain impoverished by market-led land reforms is the view that the only beneficiaries of such reform are likely to be a small elite of black commercial farmers. Reviewing ANC land reform policies since 1994, Lionel Cliffe argues that they promote 'the interests of a would-be black agrarian class, rather than those of the propertyless'.[118] The resulting emergence of a class of black capitalist farmers therefore might reconfigure the racial composition of South Africa's ruling elite, but the fate of the landless black majority would continue unchanged. For Cliffe, there is a congruence of old and new ways of thinking about land ownership: 'first, the so-called "technical" formulae of the old-fashioned paternalist white agriculturalists and equally, the black officials and policy-makers, who have brought their assumptions of World Bank-type "smallholderism"'.[119] Cliffe argues that only by challenging the shared assumptions of these two constituencies – assumptions about the priority of the market, the sanctity of individual ownership of private property and the inviolability of capitalist labour relations – can there be any hope of going beyond 'merely Africanising prevailing (massively inegalitarian) production relations'.[120] LeFeber's paraphrase of Jefferson that 'the Indians were to be "civilised" and made to act like white farmers' resonates in the post-apartheid settlement, as existing white landowners and new black landowners, who have become 'like white farmers', have been supported by their sponsors internationally (the World Bank) and nationally (the ANC government), and the landless majority have continued to confront exploitation and unemployment.


## NOTES

1. The US presence at the Cape has been accounted in commercial terms: American exports to the Cape rose from US$46,582 in 1792 to US$473,345 in 1806; and in 1806, of the 235 arrivals in Cape Town harbour, 143 ships were English, 61 American, 20 Danish, and 6 Portuguese, with the balance made up of single ships from German states (Booth, *The United States*, pp. 14, 18–19).

2. The few unsubstantiated pieces of speculation about Stout are summarised by A. Porter in the introduction to his edition of Stout's *The Loss of the Ship 'Hercules'*.

3. There is no mention of Stout in the indices of the ten volumes of Adams's *Selected Writings*, and Stout's book does not appear in the catalogue of Adams's personal library.

4. A condensed version of Stout's *Narrative* was included in Archibald Duncan's *The Mariner's Chronicle*, Vol. 2 (1805). In 1809, Stout's tale was published in two cheap London editions by Thomas Tegg: the one edition, costing a sixpence, was a 28-page summary of the 1798 edition, with Stout's tale recounted in the third person and the terrors of the sea and shipwreck prominent; and the second edition published this same version in a nautical adventure compendium, together with condensed versions of *The Guardian* (wrecked in 1789), and the *Account of an Indian Woman* discovered on Hudson Bay in 1772. In 1820, a full-length edition (including the Dedication to Adams) was published with an extra introduction exhorting the British 1820 settlers on the Cape's eastern frontier to take heart from Stout's glowing descriptions of the land they were about to settle. In 1822, a cheap Dublin edition was published, also accompanied with other shipwreck tales, where the editors singled out Stout's generous descriptions of the native inhabitants for praise. In 1842, a condensed French translation of Stout's journey was published in volume XVI of C. A. Walckenaer's *Collection de Voyages en Afrique*. The popular fascination with shipwrecks was undiminished in the second half of the nineteenth century, and George Winslow Barrington included his own summary of Stout's tale, together with 37 other shipwrecks, in *Remarkable Voyages and Shipwrecks* (1880).

5. A second edition appeared in 1805. There was a Dutch edition in 1804, and a German one in 1805. My quotations are from the 1968 edition.

6. Jasanoff, *Liberty's*, p. 6.

7. Mitchell, 'Imperial', p. 9.

8. Kelsall, *Jefferson*, p. 15.

9. Quoted in Scherr, p. 378.

10. Weeks, 'American', p. 493.

11. Quoted in Booth, *The United States*, pp. 3–4.

12. Stout's failure to stimulate American interest in Southern Africa was repeated in 1828, when another American seaman, Captain Benjamin Morrell, also wrote glowingly – but ineffectually – about Africa's potential for American investment. Morrell's editor, P. Petrie, records the captain's exasperation at the indifference his proposals encountered in America: 'I have been fated to sustain an unequal combat with the giants of prejudice and the hydras of malice and jealousy' (Petrie, *Morrell's Narrative*, p. iv).

13. Quoted in Ellis, *Passionate Sage*, p. 138.
14. Quoted in Zinn, *A People's History*, p. 70.
15. Quoted in Hill, *Democracy*, p. 217.
16. Hill, *Democracy*, p. 168.
17. Stout, *Narrative*, p. v.
18. Stout, *Narrative*, p. vi.
19. Beloff, *The Debate*, pp. 273, 275.
20. Locke, *Two Treatises*, p. 127.
21. Ibid. p. 129.
22. Ibid. p. 131.
23. Ibid. p. 132.
24. Ibid. p. 133.
25. Stout, *Narrative*, pp. x–xi.
26. Ibid. pp. xx–xxi.
27. Ibid. pp. 44–5.
28. Ibid. p. 82.
29. Ibid. p. 90.
30. Pratt invents the term 'the monarch-of-all-I-survey' (Pratt, *Imperial Eyes*, pp. 201–8) to describe the use of the elevated viewpoint, and claims it to be a pre-eminently mid-Victorian travel narrative convention. Stout's use of the elevated viewpoint precedes the examples Pratt discusses, and he displays less mastery over the landscape than later travellers.
31. On the deployment of the myth of empty land in the Eastern Cape in the eighteenth and nineteenth centuries, see Crais, 'The Vacant Land'.
32. Ibid. p. 53.
33. Ibid. p. 63.
34. Before setting out from the wreck of the *Hercules*, Stout asks the Xhosa chief to 'send a guide with us through the deserts to the first christian settlement' (Stout, *Narrative*, p. 31), and both Old and New Testament allusions to testing journeys through deserts and wildernesses recur in the text.
35. Stout, *Narrative*, pp. 85–6.
36. Ibid. p. 95.
37. Andrews, *Landscape*, p. 166.
38. Stout, *Narrative*, pp. 61–2.
39. Burke, *A Philosophical*, p. 53.
40. Stout's use of the panoramic viewpoint was shared by travellers to North America, too. For example, William Bartram, who had the same London publishers as Stout, describes North Carolina as follows: 'Having now attained the summit of this very elevated ridge, we enjoyed a fine prospect indeed; the enchanting valley of Keowe, perhaps as celebrated for fertility, fruitfulness and beautiful prospects as the Fields of Pharsalia and Vale of Tempe' (Bartram, *Travels*, p. 156).
41. David Bunn extends Barrell's arguments about the relation between landscape and the public sphere to a colonial context in his discussion of Thomas Pringle in the Cape Colony of the 1820s. Bunn argues that Pringle's version of the Eastern Cape landscape 'helps to naturalize the settler subject and establish a local version of the bourgeois public sphere' (Bunn, '"Our Wattled Cot"', p. 138).
42. Barrell, 'The public prospect', pp. 27–8.
43. Cosgrove, *Social Formation*, p. 19.
44. Ibid. p. 33.
45. Stout, *Narrative*, p. xlvi.
46. Ibid. p. 46.

47. Ibid. pp. iii, xxxiv.
48. Ibid. p. xxxviii.
49. Ibid. p. ii.
50. Ibid. pp. 58–9.
51. Ibid. p. 60.
52. Ibid. p. xxxvii.
53. Ibid. p. 84.
54. Ibid. p. 86.
55. Countryman, 'Indians', p. 361.
56. LeFeber, *The American*, p. 43.
57. Ibid. p. 43.
58. Ibid. p. ii.
59. Ibid. pp. iv–v.
60. Ibid. pp. xvii–xvii.
61. Ibid. p. xxxix.
62. It is worth noting that contemporaneous British accounts of the Cape registered with some anxiety the competitive threat posed by American traders. Based on visits to the Cape in the second half of 1796 (the same time as Stout's walk to Cape Town), and then again in 1801, Captain Robert Percival, for example, published *An Account of the Cape of Good Hope* (1804), which exhorted the British government to regain control of the Cape. In his conclusion, Percival observes: 'Other nations, Americans in particular, have already begun to share our trade in the East-Indies, and our fisheries in the South-Seas. Every circumstance that tends to obstruct our commerce in that quarter, must in the same proportion increase that of our rivals; and in this manner a door may be opened to undermine one of the most valuable branches of our resources' (Percival, *An Account*, p. 334).
63. Stout, *Narrative*, p. xxvii.
64. Ibid. p. xlv.
65. Ibid. p. 112.
66. Ibid. p. ii.
67. Ibid. p. iv.
68. Ibid. p. xxvi.
69. Ibid. pp. xxx–xxxi.
70. Ibid. p. 88.
71. In the Preface to the 1805 edition, Semple explains that his companion Charles was fictitious.
72. Semple, *Walks*, p. 67.
73. Semple, *Walks*, pp. 79–80.
74. See Van Sittert, 'The bourgeois'.
75. Semple, *Charles Ellis*, pp. 111–12.
76. Semple, *Walks*, p. 122.
77. Ibid. pp. 132–3.
78. Ibid. p. 151.
79. Ibid. p. 178.
80. Ibid. pp. 183–4.
81. Semple, *Walks*, p. 197.
82. Ibid. pp. 197–8.
83. Burke, *A Philosophical*, p. 53.
84. Semple, *Walks*, p. 175.
85. Andrews, *Landscape*, p. 167.
86. Ibid. pp. 134–5.

87. Semple, *Charles Ellis*, p. 194.
88. Ibid. p. 194.
89. Ibid. pp. 195–6.
90. Ibid. p. 196.
91. Ibid. p. 198.
92. Ibid. pp. 199–200.
93. Ibid. p. 201.
94. Ibid. p. 203.
95. Semple, *Walks*, p. 33.
96. Ibid. p. 206
97. Barnard, *The Cape Journals*, p. 178.
98. Semple, *Walks*, pp. 194–5.
99. Ibid. pp. 192–3.
100. Ibid. pp. 189–90.
101. Ibid. pp. 38–9.
102. Ibid. p. 41.
103. Ibid. pp. 64–5.
104. Ibid. p. 54.
105. Ibid. p. 86.
106. Ibid. p. 94.
107. Ibid. pp. 96–7.
108. Arendt, *On Revolution*, pp. 74–5.
109. Semple, *Walks* (1805 edition), Advertisement.
110. Ibid. pp. 184–5.
111. Booth, *The United States*, p. 23.
112. Hull, *American Enterprise*, p. 257.
113. Mbeki, 'Statement'.
114. Rantao, '"Let's be partners"'.
115. Mbeki, 'Joint Statement'.
116. Walker, *Land-Marked*, pp. 228–9.
117. Winkler, 'Land', pp. 445–6.
118. Cliffe, 'Land', p. 281.
119. Ibid. p. 285.
120. Ibid. p. 285.

# 5 Historical and Literary Reiterations of Dutch Settler Republicanism

INTRODUCTION

Reflecting upon the significance of the bourgeois revolutions of the eighteenth century, Marx warns that

> [they] storm quickly from success to success [and] outdo each other in dramatic effects [. . .] But they are short-lived, and soon reach their apogee, and society has to undergo a long period of regret until it has learned to assimilate soberly the achievements.[1]

Two of South Africa's 'revolutions' of the eighteenth century – the Graaff-Reinet and Swellendam rebellions of 1795–9 – were certainly short-lived, and they have undoubtedly been succeeded by two centuries of regret. This chapter tries to continue the process of learning to 'assimilate soberly [their] achievements' by analysing their many historical and literary rewritings. Specifically, I reflect upon the ways in which the rebellions have been refracted through three consecutive myths of Afrikaner national identity: the British imperialist construct of the Afrikaner-as-rural-degenerate propagated by the likes of John Barrow at the very end of the eighteenth century; the myth of the Afrikaner-as-God's-chosen-*volk* initiated by the *Genootskap van Regte Afrikaners* in the 1870s and elaborated by apartheid ideologues in the twentieth century;[2] and finally, the myth of the post-apartheid Afrikaner, designated 'the Promethean Afrikaner' by ex-president Thabo Mbeki, and defined by '"willingness to cross frontiers – relating the Afrikaner experience of exploitation, poverty and struggle to others who face similar experiences"'.[3] I argue that the three competing myths and associated historical and literary interpretations of the Graaff-Reinet and Swellendam rebellions are strongly marked by the pressures and limits of their respective historical moments. By extension (I suggest), a critical understanding of the economic and political pressures of the post-apartheid moment should precede the rereading of these eighteenth-century rebellions now.

The essential facts of the Graaff-Reinet and Swellendam rebellions are as follows.

In attempting to regulate escalating tensions between the burghers and the Khoikhoi and Xhosa on the Eastern Cape frontier, the VOC appointed landdrosts at Graaff-Reinet, first M. H. O. Woeke (1786) and then Honoratus Maynier (1793). Woeke's failure to pacify the contending factions led to his replacement by Maynier, but the latter's policies towards the Xhosa alienated the burghers further. In May 1793, the Second Frontier War broke out, and the burghers suffered losses in land and cattle, which intensified their sense of injustice. In April 1795, 277 burghers of Graaff-Reinet drew up a *Klagschrift* (letter of complaint), which they submitted to O. G. De Wet, commissioner for Governor A. J. Sluysken. The rebels then expelled Maynier, claimed to represent the *Volkstem* (voice of the people), constituted a 'National Convention', refused to pay taxes and wore the Dutch tricolour. Sixty burghers in Swellendam followed the Graaff-Reinet example, rejecting the Cape government and expressing the wish to be part of the new Batavian Republic in the Netherlands. While the rebellions were in progress, Britain sent troops to seize the Cape in direct reaction to the revolution in the Netherlands led by the Dutch Patriots against the House of Orange. About 170 Swellendam burghers under Commandant Petrus Jacobus Delport joined in the unsuccessful defence of Cape Town during the one-sided British invasion led by General James Craig in August 1795. The two rebellions folded when ammunition ran out, and both groups of rebels surrendered to the British. In January 1799, the arrest of Graaff-Reinet burgher Adriaan van Jaarsveld for forgery led to a second rebellion under Van Jaarsveld, Martinus Prinsloo and Coenraad Buys. Buys claimed that Xhosa forces would join their rebellion, but no such support materialised, and when 200 British and Khoikhoi troops were sent to Graaff-Reinet, the rebels capitulated without offering any resistance. Later in the same year, emboldened by the collapse of Van Jaarsveld's Rebellion, the Khoikhoi under Klaas Stuurman joined forces with the Xhosa to win substantial victories in the Third Frontier War.

## RURAL DEGENERATES

General Craig, head of the British military force at the Cape in 1795, set out how the new regime construed the actions of the Graaff-Reinet and Swellendam rebels. In a letter on 23 November 1795 to the provisional landdrost at Graaff-Reinet, Carel David Gerotz, Craig observes:

> Avarice and private ambition working upon the unenlightened minds of the people under the specious pretence of Liberty has plunged the half of Europe in an abyss of Horror and Misery which ages will not recover it from, and I am well aware that there are People even here whose views from the same Motives tend to no less than an attempt to introduce similar effects into this Colony by the same means.[4]

Craig's identification of the Graaff-Reinet rebels with the 'unenlightened minds' of Europe was reinforced in the reports of the colonial official John Barrow on his travels to the region. According to Barrow, 'Jacobinism, or subversion of all order, had industriously been propagated by the ill-disposed, among the ignorant part of the colonists, both in the town and the country districts'.[5] This subversive spirit was directed not only at the authorities in Cape Town, but also defined the set-tlers' relations with their neighbours on the eastern frontier. Barrow believed that responsibility for conflict on the frontier lay squarely with the Graaff-Reinet settlers: 'To the avaricious and covetous disposition of the colonists, and their licentious conduct, was owing a serious rupture with this nation [the Xhosa] in the year 1793'.[6] Barrow's unflattering descriptions of the Graaff-Reinet settlers were frequently cited by subsequent writers. John Philip, for example, in his influential *Researches in South Africa* (1828), repeated Barrow's anecdote about '[a] boor from Graaff Reinet, being asked [. . .] if the savages were numerous or troublesome on the road, replied, "he had only shot four", with as much composure and indifference as if he had been speaking of four partridges'.[7]

Legal confirmation of this damning assessment appeared in the court report of the 1799 Graaff-Reinet uprising, in which the *fiscaal* Willem Stephanus van Ryneveld roundly condemned the rebels and their revolutionary doctrines:

> This Patriotism [. . .] always originated from the notion the prisoners had conceived of the specious words *Liberty, Equality,* and *Fraternity,* which they presumed entitled every man to live in his own way and not to mind any divine or human Institutions, and to which they in particular added a right to treat and ill-treat the Hottentots, slaves, and their other inferiors in a most arbitrary manner.[8]

Accompanying the explanation that the rebellion was the work of a few mischief-makers pursuing a false ideology was the claim that the majority of the rebels did not grasp what was happening. The leaders of the rebellion were charged with using lies and intimidation to induce 'harmless and ignorant people to participate in their design'.[9] Van Ryneveld was not the only non-British observer to share Craig and Barrow's judgements, as several other writers less directly tied to British rule also expressed their antipathy towards the rebels. Ludwig Alberti, the German land-drost at Uitenhage during the Batavian period (1803–6), for example, impatiently dismissed the aspirations and deeds of the rebels:

> The spirit of revolution and anarchy raged in Europe and also found active sympathizers amongst the inhabitants at the southern tip of Africa. 'Good for nothings', who already earlier had been dissatisfied under all Governors, and who were deceived by a ridiculous vision of liberty, found means to spread this deception further afield in the interior of the Colony, and actually to cause an insurrection among a section of the farming community.[10]

A second observer from the Batavian period, the young official Baron A. van Pallandt, suggested that because the frontier settlers had the 'unfortunate habit [. . .] of fighting enemies who were more timid and ill-natured than dangerous, [and because of] the enormous distances from the capital', they had developed 'this spirit of independence and false liberty which [. . .] has made of the South African a tyrant in his own domain, and has rendered him so insensible to honest law that he even threatens the government with sheer disobedience'.[11] Van Pallandt then repeats an anecdote he had been told by Governor J.W. Janssens on his return from the eastern frontier:

> one of [the burghers], anxious to defend his conduct [killing 'natives'], showed the Governor by a process of reasoning of his own, that the natives are directly descended from Ham, and that the farmers [were entitled] to treat them as a people hated by God himself.[12]

A third writer with no obvious reason to echo British prejudices against the frontier settlers was the German traveller and naturalist Hinrich Lichtenstein (1780–1857), who added the trope of degeneracy in his description of the Graaff-Reinet settlers:

> The assembling together of so many uncultivated men in so remote a country, where every one, without any attention to the laws, acted only according to his own pleasure, could not fail of producing bad effects upon the general character [. . .] Without the restoration of some severe authority [. . .] it seemed very inevitable that every generation would go backwards in civilization, and that they would, at last, sink nearly as low [. . .] as the former savage inhabitants.[13]

Lichtenstein's account, however, was nuanced by his acknowledgement that there was widespread discontent amongst the settlers, which provided fertile ground for revolutionary ideas from the northern hemisphere: '[t]he separation of the American colonies from the Mother country had already awakened many wild projects among certain ill-organised heads in the colony'; and further, '[t]he speeches made by the demagogues in Holland [. . .] coincided entirely with the sentiments of most of the citizens in Cape Town'.[14] Lichtenstein notes wryly that the citizens of the Graaff-Reinet republic 'held primary assemblies; they wore the national cockade; they chose from themselves a president and secretary who could scarcely read or write; [. . .] they endeavoured to ape [the protocol] of the French popular assemblies', but he did concede that 'to their credit [. . .] no real horrors were perpetrated'.[15]

More critical of the settler rebels was the anonymous satire 'Song in Honour of the Swellendam and Various Other Heroes at the bloody action at Muizenburg on the date 7 Aug. 1795',[16] which mocks the 168 Swellendam 'heroes' under Commandant Petrus Jacobus Delport, who joined the Dutch soldiers at the Cape in attempting to resist the British invasion. Written in the collective voice of the Swellendam republicans, the second stanza ironically registers Delport's military credentials – 'That fellow has got military clout / He shot, even before we departed from home, / A great fat bontebok' – but in the subsequent stanzas, the initial bluster gives way to fear, as they face British guns, as opposed to Xhosa and Khoikhoi weapons:

We rejoice, are full of pleasure. Huzza!
The Brit could well be a Buck or a Bull.
[. . .]
But goodness, Mate, the bullets come, o woe!
We can see, it is a bomb.
Look how they jump in front of us!
O woe! That is a frightening thing, o woe!
It is no assegai, nor an Arrow. O no!

Denied easy killings, the Swellendam troops beat a cowardly retreat back to their farms: 'Come, let us now just run away, o woe! / Who can fight with such weapons? / We go to home, take up the ploughshare. / Then no bomb will fall upon our head, o woe!' The poet's pro-Orange sympathies trump any compassion for the vanquished Dutch-speaking rebels, as the poem reinforces the British master-narrative of a benevolent imperial order policing foolish dissidents.

Hostile accounts of the Graaff-Reinet and Swellendam rebels were repeated and amplified in British imperial histories throughout the nineteenth and early twentieth centuries. In his five-volume history *The British Colonies* (1851), R. Montgomery Martin declares that '[t]he timely arrival of the British fleet saved the colony from anarchy and bloodshed', and like the anonymous author of 'Songs of Honour', he describes with unsympathetic irony the Swellendam volunteers' contribution to the defence of Cape Town: '[T]he self-styled "Nationals" refused to assist in the defence of Cape Town, declaring themselves alike independent of the Dutch Company and of the English. The advocates of liberty and equality then proceeded to disperse'.[17] By the time of the Anglo-Boer War, British descriptions of the rebels were even more hostile. For example, in 1900 John Leyland described the Cape Dutch as 'ignorant, bigoted, hard in their dealings, suspicious, and unprogressive', and argued that 'the extreme neatness and preciseness of the Old Dutch life at home was impaired, and on the rough borders, where the Boer waged his war with the savage, it vanished altogether'.[18] The Afrikaners' anti-English sentiments are located in this particular moment of eighteenth-century history:

The Boer regarded the Englishman as an hereditary enemy; when he found him exercising authority and compelling obedience, he conceived a fierce detestation of the invader [. . .] The upshot of [Afrikaner] resistance [. . .] was an insurrection in the district of Graaff-Reinet.[19]

An index of how British attitudes hardened at the end of the nineteenth century is evident in the shift in Cape historian Alexander Wilmot's descriptions of the Graaff-Reinet and Swellendam rebellions. In his 1869 *History of the Colony of the Cape of Good Hope*, Wilmot criticised Barrow for taking on trust the testimony of Maynier, and insisted that had he known all the facts, 'he would not have so sweepingly condemned the Boers'.[20] In his 1901 *The History of South Africa*, however, Wilmot's tone is quite different, as he writes with heavy irony of the revolutionary pretensions of the republicans, describing the Swellendam leader as 'this South

African Cromwell'.[21] Similarly dismissive views were expressed in histories by James Cappon and Ian Colvin. Cappon contrasted the rebels, 'the most turbulent spirits of the colony were congregated there, genuine frontier ruffians', with Maynier, who was 'an able, honest, and very courageous man'.[22] Colvin argued that the rebels 'formulated a series of highly ridiculous demands, which showed that their hold on the principles of the French Revolution was a trifle imperfect',[23] and he pointed in particular to the inconsistency of their demand to keep captured 'Hottentots' as slaves for life. Such opinions did not disappear with Union; novels set in South Africa like Birch L. Bernstein's *Tomorrow is Another Day* (1951) continued to denigrate the Graaff-Reinet rebels well into the twentieth century. In Bernstein's historical romance, the young Dutch hero Gys Wentzel is initially swept along by Jacobin ideals, but his father Piet's damning judgement of the rebels is ultimately vindicated:

'Look here, Gys, you know that I am a Republican and have no desire to be ruled by the Company or by the English. But I will not be ruled by wild men who will destroy us all in their stupidity. If these men are to lead us, I will have none of it. If they bring the Kaffirs then I will oppose them. If necessary, I will fight my own people to stop such madness.'[24]

Respect for order, and in particular the racial order, thus prevails over Gys's enthusiasm for joining the cause of the Graaff-Reinet rebels.

Most (but not all) of these accounts had a vested interest in representing the Graaff-Reinet and Swellendam republicans in the most negative possible light. Writing on behalf of the new British authority at the Cape, Craig, Barrow and Van Ryneveld scripted the rebellion in close accordance with the meta-narrative of British imperial progress, defined in particular by antipathy towards the French and American revolutions. Later historians like Wilmot, Leyland and Colvin consolidated this version, and supplemented it with additional insults. The 'rural-degenerate' image of the settler republicans can be summarised as follows: they were unenlightened men motivated by avarice and private ambition (Craig); they were inspired by Jacobinism, dedicated to the subversion of all order, ignorant, avaricious, covetous and licentious (Barrow); they treated the local inhabitants with great cruelty (Barrow, Philip); they ignored all human and divine institutions, and ill-treated 'Hottentots, slaves and their other inferiors' (Van Ryneveld); they were 'good for nothings' deceived by 'a ridiculous vision of liberty' (Alberti); their anachronistic racial prejudices dictated their cruel treatment of the indigenes (Van Pallandt); they were uncultivated and lawless men, with every generation going 'backwards in civilization, and [sinking] nearly as low as the former savage inhabitants' (Lichtenstein, Cappon, Bernstein); they were brave when slaughtering antelope or poorly armed indigenes, but cowardly when faced with British guns ('Song in Honour', Martin); and in their actions, they either contradicted or failed to live up to the revolutionary ideals they espoused (Wilmot in 1901, Colvin).

## GOD'S CHOSEN *VOLK*

The documents in which the setter rebels represent their own cause are an appropriate starting point for establishing how the 'rural degenerate' myth has been challenged. Unsurprisingly, the *klagschrift* submitted to Sluysken and signed by the 277 Graaff-Reinet rebels in April 1795 constitutes a very different picture of the rebels:

> We offer for Your Honour's consideration whether it is not a most grievous hardship for a citizen to have to see himself robbed of his cattle, his servants murdered, himself to go in danger of his life; and then not to be allowed to pursue such murderers and arsonists, or to avenge himself upon them, but to be allowed only to go out with a small force, which neither dares to, nor is able to, take back his lawful property from the enemy. We ask with respect whether it were then not better, when the Kaffirs come to attack us, if we were to surrender ourselves to their command and desire, with wife and children, with all we possess, without offering any resistance, than to continue under such a restriction. To subject ourselves to our enemy, who murders, robs and destroys us, – we ask under respectful correction – is that a law? Do our God and the laws of nature not teach us that, when another would take my life, or would make himself master of my property, I may and must meet force with force? [. . .] Oh Great and Honourable Lord, consider it yet, is this not hard and sorrowful for your poor, miserable and suffering citizens? [. . .] Does this not cry out against God and all righteousness?[25]

Three overlapping discourses are compressed in the *klagschrift*: a religious discourse appealing to a Christian god to intervene on their behalf as they struggle against merciless adversaries; a legal discourse – 'the laws of nature' – appealing to the Old Testament law of an eye-for-an-eye; and a political discourse enunciating their rights as citizens within a democratic republic. The settlers' self-representation in the *klagschrift* thus contradicts at every point the 'rural-degenerate' myth: they are Christian citizens observing the laws of nature in defending their lives and property.

In a second document drafted a year later, the settlers produced a version of their past consistent with this heroic self-image. A proposition submitted by fourteen representatives of the Graaff-Reinet republic to the new landdrost F. R. Bresler in March 1796 repeats their political claims, and then proceeds to identify their historical (including Biblical) antecedents:

> 6 That in all this it might, in some slight measure, be presumed that this idea might accord with the wish of our Supreme Ruler, who has promised freedom to all who believe and trust in Him. This was so when he led Israel from the land of the Pharoah and the people desired a king to reign over them. He lamented that His people had turned from the living fountain to the broken cup that held no water and said to His prophet Samuel: They have not rejected thee, but me, who is their King.

7 As the Lord God later released His people from the monstrous tyranny of the Spanish yoke of iron and led them to freedom after eighty years of bloody war, we, who are aware of the precedent of that time, would sin twice as grievously as the unsuspecting people did then, as one finds no word in the New Testament to the effect that a people who have taken the Messiah as their King need a temporal king as well.[26]

This religious/historical narrative inscribes the Graaff-Reinet rebels in a venerable tradition of righteous insurgents defying tyranny, as it combines Biblical references to the Israelites fleeing slavery in Egypt, and historical references to the Dutch resisting 'the Spanish yoke of iron'. These precedents legitimise a republican conclusion: God supports brave rebels in their struggles for freedom, and obeisance to a 'temporal king' is contrary to God's way.

The Dutch Patriot Huibert Dirk Campagne, who worked as a school teacher in Swellendam from 1788 to 1793, and served on commando in the Second Frontier War before being deported from the Cape in 1796, wrote two lengthy reports on the rebellion for the Council for Asiatic Possessions of the Batavian Republic in 1797 – Memoriën en Bijzonderheeden wegens de overgave der Kaap de Goede Hoop and Berigt nopens den oorsprong, voortgang en ruptures der Kaffers[27] – in which he stoutly defended the rebels and attacked their adversaries, especially the landdrost Maynier. Campagne distilled his strongly held views in the short poem 'Thoughts on the contemplation of the past and future lot of the Cape' (1802),[28] which provided a wholly positive image of the Swellendam and Graaff-Reinet republicans. Campagne's Cape history begins with an idealised picture of the Cape under Jan van Riebeeck – 'How blissful was this corner then! / It was all springtide – all green!' But as with Adam and Eve in the Garden of Eden, so too at the Cape, 'the quiet peace has been driven away / And with the peace prosperity as well'. In the third stanza, Campagne pays extravagant tribute to the citizens of Swellendam and Graaff-Reinet: 'My true Africans / Your welfare still remains the highest law: / Rejoice Zwellendam! – rejoice Graaf Reinet!' Poet and rebel are united in their love of liberty and their sense of injustice: 'I feel, as much as You do, my heart burning for liberty, / Insulted – am I, the human being, just as You'. More than simply a tribute to the rebels, however, Campagne's poem registers that the meaning of the Swellendam and Graaff-Reinet rebellion is being contested, and singles out Van Ryneveld for traducing the rebels' reputations: 'Yet such a Rijneveld [. . .] such wily Sirens / Banish by their magic lutes / The truth from the auditorium'. In the penultimate stanza, Campagne returns to this theme, with the despairing declaration that 'I cannot save the honest man / Not through language or truth; / Since everything has been wrapped up in cunning, as in a cloud!' If somewhat clumsy, this imagery reinforces the poem's fall-from-grace telos: the green springtide of truth and righteousness initiated by Van Riebeeck and honoured by the Swellendam and Graaff-Reinet rebels is shadowed by the deceitful clouds generated by Van Ryneveld and his ilk.

In the second half of the nineteenth century, there were further sympathetic accounts of the Graaff-Reinet and Swellendam rebels. S. J. du Toit, the guiding spirit of the Genootskap van Regte Afrikaners, rejected the aspersions cast upon

Delport's Swellendam farmer-soldiers trying to help defend the Cape in 1795. In *Di geschiedenis van ons land in di taal van ons volk* (1877), Du Toit summarises the bare facts of the republic's rebellions in a paragraph, and then proceeds to speculate upon the reasons for the unsuccessful Dutch defence of Cape Town:

> But there was no help from the [regular Cape] soldiers and so [the Swellendam volunteers] were obliged to withdraw, after they had killed and wounded several English. Had the Dutch soldiers and commandant done their duty on the day, they would have prevailed.[29]

A more scholarly but no less ideological account was provided by George McCall Theal. Theal repeated his version of the rebellions in several different publications, but the one which enjoyed the widest readership was his *Short History of South Africa (1486–1826) for the Use of Schools* (1890):

> The landdrost [Maynier] took no notice of [the Graaff-Reinet burghers'] complaints, and while the colonists were being plundered and harassed, he reported everything as being in a quiet and orderly state. The burghers then sent delegates to Capetown, with a mass of evidence to show how matters stood, and to request that Maynier might be recalled; but Commissioner Sluysken would not hear what they had to say. By this treatment the patience of the colonists was at length exhausted. In February 1795 a party of burghers assembled at the village of Graaff-Reinet, and expelled the landdrost and his partisans from the district. As the Company's officers wore orange cockades, the burghers displayed the tricolour, and called themselves 'Nationals.' They declared that they were not acting against the States-General, but against the corrupt servants of the East India Company [. . .] In Swellendam the people acted in a similar manner.[30]

Du Toit and Theal thus vilified Maynier, and in their descriptions of the Graaff-Reinet and Swellendam rebels directed their efforts towards reversing the damning British images of the rebels.

The most explicit appropriation of the Graaff-Reinet rebels to contemporary Afrikaner political imperatives, however, appeared not in these histories, but in the didactic Dutch historical novel *De Grensbewoners* (1920) by D'Arbez (the pseudonym of J. F. van Oordt). The novel was published in D'Arbez's 'Zuid-Afrikaanse Historie Bibliotheek', the first series of which appeared between 1896 and 1898, and the second (republishing many of the same novels in 'improved print and simplified spelling') between 1918 and 1921. *De Grensbewoners* concerns the fictional Koos Botha's participation in the rebellions of 1795 and 1799, and provides a sympathetic account of the rebels, with the landdrosts, the VOC, the English and the Xhosa all painted in various shades of ignominy. The conclusion of the novel identifies a tradition of failed insurrections originating in the eighteenth century:

> The uprisings of 1795, 1799 and 1816 are all links in the great historical chain, which started in 1783, and only ended in 1902 [. . .] when they decided to

end the tragedy with the peace treaty of Vereeniging. Historically, the current Nationalist Party owes its origins to the Nationalists of Graaff-Reinet in 1795, and what Tielman Roos and other leaders of the Party declare, namely Republicanism, is nothing other than a repeated echo of what Cornelis Edelman, Hendrik Campagne and Woyer preached in the year 1795. History is a great wheel, which is still turning, and by which causes and consequences follow inevitably, – even though men only see the connection years later –, and the task of the true historian is to track that connection, and follow up on its influence.[31]

Thwarted Afrikaner attempts at self-determination are thus cast in the genre of 'tragedy', and the Afrikaners are condemned to repeated disappointments by the 'great wheel of History'. But D'Arbez identifies a way out of this pessimistic cycle: interpret the historical connections and their influences, and thus break free of the chains of the past. It is striking, however, that for D'Arbez it is the historical novel – rather than the conventional history – which provides the appropriate form for expressing the connections between Graaff-Reinet (1795) and Vereeniging (1902), and for pointing the way to a liberated political present.

Further positive qualities were attributed to the Graaff-Reinet and Swellendam rebels in twentieth-century Dutch and Afrikaans histories. In her sympathetic account, the Dutch historian Petronella Wieringa (1921) emphasised the inspiration provided by the northern-hemisphere revolutions for the settlers, but she also registered that 'the weightiest question in South Africa, then and now, was to find a way of living with the "Kaffer", with [white settler interests] paramount'.[32] Afrikaner histories in the inter-war years by Coenraad Beyers (1929), Gustav Preller (1937) and C. C. Nepgen (1938) also praised the rebels, but they held different views with respect to the impact of eighteenth-century European thought at the Cape. For Beyers, the Enlightenment had a positive effect in that it inspired the Dutch settlers in their struggles for political representation, and in the idea of the *Volkstem* – 'an idea [which] has in its origins, something mystical, something awe-inspiring'[33] – it provided an enduring aspiration for the Afrikaner *volk*. Beyers traces the idea of the *Volkstem* from the petitions of the Cape Patriots in 1779–84 to the writings of the Swellendam and Graaff-Reinet rebels in 1795–9, and on to the declarations of the Voortrekkers in 1836. Preller acknowledged that the French and American revolutionaries' ideas had inspired the Cape burghers, but he expressed concern over their unregulated dissemination. He noted that '[t]he ideals of the French Revolution, liberty, equality and the brotherhood of all men were preached to these savages', but objected that these ideals contradict the fundamental principle that 'the native [. . .] should be "kept in place," i.e. keep to his side of the border, and afterwards, that no equality between them was to be permitted'.[34] More sociological than historical, Nepgen's study distinguished between, on the one hand, seventeenth- and eighteenth-century Dutch democratic traditions, which 'were maintained and developed by [the Cape Colony] pioneers', and, on the other hand, the European and North American revolutionary traditions of the late eighteenth century, which resonated at the Cape only in very exceptional cases – 'in Graaff-Reinet and

Swellendam we have an indication of the presence of revolutionary elements among the Afrikaners; but they are not typical of the genuine Afrikaner'.[35]

Rehabilitating the reputations of the Graaff-Reinet and Swellendam rebels was not left exclusively to historians; three novelists also made contributions – Stuart Cloete in *Waiting for the Dawn* (1939), J. Albert Coetzee in *Die Ruiters van Slagtersnek* (1949), and Sarah Gertrude Millin in *The King of the Bastards* (1950) and *The Burning Man* (1952). None of these historical novels place the Graaff-Reinet and Swellendam rebellions at centre of their story, with Cloete and Coetzee focusing principally upon the Slagtersnek Rebellion, and Millin fictionalising the lives of Coenraad Buys (1761–1821) and Johannes van der Kemp (1747–1811), but they do all cast the settlers in a favourable light. Cloete's coming-of-age novel follows the adventures of Kaspar van der Berg, a young Cape Town trader caught up in the frontier conflicts of 1815. Kaspar learns the history of the Eastern Cape burghers listening to a speech by old Frederik Bezuidenhout:

> And what do you, who are children, know of the history of this land? Can you remember old Adriaan van Jaarsveld, who led us against the Kaffirs in eighty-one, and the battle at Naude's Hoek when we killed three hundred and took five thousand head of cattle? [. . .] Or the little republic we made in ninety-five with old Carel David Gerotz as Landdros and Adriaan captain general? Or how in ninety-nine they took ons Adriaan and we took him back? Or how, later, he was betrayed and finally taken?[36]

Old Frederik's rhetorical questions function as an exhortation to the settlers to unify and resist the intrusions of the British government. Seen through Kaspar's eyes, the settlers are presented sympathetically, with their distance from urban vices and proximity to God emphasised:

> these people were different, less grasping, less cynical, less wise, perhaps, but cleaner in their minds, more urgent in their natures than those of the south. A folk that some might call simple; but their simplicity was that of innocence. They were children; but with the passions and feelings of men and a great faith in God.[37]

This first impression, however, is modified as Kaspar registers that the frontier is 'a place that seemed lawless because under such conditions the law, in its letter, could scarcely apply'.[38] When he participates in a Bushmen-killing commando under Coenraad Buys, his confused thoughts are conveyed with bitter irony: 'To-day they had done a great thing. To-day, by means of gunfire, they had demonstrated the power of civilisation'.[39] The experience provokes him to ask further difficult questions: 'Kaspar had come to the north because he had thought in the wilds he would find freedom. Instead, he had found carnage [. . .] Injustice and cruelty reigned here too. Perhaps it was a natural law that such things should be'.[40] Ultimately this fatalistic view of history is endorsed, with the words of another exhausted patriarch closing the novel. Reflecting on the hatred generated by the hanging of the

Slagtersnek rebels, Oom Christiaan van Ek (like D'Arbez) resigns himself to endless cycles of retaliatory violence. But in the face of this unhappy prospect, he rejects the eye-for-an-eye 'precepts of the Reformed Church',[41] and counsels Kaspar to seek peace.

No such moral dilemmas complicate J. Albert Coetzee's polemical novel *Die Ruiters van Slagtersnek*. In several works of non-fiction, Coetzee argued that the Graaff-Reinet and Swellendam rebels were inspired by republican ideals which laid the foundation for twentieth-century Afrikaner political thought.[42] He repeats this argument in the foreword to *Die Ruiters van Slagtersnek*, describing the years 1795–1816 as 'the beginning of the independence movement which in *this* period culminated in the gallows of Slagtersnek',[43] and arguing that the ideal of freedom which underwrote the Graaff-Reinet and Swellendam republics was kept alive by Marthinus Prinsloo and his son Hendrik. In a lengthy speech on the eve of the second Graaff-Reinet rebellion, Marthinus retells the history of the first settler uprising:

'You know how in '95 we drove Maynier out of Graaff-Reinet because of his favouritism towards the Kaffers and how the English came and took our land. You know how we took down their flag in Graaff-Reinet, but we were too few in number, too divided, and we did not have enough ammunition to resist the large English force.'[44]

Having listed the many injustices and humiliations suffered by the settlers, he switches tack to proclaim his political solution:

'Listen, friends, this is *our* country. *We* are the ones who civilised the country. We are no longer Dutch or French or German like our ancestors: We are [. . .] *Afrikaners!* We have only *one* country and it is this country. We are busy building a new nation!' [. . .] 'Brothers and sisters,' continued Marthinus Prinsloo, 'here at the foot of the Bosberg a new nation is being built – the Boer nation! And it is this nation which broke the might of the barbarians and established civilisation in Africa. You have seen with your own eyes how our civilisation can be lost if entrusted to foreign officials [. . .] Friends, it is now the time to be free, just like the Americans twenty years ago won their freedom, and the French ten years ago stormed the castles of tyrants!'[45]

Immediately after Prinsloo's speech, Sias van Aard cautions, 'we must remember one thing, namely: The Boer nation is a creation of God established to protect civilisation in Africa.'[46] Coetzee's novel strives to provide what Georg Lukács describes as 'an objective prehistory of the present'.[47] Published a year after the National Party won power, *Die Ruiters* projects the political anxieties of 1948 onto the conflicts of the 1790s. In the concluding words of an influential study of Afrikaner nationalism, '*Volkseenheid* (Afrikaner unity) had been the central motif of the economic movement in the 1940s'.[48] Against the enemies of the Boer nation in the 1790s ('barbarians' and 'foreign officials' alike), and the constant threat of internecine conflict,

Prinsloo's passionate appeal for unity in 1799 articulates precisely Coetzee's political aspirations for his own times.

Published a year after *Die Ruiters van Slagtersnek*, Millin's *King of the Bastards* has a foreword by Jan Christian Smuts, in which he singles out for particular praise Millin's depiction of 'the white burghers striving for a new freedom and establishing their abortive republics under the inspiration of the French Revolution'.[49] Millin emphasises the role of Buys in both the uprisings, but bathos deflates her descriptions of them: '[In 1795], the European population of America was three million; of the Cape it was ten thousand; the centre of the Republic of Graaff Reinet had twenty houses; the centre of the Republic of Swellendam had forty houses'.[50] Millin further undercuts the revolutionary claims of the republican rebels by quoting their decree that '"every Bushman or Hottentot, male or female, whether made prisoner by commandoes or caught by individuals [. . .] shall for life be the lawful property of such burghers as may possess them, and serve in bondage from generation to generation"', and then commenting ironically, 'How good was freedom!'[51] Millin's tone in her summary description of the second rebellion of 1799 is also hardly hagiographic, as the rebels led by Adriaan van Jaarsveld, 'the respected Boer commandant charged with forgery',[52] capitulate without firing a shot. In Millin's equivocal descriptions, the settler rebels might not acquire heroic status, but they do not succumb to Buys's tragic flaw, which Smuts takes to be 'his intense pride and self-will',[53] but which the novel itself suggests is his desire for black women. Millin's anxieties about miscegenation are also central to *The Burning Man*, which is about the missionary Johannes van der Kemp. As in *King of the Bastards*, the Graaff-Reinet rebels are secondary, but in this later novel, they are depicted without any critical irony. Van der Kemp and Maynier arrive in Graaff-Reinet late in 1799, and Schoeman and Marais, two (fictitious) burghers, explain their grievances to them as follows:

> 'My ancestors fled here from France for freedom's sake, and freedom I shall have, or perish [. . .] For a hundred and fifty years we have been the slaves of the Dutch East India Company and the House of Orange. We fled from their monopolies, their extortions and penalties and they pursued us. We had a chance at last of being freed by our French brothers of the Revolution. What happened? Englishmen undertook to hold us bound to Orange.'[54]

The exchange concludes with the genial burghers inviting Maynier and Van der Kemp for a meal, an offer awkwardly declined. With Millin treating Van der Kemp's story (like Buys's story) as a warning against the dangers of miscegenation, the Graaff-Reinet burghers in this instance represent a racially pure moral reference point.

Following South Africa's departure from the British Commonwealth in 1961, several nationalist writers invoked the Graaff-Reinet and Swellendam rebellions as the originating moment in the Afrikaner *volk*'s long journey from uncertain eighteenth-century beginnings to an independent twentieth-century republic. In *Republieke en Republiekeine* (1960), M. C. E. van Schoor and J. V. van Rooyen make the argument as follows:

In the struggles of the colonists, specifically the Patriot movement and the rebellions in Graaff-Reinet and Swellendam, the roots of Afrikaans republican aspirations must be sought, because [. . .] in these struggles of the late eighteenth century, the colonists for the first time demanded a voice in government, but it was a voice which rested upon the principles of the representation of the people and the sovereignty of the people.[55]

Six years later, a collection of essays edited by F. A. van Jaarsveld[56] and G. D. Scholtz was introduced by Prime Minister H. F. Verwoerd, who insisted that Republicanism was integral to solving South Africa's twentieth-century political challenges, from 'the problem of white poverty' to 'the race problem'.[57] Several essays trace the history of republicanism from the Netherlands in the sixteenth century to contemporary South Africa, with P. J. Meyer stressing the significance of the settler rebellions of the eighteenth century:

The full meaning and the consequences of the principles of the French Revolution were not assimilated in the events of Graaff-Reinet and Swellendam, but nonetheless in this period, new influences in our progress as a people were registered, influences which would be incorporated at a constitutional level in our subsequent history.[58]

Meyer proceeds to identify these influences in the Great Trek in 1834, the First Language Movement in 1875, the Rebellion of 1914 and the replacement of Dutch with Afrikaans as an official language in 1925.

The most detailed version of this argument was set out by G. D. Scholtz, who believed that the key to understanding the frontier conflict lay in the clash of two European racial ideologies: on the one hand, the settlers' seventeenth-century perception of Africans as 'sons of Ham', and on the other hand, the Cape officials and missionaries' embrace of Rousseau's view of Africans as 'noble savages'.[59] In addition to clinging to antiquated ideas about race, Scholtz argues that the barely literate settlers had an imperfect grasp of the meaning of the French Revolution:

The people of Graaff-Reinet [. . .] sometimes used the language of the revolutionaries in Europe, but this does not mean at all that they were committed to the same principles. They were only making use of the words and phrases that were available at the time, without being particularly worried about their meaning or content.[60]

Scholtz concedes further that an examination of the documents produced by the Graaff-Reinet rebels might suggest that they were 'a bunch of people so degenerate that they showed no inclination to develop law and order',[61] but he nonetheless insists that they belong to an honourable tradition of Christian opposition to injustice:

Just as their Dutch antecedents were not prepared to bear the Spanish yoke, so the people of Graaff-Reinet were not prepared to bear the yoke of Maynier on their necks [. . .] Even if the Graaff Reinet Afrikaners did not directly acknowledge the Calvinist [opponents of tyranny], their actions were indirectly based on them.[62]

Scholtz's mild criticisms of the rebels do not compromise his construction of a continuous if at times contradictory tradition of Dutch/Afrikaans Christian republicanism. His ideas were repeated by several other writers in the 1960s and 1970s,[63] as the redemption of the Graaff-Reinet and Swellendam republican rebels reached its apotheosis.

As with the 'rural-degenerate' image of the rebels, so too with these sympathetic historical and literary accounts, the reading of the past is closely tied to the political imperatives of the present. This is particularly the case with the Afrikaner nationalist histories of the 1960s, which constituted the rebels as the 'founding fathers' of a democratic-republican tradition. While the stories of the rebellions were repeated over many decades and in several different genres – popular histories, poems, novels, academic histories – there was broad consensus within this tradition as to the key facts and the character of the participants. The adversaries of the rebels are described in consistently negative terms: the VOC government at the Cape (backed by the House of Orange) was corrupt, inefficient and made no effort to protect the frontier settlers (Campagne, Theal); the British likewise were blind to the hardships faced by the settlers (Coetzee); the landdrost Maynier was a naïve adherent of Rousseau's myth of the 'noble savage', and blindly favoured the indigenes at the expense of the settlers (Theal, Scholtz); and the Xhosa and Khoikhoi were lazy savages intent on plunder, theft and destruction (Theal, Preller). The rebels by contrast displayed many admirable virtues: they were devout Christians (Cloete, Coetzee, Scholtz); they were republicans who embraced without fully understanding the democratic principles of the Enlightenment and the French Revolution (Beyers, Wieringa, Nepgen, Scholtz); they were brave soldiers let down by pusillanimous VOC mercenaries (Du Toit); they were a community which demonstrated kindness to (white) strangers, and they treated opponents fairly (Millin, Scholtz); and they were courageous in standing up to the tyranny of the VOC and the British (Cloete, Coetzee). In displaying this final quality, they joined a long tradition of brave heroes who have opposed tyrants: the Israelites in Egypt; the Dutch fighting the 'Spanish yoke'; and the French Huguenots resisting Catholic oppression (Millin, Van Schoor and Van Rooyen, Scholtz). Furthermore, their principled resistance inspired subsequent moments of Afrikaner opposition, most notably the Great Trek, the Anglo-Boer War, and the 1914 Rebellion, and even although they were defeated, they represented an early but essential step in the long-term victory of Afrikaner Nationalism, which was reflected in the declaration of the Republic of South Africa in 1961 (Van Jaarsveld, Meyer).

## THE PROMETHEAN AFRIKANER

Succeeding but also overlapping with the myths of the Afrikaner as 'rural degenerate' and 'God's chosen *volk*', the myth of the Promethean Afrikaner is nicely captured in a speech by Thabo Mbeki at the funeral of the Afrikaner cleric Beyers Naudé in 2004. Mbeki applauds Naudé's opposition to apartheid and his commitment to an alternative, more humane, tradition of Afrikanerdom:

When [Naudé] spoke about the most difficult moments in his life, he said his actions demonstrated 'that side of Afrikanerdom which (others) have never been able to tame. It is an Afrikaner willingness to cross frontiers – relating the Afrikaner experience of exploitation, poverty and struggle to others who face similar experiences.'[64]

Mbeki likens Naudé's anti-apartheid struggles to Prometheus taking on the gods:

While he lived, Beyers Naudé like Prometheus, defied power that seemed omnipotent. He suffered woes, which hope thought infinite. Despite his pain, he did not change, falter or repent [. . . He was] an Afrikaner who refused to be tamed, an Afrikaner Prometheus Unbound. Like Shelley's Prometheus, Beyers Naudé also spoke out and said: 'I would fain / Be what it is my destiny to be, / The saviour and the strength of suffering man, / Or sink into the original gulf of things.' It was Beyers Naudé's destiny to be a new Voortrekker, the saviour and strength of our suffering people, incapable of sinking into the original gulf of things into which he was born, because an inner voice summoned him to cross many frontiers.

Mbeki thus distinguishes the Promethean Afrikaner from apartheid-racist Afrikaner, and explains that the former is supremely qualified to enter the happy fellowship of the new South Africa:

[Naudé] understood that nothing but a shared sense of brotherhood, sisterhood and community would give us the space to heal the wounds we all carry on our bodies and on our souls. He called on all of us to understand that the reconciliation we need for the peace and the progress of our country and all our people requires that we work together to achieve that peace and progress.

Mbeki's speech incorporates both older elements of Afrikaner identity and foregrounds previously neglected elements in constituting a rainbow-nation Afrikaner identity: a long history of racial and linguistic mixing; an appetite for justice, democracy and the rule of law; a capacity for tolerance and compassion; an ability to adapt and thrive in changed circumstances; and the courage to stand up to oppressors and tyrants.

Mbeki's designation of the Promethean Afrikaner might belong to the moment of post-apartheid nation-building, but there have long been Afrikaner identities and traditions at odds with both the British imperial myth of 'rural degenerates' and the apartheid myth of 'God's chosen volk'. In the specific context of the Graaff-Reinet and Swellendam rebellions, in the 1940s the historians C. W. de Kiewiet and J. S. Marais challenged these polarised myths, and described the landdrost Maynier as (in Mbeki's terms) a kind of 'proto-Promethean'. De Kiewiet's 1941 survey history of South Africa dealt with the rebellions briefly, but instead of attributing the rebels' actions to rural degeneracy or a sense of religious destiny, he emphasised the powerful economic pressures determining their lives. He argues further that

> [t]he connexion [between the French Revolution and the rebellion of the burghers] was very slight and cannot obscure the truth that the uprising was the result of what the burghers considered an unwarranted invasion upon their freedom to deal with their Kafir neighbours as they saw fit.[65]

A more detailed analysis of the rebellions was provided in 1944 by Marais, who based his arguments on a thorough examination of the Cape archives, and argued that '[w]hat was uppermost in the insurgents' minds was still the question of Xhosa policy'.[66] He too believed that the northern-hemisphere revolutionary terms assumed quite different meanings on the frontier:

> [D]uring the years 1795–6 there were current in Graaff-Reinet certain words and phrases derived from the stock-in-trade of the contemporary revolutionary movement in western Europe [. . .] By the time they reached the frontier farms, the phrases I have listed ['volkstem', 'representatives of the people', 'citizen', 'aristocrats'] had lost much of their content.[67]

Marais concludes emphatically: 'It is, in fact a mistake to suggest that "Revolutionary ideas" are of much assistance in explaining the revolts in Graaff-Reinet [. . . The causes] must be sought on the spot – in the character and experiences of an isolated community'.[68] On this basis, Marais sees the character of the rebel leader Adriaan van Jaarsveld as neither rural degenerate nor as Israelite-in-the-wilderness, but rather as a politically astute opportunist: 'What seems more likely is that this man, who was undoubtedly smart and even, at times, perspicacious, possessed little strength of character and was inclined, therefore, to trim his sails to suit the wind'.[69] Marais complemented this more complex characterisation of the frontier rebels with a generous reading of Maynier. Declaring Maynier to be 'perhaps the most misunderstood figure in South African history',[70] Marais rejects as character assassination the histories of Campagne and Theal, and concludes that although 'Maynier's humanity undoubtedly owes something to the intellectual climate of his age [and] he hated cruelty and injustice [. . .] he was neither a sentimentalist nor a visionary'.[71] His 'mistake', according to Marais, was that 'in reports of marked ability, he laid great stress on the crimes and shortcomings of fellow Europeans'.[72]

Marais's reading of the Graaff-Reinet and Swellendam rebellions had very little influence on the Afrikaans histories of the 1960s, which as we have seen simply repeated the arguments of Theal with longer footnotes. In 1974, however, Hermann Giliomee took up Marais's interpretation once again, and insisted in particular upon the role of material interest in determining the rebellion:

> If taken at face value these expressions indicate a certain degree of revolutionary fervour. Read in context, however, it is quite obvious that phrases like *volk-*

*stem* and *Representanten* had [. . .] been used to cloak the material interests of a specific section of the frontier who wished to impose their will on the whole frontier district of Graaff-Reinet [. . . T]he very use of revolutionary phrases by frontiersmen who by force of circumstances were not very literate should not be taken as sufficient proof that these phrases were properly understood or that they spurred people into action.[73]

The implication is that if the rebels *had* 'properly understood' the principles of the French Revolution – a metonym for western liberal democracy – they would have renounced the racist violence and exploitation they perpetrated on the colonial frontier. Giliomee repeated this argument in summary form in several subsequent publications,[74] and elaborated it again in detail in 2003. He acknowledges that the rhetoric of the Graaff-Reinet rebels has been 'analyzed and interpreted as if they represented the dawn of a new democratic scheme of thought', but argues *contra* that the significance of the rebellions lies 'in the evidence they offer of the breakdown of orderly government and the rise of anarchic tendencies'.[75] In describing the main actors, Giliomee repeats substantially Marais's assessment of Van Jaarsveld – '[e]nergetic, enterprising, more literate than most frontier burghers, Van Jaarsveld was also egotistic, hot-tempered, and devious',[76] but he is less effusive than Marais in his assessment of Maynier:

Maynier [. . .] was an exceptionally well-educated man from the circle of the most prominent Company servants and burghers of the western Cape, but he had no military experience [. . .] Maynier has been depicted as a negrophile, but he was rather a typical Company servant, whose first concern was to avoid trouble with the Xhosa because war would be risky and expensive [. . . H]e was ill suited to his office. He had a curious inability to understand that in the absence of military force to intimidate he could function only through the sustained support of some influential burghers.[77]

Of the early sources, Giliomee attaches the most weight to Lichtenstein, agreeing that the frontier settlers were made up of '[s]ome very rough characters',[78] and further, he defends the settlers against General Francis Dundas's accusations of cowardice in the Third Frontier War by stressing their severe shortage of ammunition.

Like Marais and Giliomee, Noël Mostert viewed the radical-democratic credentials of the rebels sceptically, but unlike Giliomee, expresses unequivocal sympathy for Maynier in his fraught negotiations with them: 'Poor Maynier! To have retained the courage of his convictions with so little behind him and even less with which to assert his authority, alone says a great deal for the man.'[79] In his critical descriptions of the Graaff-Reinet burghers, Mostert dwells in great detail on the racist violence they perpetrated against their Khoikhoi servants:

[I]t is impossible to escape the impression, and evidence, that Graaff Reinet was unique in the consistency of its brutal habits and attitudes, in its self-justification, in its vicious temper, in its random cruelty and, most especially, in the strange and perverse hatred of the Khoikhoi who for the most part faithfully and honestly served the Boers, who died for them, whose beds they shared, whose children so often were their offspring.[80]

Mostert is unusual among historians in splicing his history of the eighteenth-century Cape with brief reflections on the imprint of that history on twentieth-century apartheid politics. In this spirit, he suggests that 'the shabby and impoverished village of Graaff Reinet thus became the first point of focus for international outrage and agitation over race relations in South Africa'.[81]

In a recent study of the Graaff-Reinet rebellion, Susan Newton-King is rather closer to Marais and Mostert than to Giliomee in her characterisation of the frontier antagonists. For Newton-King, Maynier's advice to the frontier burghers that they should treat their Khoisan servants in a fair and just manner in order to ensure peace is both 'excellent' and 'wise'.[82] The outbreak of the Third Frontier War in which Khoisan servants joined the Xhosa in attacking the burghers proved that Maynier's warning not to neglect Khoisan rights 'had been proved absolutely right'.[83] Newton-King concedes that Maynier had 'failed to grasp the depths of the farmer's outrage at the extension of Christian "privileges" to the heathen',[84] but her ultimate assessment of his record on the frontier is positive:

> Maynier's achievements were more lasting than he himself realised. His role as official intermediary in 1799–1801 had given the Khoisan of the eastern Cape a breathing space, however brief. His insistence upon their free status, his attempts to protect them from arbitrary brutality and his collaboration with the missionaries Van der Kemp and Read helped lay the foundations of a vision of equal justice within an ethnically diverse society which their descendants – inhabitants of the mission stations and later, the Kat River Settlement – were to nurture and promote.[85]

With regard to the settler rebels, Newton-King perceives them in much the same way as Giliomee – racist, poorly educated, fractious, resourceful, violent, religious – but where he presents them as intimidating ('very rough characters'), she sees them as somewhat ludicrous. For example, Newton-King quotes Barrow's description of the British soldiers stifling their laughter at the 1799 rebels struggling to dismount their horses '"on account of the protuberance of their bellies"'[86] when they surrendered to General Vandeleur. Newton-King is also far less ready than Giliomee to accept the shortage of ammunition as an excuse for the Graaff-Reinet burghers' feeble resistance. Accepting Orlando Patterson's argument that the masters in slave societies derive their identity from their slaves, and that when slaves resist/refuse to be slaves any longer, the masters are left 'reeling, "timid beyond example"', Newton-King applies the argument to the Graaff-Reinet burghers: 'the metamorphosis of trusted servants [. . .] had struck at the roots of their self-confidence and undermined their sense of (masculine) identity'.[87]

Recent literary returns to the period of the Graaff-Reinet rebellion have typically featured gentle white men struggling to find their way amidst the racial violence of the frontier. Both Aart van der Lingen in Elsa Joubert's *Missionaris* (1988) and the young Dutch traveller in the service of Governor Janssens in Karel Schoeman's *Verkenning* (1996)[88] are troubled figures who fail to impose their humane sensibilities upon the frontier. Joubert and Schoeman's protagonists are antipodes of the Graaff-Reinet rebels, but in their respective efforts to distance themselves from the racist cruelty of the colony, they share many of Maynier's qualities. André Brink's contemporary hero Thomas Landman in *An Act of Terror* (1991) is as sensitive to racism as Schoeman and Joubert's protagonists, but he also displays physical courage and sex appeal. Landman is a photojournalist caught up in the anti-apartheid confrontations of 1980s Cape Town, but Brink complicates the page-turning momentum of the thriller genre by adding a 200-page supplement 'The Chronicle of the Landman Family', in which Thomas narrates his family history, from Hendrik Willemszoon Landman (c. 1604–78) to his own father, Christiaan Beyers Landman (1927–88). Brink's choice of epigrams – notably T. S. Eliot's lines 'The past experience revived in the meaning / is not the experience of one life only / But of many generations [. . .]'[89] – makes it clear that the historical past weighs heavily on the characters and events of the 1980s. Seeking a pattern, Thomas muses that his ancestors were alike in that they had all 'fought against the confines of their crude or unintelligible world, each in his own way'.[90] Thomas relates how at the close of the eighteenth century, his ancestor Benjamin Landman (1766–1811), estranged son of Jan-Jonas Landman and the Khoikhoi woman Toas/Eva, was caught up in the Graaff-Reinet rebellion. In Thomas's recollection, Maynier becomes (in an unacknowledged return to Theal) 'a man imbued with Rousseau's philosophies' confronting 'the popular commander Adriaan van Jaarsveld – a young John Wayne, I like to imagine him'.[91] According to the fragments of the Landman family history, Benjamin had been active in the first rebellion, but in Thomas's imagination, his role was embellished: 'I like to believe there was a touch of pure revolutionary fervour about my ancestor'.[92] Thomas's projection is transparent: like himself, Benjamin is a revolutionary, but not a racist. The psychological basis of Benjamin's revolutionary fervour is explained as oedipal rage against his white father, so that when he sees Jan-Jonas in the ranks of the rebels at the second uprising, his commitment suddenly dissipates, and he withdraws.[93] In characterising Benjamin as non-racist revolutionary, and favouring an individualistic, oedipal reason for his radical fervour, Thomas exonerates his ancestor from the main charge against the rebels, namely that their revolutionary rhetoric cloaked a violent racist hatred towards the Xhosa and Khoikhoi.

Filtered through the myth of the Promethean Afrikaner, the Graaff-Reinet and Swellendam rebellion assumes a fresh meaning. Material interest is identified as a major factor in determining the behaviour of the rebels, and their revolutionary words are interpreted as but a convenient mask concealing their greed for cattle and land (De Kiewiet, Marais, Giliomee, Newton-King). Of the major adversaries, the rebels led by Van Jaarsveld are neither backward farmers nor Christian warriors; rather, they are resourceful and shrewd agents in the single-minded protection and pursuit of their sectional interests (Marais, Giliomee). From certain other angles, however, they might also be identified as paradigmatic Afrikaner racists (Mostert), as faintly ridiculous (Newton-King) or even as glamorous (Brink). Maynier is described in Brink's novel as a naïve follower of Rousseau, but in all other accounts he appears in a positive light, a well-educated and humane interlocutor committed to equal justice for all the warring parties. Unrealistic perhaps in his expectations of how the settlers might respond to government intervention (Giliomee), Maynier nonetheless appears as a principled pragmatist faced with an impossible task (Marais, Newton-King). Further, the fiction set in the period suggests that Maynier was not unique in his commitment to equal justice for all races – the sympathetic characters in the novels by Joubert, Schoeman and Brink all display similar qualities. Indeed, in terms of myth-making, in much the same way that Van Jaarsveld was inaugurated as the progenitor of the white Afrikaner Republican tradition by 1960s Nationalists, Maynier might as plausibly be constituted as the first in a tradition of Promethean Afrikaners by rainbow-nation intellectuals. Brink's 'The Chronicle of the Landman Family' is an obvious fictional addition to such a tradition, but historical figures like Andries Stockenström[94] have also been re-interpreted in recent years in ways that enable them to join the line of Prometheans running from Maynier to Beyners Naudé.

## CONCLUSION

In trying to 'assimilate soberly the achievements' of South Africa's eighteenth-century 'revolutions', I have argued that they have been framed by three myths of Afrikaner identity. Reading the rebellions through the British imperialist myth of the Afrikaner as rural degenerate, the French and American Revolutions were imperfectly understood by an uneducated group of semi-civilised burgher racists, who sought to dignify their killing and enslavement of the Khoikhoi and Xhosa by recourse to libertarian republican discourses. Second, reading the rebellions through the apartheid myth of the Afrikaner as God's chosen *volk*, the northern-hemisphere revolutions inspired a beleaguered Christian people beset by marauding African foes to stand up to the tyrannical VOC and British governments in Cape Town and their meddling officials. Finally, reading the rebellions through the post-apartheid myth of the Promethean Afrikaner, material interest dictated an opportunistic reception of the northern-hemisphere revolutions by the burgher rebels, as revolutionary discourse concealed the land-and-cattle greed of most of the white community, while a heroic minority (historical figures like Maynier; fictional characters like Benjamin Landman) united word and deed, and stood up for equality and racial justice.

It might be tempting to conclude from these many versions of the Graaff-Reinet and Swellendam rebellions that the partisan extremes represented by the myths of the Afrikaner as rural degenerate and of the Afrikaner as God's chosen *volk* have been transcended by the myth of the Promethean Afrikaner; that by a dialectical process, two contending opposites have progressed to a mediating synthesis. But such a reassuring conclusion should be resisted. Historians and novelists invested in the myth of the Promethean Afrikaner might well be correcting the past excesses of imperialist and apartheid myth-making, but they are at the same time directing their intellectual labour to the ideological project of the ANC's rainbow nation.

One of the great political challenges of post-apartheid nation-building has been to incorporate white Afrikaners into the new nation, and the challenge has been met in part by generating a redemptive Afrikaner identity – pre-eminently Mbeki's Promethean Afrikaner, but also continued in Jacob Zuma's emollient words proclaiming Afrikaners as the only white tribe in Africa.[95] Consequently, when critical questions are raised about the post-apartheid polity, they should be extended to the constitution of the Promethean Afrikaner. For example: the question, 'what is the relationship between the political equalities proclaimed in South Africa's new constitution and the economic inequalities generated by the ANC's commitment to neo-liberalism?' might translate as, 'to what extent have "Promethean Afrikaners" – businessmen, politicians, intellectuals – been incorporated into the ANC's support base in exchange for their silence about systemic (black and white) poverty?' Extending such a question to our reading of the past, instead of focusing exclusively on scouring South African history for, or writing novels about, early versions of Beyers Naudé, it might in addition be worth asking once again: 'what was the relationship between the egalitarian discourses of the northern-hemisphere revolutions as deployed on the Cape frontier and the violent expansion of capitalist economic relations into Xhosa and Khoikhoi societies?' Only by continuing to raise such kinds of questions about the connections between the historical past and the political present can we avoid incorporation into a new phase of nationalist historiography and literary production.

## NOTES

1. Marx, *The Eighteenth*, p. 150.
2. See Du Toit, 'No Chosen People', pp. 920–52, and Thompson, *The Political*, pp. 25–68.
3. Mbeki, 'Speech of the President at the Funeral'.
4. Theal, *Records of the Cape Colony*, Vol. 1, pp. 236–7.
5. Barrow, *An Account*, p. 52.
6. Ibid. p. 111.
7. Philip, *Researches*, p. 53.
8. Theal, *Records of the Cape Colony*, Vol. 3, pp. 232–3.
9. Ibid. pp. 242, 285.
10. Alberti, *Ludwig*, p. 100. On Alberti, see Huigen, *Knowledge*, pp. 191–208.
11. Van Pallandt, *General Remarks*, pp. 11–12.
12. Ibid. p. 12.
13. Lichtenstein, *Travels*, pp. 453–4.
14. Ibid. p. 455.
15. Ibid. pp. 456–7.
16. 'Lied ter Eere', p. 7 (own translation). All subsequent quotations from the poem from the same source. See Conradie, *Hollandse*, pp. 117–18.
17. Martin, *The British Colonies*, Vol. IV, p. 30.
18. Leyland, 'The Story', pp. 14–15. For similar views, see Bryce, *Impressions*, pp. 130–1.
19. Leyland, 'The Story', p. 15.
20. Wilmot and Chase, *History of the Colony*, p. 220.
21. Wilmot, *The History*, p. 69.
22. Cappon, *Britain's Title*, pp. 97, 108.

23. Colvin, *Romance*, p. 179.
24. Bernstein, 'Tomorrow', p. 156.
25. Du Toit and Giliomee, *Afrikaner Political Thought*, p. 152.
26. Ibid. p. 269.
27. Campagne, Cape Archives, V. C. 76, pp. 205–85. See Marais, *Maynier*, pp. 151–3.
28. Campagne, 'Gedachten', pp. 7–8 (own translation). All subsequent quotations from the poem are from the same source. See Conradie, *Hollandse*, pp. 118–20.
29. Du Toit, *Di geschiedenis*, p. 38 (own translation). For similar such histories, see Bezuidenhout, *De Geschiedenis*, pp. 3–5 (on Slagtersnek); Van Oordt, *Slagtersnek*, pp. 13–15 (on the 1790s); and Leyds, *De eerste annexatie*, pp. 8–12 (on the 1790s).
30. Theal, *Short History*, pp. 146–7.
31. D'Arbez, *De Grensbewoners*, p. 259 (own translation). For an analysis of D'Arbez, see Huigen, *De weg*, pp. 114–49.
32. Wieringa, *De oudste*, p. 86 (own translation).
33. Beyers, *Die Kaapse*, p. 163 (own translation).
34. Preller, *Day-Dawn*, p. 130.
35. Nepgen, *Die Sosiale*, pp. 117, 119 (own translation).
36. Cloete, *Waiting*, p. 38.
37. Ibid. p. 39.
38. Ibid. p. 47.
39. Ibid. p. 180.
40. Ibid. p. 181.
41. Ibid. p. 381.
42. Coetzee, *Politieke*, pp. 22–3; and *Nasieskap*, pp. 42–3.
43. Coetzee, *Die Ruiters*, foreword (own translation).
44. Ibid. p. 67.
45. Ibid. pp. 68–9 (emphasis in original).
46. Ibid. p. 69.
47. Lukács, *The Historical*, p. 277.
48. O'Meara, *Volkskapitalisme*, p. 255.
49. Millin, *The King*, p. vi.
50. Ibid. pp. 41–2.
51. Ibid. p. 42.
52. Ibid. p. 58.
53. Ibid. p. vii.
54. Millin, *The Burning*, p. 154.
55. Van Schoor and Van Rooyen, *Republieke*, p. 39 (own translation).
56. F. A. van Jaarsveld's views on Afrikaner history and politics mutated in the course of his prolific career. For a critical analysis of his contribution, see Mouton, *History*, pp. 159–95, 233–42. For a sense of Afrikaans history-writing in the 1950s and 1960s, see Giliomee, 'Herontdekking', pp. 19–25.
57. H. F. Verwoerd, 'Herinneringe', in Van Jaarsveld and Scholtz, *Die Republiek*, pp. 7–8 (own translation).
58. P. J. Meyer, 'Nasionalisme', in Van Jaarsveld and Scholtz, *Die Republiek*, p. 300.
59. Scholtz, *Die Ontwikkeling*, pp. 300–1.
60. Ibid. p. 314.
61. Ibid. p. 315.
62. Ibid. p. 316.
63. See Van Jaarsveld, *Van Van Riebeeck*, pp. 47–62; and Muller, *Die Oorsprong*, pp. 42–3.
64. Mbeki, 'Speech of the President at the Funeral'.
65. De Kiewiet, *A History*, p. 31.

66. Marais, *Maynier*, p. 87.
67. Ibid. p. 89.
68. Ibid. p. 90.
69. Ibid. p. 92.
70. Ibid. p. v.
71. Ibid. p. 36.
72. Ibid. p. 36.
73. Giliomee, 'Democracy', p. 44.
74. Giliomee, 'The Eastern Frontier', pp. 440–3; and Du Toit and Giliomee, *Afrikaner Political*, pp. 235–42.
75. Giliomee, *The Afrikaners*, p. 74.
76. Ibid. p. 64.
77. Ibid. p. 72.
78. Ibid. p. 74.
79. Mostert, *Frontiers*, p. 253.
80. Ibid. p. 280.
81. Ibid. p. 279.
82. Newton-King, *Masters*, p. 149.
83. Ibid. p. 224.
84. Ibid. p. 227.
85. Ibid. pp. 230–1.
86. Ibid. p. 215.
87. Ibid. p. 222.
88. On *Verkenning*, see Van Vuuren, '"Op die limiete"', pp. 57–78; Roos, 'Die "vaslê"', pp. 1–20; and John, 'Die abjekte', pp. 164–85. On *Missionaris*, see Renders, 'Base', pp. 80–2.
89. Brink, *An Act*, p. 635.
90. Ibid. p. 692.
91. Ibid. p. 715.
92. Ibid. p. 716.
93. Were one to apply the strict protocols of history-writing to Brink's fiction, Thomas's explanation would not quite work. The dates for his two ancestors do not tally, as Jan-Jonas dies in 1798, and the second rebellion occurs in 1799.
94. See Du Toit, 'Experiments', pp. 422–30.
95. See 'Zuma hails'.

# 6 Literature and Cape Slavery

Unlike Atlantic slavery, Cape slavery yields very few first-person accounts of slave experience. Whereas Atlantic slavery is described in the spiritual autobiographies and polemics of ex-slaves like Olaudah Equiano, Quobna Ottabah Cugoano and Mary Prince, Cape slavery is only rarely described in the words of the slaves themselves. In the Cape, there are only a couple of surviving examples of letters written by slaves; the official records of the Council of Policy give limited information about slaves (as opposed to their owners); and the annual census records merely list slaves alongside the livestock of the white burghers. By far the richest source for accessing slave experiences at the Cape is the records of the Court of Justice, and historians in the last thirty years have drawn extensively on this archive in order to reconstruct the cultural and social worlds of Cape slaves.[1] Historians have not been alone in returning to the slave testimonies in these court records in order to try and recover the slave experience; novelists and dramatists have also used them in order to try and recreate imaginatively the consciousness of Cape slaves.

It is always reassuring to assume that Literature tells us more about the Human Condition than the prosaic discourses of History and Law. However, in this case, I argue that far from transcending the silences of legal and historical texts in their imaginative recreations of slave consciousness, the literary works on Cape slavery project the anxieties and concerns of their contingent political present(s) onto the pasts of Cape slavery. In other words, these fictional texts reveal far less about the worlds of Cape slavery and the experiences and consciousness of slaves than they do about their own worlds: the colonial Cape; South Africa under segregation and apartheid; and post-apartheid South Africa. They also fail to satisfy Georg Lukács's principal criterion for the historical novel, namely that it should represent the past as 'the concrete precondition of the present'.[2] In the context of slave histories, this would require restoring the continuities from slavery to capitalism, what Saidiya Hartman describes as the journey between 'a travestied emancipation and an illusory freedom'.[3] Instead, the fictions of Cape slavery (with one exception) imagine the past of slavery as the illegitimate and unconnected antithesis of a present defined by free labour and democracy.

## LITERATURE AGAINST SLAVERY

In the final years of Cape slavery, literature across the major genres joined the abolitionist cause. The most effective instance of literature in the service of abolitionism was in July 1832, when the Cape Town theatre company of British Amateurs produced an evening of Thomas Morton's comedy *A Cure for Heartache*[4] and the farce *Raising the Wind* in aid of the Philanthropic Society for the Redemption of Female Slave Children. The lengthy review on the front page of John Fairbairn and Thomas Pringle's *The South African Commercial Advertiser* prefaces a vigorous attack on slavery by appealing to the humanity of its readers:

> It is often affirmed, that slavery exists at the Cape in its mildest shape. But without stopping to dispute the proposition, it should not be forgotten that still Slavery *does* exist; and although its alleged mildness of character might be honourable to the Colony, yet we must remember that the paralysing Chain still hangs round the necks of thousands, who feel the iron enter into their souls as acutely as *elsewhere* in which this rank evil prevails in greater magnitude; and that it is the duty of every man who enjoys Freedom to assist, to the extent of his power, in obtaining that choicest blessing for his fellow-creatures in bondage.[5]

Like the many other abolitionist tracts at the Cape during this period,[6] the review constitutes a readership with the capacity to empathise with the sufferings of slaves, and with a willingness to act on those feelings (including to part with their money). The reviewer notes that the Philanthropic Society has already funded the emancipation of over one hundred female slave children, before proceeding to describe in detail the two plays and the fine performances of the actors. The review concludes by reporting that the clear profit from the evening of 1000 rix dollars would pay for the freedom of four young female slaves.

Similar sentiments – if not the same efficiency in extracting cash to emancipate young female slaves – were to the fore in a number of poems written at the Cape in the same period. In 1825, the satirist Frederick Brooks published an ambiguous poem called 'Nature's Logic', which imagined a conversation between 'Isaak van Batavia' and his master, and concludes with 'Isaak' declaring,

> Adam *my father* was, and *thine*,
> O! let I pray your heart incline,
> Without a wrangle and no bother,
> To hail *me* as a *Man* and *Brother*.
> For fleecy locks and black complexion
> Cannot alter nature's claim:

Skins may differ, but affection
Dwells in *Black* and *White* the same'.[7]

The most substantial Cape anti-slavery poems, however, were Thomas Pringle's, which were published in both the Cape and in England. Pringle's abolitionist ethic is conveyed in his sonnet 'Slavery', which, like Brooks's effort, juxtaposes the experiences of the master and slave:

SONNET ON SLAVERY
(*Written in South Africa*)
Oh, slavery! Thou art a bitter draught!
And twice accursed is thy poison'd bowl,
Which taints with leprosy the white man's soul
Not less than his by whom its dregs are quaff'd:
The slave sinks down, o'ercome by cruel craft,
Like beast of burden on the earth to roll;
The master, though in luxury's lap he loll,
Feels the foul venom, like a rankling shaft,
Strike through his reins. As if a demon laugh'd,
He, laughing, treads his victim in the dust –
The victim of his avarice, rage, or lust:
But the poor prisoner's moan the whirlwinds waft
To heaven – not unaveng'd: the oppressor quakes
With secret dread – and shares the hell he makes![8]

Addressing the personified figure 'Slavery', Pringle assumes the voice of the abolitionist observing how the venom of slavery poisons master and slave alike. Whereas the theatre reviewer from the *Advertiser* appeals to the readers' capacity for empathy with slaves and their shared humanity, Pringle's sonnet attempts to promote emancipation through fear. However, the sonnet threatens the masters not with the violent rebellion of the brutalised slaves, but with God's judgement: the slaves' cries 'waft / to heaven', and He will avenge the slaves by consigning the masters to hell.

## SETTLER COLONIALISM: REASON, SENTIMENT AND SATIRE

The first novels under consideration here were published in the decade of slave emancipation – slaves were emancipated on 1 December 1834, subject to them serving a four-year apprenticeship[9] – so were produced with an economy based upon free labour imminent. All three belong to the sub-genre of colonial novels defined by Patrick Brantlinger as 'emigration narratives', which he characterises as 'critical of the domestic problems that caused people to leave, but grateful for the colonies and the United States as places for them potentially to thrive'.[10] Harriet Martineau's *Life in the Wilds. A Tale* (1832), the first in her series *Illustrations of Political Economy*, is set in the Cape Colony, and describes the tribulations of an English settler community. Reduced by a 'Bushman' attack to the bare essentials, they ultimately prevail in their hostile environment through collective endeavour and the application of the rational principles of 'political economy'. Martineau emphasises that their most urgent need was to find the 'the means of shortening and easing labour',[11] and that this was to be achieved by the acquisition of appropriate machinery, and not by the exploitation of slaves. Martineau does not include Cape slaves as characters in her tale, but her arguments against slavery in *Demerara* (1833), another of her twenty-five *Illustrations of Political Economy*, can be extrapolated to the Cape. Like *Life in the Wilds*, much of *Demerara* is concerned with applying the principles of political economy to a colonial setting, and Martineau argues that 'slavery was a perishing system, – a system that must perish ere long under any kind of management. High price, rich lands, and scarcity of people, in conjunction [. . .] are the only supports of slavery'.[12] However, Martineau combines reason with sentiment, as *Demerara* closes with an allegory comparing a slave in the West Indies to a canary in captivity: in the same way that it is difficult to imagine how 'that tame little creature [might] flit about its native lands and warble unchecked till twilight', so too we

> can never guess from looking at the negro sulking in the stocks, or tilling land which yields him no harvest, what he might be when there is no white man to fear and hate, and where he may reap whatever he has sown'.[13]

Slavery is therefore simultaneously uneconomical and immoral, and the future portends a society based upon free labour and rational management.

No such didactic ambitions mark the anonymous three-volume adventure yarn, *Makanna; or the Land of the Savage* (1834), but its representation of slavery too is negative. The convoluted plot is set in motion with the mutiny and then shipwreck of the ship the *Ganges* in 1807 off the Southern African coast,[14] and then follows the survivors in their many adventures, most prominently a confrontation with the Xhosa chief Makanna. A subsidiary plot, however, follows one of the villains, Stunted Mic, in his flight towards Cape Town. En route, he is employed by Hugo Drakenstein, a violent and lazy Dutch farmer, whose patronage extends to a Miss Falkland and her slave, Javan. The passages describing Javan are of interest:

> The first sounds that Javan remembered were the agonizing groans of his kindred; – and the rude hands of the stern Hugo, when they tore him screaming from the bosom of his dying mother, were reeking and purple with his father's blood! Perchance it was the gnawing recollection of these horrors, that had given a premature growth to his infantine faculties; but however that might be, every day brought its unrequited injury, and the passion of revenge, – one, be it remembered, nearly allied to virtue in the breast of a savage, who knows no other form of justice, – gave to the young 'Bosjesman' a stoical fortitude, and a quickness of perception, which might have challenged a milder fate. As the unrelenting foes of his race, and the ceaseless persecutors of himself, the glance of Javan never met the face of either Drakenstein, or any of his dependents,

without betraying the restless annoyance of a chained wolf, that longs to bite and cannot.[15]

Miss Falkland's kind treatment softens Javan's character, so that he comes to idolise her, and within pages is rescuing her from Stunted Mic's attempts to rape her. *Makanna* generates and embellishes all the racist binaries of British colonial discourse with great energy, but makes an exception of Javan. The violent hostility of the 'Bushmen' slaves is not intrinsic to their nature; it is a consequence of colonial violence. And this insight is the basis for appealing to the readers' sentiment.

The third novel is Edward Augustus Kendall's three-volume *The English Boy at the Cape* (1835). Conforming closely to the generic requirements of the 'emigration narrative', Kendall's novel elaborates upon the expanding gulf between rich and poor in Britain. The solution of immigrating to the Cape is taken by John Laleham and his young son Charles, but after John's death in a shipwreck north of Cape Town, Charles is left to fend for himself. For much of the novel, slaves are a peripheral presence – for example, after a death during a journey to the Eastern Cape, the narrator notes, 'The slaves and Hottentots, and other members of the party, were partakers in the consternation and grief'[16] – and only when Charles returns to Cape Town is there an incident which foregrounds slave society. The lonely and ill-treated Charles is rescued from his heartless Dutch 'benefactor' by the ex-Malay-slave, Namal, who 'inwardly grieved over the neglect of which he saw his "pitty English boy" the victim'.[17] Kendall's critical representation of the slave-owning Dutch extends to his descriptions of the English at the Cape. Describing the interruption and destruction of a Malay religious festival attended by Charles and Namal by English sailors, Kendall generalises: 'They were full of the Englishman's vice, upon every distant shore and soil; that of despising and insulting, and sometimes even of substantially outraging, everything that is not English'.[18] The implication is that the Englishman true to his nation (like young Charles) will behave abroad in a proper fashion, and engage in a dignified manner with the 'natives'. In less lurid prose than *Makanna*, Kendall's novel ultimately consolidates the racist binaries of colonial discourse, but the critical descriptions of the English and the sentimental representation of the Malay-slave 'other' complicate the narrative.

Later in the nineteenth century, satire becomes the dominant trope in novels representing Cape slavery. A good example is provided in the slight historical romance, Thomas Mcintosh McCombie's *Governor van Noodt's Revenge, 1727* (1887), which opens on a Western Cape wine farm with a slave being taken off to be whipped. The sons of the wine farmer call their sister to come and watch the whipping, but she refuses:

Margherita turns, with a *moue* of disgust, away. She will not join the boys at the wagon house where the horrid spectacle takes place, but scarce will her meditations on the romantic volume in her hands be disturbed by the screams that will issue therefrom. The treasure is no less than the first copy of *Gil Blas de Santillane* which had reached the Colony.[19]

As slavery as an institution recedes further into the past, novels appealing to reason and sentiment in their condemnatory depictions of slavery are therefore superseded by satirical portraits of slave-owner hypocrisy.

Certain generalisations about the literary representation of Cape slavery in the nineteenth century might now be attempted: slaves and indigenes alike are the victims of settler avarice; slavery is the unreasonable and uneconomical anteced-ent of an economy based upon rational principles and free labour; the liberation of slaves in the Western Cape is subordinate to the more challenging confrontation between 'the settler' and 'the savage' on the eastern frontier; and the slave owners' 'culture' cloaks their lack of human feeling. Slavery thus functions as a safe target, as deserving the righteous loathing of a self-congratulatory readership. In these novels, the recent past of Cape slavery is therefore represented not as a concrete precondition of the present (the 1830s or 1870s); rather, slavery is an embarrassing aberration contrary to sentiment, reason and the progressive march of history, and its beneficiaries are legitimate targets of satire. A firm line is thus drawn, with slavery consigned to the unhappy past, and free labour the axis of the present and future.

## SEGREGATION/APARTHEID: NOSTALGIA AND REBELLION

The genre of the historical romance continued to be popular in twentieth-century South Africa with white novel readers. Those novels set in the Cape of the pre-vious century followed the pattern established in novels like *The English Boy at the Cape*, with plots structured in terms of the opposition between the 'civilised' Western Cape and the 'savage' Eastern Cape.[20] A typical example is Brigid Knight's *Walking the Whirlwind* (1940), which begins in 1808 with Colonel Hugo Vernon, an Englishman at the Cape, acquiring the farm La Dauphine (which he renames Ashenden) by marrying Cécile, the only daughter of the 'pure' Huguenot aristocrat Jean de la Rocque. The nostalgic description of the farm echoes *Gone with the Wind* (1936), with its benevolent patriarch, happy slaves, and stable social hierarchy:

[All Cécile's slaves and body-servants] loved the newcomer, Hugo Vernon, and looked to him. He had not failed them. He was impartial, and accorded to the Negro field hands who did the rough work of the farm the same considera-tion that the Malays received; for the Malays, being more skilled and efficient, were the house servants and held the positions of trust. Harsh and overbearing as he might be at times, Hugo Vernon was always just and, for the most part, generous, with humanity enough to order nothing beyond a flogging in extreme cases. The slave code of the mid-eighteenth century with its grisly penalties was still close enough to render them deeply appreciative of a master who erred on the side of leniency [. . .] Ai, thought [the slave] Jonas, his mind vaguely on the ancient wrongs of the unfree and actively on the man before him, there was more than mere gratitude to account for the esteem in which this master was held. He was an imposing man, the master, a man with money and position and power, and, and, as he towered head and shoulders above his fellows by virtue of his personality and his possessions, so their own status rose. To them he seemed nearer than God, and more kind.[21]

With this heart-warming image in mind, it is no surprise that Hugo's daughter Alison contemplates the emancipation of the slaves twenty years later without too much apprehension:

> With all this talk of emancipation in the air the slaves are restless [but] I am not really concerned. So many of our slaves have been in the family for generations that I cannot believe that they will take advantage of their freedom. I shall have Jonas and his family [. . .] for the rest of their lives. They are very loyal'.[22]

True to the requirements of the genre, the rest of the novel shifts to the frontier wars of the Eastern Cape, and concludes on a sombre note, as the two white romantic leads resolve their differences, and contemplate 'the wooded hills that lay between them and Grahamstown; and silently, closing in on them, the Kaffirs stole like shadows through the bush'.[23] The Western Cape wine farm with its contented slaves functions as a secure refuge for the white characters, who venture eastwards at their peril, as they risk their lives in confronting violent African resistance.

A novel in the tradition of the South African historical romance, which deviates from the norm by dealing at length with Cape slavery, is V. M. Fitzroy's *When the Slave Bell Tolled* (1970). Starting with the arrival of the first slave in the seventeenth century, and concluding with emancipation in 1834, Fitzroy's novel is extensively researched, drawing not only on available histories, like Isobel Edwards's *Towards Emancipation: A Study of South African Slavery* (1942) and Victor de Kock's *Those in Bondage: An Account of the Life of the Slave at the Cape in the Days of the Dutch East India Company* (1950), but also on the newspapers of the early Cape and the legal records of the slave courts in the Cape Archives. The omniscient narrator alternates between social and economic history, and passages of dialogue between historical and invented characters. Unlike Knight, Fitzroy describes the violence of slavery throughout the novel, frequently juxtaposing the gentility of white Cape Town with the desperation of servitude: Riebeeck Square by night 'was unwontedly gay with torches and jingling horses and pretty gowns', as the governor and his friends went to watch Shakespeare plays, but by day, it 'was not so light-hearted a place. Government flogged its criminals here, and people living in the neighbourhood found their screams a matter for serious complaint'.[24] The cruelty and hypocrisy of the slave-trading and slave-owning classes are satirised, particularly in the first half of the novel, and by means of internal focalisation, Fitzroy attempts to convey slave consciousness. The agents of the emancipation of the slaves, however, are not the slaves themselves, but the long line of humane white people who challenged slavery, from Hendrik van Rheede (1636–91), who 'saw [slaves] not as chattels but as beings with souls', to John Fairbairn (1794–1864), whose 'leaders [in *The Commercial Advertiser*] were taken up more and more with the subject of slavery and its abolition'.[25] Given the novel's detailed treatment of the decades leading up to emancipation, the failure to mention either the 1808 slave uprising,[26] or the 1825 rebellion led by the slave Galant,[27] is particularly striking. The primary material for both rebellions has long been available in the Cape Archives, and Fitzroy would have been unable to avoid the lengthy coverage of them in the volumes of the early Cape historian, George McCall Theal.[28] *When the Slave Bell Tolled* avoids Knight's nostalgia of happy-slaves-on-Cape-wine-farm, but instead sentimentalises the urban landscape of 1830s Cape Town: 'Here was no colour bar. Here was no cat-o'-nine-tails, nor bo'sun's lash, nor slave bell, nor smith's fetters. Nor sergeant's berating. Here was freedom from the censure of the respectable'.[29] This passage coincides with descriptions of the emancipation of the slaves, and with the marriage of the slaves Jonas and Grietje. Fitzroy's novel thus excludes the struggles of the Cape's impoverished classes which continued beyond 1834, and as such is in accord with the political temper of 1960s South Africa, a decade during which the apartheid state successfully excluded and contained anti-apartheid resistance.

Written in the aftermath of the Soweto Uprising of 1976,[30] André Brink's *A Chain of Voices* (1982) fills one of the silences in Fitzroy's novel, as it is based upon the court records of the unsuccessful 1825 slave uprising led by Galant. The judgment laid down in the trial paraphrases Galant's motivation for the rebellion, thus providing an indirect route to understanding his motives and consciousness:

That the First Prisoner Galant (as he said) had also been informed, that several newspapers had come out, in which the freedom of the slaves was made known and that he the First Prisoner learned himself from different discourses which his master had held with other persons, that such was the intention of the English Government, but that it would not be carried into effect because the farmers had opposed it, and that in consequence of these discourses, he had heard his master, as well as others say, that they never would allow, still less lend a hand to it, but that they would much rather kill the slaves as well as those who wanted to make them free. That the First Prisoner Galant, dissatisfied with the treatment, which he asserts to have suffered from his master, and actuated by the promise of the general freedom of the slaves not having been fulfilled at the appointed time, had formed the plan to procure that freedom by force; for which purpose he on sundry occasions applied to the people of the different places for assistance, which declared their willingness to lend him a helping hand therein.[31]

Bearing in mind that Galant testified with the sure knowledge that he faced the death penalty, his reasons for rising up and killing his master are quite clear from the judge's summary: he had heard rumours that the English Government intended to free the slaves at the Cape; he had heard further that the white farmers (including his master) opposed emancipation to the extent that they would rather kill the slaves than see them go free; and he was 'dissatisfied with the treatment [. . .] he asserts to have suffered from his master'. Accordingly, as freedom had been delayed, he formed the plan 'to procure that freedom by force' by recruiting other slaves and sympathisers to join his uprising.

Brink establishes the causes of Galant's rebellion by starting the story several decades before 1825. He has subsequently explained the creative process he pursued in turning the legal records of the slave uprising into the fiction of his novel:

> When I was working on A *Chain of Voices* I came to know almost by heart the archival documentation about the slave revolt the novel tried to re-represent [. . .] But *knowing* all this was to no avail. It was only when I attempted that dangerous fire-leap from self to other, that history came what it had always yearned to be, namely *story*: and for this it was necessary to try to *imagine* what it is like to be a slave who has been promised his freedom and sees that hope frustrated; to imagine what it is like to be a woman who has to sacrifice her independence to the inarticulate domination of her husband; to imagine what it *means* to be a fierce patriarch or uncomprehending child or dour matron or protective mother or wild adventurer – slaves, all of them, locked in an inescapable chain of voices, sprung from earth, cleansed in water, wanton with wind.[32]

Brink indeed imagines the events of the rebellion from multiple perspectives by borrowing the form of William Faulkner's *As I Lay Dying* (1930), although there is only limited individuation of the many competing narrative voices. He is especially imaginative in narrating the escalating sexual tensions on the farm, with much emphasis on the sexual humiliations inflicted upon Galant: his childhood exclusion from intimacy with the white Hester; the death of his child with Bet at the hands of his white owner Nicolaas; and Nicolaas's seizing and impregnating of Galant's woman Pamela. Galant's speech to the slaves on the eve of the rebellion echoes the court record in that it appeals to their shared suffering and common struggle – "'We are all together here [. . .] We all speak with one voice [. . .] All these years we have been bearing it in silence. Bad food. Harsh words. Floggings. Cold. Heat. Hunger.'"[33] – but these economic and political oppressions are ultimately subordinated in the structure of the novel to the slaves' sexual frustrations. The final voices before the concluding Verdict are those of Hester and Galant describing their transcendent sexual encounter in a loft during an hour-long hiatus in the rebellion. For Hester, forbidden sex with Galant represents a kind of existential freedom, 'a shameless affirmation: I am – I am – I am. Thresh me, break me, shape me: running with fire. –'.[34] For Galant too, the encounter is about much more than sex: 'All right: so it was not the freedom we dreamed of, open and visible, and shared by all. In that sense we failed. But perhaps freedom can never really be other than this, a small and private thing'.[35] He also believes that his having sex with a white woman 'is the one freedom that truly threatens them',[36] and this knowledge reconciles him to his death. Whether Hester and Galant's emotional vocabulary replicates that of their historical predecessors is open to question; what is more certain, however, is that their words carry heavy traces of Brink's own Paris-1960s existentialism, schematic Freudianism and Romantic individualism. In his efforts to turn 'history' into 'story', Brink ultimately produces a narrative in which an individual slave fails to lead a rebellion against his master, and finds consolation in sex with a white woman. What is striking is how closely Brink's narrative of the Cape in the 1820s conforms to commonplace liberal responses to 1970s South Africa: acts of violent rebellion (the black consciousness movement, the trade unions of Natal, the schoolchildren of Soweto) ultimately fail to trouble the all-powerful apartheid state, and limited freedom exists precariously in forms of personal (including sexual) community.

None of these novels attempt to represent the continuities from slavery to capitalism. Rather, they dramatise three distinct forms of white consciousness: Knight in 1940 combines nostalgia about docile black farm workers in the Western Cape and fear of violent black insurgents on the Eastern Cape frontier; Fitzroy in 1970 ignores histories of black rebellion, and imagines Cape Town as a peaceful melting pot; and Brink in 1982 registers the exploitation and violent rebellion of the black oppressed, but restricts their prospects of freedom to brief moments of cross-racial personal and sexual intimacy.

## POST-APARTHEID: SUBJECTIVITY, SEXUALITY AND RESTITUTION

Since 1994, there have been more literary texts on Cape slavery than ever before,[37] with many drawing upon the old legal sources in the Cape Archives and the new historiography. Rayda Jacobs's *The Slave Book* (1998) is typical in displaying a sure knowledge of the histories of Cape slavery by Ross, Worden and Shell. The novel is introduced by the first-person narration of Sangora, an emancipated Malay slave, who is swiftly replaced by an omniscient narrator recounting the love story of Sangora's and his step-daughter Somiela's experiences during the final years of slavery. The narrative conforms to the genre of the popular romance, as it follows Somiela being sold at the slave auction to a violent and sexually predatory white farmer; her and Sangora's struggles against economic and sexual oppression on the farm; her experiences of support and solidarity with certain of the other slaves on the farm; her love affair with the affluent half-white/half-Sonqua Harman,[38] which culminates with emancipation, and their escape into the interior to be reunited with his family. The novel returns in conclusion to Sangora, who addresses the reader as if showing photographs of the characters in their later life, and summarising their various fates (including the death of Harman). This *telos* provides a version of the liberal discourse of freedom in which the sins of slavery recede ever further into the past with the arrival of the post-emancipation promised land. In concluding with the emancipation of the slaves and the leading slave characters getting married, *The Slave Book* repeats the happy ending of Fitzroy's *When the Slave Bell Tolled*. However, the 'present' of 1970 and the 'present' of 1998 produce different meanings. Whereas Fitzroy's ending suggests white complacency about black resistance at the zenith of apartheid, Jacobs's ending suggests an optimistic embrace of the post-apartheid rainbow-nation settlement. Read as national allegory, *The Slave Book* plots the journey of coloured South Africans struggling through the final years of apartheid and ultimately finding love and freedom in a racially mixed society.

Superficially different to *A Chain of Voices*, André Brink's *The Rights of Desire* (2000) engages with the past of slavery via the story of the ghost of an unjustly executed eighteenth-century slave woman haunting a Cape Town house in post-apartheid South Africa. The legal records which provide the basis of the story of the slave woman are contained in the Cape Archives, some of which have been republished,[39] but Brink relies less on these primary sources than on the historian Nigel Penn's essay 'The Fatal Passion of Brewer Menssink. Sex, beer and politics in a Cape Family, 1694–1722' (1999).[40] Brink's central plot is set in the 1990s, and concerns Ruben Olivier, a retired librarian (the narrator) renting a room in his large house to Tessa Butler, a young woman, and his obsessive desire for her. The librarian/narrator's lust for the young woman repeats that of the house's eighteenth-century inhabitants: the brewer Mostert's pursuit of the slave woman Antje of Bengal. The historical dimensions of the plot are filtered through the perceptions and experiences of the narrator and principal characters, with reports of township violence from Magrieta Daniels, Olivier's domestic worker, regularly punctuating the white suburban existence. The engagement with the Cape's slave past in *The Rights of Desire* is more oblique than in *A Chain of Voices*, but Brink's later novel again foregrounds sex and existential self-discovery. Towards the end of the novel, when Ruben finds Antje's bones in the cellar of the house, he concludes, 'For nothing can match the memory of the lover. Nothing is as durable as desire'.[41] The final pages comprise Ruben's self-lacerating declarations about his lifelong failure to connect with other people – 'How many other voices have there been shouting for help throughout my life, shouting for me to help?' – and his ultimate consolation in his solitary old age is that 'My desire is intact'.[42] A lonely and self-pitying old white man, Ruben fails to inhabit any kind of post-apartheid rainbow community. However, like Hester and Galant in the loft in *A Chain of Voices*, Ruben transcends contingent social contradictions by embracing his desires and thus achieving some form of individual self-knowledge. What Brink leaves *out* in framing the past of Cape slavery is perhaps best demonstrated by referring briefly to Penn's essay. Like Brink, Penn acknowledges the power of Messinck's all-consuming and destructive desire for slave women, but crucially, Penn insists that '[w]hile these domestic dramas were being enacted, the business of beer brewing continued',[43] and he scrupulously traces the economic pressures both aiding and frustrating Messinck's sexual predations. The contrast with Brink's novel is striking. In Brink's terms, when Penn's 'history' of Messinck became in his creative hands 'what it had always yearned to be', namely the '*story*' of Mostert and Ruben Olivier, material pressures disappear, and (as in *A Chain of Voices*) sexual desire supersedes all other social determinants.

A more substantial engagement with the history of Cape slavery is provided in Yvette Christiansë's *Unconfessed* (2006), which is based on another legal case: the conviction of the slave woman Sila for the murder of her child Baro in 1823. Loosely similar to the plot of Toni Morrison's *Beloved* (1987), the details of Sila's case are summarised in the original court record as follows:

> That the Prisoner, supposed to be between Thirty and Thirty Five years of age, having left her Master's place situated in the District of George, about three o'clock on the 24th December last year, repaired to the place of Hendrik Van Huysteen, Field Cornet of the land behind said Bay, she there, in presence of a

certain Carel Schaffer, acquainted the Field Cornet, at the same time delivering him a Clasp Knife and shedding some Tears, that she, through Heartsore
and Grief, had cut the Throat of her Child named Baro with that knife because
she, as well as the Child, were ill treated both by her Master and Mistress.[44]

The court rejected Sila's claims that she and Baro had been ill-treated by their
Master, found her guilty of murder and sentenced her to death by strangulation at
the stake. When it was discovered that Sila was pregnant, after protracted delays,
her sentence was commuted to fourteen years on Robben Island. Sila's own voice
is mediated by the legal discourse of the court; her claims of 'Heartsore and Grief'
caused by being 'ill treated both by her Master and Mistress' are noted in the judgment, but rejected in favour of the slave-owner's version of events.

*Unconfessed* opens and closes with an omniscient narrator framing the events
of the novel, but Sila's voice then dominates, as she looks back on her life from
Robben Island, and recounts her many struggles to several sympathetic interlocu-
tors – her son Baro; her lover, the slave woman and fellow prisoner Lys; and an old
slave from her youth, Johannes. Patriarchal violence perpetrated against Sila by
her masters Theron and Van der Watt is sanctioned by the law, and the conflict
between instrumentalist legal discourse and Sila's own voice runs through the novel:
at an early stage of the novel, Sila asks, 'And do I not know of the thinness of laws
and the words that speak them?'[45] Of her inability in the courtroom to articulate her
case and disrupt the master's judgements of her conduct, Sila explains:

> They asked me to speak for myself, me who was so offensive to them. They
> wanted to come inside my heart. It was not an entry I could permit [. . .] I
> thought, oh, that it could be in wonder that they would listen to me if I had
> words they understood. But no, Baro, your mother is not a fool. There is no
> language to make them ashamed. Nothing I have to say could be beautiful. Not
> after things done.[46]

Sila asserts her subjectivity independent of colonial discourse, distinguishing her
authentic self from the identity imposed by her masters and the courts: in an address
to Johannes, for example, she declares, 'I am not a bad person. I am not this Sila who
cuts people, or who hits people. This is not me. I want to be [. . .] I feel I am [. . .]
A person who is me hides nearby'.[47] Sila's allies in her efforts to claim some limited
autonomy are her fellow slaves, and more particularly, her lover Lys. The experiences of shared oppression produce but fleeting moments of collective consciousness: Sila tells Baro that after a particularly cruel humiliation, 'We [the slaves] were
like dogs chasing our tails. Because that was all we were. Dogs and cows, pigs and
horses.'[48] Towards the end of the novel, however, Sila strikes a more defiant note,
when she asks Baro to tell other generations of slaves,

> I am sending you to say we are a trapped people, we are a wounded people, we
> long for freedom, we long for things we have been taught to admire and desire,
> we long for the courage to desire such things, and we are a jealous people.[49]

Sila draws constant support from Lys, whose love sustains her on Robben Island: she recalls Lys's intervention in a conflict with another prisoner: 'Lys says, enough, we must be strong together, Sila. We share this life and we must be as a wall against it'.[50] Sila reflects, 'what kind of woman are you, Sila van den Kaap? I ask myself because there is no one who can tell me. Except, perhaps, Lys'.[51] In a tender moment, Sila says, 'You are my good, quiet day, Lys. You make a place for my back to rest and all aching stops, and when my face relaxes, I know that it was pulled up, strained'.[52] And Sila tells Johannes that 'Lys is the one who brings me warmth. We reach out and we are there. Being woman is enough. Ja'.[53] Sila's love for Lys in *Unconfessed* therefore has a similar redemptive function in the context of Cape slave society to Hester and Galant's stolen hour in the loft in *A Chain of Voices*.

Like the slave novels by Knight, Fitzroy, Brink in *A Chain of Voices*, and Jacobs, *Unconfessed* is set in the final decades of Cape slavery, but emancipation is less cause for celebration, as Sila's prison sentence on Robben Island continues well beyond 1834. However, the final lines of the novel are ambiguous, and the possibility of a happy ending for Sila is allowed: '*a child of a child came, a guard swallowed astonishment and she hers – hah! – A quiet freedom in the shadow of Signal Hill*'.[54] There is no mention in *Unconfessed* of the slave uprisings of 1808 and 1825. Such a silence is plausible given Sila's geographical location within the Cape Colony, but by choosing to ignore them, Christiansë (like Fitzroy and Jacobs) excludes the possibility of imagining resistant forms of collective subjectivity. A more difficult question is whether the novel can be read as an allegory of the end of apartheid. In *Unconfessed*, the resources of lesbian love and fragile moments of solidarity with fellow oppressed help Sila to survive slavery, patriarchal violence and the law's complicity with power. Similar such resources doubtless sustained oppressed and embattled individuals in the final decades of apartheid and since. However, as a political response to post-apartheid inequalities, the literary privileging of a personal/individual 'solution' here forestalls critique of the systemic continuities – and the collective struggles against them – in the transition from slavery to capitalism, and from apartheid to post-apartheid society.[55]

Expecting *Unconfessed* to imagine further forms of slave resistance, or to speak to South Africa's political present more directly, might seem unreasonable, but literary works in other genres have come closer to meeting such expectations. For example, the Jazzart Dance Theatre and Magnet Theatre collaboration *Cargo* (2007) directed by Mark Fleishman commemorated the bicentenary of the end of the slave trade by seeking to recover the pasts of Cape slavery in order to pose challenging questions about contemporary Cape Town. The programme notes summarise the production's ambitions:

For many centuries, cargo has come to this place, our city, the Cape of Good Hope. Porcelain and silk and spices and slaves. Slaves from Mozambique, from Madagascar, from India and the Indonesian archipelago. For 186 years between 1652 and 1838 slaves were a major part – sometimes the major part – of the unique and diverse society in formation at the Cape. Today, slavery still haunts the city, an incrustation of the past at the heart of the present. It is 'a past that will not pass' and yet it is little remembered. Our *Cargo* is a performative engagement with the archive of slavery at the Cape [. . .] The work is an attempt to use performance to get at what has been left out, the voices and their bodies 'exiled on the borders of discourse [. . .] the murmur and the noises from which the process of scriptural reproduction distinguishes itself' (De Certeau). It is a difficult task because the bodies are not immediately or easily available [. . .] To remember is not to forget, it is also to make present, and, most importantly, it is to put the body back together again.[56]

The final section of *Cargo* enacts the discovery in 2003 of over 1000 slave skeletons in the prime real estate zone of Prestwich Place in Greenpoint, Cape Town, a discovery which confirmed that Cape Town 'was built over the graves of slave ancestors, and its continued construction represented an architecture of erasure, a concrete covering over of the material traces of memory'.[57] The political debates precipitated by the discovery of the Prestwich Place slave skeletons, and dramatised in *Cargo*, confront not only the continuities from slavery to capitalism, but also the function of historical memory in constituting national identity, and the question of economic restitution for descendants of slaves.[58] Of a quite different temper to the novels of Jacobs, Brink and Christiansë, *Cargo* registers histories of collective slave suffering, and demands social/political as much as individual/subjective responses of contemporary audiences.

## CONCLUSION

Literary works on Cape slavery have typically ignored, denied or repressed the continuities between exploitation under slavery and exploitation under capitalism. Slavery has been imagined not as the concrete precondition of the present, but as the unconnected antecedent of a happy present defined by free labour and democracy. As literary subject matter, slavery has functioned as a means of negotiating a variety of contemporary anxieties, from the Eastern Cape frontier wars of the nineteenth century to the politics of identity and sexuality in the post-apartheid period.

In contrast to these literary works (*Cargo* excepted), former president Thabo Mbeki's political writings explicitly connect slaveries past and present. In his 2007 Internet letter 'Nobody ever chose to be a slave', Mbeki bemoans the fact that commemorations of the bicentenary of the founding of Haiti as the first ever independent black republic on 1 January 1804 had been more subdued than the celebrations for the bicentenary of the ending of the slave trade in 2007. He quotes Adam Hochschild and Karl Marx to illustrate both the human cost of slavery and its economic importance, and pays tribute to those who brought about the end of the slave trade, 'the African slaves of Haiti, and their colleagues throughout the "New World" [and] people of conscience in the slave-owning countries'.[59] He hails the tradition of international solidarity running from the abolitionist movement to the anti-apartheid movement, and quotes with approval the argument of the Archbishop of Canterbury, the Most Reverend Rowan Williams, that "'the slave trade yielded considerable profit for institutions'", and that reparations should be sought "'to help most effectively those suffering because of the legacy of slavery'".[60] Aside from reparations, Mbeki identifies another echo of chattel slavery in contemporary forms of exploitation: 'the contemporary global economy and society have given birth to various forms of economic activity affecting millions of human beings, that are akin to the loss of personal freedom experienced by the classical slaves'.[61] Mbeki quotes Marx a second time, and then attributes to him the view that 'economic systems predicated on private gain will always seek ways to enslave the people who work for others'.[62] In the climax of Mbeki's letter, the shocking statistics on 'the new slavery' provided by the International Labour Organization (ILO) in 2005 are quoted in full, and he draws particular attention to the exploitation of Africans 'who, driven by dire poverty, daily risk their live to reach Europe in search of even the meanest jobs', and find themselves 'in conditions of disguised slavery'.[63] Mbeki calls finally on 'comrades-in-arms' to address their campaigns against 'those who benefited from the open and old slavery, and those who benefit from disguised, contemporary slavery' in order to 'help most effectively those suffering because of the legacy of slavery'.[64]

How much weight should be attached to Mbeki's anti-slavery declarations? Looking beyond South Africa's borders, there is a long tradition of opportunistic politicians condemning slavery. In the US, for example, Walter Johnson reflects upon the many presidents who have delivered pious anti-slavery speeches, and in particular upon ex-president George Bush's speech on Gorée Island in 2003, and concludes:

> In the historical vision expressed by (though certainly not limited to) Bush's address, slavery has been turned into a cliché, a set of images that have been emptied of historical meaning through their sheer repetition in connection with their supposed extinction at the hands of freedom. In this way, the image of slavery has been put to work in the service of whatever meaning is given to that latter idea.[65]

Johnson contends that the past of slavery has been 'put to work' pre-eminently in the service of 'a single story of story of progress organized around successive modes of production and the achievement of citizenship: the story of racial liberalism, of black freedom and racial acculturation, of how black slaves became American citizens'.[66] Mbeki's speech does not replay quite this crude teleology; indeed, his reconnecting slaveries past and present resists such complacency. Nonetheless, in relation to the specifics of South African history and post-apartheid politics, Mbeki assumes a story of progress from servitude to free labour and (after 1994) democratic citizenship. And the most striking aspect of his letter on the anniversary of 1807 is the fact that he never refers directly to the history of Cape slavery, and nor does he mention the plight of Africans who, 'driven by dire poverty', cross the South African border in search of the 'meanest jobs' in the Republic.

## NOTES

1. For their utilisation of the records of the Council of Justice, see the monographs by Ross, *Cape of Torments*; Worden, *Slavery*; and Shell, *Children*, as well as the special issues on Cape slavery of the journals *South African Historical Journal* (34: 1996) and *Kronos. Journal of Cape History* (28: 2002). Directly focused on the Cape legal records are Heese's *Reg*, which catalogues and analyses the criminal cases involving slaves, and Worden and Groenewald's *Trials*, which introduces and reproduces a large sample of slave trials between 1704 and 1795.
2. Lukács, *The Historical*, p. 18.
3. Hartman, *Scenes*, p. 119.
4. *A Cure for Heartache* makes no explicit reference to slavery, but the plot of Morton's later melodrama *The Slave* (performed at Covent Garden from 12 November 1816) is centred on the love affair between the slave Gambia and Zelinta. See Taylor, 'Anti-slave', p. 16.
5. 'The Philanthropic', p. 1
6. See Meltzer, 'Emancipation'; and Watson, *The Slave*, pp. 67–92.
7. Brooks, 'Nature's Logic', p. 32.
8. Quoted in 'A Resident', p. 16. Pringle's sonnet was much anthologised, and he published it again himself in his short-lived journal in England, *The Tourist; or Sketch Book of the Times* 1, 25 (11 February 1833): 203. See Voss, '"The Slaves"'.
9. See Dooling, *Slavery*, pp. 112–58; and the essays in Worden and Crais, *Breaking*, by Worden, pp. 117–44, and Ross, pp. 145–67.
10. Brantlinger, *Victorian*, p. 24.
11. Martineau, *Life*, p. 56
12. Martineau, *Demerara*, p. 120.
13. Ibid. p. 139.
14. The plot is based on an actual shipwreck, which was subsequently written up by T. Harington and published by Thomas Tegg in 1808.
15. *Makanna*, Vol. 2, pp. 229–30.
16. Kendall, *The English Boy*, Vol. 2, p. 38.
17. Ibid. Vol. 3, p. 83. Kendall anticipates I. D. Du Plessis's sentimental construction of the Cape Malay in the 1940s and 1950s. See Ward and Worden, 'Commemorating,' p. 208.
18. Kendall, *The English Boy*, Vol. 3, p. 115.
19. McCombie, *Governor*, p. 2.
20. Examples of the sub-genre include Nan K. Lock's *No Wine for the Governor* (1946), H. Watkins-Pitchford's *In God's Good Time* (1949), Birch L. Bernstein's *Tomorrow is Another Day: An Historical Romance of South Africa – 1652 to the Present Day* (1951), and Iris Vaughan's *O Valiant Hearts* (1984). Also of this moment is Madeleine Masson's short story collection *The Slave Bell and Other Stories* (1946).
21. Knight, *Walking*, pp. 20–1.
22. Ibid. p. 81.
23. Ibid. p. 343.
24. Fitzroy, *When*, p. 201.
25. Ibid. pp. 34, 195.
26. On the 1808 rebellion, see Worden, '"Armed"'.
27. On Galant's rebellion, see Van der Spuy, '"Making"'.
28. The court judgment on the 1808 rebellion is in Theal, *Records of the Cape Colony*, Vol. 6, and the slaves' testimonies are in the Cape Archives Depot, CJ 515–CJ 516. The court judgment of Galant's rebellion is in Theal, *Records of the Cape Colony*. Vol. 20, and the slaves' testimonies are in the Cape Archives Depot, CJ 633 and CJ 819.
29. Fitzroy, *When*, p. 196.

30. Two other novels on slavery from the 1980s are Wilma Stockenström's *The Expedition to the Baobab Tree* (1983) and Mohammed Cassiem D'Arcy's *The Golden Kris; Saga of Dein, Slave at the Cape* (1988).

31. Cape Archives Depot, CJ 819, pp. 169–74.

32. Brink, *Reinventing*, p. 199.

33. Brink, *A Chain*, p. 363.

34. Ibid. p. 481.

35. Ibid. p. 483.

36. Ibid. p. 484.

37. In addition to the works discussed in this essay, there have been many novels with plot lines about Cape slavery – Karel Schoeman's *Verkenning* (1996), Thomas Pynchon's *Mason and Dixon* (1997), Daniel Sleigh's *Islands* (2002), Therese Benadé's memoir *Kites of Good Fortune* (2004), Russel Brownlee's *Garden of the Plagues* (2005) and Botlhale Tema's *The People of Welgeval* (2005); several well-received plays – the musical *Rosa* (1996), David Kramer and Taliep Petersen's musical *Ghoema* (2005) and the play *Salaam Stories* (2003); one film – John Badenhorst's film *Slavery of Love* (1999); short stories – Moosa Patel's 'Tell-a-Tale: the Final Hour of Slamath' (1999) and Wendy Woodward's A Cape Town Story' (1999); and popular social/family histories – Winnie Rust's *Martha: 'n Verhaal oor Martha Solomons, Countess of Stanford* (2004) and Diana Ferrus's *Ons komvandaan* (2005). There have also been a number of popular histories: Alan Mountain's *An Unsung Heritage: Perspectives on Slavery* (2004), Jackie Loos's, *Echoes of Slavery* (2004) and R. E. van der Ross's *Up from Slavery: Slaves at the Cape, Their Origins, Treatments and Contributions* (2005).

38. Pumla Gqola argues persuasively that the coloured characters in *The Slave Book* exceed colonial and apartheid stereotypes, but that the black characters associated with the African side of Harman's family do not. See Gqola, '"Slaves"'.

39. The historical case concerns Tryntjie of Madagascar. The records (in Dutch) are in Cape Archives Depot, CJ 5 and CJ 317. Heese has republished the court sentence for Tryntjie's case in *Reg*, pp. 113–21.

40. See Penn, *Rogues*, pp. 9–72.

41. Brink, *The Rights*, p. 281.

42. Ibid. pp. 299, 306.

43. Penn, *Rogues*, p. 21.

44. Cape Archives Depot, CJ 817, pp. 239–40.

45. Christiansë, *Unconfessed*, p. 69.

46. Ibid. pp. 230–1.

47. Ibid. p. 313.

48. Ibid. p. 114.

49. Ibid. pp. 279–80.

50. Ibid. p. 127.

51. Ibid. p. 127.

52. Ibid. p. 198.

53. Ibid. p. 314.

54. Ibid. p. 341.

55. A recent British novel which imagines the complexities of collective struggles against slavery and capitalism in Britain and the United States in the nineteenth century is Richard Bradbury's *Riversmeet* (2007).

56. *Cargo* 2007.

57. Grunebaum, 'Unburying', p. 213.

58. On the relationship between Cape slavery, the heritage industry and post-apartheid nation-building, see Worden, 'The changing'.

59. Mbeki, 'Nobody'.

60. Ibid.
61. Ibid.
62. Ibid.
63. Ibid.
64. Ibid.
65. Walter Johnson, 'Slavery', p. 43.
66. Ibid. p. 46.

# 7 History and the Griqua Nation: Andries Waterboer and Hendrick Hendricks

## INTRODUCTION

How did the indigenes of the Cape write back to the northern-hemisphere discourses of nation and colony at the start of the nineteenth century? This final chapter addresses this question by reflecting upon histories by the Griqua leaders, Andries Waterboer (1789–1852) and Hendrick Hendricks (c. 1795–1881). Waterboer's *A Short Account of Some of the Most Particular and Important Circumstances Attending the Government of the Griqua People* (1827) and Hendricks's 'Oppressions of the Griquas' (1830) have been carefully mined by social historians in order to reconstruct the complicated events of the Cape's northern frontier from 1770 to 1830.[1] My aim here is somewhat different. Rather than reading these texts for the information they disclose about the facts of Griqua history, I am interested in how they narrate the relationship between the origins, the early history and the contemporary politics of the Griqua nation. In other words, I am less interested here in assessing whether Waterboer or Hendricks describe Griqua history accurately than with understanding how they 'imagined' the emergence of the Griqua nation. To appreciate Waterboer's *Short Account* and Hendricks's 'Oppressions of the Griqua', an extended preliminary is required, namely a detailed analysis of the northern-hemisphere accounts of the Griqua between 1800 and 1830. Traces of all the northern-hemisphere nationalisms in Chapters 1 to 5 are inscribed in missionary and traveller accounts on the Griqua. These different accounts – sometimes competing, sometimes in agreement – scripted the communities and loose assemblages of the northern Cape frontier through the images, narratives, histories and mythologies of European and US nationhood. As such, they constitute the discursive pressures and limits determining Waterboer and Hendricks's histories of the Griqua.

## FROM 'LITTLE ABOVE THE BRUTES' (1800) TO 'TYRANNICAL USURPERS' (1827)

During the 1750s, an emancipated slave, Adam Kok (c. 1710–c. 1795) acquired grazing rights in the Piketberg region 70 miles north-east of Cape Town, and attracted a following made up of the remains of the Khoi community of Chaguriqua, 'Bastaards' or 'Basters' (the offspring of white men and Khoi women), escaped slaves, and deserting sailors and soldiers in flight from VOC rule at the Cape. Kok was recognised by the VOC as a *kaptyn* (captain, chief, patriarch), and presented with a staff of office like those given to chiefs of other indigenous groups. Coming under pressure from white farmers in the 1770s, Kok's community moved further north, and by the final decades of the eighteenth century, his son Cornelius Kok I (c. 1740–1820) had displaced Khoi and San hunter-gatherer groups first in Namaqualand and later in the region of the Orange River. They lived by hunting, stock-raiding, grazing their livestock and trading, and their leaders accumulated significant wealth – in 1800, Kok was reckoned to own 25,000 sheep. Missionaries from the London Missionary Society (LMS) arrived in Southern Africa in 1799, and their representative on the northern frontier, William Anderson (1769–1852) and the Dutch lay-missionary C. A. Kramer (1778–1851) attached themselves to Kok's peripatetic community in the Namaqualand region in 1800. Further European travellers and missionaries visited the Griqua in the opening decades of the nineteenth century: William Somerville (1771–1860) and Petrus Borcherds (1786–1871) in 1801–2; Hinrich Lichtenstein in 1805; William Burchell (1781–1863) in 1811–12; John Campbell (1766–1840) in 1813 and 1820; Robert Moffat (1795–1883) in 1820; and George Thompson (1796–1889) in 1823.[2]

The son of a London merchant, Anderson was present at the founding of the LMS in London in September 1795. He and Kramer spent their first four years travelling around with Kok's community, but in 1804 finally succeeded in persuading them to settle at Klaarwater. Looking back some years later, he describes the transformation of the Griqua under his guidance:

> When I went among the Griquas, and for some time after, they were without the smallest marks of civilisation [. . .] Their wretched appearance and habits were such as might have excited in our minds an aversion to them, had we not been actuated by principles which led us to pity them, and served to strengthen us in pursuing the object of our missionary work; they were, in many instances, little above the brutes [. . .] When we went among them, and some time after, they lived in the habit of plundering one another; and they saw no moral evil in this nor in any of their actions. Violent deaths were common [. . .] Their usual manner of living was truly disgusting, and they were void of shame; however, after a series of hardships, which required much faith and patience, our instructions were attended with a blessing which produced a great change. The people became honest in their dealings; they came to abhor those acts of plunder which had been so common among them [. . .] They entirely abandoned their former manner of life, and decency and modesty prevailed in their families

[. . . I]n wandering about with them, we constantly endeavoured to impress upon their minds the superior advantages they would derive from cultivating the ground, and having fixed habitations. After a considerable time had elapsed, we prevailed upon them to try the experiment, and a commencement was made. This event was preceded and followed by a great and visible improvement among them as a body.[3]

The principle narrative underlying Anderson's account of the Griqua is the Christian conversion of the heathen: from shameless and amoral brutes, they are converted into a decent and modest Christian community. But complementing and entwined with Anderson's religious discourse are economic and political teleologies. The Griqua's economic 'evolution' requires that they give up 'plundering' in favour of becoming 'honest in their dealings', a change which might alternatively be expressed as relinquishing communal forms of ownership for the laws of private property. In terms of political development, he scripts the Griqua journeying from a Hobbesian state of nature ruled by violence, brutality and mutual plunder, to become a law-abiding political 'body'. The Griqua's transition from a wandering life to one based on 'fixed habitations' follows the first three stages of the Scottish Enlightenment developmental *telos*: they evolve from the first stage of civilisation (hunter-gatherers) through the second stage (pastoralists) to the third stage (settled agriculture).[4] Anderson's faithful application of the stadial theory to the Griqua at the Cape, however, displays none of the qualifications, doubts or anxieties about 'the progress of empire' expressed by Smith, Ferguson and Millar in Scotland (see Chapter 3).

Anderson's themes are repeated in the writings of subsequent travellers. William Somerville was born and educated in Edinburgh, and served as a hospital assistant in General Craig's invading army of 1795, before being appointed in 1797 by Governor Macartney to the post of Secretary of the Court of Appeal. The political instability precipitated by the Graaff-Reinet rebellions and Third Frontier War of 1799, coinciding with crop failures in the Western Cape in 1800, prompted the Cape government to send Somerville on two extended journeys to the interior: his first in December 1799 was to accompany Maynier on delicate peace negotiations on the eastern frontier, and his second in October 1801 was to accompany Petrus Johannes Truter (1775–1867) to the northern frontier in search of cattle for the Colony. It was on the second journey that Somerville encountered the nascent 'Bastard' community living with Anderson and Kramer. More educated in eighteenth-century philosophy than Anderson, Somerville's commentary on this community was framed by his rejection of French Enlightenment ideas of African innocence:

Those who have only seen man in the highly polished state in which the European lives, have been by daily experience and observation convinced that in every station the life of the most happy is chequered by many cares and toils, which they have ascribed to his civilisation from which the natural propensity to reason by contrast has easily led the poetical fancy of a Rousseau to paint the state of nature on [sic] the only one in which true happiness is to be attained, and every deviation from this to be a corruption of the original purity of the human race: if this reasoning were true, it would be very inapplicable to any of the tribes in the SW corner of Africa with which I am acquainted. To none does the state of nature supply a competent quantity of food for the consumers [. . .] Few I am persuaded of those whose lot in polished societies is deemed the most unhappy would willingly change conditions with the most envied of the African chiefs. An idea of pastoral happiness from the alluring descriptions of Arcadian happiness would be found realised only in the elegant imagination of Fenelon. Here hunger, thirst, and dread of danger from the robber or the beasts of prey ever press upon the Savage.[5]

Embedded in the traditions of British empiricism, Somerville asserts the authority of his own direct experiences and observations of Africans in Africa in order to discredit what he regards as the fanciful imaginings of Rousseau and Fenelon. Limited by their exposure only to European societies, Rousseau and Fenelon create fantasies of Africa in order to criticise the limits of their own European world, but in the process generate false myths about Africa. Although he does not make an explicit link between Rousseau and the missionaries at Klaarwater, Somerville also accuses the latter of failing to register (what he sees as) the realities of African indolence. Recording his impressions in his journal entry of 8 November 1801, Somerville criticises the missionaries:

> Many of them are the people called Bastards, who are sprung from white people and Hottentots, they are the most faithful and intelligent servants that the farmers can employ, it is to be apprehended that many of these have made their desire of instruction a pretext for indulging in habits of idleness, they have left their service and followed the missionaries, by which not only the individuals who employed them but the colony at large materially suffers [. . .] These people attend divine service morning and evening with regularity, but the influence of the principles they are taught upon their moral conduct is not very apparent, not one of them has shewed the least mark of industry or drive to learn any useful art, the whole day is spent in sleeping or smoking.[6]

The expedition met with 'Kocks Horde'[7] on its return journey, and Somerville expanded upon his first impressions in his journal entry of 11 March 1802. He notes their credulousness – 'the Bastards composing this Horde [. . .] have docility of character which renders them easily operated upon'[8] – and describes how this quality has been exploited by unscrupulous colonists. As a consequence, the members of 'Kocks Horde' have been filled 'with a dread of Government as a source from which every thing bad is to be apprehended and nothing good expected'.[9] Somerville recounts an example of how a dispute between a colonist and a member of 'Kocks Horde' over 600 sheep was settled in favour of the former on the basis that the colonist 'is a Christian and [the Bastard-Hottentot] but a Heathen'.[10] But Somerville shifts abruptly in the next sentence from this critical exposé of colonial justice to a final negative image of 'Kocks Horde':

> The Bastards are indolent and slothful as all Hottentots are, and as I believe all people who lead a pastoral life are. The cattle breed without any care or active exertion on their part. Fenelon's enchanting pictures of Arcadia's felicity but ill accord with the scenes of South Africa.[11]

The positive qualities Somerville attributes to 'Kocks Horde' – 'faithful and intelligent servants' and 'docility of character' – are outweighed by the negative: they are prone to 'habits of idleness'; they use their ostensible embrace of Christianity to escape work; and they take advantage of the trusting but naïve missionaries.

Travelling with Somerville was fifteen-year-old assistant secretary Petrus Borcherds, who provides a contrasting and more sympathetic picture of the 'Bastard Hottentots'. Writing in the spirit of Rousseau and Levaillant, Borcherds introduces them as 'the race' on the Orange River which enjoys 'a degree of independence and power but little known in the colony':[12]

> [They are] a hybrid race, originating from the European and the Hottentot [. . .] In dress, manners and habits they resemble the farmers of the frontier, as also in their pursuits of cattle-breeding, and their addiction to hunting excursions [. . .] Their habitations resemble those of the Hottentots, being the same semi-circular huts covered with matting, but larger; they differ from the last-mentioned race by being more prudent in making provision for future wants [. . .] They are served by Kora or Koranah servants [. . .] and by Bushmen [. . .] Manual labour is seldom used in cultivation of land, or any other purpose. Cattle seem to supply their wants abundantly, and this naturally leads to a pastoral, inactive life. Undisturbed from without and contented with few wants, they appear to enjoy a tranquillity unknown to those engaged in the business and bustle of civilized society.[13]

'Kocks Horde' in Somerville's account thus becomes 'a hybrid race' in Borcherds's memoir, and whereas Somerville firmly locates the 'Bastard Hottentots' between hunter-gatherer and pastoralist in the four-stage journey, Borcherds echoes Rousseau's proto-Romanticism by describing Kok's community free from 'the business and bustle of civilized society'. However, Borcherds's French Enlightenment image of the 'Bastard Hottentots' was superseded, and all subsequent accounts imposed the stadial theory on the Griqua. Even Thomas Arbousset (1810–77) and François Daumas (1812–71) from the Paris Evangelical Missionary Society, who visited the northern frontier in 1836, displayed no trace of Rousseau's influence, and repeated what had become the hegemonic narrative:

> Like the Bastaards, the Griqua are indolent, apathetic, and content with little [. . .] Notwithstanding their natural indolence, they have – thanks to their religious instructors,– made considerable progress in civilisation and improvement. Thirty years ago, Mr. Anderson, to whom they are indebted for their advancement, found them poor, barbarian, and pagan, wandering about on the banks of the Gariep, with a few flocks, knowing nothing of Europeans, but their names and their vices.[14]

The next significant European account of the Griqua after Somerville's was that of the German Lichtenstein, who travelled to the northern frontier under the auspices of the short-lived Batavian Republic at the Cape. Born in Hamburg, and educated in Jena and Helmstedt, Lichtenstein arrived at the Cape as part of the entourage of the Batavian governor Jan Willem Janssens. The third of Lichtenstein's journeys into the interior of the Colony took place between April and August 1805, and included a visit to the 'Bastards' and their resident missionary Anderson in June 1805. Lichtenstein's descriptions of the 'Bastards' should be read in the context of his broader vision of how European power should be expressed on the frontier:

> The hordes ['Die kleinen Horden'] who now live upon the borders of the colony, or within its boundaries, are become more peaceable than their distant brethren: those, in particular from whom the present embassy was sent, have for several years together, abstained from plunder. But since the Bosjemans have no national interest ['Kein National-Interesse'] and any compact made with them, even if it were ever so well observed, could have merely a partial effect, binding individuals only, not the whole nation ['ganze Nation'], it is easy to see how little such agreements can afford luxury to the colony at large. The experience of the following years only shewed, alas! the inefficiency of the compact made with them at this time. More distant hordes came down, and not only made terrible devastations upon the property of the colonists, but vented their rage equally upon their own peaceable countrymen, when they found the latter would not make common cause with them [. . .] There seems, however, to be nothing better to do at present, if the utter extirpation of the whole race is not desired (an idea which must be deprecated by every person of common humanity), than to endeavour, by conciliatory measures, to purchase the good-will of the numberless scattered hordes, though this may not be an easy thing to accomplish. I shall not enter further in this place into the modes of life of these untamed people ['als halbwilden Menschen'].[15]

It is worth pausing to elaborate Lichtenstein's sense of the colonial encounter more carefully. The Europeans extending their reach on the frontier do so as members of unified and coherent nations, whereas the distant indigenes of the northern Cape function as individuals, and are incapable of collective or unified action. In a sense, 'the numberless scattered hordes'/'these untamed people' are pre-national, and Lichtenstein counsels efforts to purchase their goodwill. What optimism he feels with regard to promoting their journey from 'individuals' to 'whole nations' derives from his sense that those 'hordes' which have had more contact with Europeans are more 'peaceable', more likely to 'abstain from plunder' and therefore more amenable to progressing towards European forms of political community.

Lichtenstein identifies precisely where on the journey from savagery to nation-hood the 'Bastards' were located. In line with his adjective 'halbwilden', he describes them as 'a thousand men, whose regulations as a community [. . .] exhibit a curious intermediary state between savage and civilised life. They have only recently begun, under the conduct of [. . .] missionaries, to unite in one general and firm bond of union.'[16] He then expands upon their heterogeneous origins, starting with 'Bastard-Hottentots, descended, in part, from old Christian families [. . .] in whose veins Christian blood often flowed [. . .] and [who] were [. . .] as good Christians as the pure offspring of the Europeans'.[17] Having been driven out by the 'white children of the colonists', these 'Bastard Hottentots' sought asylum in remote parts, where they were united with 'several hordes of pure Hottentots, who lived wandering lives along the banks of the [Orange] river [. . . and whose] only idea was to live in indolence.'[18] To this mix of 'Bastard Hottentots' and 'pure Hottentots' then 'were added rabble of every kind, free blacks and slaves who had escaped from their servitude; some even of Africanus's band were to be found among the motley assemblage.'[19] Implicit in Lichtenstein's listing of these constituent elements is a racial hierarchy: from the 'most white'/most-European/civilised/ 'Bastard Hottentots' descended from Christian families, to the 'most black'/ least-European/savage/members of 'Africanus' band'. The challenge facing Anderson was to find a means of transcending these internal divisions, and somehow to constitute a stable Christian community. The most important strategy in achieving this end – promoted by Anderson and warmly endorsed by Lichtenstein – was to replace their nomadic lifestyle with one based upon permanent settlements and crop cultivation. According to Lichtenstein, Anderson had made very limited progress in his first four years as a missionary, but this changed once they took up residence at the Klaarwater station:

> Since that time, he could perceive among them an increasing spirit of industry, of docility, and desire of improvement [. . .] His great object at present was to keep the institution fixed, and [. . .] to excite a spirit of attention to agriculture, and to wean them from their attachment to the nomade [sic] life.[20]

Lichtenstein notes how difficult it is to categorise this nascent community of 'harmless men' in terms of colonial relationships, since they consider themselves 'fellow citizens of the colony, and subjects of the colonial government', while at the same time 'are even ignorant of the boundaries fixed by the government for the colony'.[21] This indeterminacy, however, does not prevent Lichtenstein from concluding finally that '[u]ndoubtedly this little State ['der kleine Bastard-hottentotten-Staat'] deserves not only the attention but the earnest support of the government at the Cape.'[22] The particularly German associations of the term 'state' are expressed by Lichtenstein's contemporary (and fellow product of Jena), G. W. F. Hegel (1770–1831) in his 1802 essay 'The German Constitution'. For Hegel, to be counted as a 'state', a political community requires a centralised authority – 'all institutions in the nature of a society should proceed from the supreme public authority and be regulated, commanded, overseen, and conducted by it' – and it is particularly important that the state exercise a monopoly on violence: 'those who assail the state directly [. . .] are the greatest criminals, and the state has no higher duty than to maintain itself and crush the power of those criminals in the surest way it can'.[23] By defining the Klaarwater community as a 'state', Lichtenstein might attribute political autonomy to them, but at the same time, his designation requires that they fulfil the imperatives of statehood – the consolidation of centralised political authority and a state monopoly of violence.

Six years after Lichtenstein's visit, Burchell arrived at Klaarwater, and in the course of his stay formed a negative impression of the missionaries' endeavours. Burchell was born in London and educated at a private boarding school in Surrey. At the age of 23, he was appointed by the East India Company to the position of schoolmaster and acting botanist on the island of St Helena, and assumed his duties there on 13 December 1805. He travelled from St Helena to the Cape, landing in Cape Town on 26 November 1810, and departed on his journey to the interior on 19 June 1811. Before his final return to Cape Town in April 1815, Burchell visited Klaarwater twice: once for a four-month spell from October 1811, and a second time in May 1812. Like Lichtenstein, Burchell emphasises the 'mixed' identity of the 'Bastard' community at Klaarwater:

> [t]he tribe of Hottentots now at Klaarwater had its origins from the two families of the Mixed Race of the name of Kok and Berends [and] they were joined by others of the same race who found their life under the Boors not so agreeable.[24]

He repeats the view that they should be compelled to progress from African savagery to European civilisation, but is less sanguine about the prospects for such progress, and doubts the ability of the self-deluding missionaries to facilitate the journey:

> Every sensible and reasonable person must be too well aware of the difficulties attending the civilization of wild nations, to expect more than slow and gradual advancement, or to be disappointed or deterred by the untowardness of savages, or by their resistance to novel doctrines.[25]

Rather than teaching Christianity to the inhabitants of Klaarwater, Burchell recommends 'instruction in such arts as have for them evident utility'.[26] Without such practical instruction, he argues, the teaching of the Christian doctrine fails to promote European civilisation, not only among the '*Kora* and *Bushmen*' of the Klaarwater region, who 'continue to remove from place to place, a wild independent people',[27] but also among the 'Bastaards' under Kok and Berends, whose patriarchal authority structure is limited and 'does not seem to be so strong, as the good of their society requires'.[28] Burchell's references to 'the 'untowardness of savages' and 'wild independent people' reinforce the earlier travellers' negative images of the communities of the northern frontier.

Soon after Burchell's visit, the Scottish minister John Campbell travelled to the northern frontier to inspect LMS missions. In his *Journal of Travels in South Africa* (1815), he explains in his diary entry for 7 August 1813 how he facilitated the next major stage in the 'civilisation of the Bastard Hottentots':

> Had a meeting with the male population, to consider various points, especially regulations for the protection of the lives and property of the community. I endeavoured to explain to them the necessity and design of laws for the

government of every society [. . . I]n case they should become a much more numerous people, which was not improbable, should they remain without laws, all would be anarchy and confusion. I told them that in the history of the world there was no account of any people existing and prospering without laws; I commended them for relinquishing a wandering life, and for having become a stationary people; and said that I was happy that they were, from experience, convinced of its utility. The chiefs and people unanimously consented that laws should be made, and magistrates chosen to put them in execution; and that a meeting should be held in the afternoon to consider what laws should be adopted. It was agreed that their two captains, or chiefs, should continue to act as commanders, in things respecting the public safety against foreign attacks. The whole people likewise resolved, that henceforth they should be called Griquas, instead of Bastard Hottentots; and that the place should be called Griqua Town, instead of Klaar Water. I had drawn up fourteen laws, which were proposed and agreed to.[29]

Campbell thus claims to be the catalyst for 'creating' the 'Griqua', as he persuades them to consolidate the advantages of becoming a 'stationary people', first, by adopting laws to protect 'the lives and property of the community', and second, by replacing their pejorative name of 'Bastard-Hottentots' with 'Griqua'.

On his second visit to the Griqua in 1820, Campbell questioned their embrace of Christian values. Discovering that a significant minority of the Griquatown community merely paid lip-service to Christianity, especially with regard to their treatment of the 'Bush people', Campbell insists that 'a mixed multitude are not the materials of a church', and exhorts the Griqua leaders to be 'faithful in the exclusion of hypocrites whose works discover them'.[30] In unforgiving corporeal metaphors, Campbell declares,

> If it be necessary for the life and health of the body to amputate or cut off a corrupted member, it is equally necessary to guard against ingrafting into the Body of Christ a corrupted member lest the corruption should circulate throughout the whole body.[31]

Having thus laid down the general principle, Campbell applies it to the Griqua: 'Men of low lives and who have done acts of cruelty against the poor innocent Bush people should receive no countenance either from the pastor or the members of a Christian church'.[32] However, in the conflict between Griqua and Bushman over land and cattle, Campbell recognises the validity of their respective claims:

> The Griquas [. . .] and the neighbouring Bushmen, are much exasperated against each other. The poor Bushmen say, in defence of their conduct in stealing the Griqua cattle, – 'That the country was originally theirs, that the Griquas have seized the fountains of water, and shot almost all the game, and that they are forced to steal or starve.' On the other hand, the Griquas urge in their defence, when accused of cruelty against the Bushmen, – 'That their

chief dependence for subsistence is on their cattle; that it is hard to be deprived in one night of their principal means of support, by those savages, who will neither sow nor rear cattle.'[33]

Campbell notes that the Scottish Highlanders used the same kind of reasoning as the Bushmen, quoting a letter from the Highlander Cameron of Lochiel to the land-owner Sir James Grant, in which 'the Highland chieftain has recourse to the same ingenious sophistry [. . . reminding Grant] that the low countries were once the property of the Highlanders, and that they have a right to all they can capture there'.[34]

Campbell's 1813 constitution failed to stabilise the Griquatown community, and defections followed, triggered by the colonial government's demand in 1814 that the Griqua provide conscripts for military service, exacerbated by the inadequate water supply at Griquatown and the resulting pressure on arable land, and fuelled by the interference in Griqua politics of the frontier rebel Coenraad Buys. A year later, increasing numbers of defectors gathered on the banks of the Hart River, and assumed the designation 'Hartenaars'. The Hartenaars were themselves divided between 'accommodators' (like the future Griquatown leader Andries Waterboer), who wanted to take advantage of the patronage of the missionaries and centralise Griqua state power, and 'resistors', who rejected the missionaries and sought a return to their autonomous and nomadic lifestyle beyond the authority of the Colony. The Hartenaars' relatively democratic command structures (compared with those of Kok and Berends) meant that they were also sometimes known as the 'Patriots'. An uneasy rapprochement between the Hartenaars and the Griquatown captaincy was achieved by 1816, but continuing tensions prompted the LMS in 1820 to replace Anderson at Griquatown with Robert Moffat,[35] and this change in missionary personnel in turn facilitated the appointment on 20 December of the same year of Andries Waterboer as *kaptyn* at the expense of Adam Kok II and Berends.

Looking back on his time at Griquatown, Moffat insisted (*contra* Somerville and Burchell) that 'all methods of effecting the civilization of Africa, apart from the Gospel of Christ, have hitherto proved abortive'.[36] Philosophy and Science, he argues, have been impotent, and it must be 'universally acknowledged, that the Gospel of Christ is the only instrument which can civilize and save all kindreds and nations of the earth'.[37] In dedicating this work to Prince Albert, Moffat singles out Portugal's Henry the Navigator as the exemplary European civiliser of Africans:

Of the influence which may be exerted on a whole nation by a single Prince, enlightened by Philosophy and animated by Piety, Don Henry [. . .] as your Royal Highness will remember, has left an illustrious example. This distinguished Personage was the first royal European friend to Africa. He to whom the School of Modern Navigation owes its origin, and to whom Portugal is indebted for all the glory of her discoveries, was impelled, in all his projects, through a long life, by the spirit of Missions. His achievements, in relation to Africa, have immortalized his name; but a work immeasurably greater still remains to be accomplished, on its behalf. The honour of this work, I would fondly hope, is reserved for my beloved country; and historians of future times will record that Prince Henry of Portugal found a successor and superior in Prince Albert of England.[38]

Moffat resolutely insists upon the need to follow what he sees as Henry's example by excluding all other concerns – political, philosophical, scientific, economic – from the religious mission of civilising Africans by Christian proselytising. However, Moffat was not always consistent in following this exclusive path, as his version of how he communicated European conceptions of nationhood and statecraft to Waterboer demonstrates:

> Andries, who was not prepared for this new station [of Griqua leader], soon felt the responsibility of office. He had no opportunities of studying the science of government from books (Minos, Lycurgus and Solon were names unknown to him!) and had heard little else than the principles of law derived from the Bible, the best foundation for the law of nations. He felt his deficiency and thirsted for information, and for months together we spent several evenings a week, after it was supposed all were gone to rest, conversing on these subjects. Though I did little more than reply to his numerous inquiries, yet, having been placed there for the express object of lending my aid to abolish the old system, I naturally felt the task a delicate one. At the same time neither Mr [Henry] Helm nor I could see any impropriety in giving him what information we could on the history of nations and their political economy. From this and other circumstances he long retained a grateful sense of his obligations, and a warm friendship of many years ensued.[39]

Moffat is vague here as to precisely what version of 'the history of nations and their political economy' he transmitted to Waterboer, but his summary at least makes clear that Waterboer was instructed in the primacy of the Bible as a guide to the science of government, and that he was taught firm lessons in obeisance to missionary authority. Moffat moved from Griquatown to the LMS mission to the Tswana a year later, and his role as Waterboer's instructor-in-statecraft was filled first by the government agent John Melvill (1787–1852), who lived in Griquatown from 1822–6, and then the Lancashire-born missionary Peter Wright (1796–1843), who lived for thirteen years with the Griqua. In 1838, Moffat thought that his tutelage of Waterboer had provided the basis for the Griqua nation to enjoy a happy future comparable to that of the United States: Kuruman would be the capital of this new nation, and its citizens 'might hold their forum under the cooling shade of the tall spreading willows opposite a range of substantial buildings and awe the nations until Waterboer had become a second Washington'.[40]

Notwithstanding Moffat's reflections, Waterboer's first years as *kaptyn* of Griquatown were difficult ones. With missionary support, he pursued a more interventionist mode of governance, establishing irrigation systems for crop production, and policing infractions against the laws of the 1813 constitution more assiduously.

This precipitated further splintering, with the emergence in 1822 of two further factions: first, one under the old chiefs Adam Kok II and Berends, who relocated with their followers to the Riet River, and a second, more radical anti-missionary faction (including Hendrick Hendricks), which gathered at the Modder River, and came to be known as the 'Bergenaars' ('Mountaineers'). Despite these defections, Waterboer played a leading role in the Battle of Dithakong in 1823, in which he and the other Griqua *kaptyns* combined successfully to defend the mission stations of the northern frontier against the attack of a large force of Hlakwana and Fokeng.[41] An eyewitness to the Battle of Dithakong, the traveller George Thompson, provided yet another image of the Griqua in his extensive travel notes, which were heavily edited by his friend Thomas Pringle and published in 1827. Thompson was born in Cumberland, and had worked as a sailor, a draper and a solicitor's clerk before leaving for the Cape in 1818 for employment with a firm of merchants. Thompson turns a more practical eye on the state of the Griqua, noting the obstacles to their progress presented by the physical landscape and their internal politics:

[T]he Griqua, who have been but lately reclaimed by the missionaries from a life entirely nomadic, are as yet with difficulty excited to agricultural labours, to which the aridity of the soil and the uncertainty of the seasons are also great obstacles. Their internal dissensions have recently added another obstacle to settled pursuits and agricultural improvements.[42]

He repeats the standard descriptions of the Griqua as "'a herd of wandering and naked savages, subsisting by plunder and the chase'",[43] who had been rescued by Christianity. He concludes that '[n]o slight improvement has been wrought upon the manners and character of this wild horde by the labours of the missionaries',[44] but then criticises the Griqua's violent hatred of the Bushmen: 'towards the wretched Bushmen, I found them, in general, animated by the same spirit of animosity as the frontier boors'.[45] Thompson acknowledges the threat posed by the Bushmen, but like Campbell, he does not side unequivocally with the 'Boors' and Griqua: 'In these deplorable wars the Bushmen are doubtless, in general, the aggressors, by their propensity to depredation. Yet [. . .] have they not some cause to regard both Boors and Griquas as intruders upon their ancient territories, – as tyrannical usurpers'?[46] In Thompson's writings, the Griqua are thus interpolated within a binary which locates them on the side of the white settlers (the 'Boors') against the indigenes (the 'Bushmen'). In Lichtenstein's term from the first decade of the century, they are therefore no longer 'half-wild'; by the 1820s, they are identified with the white settler, and constituted as the antithesis of the entirely wild 'Bushmen'.

What do these colonial texts tell us about the rise of the Griqua nation? The first point is that they reproduce traces of different European discourses of nationhood: Somerville, Burchell, Campbell and Thompson subscribe to a crude version of the Scottish Enlightenment four-stage theory of civilisation, and describe the Griqua as instances of the earliest two stages; Borcherds projects a version of Rousseau's French Enlightenment state-of-nature on to the Griqua; Lichtenstein lifts the designation of 'state' from German political philosophy, and attaches it to the

Griqua; and Moffat first reaches back to proclaim the Portuguese age of discovery as the model for 'civilising' Africans on the northern frontier, and then imagines the Griqua's future in the image of the United States, with Waterboer as a second Washington. Second, these European writers impose a striking variety of collective identities onto the Griqua. As members of the Cape Colony's population in the eighteenth century, the 'Bastard Hottentots'/Griqua are described sympathetically – Somerville, for example, declares that they make 'the most faithful and intelligent servants that the farmers can employ' – but in terms that allocate them unambiguously to a subordinate function within the colonial economy. They are cheap, skilled labour. As an independent people on the fringes of the colonial borders, however, the appellations attached to them are more pejorative and more varied: they are described as 'little above the brutes' (Anderson); 'Kocks Horde' (Somerville); a 'hybrid race' (Borcherds); 'Bastard Hottentots' (Somerville, Borcherds, Burchell); a 'horde', 'half-wild', an 'untamed people', a 'rabble', a 'motley assemblage', a 'Nation', 'harmless people', 'fellow citizens of the colony', 'subjects of the colonial government' and a 'little State' (Lichtenstein); a 'tribe', a 'race' and 'wild independent people' (Burchell); a (Christian) 'body' (Anderson and Campbell); the 'Griqua' (Campbell); and 'intruders upon ancient territories' and 'tyrannical usurpers' (Thompson). Third, their 'progress' from individual 'brutes' to 'Griqua' community to 'tyrannical usurpers' is narrated in a variety of ways. For the missionaries like Anderson, Campbell and Moffat, the fundamental journey is the religious one from godless savages to Christian converts. By contrast, for the non-missionary travellers like Somerville, Lichtenstein and Burchell, the religious journey is secondary to both the economic progression from hunter-gatherer to pastoralist to settled agriculturalist, and to the political journey from an African version of Hobbes's *bellum omnium contra omnes* to a legally constituted nation-state. Finally, these writings reveal two enduring contradictions in Griqua identity: first, Lichtenstein identifies the Klaarwater community as 'citizens' and 'subjects' of the Cape Colony, on the one hand, and as members of an independent 'State', on the other; and second, whereas Somerville in 1802 describes them sympathetically as victims of settler avarice, Campbell and Thompson in the 1820s criticise them as perpetrators of murder and plunder against the indigenous 'Bushmen'.

## ANDRIES WATERBOER'S *A SHORT ACCOUNT*

At the end of 1827, four years after the Battle of Dithakong and Thompson's visit to Griquatown, Waterboer addressed a 27-page document, A Short Account of Some of the Most Particular and Important Circumstances Attending the Government of the Griqua People to Dr John Philip (1775–1851), director of the LMS in Cape Town. Translated into English and transcribed by Peter Wright, Waterboer's A Short Account represents the most extended instance in the period of the colonised 'writing back' to the coloniser. Before looking at the document in detail, Waterboer's distinctiveness as a Griqua leader should be registered: unlike the traditional Griqua *kaptyns* Adam Kok II and Berends, he was of San (as opposed to mixed race) descent, and had little personal wealth; he had been part of the Hartenaar/'Patriot' rebellion of 1815–16; his authority derived not from consanguinity but from having been elected leader; and he was mission-school educated.

A *Short Account* is structured chronologically, starting with the rule of Cornelius Kok on the banks of the Orange River in the eighteenth century, and ending with Waterboer's desperate defence of Griquatown against Bergenaar attacks in July 1827. It is striking, however, that only the first five pages are about Griqua history before Waterboer's ascension to the captaincy in 1820, with the remaining twenty-two pages allocated to describing the eventful first seven years of his regime. Waterboer describes how Cornelius Kok ruled first through the deputies Piet Berend and Lucas Hans, and after their deaths, through Jan Hendrik and Klaas Berend. At the time of the establishment of the settlement at Klaarwater, Waterboer records how Cornelius Kok replaced Hendrik and Berend with Adam Kok II and Berend Berends. Kok and Berends unfortunately displayed 'the greatest possible unfitness for their great work', and their ineptitude was compounded by their failure to curb the influence Coenraad Buys, who led the young men to rebel against 'the Captains, their laws, and the Gospel itself'.[47] Waterboer explains Buys's malign influence and the Hartenaar rebellion as direct consequences of Kok and Berends's lax rule, and suggests that even these destabilising events failed to animate them into confronting 'the uproar they were causing in the Country through their neglect and unfaithful-ness'.[48] Waterboer represents the inhabitants of Griquatown at this time as torn apart by contending factions: 'the parties attacked each other with assegais; [. . .] they wilfully destroyed each other's gardens [and] they cut the back sinews of each other's cows and oxen'.[49] Furthermore, this 'disorderly party' plundered their neigh-bours: 'they made commandoes against the poor Bechuana to steal their Cattle; the Bushmen [. . .] were by that banditti either shot dead or had their throats cut'.[50] Faced with such anarchy, Waterboer and his faction – 'Those individuals amongst us who were decent characters'[51] – were on the point of fleeing the district, when as a last resort they took matters into their own hands:

> As the last means of effecting a change in the State of Things, the people resi-dent at Griqua Town came to the resolution of choosing a Captain for them-selves, and the universal voice of the people falls on me, and I was chosen to be their Captain [. . .] I submitted to their wishes from a sense of duty, and this appointment was sanctioned by the Colonial Government.[52]

Whereas Moffat in his version of events in Griquatown in 1820 claims the credit for overseeing the appointment of Waterboer as *kaptyn*, the missionary disappears in Waterboer's own account, where his election is attributed to the collective agency of 'the people resident at Griqua Town'. As a genealogy of the rise of the Griqua nation, the opening pages of Waterboer's *Short Account* follow the sequence of an exclusively masculine oedipal drama: the benevolent paterfamilias, Cornelius Kok I, is succeeded by bad patriarchs (Adam Kok II and Berend Berends), who are in turn defeated and driven out by a brotherhood of good sons (Waterboer and the decent characters of Griquatown).

The rhetorical dichotomy established in the opening pages between Waterboer's rule (dutiful/decent/law-abiding/benevolent) and that of the old *kaptyns* (rebellious/disorderly/unfaithful/murderous) is elaborated further in the account of his years in power from 1820–7. Waterboer continued to be undermined by the endless intriguing and politicking against his captaincy by Kok and Berends, whose enmity 'was manifested continually in their misleading of the People not only against my Person, but against all good order and law'.[53] Compounding and complicating the hostility of Kok and Berends was the threat to Waterboer posed by the Bergenaars (translated as 'Mountaineers' by Wright), whom he describes variously as 'people who separated themselves from captain and Law';[54] '[their] conduct [was] an outrage on Captainship and Government and on all Law and Order';[55] 'a party that refused to submit to all peaceable terms, and seemed determined not to leave off their murderous, cattle-stealing habits';[56] '[motivated by] lawless and wicked purposes [and] too wicked and ungovernable';[57] and [committed to] rooting out Captains and Laws from the Country'.[58] Waterboer's pejorative descriptions of the Bergenaars produce another moral binary that replicates the Good vs Evil opposition of Christian discourse: on the one hand, Law/Order/Captaincy/Government/Peace/Benevolence, and on the other, Lawlessness/Disorder/'outrage against' Captaincy and Government/Warfare/Murder and Theft.

In addition to violent challenges to his authority, Waterboer was also obliged to negotiate awkward diplomatic challenges posed by missionaries and colonial administrators. The most significant such challenge was Philip's attempt to establish a peaceful settlement between Waterboer, Kok and Berends, and the Bergenaars at Griquatown in September 1825. In giving too much credence to the testimony of his adversaries, Waterboer believed:

> [I]it did not become Dr Philip as missionary to interfere in our Governing affairs [. . .] We can well appreciate the good intentions of our friend Dr Philip in this affair, but he was much too ignorant of the real state of things amongst the Griqua to effect anything that would turn out good or useful, and we are at this time heavily suffering the effects of his improper conduct.[59]

Waterboer discredits Philip by juxtaposing his own authority as 'native informant' and the outsider Philip's well-intentioned ignorance and impropriety. Waterboer thus authorises *A Short Account* by claiming not only to be law-abiding, orderly and benevolent (in contrast to the old *kaptyns* and the Bergenaars), but also to be the authentic voice of the Griqua people (in contrast to Philip).[60]

The narrative of *A Short Account* is structured by Waterboer's struggle to secure law and order against all manifestations of lawlessness. Central to this struggle for Waterboer is the imperative to consolidate his own authority as the single sovereign leader of the Griqua nation, and as such, to exercise a monopoly on state violence. Waterboer recounts how in order to eliminate competitors to his title as *kaptyn* of Griquatown, he was obliged to suppress Bergenaar opposition in a series of violent confrontations, including his defeat with the help of Cornelius Kok II of a large group of Bergenaars and his seizure of 4,000 of their cattle at Sluitel's

Poort near Fauresmith in July 1824; the Bergenaars' unsuccessful revenge attack on Griquatown while Waterboer was away in May 1825; and most damagingly, the second and much larger Bergenaar attack on Griquatown in July 1827, which was only repulsed after twelve houses had been burnt down, and 'all the pewter plates, Tea Pots [and] Copper ornaments of my People [had been] melted down into balls'.[61] In all these conflicts, Waterboer presents his own exercise of violence as the legitimate defence of political order, whereas Bergenaar violence is illegal and threatens such order. Waterboer's anecdote about melting down pewter plates and teapots into bullets is but one example in A Short Account of his obsession with ammunition. Another is his complaint that Melvill left 'Griquatown for the Cape [. . .] with all our ammunition'[62] in April 1825, thus providing a clear opportunity for the Bergenaars to attack soon afterwards. As the legitimate political authority on the northern frontier, Waterboer believes he should always have the exclusive monopoly on violence in order to guarantee order. The stark alternative – precipitated by Melvill withdrawing Waterboer's ammunition – is the kind of frontier anarchy epitomised by the Bergenaar attack. The exercise of state violence for Waterboer is expressed not only by putting down external enemies; it also extends to enforcing breaches of the law by his own citizens. In the most detailed and precise passage in A Short Account, Waterboer explains how he honoured the Griqua constitution by enforcing its laws against theft and murder in the case of eleven Bergenaars, who raided a Coranna kraal within the Griquatown captaincy, 'and shot one Woman dead and did other mischief'.[63] Having sanctioned the arrest of six of the accused, Waterboer records that they were tried and found guilty on 7 May 1827; sentenced to death on 8 May; and executed on 16 May. Although his execution of the six Bergenaars (including Hendrick Hendricks's brother) provoked counter-violence in the third and most destructive Bergenaar attack on Griquatown, and his severity in the matter led to a flood of complaints to the landdrosts against his rule, Waterboer concludes his account confident that he has done 'nothing but what is just, and [I] am not ashamed or afraid to have my conduct brought to daylight'.[64]

In certain respects, A Short Account fits Fanon's 'assimilated phase' of the native writer responding to colonialism, as Waterboer 'gives proof that he has assimilated the culture of the occupying power. His writings correspond point by point with those of his opposite numbers in the mother country'.[65] In material terms, he rejects economic subsistence based upon cattle-raiding and plunder in favour of settled agriculture; in political terms, he endorses the political forms of democratically elected government and centralised state power; and in legal terms, he embraces the rule of law, including its violent enforcement. In certain respects, the line of influence is strikingly direct, as Waterboer enacts the prescriptions handed down by his European 'opposite numbers'. For example, Campbell's exhortation in 1820 to 'amputate or cut off a corrupted member' of the political body, specifically those 'men of low lives [. . .] who have done acts of cruelty against the poor innocent Bush people', is given expression in Waterboer's execution of the six Bergenaars in 1827 for their crimes against the Coranna. Waterboer deflects accusations of misconduct against the Griqua by attributing them to the old kaptyns and the Bergenaars – he accepts Campbell and Thompson's criticisms that the Griqua murder and plunder the 'Bushmen', but blames the Bergenaars for such predations, and claims to be the true protector of the 'Bushmen'. The close correspondence between these European narratives and representations and Waterboer's *Short Account* are further reinforced by Waterboer's repeated insistence that the enemies of Griqua nation-formation are not the colonisers (missionaries, government agents or 'Boors'); rather, the rise of the Griqua nation is frustrated by adversaries who are themselves members of the colonised – the old *kaptyns* and the Bergenaars. For these reasons, within the context of anti-colonial writing, there might be a case for dismissing Waterboer's *Short Account* as the paradigmatic history of the sell-out. However, there are at least two reasons for qualifying this judgement, and both relate to how Waterboer represents his relationship to missionary patronage. First, his description of how his captaincy emerged – 'the people resident at Griqua Town came to the resolution of choosing a Captain for themselves, and the universal voice of the people falls on me' – makes no reference to the tutelage of the missionaries; Waterboer represents the Griqua people as a collective capable of democratic judgement in electing him leader.[66] Second, in rejecting the intervention of Philip in 1825 because he was 'much too ignorant of the real state of things amongst the Griqua', Waterboer claims the authority of witness and participant. Waterboer's principal binary in *A Short Account* between Europe/Christianity/Law/Order and Africa/godlessness/lawlessness/anarchy is thus interrupted, as he insists upon his own authority-as-Griqua as against Philip's interference-as-outsider.

## HENDRICK HENDRICKS'S 'OPPRESSIONS OF THE GRIQUAS'

The principal outcome of Philip's intervention in Griqua affairs in 1825 was the establishment of a new Griqua captaincy at Philippolis under Adam Kok II a year later.[67] Philip persuaded Kok and his followers, as well as a sizeable faction of Bergenaars, to relocate to Philippolis, which was the site of a small mission station for the Khoi. Kok was the official *kaptyn*, but the politics of Philippolis were more substantially influenced by Kok's son-in-law Hendrick Hendricks, secretary to the Philippolis government from 1827–50. Like Waterboer, Hendricks was educated in the Griquatown mission school, but he was more closely tied to the traditional *kaptyns* and was prominent in the Bergenaar uprisings of the early 1820s. Unlike Waterboer, Hendricks was suspicious of the missionaries, and he readily reverted to stock-raiding and ivory-trading when given the opportunity. His antipathy towards Waterboer hardened when his brother was executed as one of the six Griqua convicted of murdering the Coranna in May 1827.

'Oppressions of the Griquas' was published as a letter to the editor in the Cape Town newspaper *The South African Commercial Advertiser* on 29 September 1830. Although it was signed from 'Oppressed Griqua', Philippolis, it bears the characteristics of Hendricks's other writings and the scholarly consensus attributes it to him.[68] The *Advertiser*'s editor John Fairbairn announced the publication of the letter in the

22 September 1830 edition of the paper, framing the aspirations of the Griqua in terms of the assimilationist ideals of Cape liberalism:

> We mentioned in our last the receipt of a letter from an oppressed Griqua, and we have since ascertained that it is the composition and in the hand writing of an actual living Griqua, of pure descent from the original Natives of this part of Africa [. . .] It is the first which we have received from that quarter [. . .] When men begin to write and reason like this Griqua, it is full time to drop the Christian name of Savage, which we are accustomed to use when speaking of them. Let them once get a taste of our Civil Institutions and Laws, let the Arts and Sciences in amongst them, and they will soon become our faithful Allies and valuable Customers, if not integral portions of our community.[69]

Fairbairn's announcement echoes the optimistic, developmental narrative of the missionaries, but on the evidence of Hendricks's letter, credits the Griqua with the ability to complete the fourth stage of the journey to civilisation: the Griqua's demonstrable ability to 'write and reason' convinces Fairbairn that with the appropriate exposure to British 'Civil Institutions and Laws', and 'Arts and Sciences', they can take the final step from settled agriculture to commercial society.

Hendricks's opening rhetorical strategy is to constitute his reader(s) – both the *Advertiser's* editor and the newspaper's readers – as fair-minded Englishmen committed to justice and equality for all contending parties on the frontiers of Colony. At the outset, he addresses the editor as 'a good friend to all oppressed men', and then extends the same tribute to the King of England ('we do not believe that the King knows how it fares with us in this country, otherwise he would take care of us') and to the Governor of the Cape ('we have heard that he takes the part of the oppressed').[70] In the concluding paragraph, Hendricks asks that his readers act upon their humane convictions and intervene on the side of the oppressed of the frontier: 'Pray, Sir, please tell the Governor to come hear, or otherwise to send an Englishman [. . .] Sir, you must advise us and tell us whether the King of England will be offended if I write him a letter about these things'.[71] Hendricks thus constitutes a sympathetic readership that includes the editor of the *Advertiser*, English-speaking liberals at the Cape, the Governor at the Cape and (potentially) the King of England. There is, however, more to Hendricks's mode of address than flattery. By imputing egalitarian values to his readers, he suggests that the standards of justice in England be applied to the Griqua. He asks, 'Are we not also creatures who are destined by the same God of us all to remain on the earth?'[72] And then pointedly asks further whether the kinds of changes to colonial boundaries to accommodate 'Boer' incursions into the territory of the 'Hottentots' would be countenanced in England: 'I will ask you, Sir, whether the people of England also alter often their boundary lines when their children grow up and their cattle increase?' The key difference between England and the Cape frontier, Hendricks answers, is that 'in England will not be found Hottentots bordering on it so that they can take land from them'.[73]

In representing the Griqua, Hendricks emphasises their prior claim to the land of the Cape: 'The spot where the Cape stands and all about it has been the land of our forefathers; there they have pastured their cattle and sheep in peace and freedom'.[74] Responding to the charge that the Griqua had seized 'Bushmen' land, Hendricks retorts, '[The Boers] say it is Bosjemen land and therefore they have a right to occupy that country. I also say that it is Bosjemen land. But, Sir, where is not Bosjemen land?'[75] Having established that neither Boer nor Griqua land claims precede those of the 'Bosjemen', Hendricks concludes that 'we have as good a right to that land as the Boers', and further, that if the contest over land is to be resolved, they 'ought to restore first our country and that of the Bosjemen, and then they can talk about the land'.[76] Complementing Hendricks's insistence upon the legitimacy of Griqua land rights is his claim that the Griqua have used the land in precise accordance with British wishes. Again he introduces his argument with a rhetorical question: 'Sir, is it true that it is the will of the King of England that all the people in the world shall build houses and plough and sow and make gardens?'[77] Assuming an affirmative answer, Hendricks claims that the Griqua have obediently 'taken fifty farms in hand, have led water out, have ploughed, sowed and made gardens'.[78] What has prevented them from making even more impressive progress along this route has been the seizure of their newly cultivated land by the Boers. As a result, their progress has been blocked, and the real danger (to the Griqua and their British protectors alike) now exists that the Griqua might be forced to revert to savage ways:

> We are accustomed to clothing, and receive many other things from the Colony; we shall become very savage and wild in the interior, without clothing and other things; but, Sir, we think it is better to be naked and free than to wear clothes and be oppressed.[79]

On the awkward subject of the treatment of the 'Bushmen', Hendricks readily concedes that 'our doings have not always been good' and 'we have cause to be ashamed of some things, we must improve, we are still half savages and not so as civilised men'.[80] But in their defence, he raises two points: first, their enemies exaggerate the scale of their crimes ('our black spot is made tenfold larger than it is'), and second, they have been instructed in violence against the 'Bushmen' by the white settlers: 'We have learnt many things from them that are not good. Some of us have made in former times commandos with them and shot Caffers and Bosjesmens.'[81]

Hendricks locates the place of the Griqua within colonial society in relation to a number of different groups. In relation to the British government at the Cape, the Griqua are supplicants dependent upon the benevolent paternalism of their rulers (although Hendricks identifies inconsistency and hypocrisy in British colonial discourse). Second, in relation to the 'Christians' and the 'Boers' (Hendricks uses the terms interchangeably), the Griqua are locked in an unequal struggle over land and cattle. Third, in relation to the 'Bosjemans', the 'Caffer' and the 'Bechuana', the Griqua have a contradictory relationship. On the one hand, the Griqua share with these other indigenous groups the experience of being forced off their land by 'Boers': 'had it not been for the Christian men we would be to this day in [the Cape]'.[82] But on the other hand, the Griqua are more powerful than these other indigenous groups, and they have been obliged by Boer/Christian expansion to seize their land in turn. For example, Hendricks argues, 'if we go [into Bechuana country] we must do the same which the Christians always do; we must seize [*afvat* – in original] their country'.[83] In his final paragraph, Hendricks shifts from the history of the Griqua people to the most urgent political challenge facing them in 1830, namely the illegal occupation of Griqua land by Boer farmers, and he concludes his letter by providing the names of eight Boer farmers he believes the Cape government should evict from Griqua land.

As Hendricks's text is substantially shorter than Waterboer's account, I would like to flesh it out by referring briefly to a couple of subsequent occasions when he reflected upon Griqua history. In the minutes of a three-way meeting at Colesberg on 31 December 1842 between the British governor of the eastern province of the Cape Colony, the Griqua chief Adam Kok and a Boer farmer claiming rights over Griqua land, the following interjection from Hendricks is recorded:

> The Farmers say the Griquas now occupy the Bushmen's land, who was it that drove us there? Let the names Kaapstad, Stellenbosch, Tulbagh [towns established by the Dutch], give the answer, it was the Dutch people who sent us forward; it was not until late years – until the English name of Colesberg was heard in the land, that the Griquas had rest [. . .] It was not until England put her hand on the land, there was any resting place for the Griquas, and *never, never will there be security for the Griquas, and the black nations of Africa, until England continues to hold her hand over the whole country*.[84]

Hendricks repeats here the essentials of his 1830 history of colonial occupation: the Dutch seized 'the Bushmen's land' and imposed Dutch place names, and only when England 'put her hand on the land', and 'continues to hold her hand over the whole country', can the 'black nations of Africa' feel secure from further Dutch/Boer incursions. On his second return to Griqua history – in a deposition made on 5 February 1863 to the landdrost of Fauresmith, who was investigating land claims in the Orange Free State – Hendricks was less concerned with the competing settler powers (Boer and Briton) than with refuting Waterboer's claims to legitimacy. Hendricks insists – *contra* Waterboer's *Short Account* – that the blame for the conflicts in the Griquatown captaincy from 1816 rested not with the old *kaptyns* but with the missionaries. According to Hendricks, 'differences arose between [Adam] Kok, the Chief of Griqua Town, and the missionary residing there. The difference arose about punishing criminals guilty of capital crimes, whom [Adam] Kok wished to have punished, and against which the missionary objected'.[85] The missionaries succeeded in frustrating Kok's attempts to impose his version of frontier justice, but the cost (according to Hendricks) was increased lawlessness. The missionaries then compounded their mistake by favouring Waterboer at the expense of Adam Kok: 'As the missionaries sided with Waterboer and against Adam Kok [. . .] they contrived to effect that the British Government recognized Waterboer as Chief [in Griquatown].'[86] Of some consolation was the fact that Adam Kok was recognised by the British government as chief at Philippolis independent of Waterboer's sovereignty.

How does Hendricks write back to the colonial representations of the Griqua?

Like Waterboer, Hendricks mimics the words of the coloniser, echoing Fairbairn's claims about the superiority of English justice, accepting Lichtenstein's characterisation of the Griqua as 'half savage', and declaring that the Griqua have followed the King of England's prescribed journey to civilisation by building houses, ploughing fields and making gardens. But more striking than these traces of mimicry are the many instances of resistance to colonial discourse. If Waterboer fits loosely Fanon's 'assimilated phase' of the native intellectual, Hendricks's defiant words place him (with qualifications) in Fanon's second phase, in which the native intellectual questions the colonial master's script and asserts the pre-colonial rights of the indigene.[87] Hendricks might strategically concede that the Griqua remain 'half savages', but he insists that before the arrival of the Dutch, Africans occupied the land of the Cape in 'peace and freedom'. This is not as elaborate as the idealised images of pre-colonial societies generated by later generations of African nationalist intellectuals, but it nonetheless challenges European myths of Savage Africa. Second, Hendricks's refusal to accept the negative stereotype of pre-colonial Africa is complemented by his refusal to parrot the positive characterisation of the European coloniser. Most obviously, he criticises the Dutch settlers for murdering 'Caffers and Bosjemens' in their conquest of land and cattle, but he also questions the role of the missionaries and the British colonial government. In his 1830 letter, the 'Christians' are indistinguishable from the 'Boers' in his descriptions of how African land was plundered, and in his 1863 deposition, he blames the missionaries for interfering in Griqua politics, and precipitating damaging and enduring divisions. With his principal concern being to flatter and thus win the support of the British, Hendricks's criticisms of them are more subtle, but in pointing to the hypocrisy of colonial policy with respect to African land rights, his anger is unambiguous: in England, the laws of private property are honoured because 'in England will not be found Hottentots bordering on it so that they can take land from them'. As Griqua power waned, however, Hendricks swallowed whatever anger he might have felt, and (like Waterboer) paid obsequious tributes to the British colonial government. Third, we have noted that Hendricks flags up the Griqua's obedient journey from hunter-gatherer to settled agriculturalists. But more significant is his insistence that the journey can be reversed. For Hendricks, the Griqua in 1830 retain some choice: they can either continue to follow the European road to civilisation, or if the British do not protect them from Boer violence, they can revert to pre-colonial ways of life: 'we think it is better to be naked and free than to wear clothes and be oppressed'. It is an index of the speed and scale of colonial expansion into the Southern African interior that Hendricks has given up on this latter choice in his later writings: in 1842, he is limited to imploring the British for protection against the Boers, and in 1863, he directs his energies to internecine politics, as he seeks to discredit Waterboer.

## THE GRIQUA AND THE POST-APARTHEID NATION

Once the Griqua (or, more precisely, their Khoisan ancestors) had lost their land, rejected the fate of exploited labour within the colonial economy and migrated to the colonial border-zone, the colonial writers scripted a specific destiny and specific choices for them: they were savage bands of hunter-gatherers, who would progress under the tutelage of missionaries and ultimately form a Christian nation living by settled agriculture. Should they fail to follow this trajectory, they could either relinquish their independence and work as servants for white farmers, or could maintain their autonomy and migrate further north and east beyond the settler polities. It was in the face of this prescribed destiny and these stark choices that Waterboer and Hendricks – to adapt Marx's words – wrote their own histories, 'not of their own free will; not under circumstances they themselves chose, but under the given and inherited circumstances with which they were directly confronted'.[88] In the context of these formidable material and discursive pressures, Waterboer (substantially) repeated and Hendricks (partially) subverted the coloniser's version of Griqua history. The differences between Waterboer and Hendricks's histories, however, were accompanied by important similarities: they both appeal strategically to the purported humanity and justice of their British rulers, and they both readily acknowledge the role of the Griqua in the violent plunder of the Khoisan, although they deny personal responsibility, with Waterboer blaming the Bergenaars, and Hendricks the malign influence of Boer commandos.

How have Griqua histories been retold in relation to the new official history of post-apartheid South Africa?[89] South Africa's national historical narrative is laid down in the Preamble of the Constitution:

We, the people of South Africa
Recognise the injustices of our past;
Honour those who suffered for justice and freedom in our land;
Respect those who have worked to build and develop our country; which
Belongs to all who live in it, unified in our diversity.[90]

This history also goes through four stages: from (1) a past of injustices and suffering, to (2) a struggle for justice and freedom, to (3) a process of building and developing, and finally, to (4) a present characterised by 'unity in our diversity'. Specific efforts have been made by the ANC to incorporate the Griqua within this master narrative, most notably in Nelson Mandela's speech at the inauguration of the National Council of Traditional Leaders in Cape Town on 18 April 1997, where he paid tribute to 'the Griquas, whose long resistance to dispossession forged leaders of the stature of Waterboer, Le Fleur and Adam Kok'.[91] Mandela's generous account of Griqua anti-colonial resistance was repeated by cabinet minister Ronnie Kasrils in a 1999 speech before parliament, in which he praised 'the indigenous African people [who] struggled bravely against colonial invasion', and then listed the heroes of these struggles:

There is the epic 100 years war by the Xhosa people under the generalship of Makanda and Maqoma; the ingenuity of the Sotho under Moshweshwe; the struggle of the Griqua under Adam Kok; the astonishing defeat of the British by

Cetshwayo's Zulu impis at Isandlwana, and the brave resistance of Sekhukhune of the Pedi, Galishewe of the Tswana and of Venda kings such as Makhado.[92]

Framed by this unifying national narrative in which the Griqua have been allo-cated a place as worthy anti-colonial warriors, Griqua histories have been rewritten in a number of different ways. For Griqua political activists, the strategic necessity of conforming to the ANC version of history has seen a strong emphasis on the Khoisan origins of the Griqua, and upon their centuries of oppression under colonial rule and apartheid. For example, the Griqua National Conference (GNC)[93] in their memorandum to the United Nations Working Group on Indigenous Populations on 27 July 1995 open with a short history of the Griqua, which declares that the Griqua 'evolved from the semi-nomadic aboriginal group of people with a common identity, culture and language essentially known as the Khoi-Khoi'.[94] As a result of colonial expansion, 'displaced remnant clans withdrew from Colonial subjugation and oppression and came to be known and united as the Griqua'.[95] A more detailed version of this kind of Griqua history is provided by Johan Cronje's *The Griqua of the Northern Cape. Land Ownership, Identity and Leadership* (2006). Commissioned and published by the Sol Plaatje Trust in Kimberley, and funded by the National Lotteries Board Trust Fund, Cronje's study is based on written sources and 100 oral interviews with Griqua informants in Campbell and Griquatown, and sets out to address state policies affecting the Griqua. To contextualise present political chal-lenges, Cronje supplies a summary of nineteenth-century Griqua history, but is silent about Griqua violence against the 'Bushmen', and concludes in terms that unconsciously echo the nineteenth-century travellers like Burchell that

> [t]he alienation of [Griqua] land created even more serious problems as the mis-sionaries, the Cape and the British authorities, in succession, did not allow the Griquas the opportunity to make the transition from a nomadic people to that of settled pastoralists in a normal and progressive manner.[96]

Although Cronje diminishes uncomfortable aspects of the Griqua past, he is consci-entious in drawing attention to the specifics of Griqua poverty now, citing the grim social indicators of the Griqua inhabitants of Griquatown and Campbell.[97]

With respect to the popular historical consciousness of Griqua communities, the articulation of the ANC's national narrative and the Griqua's own histories are less synchronous. Anthropologist Linda Waldman emphasises both the importance of the oral transmission of the Griqua past[98] and the resilience of specifically Griqua histories (in opposition to national history). In the case of Griquatown, for example, Waldman notes:

> The period of historical glory, the famous leaders – Adam Kok, Andries Waterboer, Nicolaas Waterboer – and the products of their leadership, form significant markers [. . .] Such histories allowed the Griqua to retain a sense of pride and [. . .] cushioned the experience of being classified coloured and its associated deprivation vis-à-vis whites. This history remains essential to the

people who identify themselves as Griqua in Griquatown. Tourists frequently visit the *galgboom* (hanging tree) where Andries Waterboer used to hang dissidents.[99]

ANC national history has a similarly marginal function for the Eastern Cape Griqua community of Kranshoek. But the Griqua history of Kranshoek is different to the Griqua history of Griquatown. In Kranshoek (as in Griquatown), the community retains elements of the Griqua past particular to their own community, and accordingly, in Kranshoek the later Griqua leader A. A. S. le Fleur (1867–1941),[100] who played a fundamental role in the founding of the settlement, is commemorated. The anthropologist Rumi Umino observes that the *Volksgeskiedenis* (people's history) taught in the Griqua Church catechism involves 'intensive instruction in the important basic segments of the *geskiedenis*, including hymns, dates, and locations of certain events related to A. A. S. le Fleur'.[101]

Beyond histories by Griqua political groups, commissioned oral histories and the research findings of anthropologists, there have also been several literary returns to Griqua history. All but one wrestle with the tension between the specifics of Griqua history and post-apartheid national history. Not strictly 'literary', William Dicey's travelogue *Borderline* (2004) describes a canoe journey down the Orange River, and includes a visit to Griquatown (and specifically the *galgboom*). Dicey is moved by his knowledge of the Griqua past and his encounters with the Griqua present to imagine an alternative South African history:

> And yet what is the story of the Griquas, I thought, if not a story of coloured people making history. And not just their own history, but an alternative course the whole country might have followed. How different South Africa might have been had the Griqua managed to defend their multi-ethnic state against the advancing whites, a state based not so much on the racial exclusion of the Colony as on the frontier ethos of absorption and inclusion.[102]

In Dicey's reflections, the Griqua states of the nineteenth century are thus affirmed as substantial political achievements, even precursors of the rainbow nation, that were sabotaged by colonial racism and apartheid. Similar themes are also to the fore in Scott Balson's novel *Children of the Mist* (2007), in which the retelling of Griqua history is filtered through three characters: Lucas, an old Griqua, tells the history of the Griqua to Marie, a young white farm girl he rescues from a storm in the foothills of the Drakensberg in the 1930s; and Marie in turn tells Lucas's history to her granddaughter Janet, 'a pretty child with long flowing blonde hair and bright blue eyes'[103] in the post-apartheid present. Marie's history favours missionary perspectives (especially Moffat's), and invents numerous details to fill gaps in the historical archive. For example, Anderson is described teaching Hendricks (son of a 'coloured father and Korana mother') and rescuing Waterboer (a 'young Bushman'[104]). But Balson does not flinch from describing both colonial violence and violence perpetrated by the Griqua against the 'Bushmen' and each other (the *galgboom* gets a particularly lurid couple of paragraphs).[105] Like Dicey, Balson claims a prefigurative status for the Griqua – Campbell in his first impressions of Klaarwater is 'immediately struck by the multi-racial make-up of the community [. . .] This was truly the rainbow nation we talk about today'.[106] But even more so than Dicey, the tone of his thinly mediated popular history is nostalgic, even elegiac. Whereas Dicey and Balson see the Griqua 'multi-racial' state of the nineteenth century as a brave social experiment defeated by colonial racists, the protagonist of Zoë Wicomb's novel David's Story (2000) journeys from one Griqua community in Namaqualand to another in Kokstad in an effort to reconstruct a version of Griqua history in accord with his own anti-apartheid commitments. For Wicomb's David (like the people of Kranshoek), the pivotal Griqua leader is not a Kok or Waterboer or Hendricks, but rather Le Fleur, and David's determination to inscribe himself within a continuous tradition of Griqua anti-colonial/anti-segregation/anti-apartheid struggle therefore originates principally in the late nineteenth century. David's fascination with the Griqua past also extends to the eighteenth-century Saartje Baartman, but by leapfrogging over the founding decades of the Griqua nation written up by Waterboer and Hendricks, he (like his political leaders Mandela and Kasrils) evades the questions they raise about Griqua collusion with colonial violence.

The only post-apartheid novel to revisit the Griqua past without referring directly to the ANC's national history is A. H. M. Scholtz's Afrikaans novel A Place Called Vatmaar (1995), set in the first decades of the twentieth century in an imagined community on the outskirts of the Kimberley diamond fields. The old Griqua character Ta Vuurmaak tells the local children the early history of the Griqua:

> We, the Griquas and the Bushmen, are not people, the white people said. And they hunted us down like animals and stormed into our homes and killed us if we were a danger to them [. . . O]ur ancestors had respect for our women and never took a women against her will. She had to be taken through a celebration. We never stole the fruits of a woman. As I have told you, before the white men came we did not even have a word for stealing [. . . T]he Englishmen were very cunning, my children. They sent what they call men of God – their missionaries – to get us to leave our God [. . .] Then they taught us we should not steal – after they had first taught us about stealing [. . .] After many droughts our Big Brother, who had been given the new name of Captain, had become a Christian together with all his people [. . . T]he Big Brothers of our forefathers, their names have been washed away by time. But the new names of the captains, the oppressors and the sell-outs, are Andries le Fleur, Andries Waterboer, Adam Kok, Pieter Davids, and there are others too.[107]

The character Ta Vuurmaak's history of the Griqua repeats several elements of Hendricks's history: a common suffering along with the 'Bushmen' of colonial violence; a pre-colonial African world characterised by 'peace and freedom'; and experiences of hypocrisy and betrayal at the hands of the missionaries. But Ta Vuurmaak also deviates from Hendricks's history in that he adds humane gender relations to his image of pre-colonial African society, and in a more substantial deviation, he describes the kaptyns of the original Griqua factions as 'oppressors and sell-outs'.

Scholtz's narrative technique is sophisticated, and Ta Vuurmaak is not an entirely reliable witness. However, his account captures the contradictions of early Griqua history by juxtaposing the Griqua suffering colonial violence (hunted down like animals), and colluding with colonial rule (Waterboer and Kok alike cast as sell-outs and oppressors). What *Vatmaar* also points to is the inadequacy of 'nation' as a term for describing the Griqua community imagined in the novel. Social relationships include instances of communal solidarity, as well as acts of betrayal, but the people of Vatmaar never constitute a 'national community'. Rather, they form a loose assemblage of resilient characters who are sometimes united, sometimes divided, in the struggle against poverty. Tellingly, the most sympathetic characters – Suzan and Kenny – leave Vatmaar at the end of the novel in search of a more materially secure existence elsewhere in South Africa.

## CONCLUSION

The absence of any fit between Griqua communal identity and the category of the nation in the novel *Vatmaar* should be understood in the context of a long-standing dissonance between the terms 'Griqua' and 'nation'. Since the nineteenth century, nationhood on the western model has been an aspiration imposed upon the Griqua, with many Griqua leaders internalising the aspiration and pursuing Griqua nationhood with great fervour. But the achievement of Griqua nationhood has been frustrated by many factors, beginning with the model of Khoi politics inherited by the Griqua in the eighteenth century. Richard Elphick has argued that Khoi polities typically had dual leadership, which was a 'precondition for the splitting of tribes',[108] and that stability resided not in alliances between tribes but in feuds, since the 'Khoikhoi changed their allies freely but tended to keep the same enemies for decades'.[109] Waldman extends Elphick's analysis of the Khoi to Griqua politics, and notes the persistence of broken alliances, feuds, strategic coalitions and further splits. Waterboer's *Short Account* bears abundant testimony to such factionalism, and in the nineteenth century the Griqua pattern of fragmentation was perpetuated:

> the failure to amalgamate [into a unified nation . . .] is located in leaders' tendency to *trek* in search of autonomy and independence, and in the historical structures of Griqua governance which allowed a *Kaptein's* powers to be balanced, or even surpassed, by that of his deputy.[110]

In the twentieth and twenty-first centuries, this history of splitting has continued to define Griqua political identity, with internecine skirmishing alternating with strategic but short-term appeals for Griqua unity. As a result, the Griqua-as-political-community bear very little resemblance to the models of the nation forged in the northern hemisphere. The Griqua's absence of an agreed narrative of historical origins (with venerated founding fathers), or of an accepted set of unifying national symbols, or of political representatives with broad legitimacy, have confounded national leaders in Southern Africa, from British colonial officials at the Cape in the nineteenth century, to National Party and ANC leaders in South Africa in the twentieth and twenty-first centuries.

Waterboer and Hendricks's descendants have struggled to assert their distinctive histories and political identities in relation to the state-generated, post-apartheid discourses of nationhood. Their political marginalisation is compounded by their economic plight, as they survive on the margins of the post-apartheid economy. According to Waldman, in Griquatown 'they earn a bit as farm workers, occasionally they migrate to find work elsewhere, they scrounge from tourists [. . .] and, of course, they claim government pensions'.[111] They are far from alone in struggling to survive in the post-apartheid economy, and indeed, their access to government pensions gives them an advantage over the many migrant workers in South Africa. However, their contested histories and current political difficulties signal the need to look beyond the nation as a form of collective identity, and to register the complexity and resilience of alternative forms of community.

With this perspective in mind, it is worth asking finally whether this case study of the Griqua has broader resonances. Since the eighteenth century, how many other 'failed' nations like the Griqua have floundered in the wake of the global expansion of capitalism and the associated export of northern-hemisphere models of nations-as-imagined-communities? For millions of people on the receiving end of what Marx called 'primitive accumulation',[112] and what David Harvey calls 'the new imperialism',[113] the transmission of such models of nationhood has enforced difficult choices: to abandon older forms of political community; to assimilate with larger (probably national) collectives; or to cling to residual or emergent varieties of non-national assemblages. National elites in the 'developing world' might indeed 'pirate' northern models of nationhood (Anderson), or produce the 'most creative results of the nationalist imagination' by positing their *'difference'* from western models of nationhood (Chatterjee). But their nationalist projects, including pre-eminently the generating of national histories, drown out alternative (historical and literary) narratives of community, and obscure the processes of economic exploitation.

## NOTES

1. See, for example, Penn, *The Forgotten*; Legassick, *The Politics*; Ross, *Adam Kok's*; and Schoeman, *The Griqua Captaincy*.
2. This is not an exhaustive list. I have selected these particular accounts to convey the variety and range of representations of the Griqua. With these criteria to the fore, I have therefore not analysed the writings of two important figures – Andries Stockenström (1792–1864) and John Philip – who played major roles in Griqua politics. Stockenström and Philip repeat substantially the same versions of Griqua history and society as earlier observers like Anderson and Somerville.
3. Quoted in Moffat, *Missionary*, pp. 194–5.
4. To highlight that this reading of Griqua progress is ideological, it is useful to contrast Nancy Jacobs's recent environmental history of the northern Cape, which differentiates the communities of the region into three economic/linguistic groups: San groups who survived by foraging; Khoikhoi groups who kept livestock, but did not cultivate; and Bantu-speaking agro-pastoralists, 'whose men herded cattle, sheep and goats, while the women

cultivated with iron tools' (*Environment*, p. 32). Jacobs stresses that there was no inevitable progression from foraging to agro-pastoralism.

5. Somerville, *Narrative*, pp. 135–7.
6. Ibid. pp. 99–100.
7. Ibid. p. 183.
8. Ibid. p 183.
9. Ibid. p. 183.
10. Ibid. pp. 183–4.
11. Ibid. p. 184.
12. Borcherds, *An Auto-Biographical*, p. 116.
13. Ibid. p. 117.
14. Arbousset and Daumas, *A Narrative*, p. 19.
15. Lichtenstein, *Travels*, Vol. 1, p. 144. German original, Lichtenstein, *Reisen*, Vol. 1, pp. 186–7.
16. Lichtenstein, *Travels*, Vol. 1, p. 302.
17. Ibid. p. 303.
18. Ibid. p. 304.
19. Ibid. p. 305.
20. Ibid. p. 324.
21. Ibid. p. 326.
22. Ibid. p. 327. German original, Lichtenstein, *Reisen*, Vol. 2, p. 423.
23. Hegel, *Hegel's Political*, pp. 161, 21.
24. Burchell, *Travels*, Vol. 1, p. 361.
25. Ibid. p. 358.
26. Ibid. p. 358.
27. Ibid. p. 361.
28. Ibid. p. 363.
29. Campbell, *Journal*, pp. 167–8.
30. Quoted in Schoeman, *The Mission*, p. 105.
31. Ibid. p. 110.
32. Ibid. p. 110.
33. Campbell, *Travels*, pp. 242–3.
34. Ibid. p. 243.
35. For a nuanced discussion of Moffat, see Elbourne, *Blood*, pp. 318–24.
36. Moffat, *Missionary*, p. ii.
37. Ibid. p. ii.
38. Ibid. pp. iii–iv.
39. Ibid. pp. 200–1.
40. Quoted in Legassick, *The Politics*, p. 250.
41. For an account of the Battle of Dithakong, see Hartley, 'The Battle'. Hartley discusses Thompson's role as observer, pp. 398–400.
42. Thompson, *Travels*, Vol. 1, p. 75.
43. Ibid. p. 76.
44. Ibid. p. 77.
45. Ibid. p. 77.
46. Ibid. p. 78.
47. Waterboer, *A Short Account*, p. 2.
48. Ibid. p. 3.
49. Ibid. pp. 3–4.
50. Ibid. p. 4.
51. Ibid. p. 4

52. Ibid. pp. 4–5.
53. Ibid. p. 6.
54. Ibid. p. 7.
55. Ibid. p. 14.
56. Ibid. p. 19.
57. Ibid. p. 21.
58. Ibid. p. 26.
59. Ibid. pp. 14–15.
60. It is important to note that Waterboer did not remain consistent in his criticism of Philip, and subsequently formed a close alliance with Wright and Philip. For example, in an 1837 letter to Wright, Waterboer declared, 'We owe everything to the blessing of God upon the labours of the missionaries in the service of the London Missionary Society. We were no people when the missionaries found us, and it was under these circumstances we became a people. We had no country of our own when the missionaries came among us, but were wandering about as fugitives without a settled abode; and it was the missionaries that found a country for us, and persuaded us to settle on it and cultivate the land' (Great Britain, *Report*, p. 624). For a letter from Waterboer to Philip in December 1832 expressing similar sentiments, see Legassick, *The Politics*, pp. 242–3.
61. Waterboer, *A Short Account*, p. 26.
62. Ibid. p. 11.
63. Ibid. p. 23.
64. Ibid. p. 27.
65. Fanon, *The Wretched*, p. 178.
66. Waterboer's argument that both pre-colonial and more democratic political structures continued to influence Griqua state formation is supported by a number of recent historians. See Carstens, 'Opting'; Ross, 'Griqua'; Lye, 'The Emergence'; and Kinsman, 'Populists'.
67. For a summary of the competing accounts of the founding of the Griqua captaincy at Philippolis, which includes extensive quotations from the primary documents, see Schoeman, *The Griqua*, pp. 39–59. See too Keegan, *Colonial*, pp. 170–84.
68. See Schoeman, *The Griqua*, pp. 65–9.
69. 'Editorial', p. 2.
70. Hendricks, 'Oppressions', p. 2.
71. Ibid. p. 2.
72. Ibid. p. 2.
73. Ibid. p. 2.
74. Ibid. p. 2.
75. Ibid. p. 2.
76. Ibid. p. 2.
77. Ibid. p. 2.
78. Ibid. p. 2.
79. Ibid. p. 2.
80. Ibid. p. 2.
81. Ibid. p. 2.
82. Ibid. p. 2.
83. Ibid. p. 2.
84. Chase, *The Natal*, Vol. 2, p. 270.
85. Lindley, *Adamantia*, p. 36.
86. Ibid. p. 37.
87. Fanon, *The Wretched*, pp. 178–9.
88. The original refers to 'men making history'. See Marx, *The Eighteenth Brumaire*, p. 146.

89. I have written about the Griqua in post-apartheid South Africa in relation to academic and political discourse in 'The First', and in relation to land rights in 'Theorizing'.
90. Republic of South Africa, Constitutional Assembly, 'The Constitution'.
91. Mandela, 'Address'.
92. Kasrils, 'Speech'.
93. For summaries and analyses of the competing Griqua political and cultural organisations, see Waldman, *The Griqua*; Besten, 'Transformation'; and Kitching and Meiring, *A Conceptual*.
94. Griqua National Conference, p. 1.
95. Ibid. p. 1.
96. Cronje, *The Griqua*, p. 55.
97. Ibid. pp. 46–8.
98. See Waldman, 'The Past'. Also of interest in this context are Legassick's efforts at practising 'applied history' to support land claims in the Northern Cape by Baster families closely related to the Griqua. See Legassick, 'Reflections', pp. 129–33.
99. Waldman, 'Klaar'.
100. On A. A. S. le Fleur, see Edgar and Saunders, 'A. A. S. le Fleur'.
101. Umino, 'A Backyard', p. 37.
102. Dicey, *Borderline*, p. 62.
103. Balson, *Children*, p. 1.
104. Ibid. pp. 87, 89.
105. Ibid. pp. 108, 123.
106. Ibid. p. 100.
107. Scholtz, *A Place*, pp. 112–15.
108. Elphick, *Kraal*, p. 47
109. Ibid. p. 55
110. Waldman, *The Griqua*, p. 37.
111. Ibid. p. 213.
112. Marx, *Capital*, Vol. 1, p. 873.
113. Harvey, *The New*, p. 229.

# Conclusion

Having started with a speech by Thabo Mbeki that invoked successful anti-colonial resistance to European incursions in Table Bay in 1510, I want to conclude with another Mbeki speech in which he acclaimed an earlier moment of co-operation between the peoples of Europe and Southern Africa. In this second speech, delivered to the Mozambican National Assembly on 2 May 2002, Mbeki referred to the arrival of Vasco da Gama on the shores of Mozambique:

> As we know, the first recorded contact between whites and blacks in southern Africa happened on the 11th January 1498 when Vasco da Gama anchored his ships up the coast off a small river identified as Inharrime, south of Cape Corrientes [. . .] With further attempts they anchored at Inharrime and found such friendly people that they named the place Terra da Boa Gente, the Land of Good People. Today we are happy to be amongst *boa gente*. In fact, we will all agree that there are very few Africans, across the entire continents, who are themselves not *boa gente*. I am recalling this story of the *boa gente*, to indicate that these good people of Africa, who comprise many nations, speak many related languages, displayed to the strangers who appeared at their shores the spirit of ubuntu, which is the spirit of kindness, selflessness, solidarity, service to the people and innate humanism.[1]

The shift from third to first person fails to disguise Mbeki's implicit identification with Da Gama. Both of them are outsiders arriving to a warm welcome from the good people of Mozambique: in 1498, 'they [Da Gama and his Portuguese followers] anchored at Inharrime and found such friendly people that *they* named the place Terra da Boa Gente'. In 2002, '*we* [Mbeki and his South African followers] are happy to be amongst *boa gente*'. At first glance, Mbeki's invocation of Da Gama's words might be dismissed as the work of careless speech-writer, as there would appear to be little to link the progenitor of Portuguese imperialism in East Africa and the post-apartheid president celebrating the good people of Mozambique and the African values of 'ubuntu'. However, I want to argue in conclusion that there is indeed a connection between Da Gama and Mbeki by briefly referring first to the histories of the Cape Colony and Mozambique, and then to post-apartheid South Africa's relationship with Mozambique. The relation between the Cape and Mozambique is read metonymically, not as the exclusive key to reading South African nationalisms, but this final juxtaposition of the colonial and the postcolonial illustrates the blind spots and exclusions endemic in the imagined political communities of the Cape Colony and post-apartheid South Africa alike.

## COLONIAL AND APARTHEID HISTORIES

Even the most superficial run-through of Mozambique's history reveals how Da Gama's tribute to the 'boa gente' was an anomalous precursor to centuries of plunder: in 1550, the first Jesuit mission to the region arrived, and a decade later, the Portuguese developed Inhambane (just to the north of the Inharrime River) as an ivory trading port; in 1678, a smallpox epidemic which started at Mozambique Island killed many of the local Tonga people; in 1727, the discovery of a Dutch ship trading at Inhambane prompted the Portuguese to establish a permanent settlement, a project secured by the army of Domingos Lopes Rebello marching 200 miles south from Sofala to Inhambane, killing or enslaving villagers, burning fields and seizing cattle; by 1762, 400 slaves a year were being captured and transported from Inhambane to the French Indian Ocean islands;[2] and by the time of the abolition of slavery at the Cape, thousands of Mozambicans had been transported to the Cape Colony (26.4 per cent of the total slaves imported between 1661 and 1808: about 25,000).[3]

White writers at the Cape produced a typology of slaves, with those from Mozambique being attributed certain positive qualities. Levaillant in 1790 declared that the 'Negroes from Mozambique [. . .] are considered the strongest labourers and most loyal to their masters'.[4] Samuel Hudson in about 1803 provided a more detailed characterisation:

> The Mosambiques are mild, peaceable and patient under this slavery [. . .] These [Mozambican] slaves are therefore most useful in the colony for hard labour and all agricultural concerns. They are capable of carrying heavy burthens which they do without murmuring [and they] are affectionate and faithful to those who treat them well [. . .] Prejudice has stamped them a dull, stupid link in the great chain and 'tis hard to do away [with] these errors which long custom has rendered sacred. Was I permitted to make choice of slaves for a continuance in the colony, I would certainly make choice of Mosambiques for fidelity and a mild disposition.[5]

Semple in the same year re-emphasised the obedience and good nature of the Mozambican slave:

> in his inoffensive and humbled countenance, you may read that he has often submitted to blows and unmerited reproaches without for a moment thinking

of revenge [. . . He is] occupied only with the present, thinks neither of the hours of bitterness which are past, nor of those which are to come.[6]

And William Wilberforce Bird in 1822 praised the Mozambican slaves' capacity for hard work: 'These slaves are chiefly hewers and carriers of wood, and drawers of water, coolies, or public porters for hire, and also employed by the boers and others as the hardiest labourers of the field.'[7] There is no explicit connection from the '*boa gente*' of Inharrime in 1498 to the 'loyal' Mozambican slaves of the Cape in 1800, but once again the people of Mozambique are inscribed sympathetically within colonial discourse, with the later descriptions appreciating in particular the contribution of Mozambican slaves to the Cape's economy.

After the abolition of slavery at the Cape in the 1830s, Mozambican slave traders continued to send slaves to South America (in Rio de Janeiro, for example, 'Inhambanes' formed a significant slave community),[8] and the transfer of labour from Mozambique to the Cape Colony also continued, but in a different form. It has been calculated that 'from roughly 1780 to 1880, about 25,000 Mozambicans were brought to [the Cape]: firstly as slaves, then as prize Negroes or liberated slaves, and finally as contracted and free workers'.[9] In the nineteenth century, Mozambicans formed a substantial and clearly defined community at the Cape, but in the twentieth century, under escalating pressure from the state's system of racial classification, 'Mozbiekers chose to meld into the large mixed race community in the Western Cape [. . .] abandoned the formal the use of this word ["Mozbieker"] and no longer saw themselves as forming a separate community'.[10] Unlike northern-hemisphere travellers and settlers, the Mozambicans forced to migrate to the Cape Colony have left few written records of their community at the Cape. As a consequence, despite their significance as an economic resource for the Cape economy, they are invisible in South Africa's political/national narratives of the nineteenth and twentieth centuries.

Beyond the Cape, people from Mozambique played a major role in generating wealth for the South African economy. From about 1860, the first Mozambicans were transported to work on the sugar-cane plantations of Natal, and then from the 1870s on the diamond mines of Kimberley and the gold mines of the Witwatersrand.[11] During the period 1890–1920, a formalised contract labour system was introduced to regulate the supply of cheap migrant workers for the South African mines. The principal piece of legislation regulating migration, the 1937 Aliens Control Act, cohered entirely with the needs of the mining industry, ruling that migrant workers would never become South African citizens by laying down the requirement that prospective citizens must 'be readily assimilable by the white inhabitants [and not threaten] the language, culture, religion of any white ethnic group'.[12] As African colonies won independence in the 1960s, the attitude of the apartheid regime towards migrants from the north hardened – border posts were erected, passport requirements were tightened, and foreign women in South Africa in particular were targeted and expelled by police. Acquiring South African citizenship through naturalisation remained impossible, as the 1937 Aliens Act remained on the statute book until 1991. In the 1980s, there was a further influx of approximately 350,000 refugees from Mozambique to South Africa escaping the civil war between the FRELIMO government and the US- and apartheid-backed RENAMO forces. Bordering countries such as Malawi, Zimbabwe and Swaziland took in refugees, while South Africa tried to keep them out, electrifying border fences and deporting as many refugees as it could.[13]

From the colonial period to the end of apartheid, Mozambicans in the Cape Colony and South Africa were therefore units of labour and objects of surveillance (and occasionally of sympathy). But they were never inscribed within the formal political communities of the Cape or of South Africa. In the eighteenth century, their slave status by definition precluded them from citizenship, and after the Union of South Africa in 1910, the ex-slave communities of Mozambicans at the Cape gradually merged with other black and coloured communities, and Mozambican mine and farm workers further north were denied South African nationality by the legislation regulating the state's migrant labour system.

## POST-APARTHEID CONTINUITIES

Since 1990, these long-entrenched patterns of national exclusion and economic exploitation have persisted. In terms of trade, South Africa's post-apartheid policy-makers have taken their cue from IMF imprimaturs promoting trade liberalisation, and as a consequence have used the Southern African Development Corporation (SADC) and the New Partnership for Africa's Development (NEPAD) to enforce differential terms of trade with the rest of the region. In the mid-1990s, European negotiators in trade talks with South Africa applied a version of the venerable mix of free trade and protectionism, with Europe protecting its markets from cheaper South African exports, while at the same securing generous access for European goods to Southern African markets. According to a Mozambican negotiator at subsequent Southern African trade talks at the end of the decade, 'the South African government learnt a series of hard lessons that it didn't hesitate to apply during the negotiations for the implementation of the SADC Trade protocol'.[14] Exploiting its position as the region's most powerful trading nation, South Africa applied to Mozambique (and the other former frontline states) the same tactics it had endured in negotiations with the EU, with the result that South Africa secured preferential trading rights with its poorer neighbours.[15]

In terms of investment policy, a similar pattern can be discerned. There has been a massive increase in investment by South African capital in Mozambique, rising from ZAR107 million in 1997 to ZAR4298 million in 2001, but it has been investment of very specific kind. In the period 1990–2000, South African investment has been concentrated heavily in the south of Mozambique, with 183 of the 279 projects and US$2,180 million of the US$2,568 million total investment directed to Maputo province. Investment has been focused principally upon meeting South Africa's Gauteng province's need for a reliable port infrastructure in Maputo. The limitations of these kinds of capital-intensive investments have been pointed out by many development economists: they exacerbate existing disparities and tensions between the Maputo region and the rest of Mozambique; the most generous estimates calculate that this investment has created only about 31,000 jobs, most of them short-term; such investment has few linkages with Mozambique's host economy because South African retail, mining, telecommunications, financing and manufacturing companies operating in Mozambique all tend to import the bulk of their products from South Africa, thus displacing local production.[16] The most controversial South African investment initiative has been the ANC-FRELIMO agreement to enable white South African farmers to acquire eight million hectares of agricultural land for commercial farming in Mozambique. This initiative prompted one critic to conclude that 'the transfer of nominal power by the apartheid regime in 1994 rather than restraining the white dominated economic system, has in fact created the pre-conditions for its advancement, both within South Africa and the region'.[17]

The gulf between declarations of a common African humanity and economic profiteering is clearest in the state policies regulating the migration of labour. These policies were vividly exposed in August 2010, when South African security guards shot and killed four foreign mine workers at the Aurora gold mine, which is owned by relatives of Nelson Mandela and President Jacob Zuma.[18] Migration policy in South Africa remained substantially the same after the end of apartheid, with the continuation of what has been termed the 'two gate' system – one system for mine workers, regulated by bilateral agreements between mining companies and supplier governments, and a second system for all other migrants, regulated by the Aliens Control Act. As regards mine workers, the industry as a whole has seen the large-scale retrenchment of both South African and foreign miners (from 1983 to 1994, the number of South African gold- and coal-miners dropped from 495,000 to 321,500, while during the same period the number of non-South African miners dropped from 183,000 to 147,000). By 2000, the ratio of South African to non-South African miners had stabilised at 50 per cent, but the wage gap between South African and foreign miners remains substantial: foreign miners are paid on average up to 40 per cent less than their South African counterparts. The second 'gate', the Aliens Control Act, continued to regulate migrants in South Africa outside the contract labour system. The Act was amended in 1991 to delete the explicit racial exclusions of the 1937 Act, but its key requirement remained in place – that to employ foreign workers, South African employers had to convince the Department of Home Affairs that no South Africans were available for the relevant job. This policy was confirmed in the 1996 Amendment Act, which explicitly excluded the issuing of work or immigration permits to foreign workers seeking employment in occupations where there are sufficient South Africans, and which criminalises migrant workers entering South Africa without the requisite permits. They are protected to some extent from prosecution by their South African employers, who are reluctant to relinquish their cheap and non-unionised labour.[19]

# CONCLUSION

I do not know what the Mozambicans listening to Mbeki's 2002 speech made of his words. Were they flattered to be described once again as '*boa gente*'? Or did they uneasily recall the centuries of violent dispossession and economic subordination that followed Da Gama's generous words? What they will have known is that the relationship between the words of politicians and the economic ambitions underlying them requires scrutiny. Da Gama's tribute to the '*boa gente*' of Inharrime in 1498, the sympathetic descriptions of Mozambican slaves at the Cape around 1800, and Mbeki's Pan-African embrace of Mozambique's '*boa gente*' in 2002, belong to quite distinct moments of colonial and postcolonial history. But when each of these statements is read in its context(s), and in particular with an eye to the articulation of political community and economic production, more troubling and complicated meanings beyond the words become apparent. Such contextual readings reveal submerged patterns of exploitation linking past and present, and point in particular to what is suppressed in the imagining of political community under neo-colonialism.

## NOTES

1. Mbeki, 'Address by the President'.
2. See Alan K. Smith, 'The Peoples'; Harries, 'Slavery'; Vail and White, *Capitalism*, pp. 7–50; and Newitt, *A History*, pp. 160–6.
3. See Harries, 'Culture'; and Shell, *Children*, pp. 41–2.
4. Levaillant, *Travels*, p. 49.
5. Shell, 'Introduction', pp. 46–7, 49.
6. Semple, *Walks*, p. 47.
7. Bird, *State*, p. 73.
8. See Karasch, *Slave Life*, pp. 21–5.
9. Harries, 'Culture', p. 29.
10. Ibid. p. 48.
11. See Crush et al., *South Africa's*; and Harries, *Work*.
12. Quoted in Peberdy, *Selecting*, p. 64. Peberdy explains how the 1937 Act was also aimed at preventing Jews fleeing persecution in Europe from entering South Africa.
13. See Johnston, 'The Point'.
14. Pallotti, 'SADC', p. 517.
15. On post-apartheid South Africa's economic relationship with Mozambique, see Pallotti, 'SADC'; and Bond, 'The ANC's'.
16. On the changes in Mozambique's internal economy since the end of apartheid, see Hanlon, *Peace*; and Pitcher, 'Recreating'.
17. Chossudovsky, 'Exporting', p. 394.
18. See David Smith, 'South'.
19. See Crush and Williams, 'Labour'.

# References

Abrahams, Yvette, 'Colonialism, dysfunction and disjuncture: Sarah Bartmann's resistance (remix)', *Agenda* 58 (2003), pp. 12–26.

'Adamastor: The Titan of Table Mountain', *Cape Monthly Magazine* 5, 29 (May 1859), pp. 310–17.

Ahmad, Aijaz, *In Theory: Classes, Nations, Literatures* (London: Verso, 1992).

Alberti, Ludwig, *Ludwig Alberti's Account of the Tribal Life and Customs of the Xhosa in 1807*, trans. W. Fehr (Cape Town: Balkema, [1815] 1968).

Anderson, Benedict, *Imagined Communities: Reflections on the Origin and Spread of Nationalism* (London and New York: Verso, 2006).

——, 'Responses', in Pheng Cheah and Jonathan Culler (eds), *Grounds of Comparison: Around the Work of Benedict Anderson* (New York and London: Routledge, 2003), pp. 225–45.

——, *The Spectre of Comparisons: Nationalism, Southeast Asia, and the World* (London: Verso, 1998).

Andrews, Malcolm, *Landscape and Western Art* (Oxford: Oxford University Press, 1999).

Arbousset, T. and F. Daumas, *A Narrative of an Exploratory Tour to the North-East of the Colony*, trans. John Croumbie Brown (Cape Town: A. S. Robertson, 1846).

Arendt, Hannah, *On Revolution* (Harmondsworth: Penguin, [1963] 2006).

Arkin, Marcus, 'John Company at the Cape', *Archives Yearbook for South African History* II (1960), pp. 179–344.

Arrighi, Giovanni, *The Long Twentieth Century* (London: Verso, 1994).

Atkinson, Geoffrey, *The Extraordinary Voyage in French Literature*, Vol. 2: *From 1700–1720* (Paris: Champion, 1922).

Avelar, Ana Paula M., *Fernão Lopes de Castanheda: Historiador dos Portugueses na Índia ou Cronista do Governo de Nuno da Cunha?* (Lisbon: Edições Cosmos, 1997).

Axelson, Eric, *Portuguese in South-East Africa 1488–1600* (Cape Town: Struik, 1973).

'The Bad Sex Award winner and longlist', *Guardian* 14 December 2004', http://books.guardian.co.uk/news/articles/0,,1373416,00.html (accessed 10 December 2005).

Bakhtin, M. M., *The Dialogic Imagination*, trans. C. Emerson and M. Holquist (Austin: University of Texas Press, 1981).

Ballard, Richard, Adam Habib, Imraan Valodia and Elke Zuern, 'Introduction: From Anti-apartheid to Post-apartheid Social Movements', in Richard Ballard, Adam Habib and Imraan Valodia (eds), *Voices of Protest: Social Movements in Post-apartheid South Africa* (Scottsville: University of KwaZulu-Natal Press, 2006), pp. 1–22.

Balson, Scott, *Children of the Mist: The Lost Tribe of Africa* (Wellers Hill, Australia: The Author, 2007).

Banks, Jared, 'Adamastorying Mozambique: *Ualalapi* and *Os Lusiadas*', *Luso-Brazilian Review* 37 (2000), pp. 1–16.

Barnard, Lady Anne, *The Cape Journals of Lady Anne Barnard 1797–1798*, ed. A. M. Lewin Robinson, Margaret Lenta and Dorothy Driver (Cape Town: Van Riebeeck Society, 1994).

Barrell, John, 'The public prospect and the private view: the politics of taste in eighteenth-century Britain', in Simon Pugh (ed.), *Reading Landscape: Country – City – Capital* (Manchester: Manchester University Press, 1990), pp. 19–40.

Barros, João de, Da Asia, *Of the Deeds which the Portuguese Performed in the Conquest and Exploration of the Lands and Seas of the East* (1553), in G. M. Theal (trans. and ed.), *Records of South-Eastern Africa*, Vol. 6 (Cape Town: Struik, [1900] 1964), pp. 298–306.

Barrow, John, *An Account of Travels into the Interior of Southern Africa in the Years 1797 and 1798*, Vol. 1 (London: T. Cadell and W. Davies, 1801 and 1804).

Bartram, William, *Travels through North and South Carolina* (1792), repr. in Tim Fulford and Carol Bolton (eds), *Travels, Explorations and Empires*, Vol. 1 (London: Pickering and Chatto, 2001), pp. 141–60.

Bassani, Ezio and Letizia Tedeschi, 'The image of the Hottentot in the seventeenth and eighteenth centuries: an iconographic investigation', *Journal of the History of Collections* 2, 2 (1990), pp. 157–86.

Bearce, George D., *British Attitudes Towards India 1784–1858* (Oxford: Oxford University Press, 1961).

Bell, Aubrey, *Gaspar Corrêa* (London: Hispanic Notes and Monographs, 1924).

——, *Luis de Camões* (London: Oxford University Press, 1923).

Bell, David A., *The Cult of the Nation in France: Inventing Nationalism, 1680–1800* (Cambridge, MA: Harvard University Press, 2001).

Beloff, Max (ed.), *The Debate on the American Revolution, 1761–1783* (Dobbs Ferry, NY: Sheridan House, 1989).

Benjamin, Walter, *Illuminations*, trans. Harry Zohn, ed. Hannah Arendt (New York: Schocken Books, 1968).

Bennett, Herman L., '"Sons of Ham": text, context, and the early modern African subject', *Representations* 92, 1 (2005), pp. 16–41.

Bernardin de Saint-Pierre, Jacques-Henri, *Journey to Mauritius*, trans. Jason Wilson (Oxford: Signal Books, [1773] 2002).

Bernstein, Birch L., *'Tomorrow is Another Day': An Historical Romance of South Africa – 1652 to the Present Day* (Cape Town: Juta, 1951).

Besten, Michael Paul, 'Transformation and reconstitution of Khoe-San identities: A. A. S. Le Fleur I, Griqua identities and post-apartheid Khoe-San revivalism (1894–2004)' (Leiden: University of Leiden, unpublished PhD thesis, 2006).

Beyers, Coenraad, *Die Kaapse Patriotte 1779–1791* (Cape Town: Juta, 1929).

Bezuidenhout, C. P., *De Geschiedenis van het Afrikaansche Geslacht, van 1688 tot 1882, Vergeleken met Psalm 80, Vers 9 tot 16* (Bloemfontein: Oranjevrijstaat Nieuwblad Maatschappij, 1883).

Bird, William Wilberforce, *State of the Cape of Good Hope in 1822* (London: John Murray, 1822).

Blackburn, Robin, *The Making of New World Slavery: From the Baroque to the Modern, 1492–1800* (London: Verso, 1997).

Bolton, Carol, *Writing the Empire: Robert Southey and Romantic Colonialism* (London: Pickering and Chatto, 2007).

Bond, Patrick, 'The ANC's "Left Turn" and South African sub-imperialism', *Review of African Political Economy* 31, 102 (2004), pp. 599–616.

——, *Elite Transition: From Apartheid to Neoliberalism in South Africa* (London: Pluto Press, 2000).

Booth, Alan R. *The United States Experience in South Africa, 1784–1870* (Cape Town: A. A. Balkema, 1976).

Borcherds, Petrus Borchardus, *An Auto-biographical Memoir* (Cape Town: A. S. Robertson, 1861).

Boucher, Maurice and Nigel Penn, *Britain at the Cape: 1795–1803* (Johannesburg: Brenthurst, 1992).

Bowen, H. V., *The Business of Empire: The East India Company and Imperial Britain, 1756–1833* (Cambridge: Cambridge University Press, 2006).

Boxer, C. R., *João de Barros: Portuguese Humanist and Historian of Asia* (New Delhi: Concept Publishing House, 1981).

——, *The Portuguese Seaborne Empire 1415–1825* (London: Hutchinson, 1969).

Bradlow, Frank, R. *Francis Masson's Account of Three Journeys at the Cape of Good Hope 1772–1775* (Cape Town: Tablecloth Press, 1994).

Brantlinger, Patrick, *Victorian Literature and Postcolonial Studies* (Edinburgh: Edinburgh University Press, 2009).

Braudel, Fernand, *The Perspective of the World: Civilization and Capitalism 15th–18th Century*, Vol. 3, trans. S. Reynolds (London: Phoenix Press, [1979] 2002).

Brink, André, *An Act of Terror* (London: Vintage, [1991] 2000).

——, *A Chain of Voices* (London: Vintage, 1982).

——, *The First Life of Adamastor* (London: Vintage, [1993] 2000).

——, 'A myth of origin', in Ivan Vladislavic (ed.), *T'kama-Adamastor: Inventions of Africa in a South African Painting* (Johannesburg: University of Witwatersrand Press, 2000), pp. 41–8.

——, *Reinventing a Continent: Writing and Politics in South Africa, 1982–1995* (London: Secker and Warburg, 1996).

——, *The Rights of Desire* (London: Vintage, 2000).

—— with R. Nethersole, 'Reimagining the past', in Ivan Vladislavic (ed.), *T'kama-Adamastor: Inventions of Africa in a South African Painting* (Johannesburg: University of Witwatersrand Press, 2000), pp. 49–58.

Brooks, Frederick, 'Nature's Logic', *South Africa Grins; or, The Quizzical Depot of General Humbug* (Cape Town: William Bridekirk, 1825).

Brown, Stewart J. (ed.), *William Robertson and the Expansion of Empire* (Cambridge: Cambridge University Press, 1997).

Bruce, John, *Historical View of Plans for the Government of British India, and Regulation of Trade to the East Indies and Outlines of a Plan of Foreign Government, of Commercial Economy, and of Domestic Administration, for the Asiatic Interests of Great Britain* (London: J. Sewell and J. Debrett, 1793).

——, *Report on the Negociation between the Honourable East-India Company and the Public, respecting the Renewal of the Company's Exclusive Privileges of Trade, for Twenty Years from March, 1794* (London: Black, Parry and Kingsbury, 1811).

——, *Sketches of the Political and Commercial History of the Cape of Good Hope* (London: State Paper Office, 1796).

——, 'Speech in the Committee of the House of Commons on India Affairs', *The Parliamentary Debates from the Year 1803 to the Present Time*, Vol. 26. *Comprising the Period from 11 May to 22 July 1813* (London: Hansard, 1813), pp. 414–37.

Bryce, James, *Impressions of South Africa* (London: Macmillan, 1897).

Buchan, John, *Prester John* (Harmondsworth: Penguin, [1910] 1956).

Bunn, David, '"Our wattled cot": mercantile and domestic space in Thomas Pringle's African landscape', in W. J. T. Mitchell (ed.), *Landscape and Power* (Chicago and London: University of Chicago Press, 1994), pp. 127–73.

Burchell, William, *Travels in Southern Africa* (Oxford: Oxford University Press, [1822] 1935).

Burke, Edmund, *A Philosophical Enquiry into the Origin of our Ideas of the Sublime and the Beautiful* (Oxford: Oxford University Press, [1757] 1990).

Byron, Lord George Gordon, *The Major Works*, ed. Jerome McGann (Oxford: Oxford University Press, 1986).

Cain, Peter J. (ed.), *The Wellesley Series II: Free Trade and Protectionism, Vol. 1. Origins of Free Trade to 1850* (London: Routledge/Thoemmes Press, 1996).

Camões, Luís Vaz de, *The Lusíads*, trans. Landeg White (Oxford: Oxford University Press, 1997).

Campagne, H. D., 'Gedachten bij de beschouwing van het voorleeden en toekomstig lot van de Kaap', *Hollandsch Zuid-Afrika* (15 July 1920), pp. 7–8.

——, *Memoriën en Bijzonderheeden wegens de overgave der Kaap de Goede Hoop; Berigt nopens den oorsprong, voortgang en ruptures der Kaffers*, Cape Archives, V. C. 76, pp. 205–85.

Campbell, John, *Journal of Travels in South Africa Among the Hottentot and Other Tribes; in the Years 1812, 1813, and 1814* (London: Religious Tract Society, [1815] 1834).

——, *Travels in South Africa, Undertaken at the Request of the London Missionary Society; Being a Narrative of a Second Journey in the Interior of that Country*, Vol. 2 (London: Francis Westley, 1822).

Cape Archives Depot, CJ 5. Original Rolls and Minutes (Criminal and Civil) (1713).

——, CJ 317. Crimineel Processtukken (1713).

——, CJ 515–CJ 516. Documents in Criminal Cases (October 1808).

——, CJ 633. Documents in Criminal Cases, Case 8 (March 1825).

——, CJ 819. Documents in Criminal Cases, Case 9 (14 March 1825).

Cappon, James, *Britain's Title in South Africa, or, The Story of Cape Colony to the Days of the Great Trek* (London: Macmillan, 1901).

*Cargo* 2007, http://www.magnettheatre.co.za/productions/ (accessed 15 December 2009).

Carstens, Peter, 'Opting out of colonial rule: the brown voortrekkers of South Africa and their Constitutions', *African Studies* 42, 2 (1983), pp. 135–52; 43, 1 (1984), pp. 19–30.

Castanheda, Fernão Lopes de, *History of the Discovery and Conquest of India by the Portuguese* (1551), in G. M. Theal (trans. and ed.), *Records of South-Eastern Africa*, Vol. 5 (Cape Town: Struik, [1901] 1964), pp. 466–9.

Catz, Rebecca, 'Consequences and repercussions of the Portuguese expansion on literature', in G. D. Winius (ed.), *Portugal, The Pathfinder: Journeys from the Medieval toward the Modern World 1300 – ca. 1600* (Madison: Hispanic Seminary of Medieval Studies, 1995), pp. 329–40.

Caudle, J. J., 'Mickle, William Julius (1734/5–1788)', *Oxford Dictionary of National Biography* (Oxford: Oxford University Press, 2004), http://www.oxforddnb.com/view/article/18661 (accessed 25 May 2007).

Chandler, James, *England in 1819: The Politics of Literary Culture and the Case of Romantic Historicism* (Chicago: University of Chicago Press, 1998).

——, 'History', in Iain McCalman (ed.), *An Oxford Companion to the Romantic Age: British Culture, 1776–1832* (Oxford: Oxford University Press, 1999), pp. 354–60.

Chapman, Michael, 'Roy Campbell, poet: a defence in sociological times', *Theoria* 68 (1986), pp. 79–93.

Chase, John Centlivres (ed.), *The Natal Papers: A Reprint of All Notices and Public Documents Connected with that Territory*, 2 vols (Grahamstown: n.p., 1843; reprinted Cape Town: n.p., 1968).

Chatterjee, Partha, *The Nation and its Fragments: Colonial and Postcolonial Histories* (Princeton: Princeton University Press, 1993).

Choisy, Abbé François-Timoléon de, *Journal of a Voyage to Siam*, ed. Michael Smithies (Kuala Lumpur: Oxford University Press, [1687] 1993).

Chossudovsky, Michel, '"Exporting apartheid" to Sub-Saharan Africa', *Review of African Political Economy* 24, 73 (1997), pp. 389–98.

Christiansë, Yvette, *Unconfessed* (New York: Other Press, 2006).

Cliffe, Lionel, 'Land reform in South Africa', *Review of African Political Economy* 84 (2000), pp. 273–86.

Cloete, Stuart, *Waiting for the Dawn* (London: Fontana, [1939] 1974).

Coetzee, J. A., *Die Ruiters van Slagtersnek* (Pretoria: Persbou, 1949).

——, *Nasieskap en Politieke Groepering* (Pretoria: Transvaalse Uitgewersmaatskappy, 1969).

——, *Politieke Groeperinge en die Wording van die Afrikanernasie* (Johannesburg: Voortrekkerpers, 1941).

Cohen, Walter B., *The French Encounter with Africans: White Response to Blacks, 1530–1880* (Bloomington and London: Indiana University Press, 1980).

Colvin, Ian, *Romance of Empire: South Africa* (London: T. C. and E. C. Jack, 1909).

Conradie, E. J. M., *Hollandse Skrywers uit Suid-Afrika: Deel 1 (1652–1875)* (Pretoria: J. H. de Bussy, 1934).

Cooper, Frederick, 'Postcolonial Studies and the Study of History', in Ania Loomba, Suvir Kaul, Matti Bunzl, Antoinette Burton and Jed Esty (eds), *Postcolonial Studies and Beyond* (Durham, NC and London: Duke University Press, 2005), pp. 401–22.

Corrêa, Gaspar de, *Legends of India* (1858), in G. M. Theal (trans. and ed.), *Records of South-Eastern Africa*, Vol. 2 (Cape Town: Struik, [1898] 1964), pp. 45–7.

Cosgrove, Denis, *Social Formation and Symbolic Landscape* (Madison: University of Wisconsin Press, [1984] 1998).

Countryman, Edward, 'Indians, the colonial order, and the social significance of the American Revolution', *The William and Mary Quarterly* 53, 2 (1996), pp. 342–66.

Craig, David M., *Robert Southey and Romantic Apostasy* (Woodbridge: The Royal Historical Society, 2007).

Crais, Clifton, 'The vacant land: the mythology of British expansion in the Eastern Cape, South Africa', *Journal of Historical Sociology* 25, 2 (1991), pp. 255–75.

—— and Pamela Scully, *Sara Baartman and the Hottentot Venus: A Ghost Story and a Biography* (Princeton: Princeton University Press, 2009).

Crewe, Jonathan, 'The spectre of Adamastor: heroic desire and displacement in "White" South Africa', *Modern Fiction Studies* 43, 1 (1997), pp. 27–52.

Cronin, Jeremy, 'Turning around: Roy Campbell's "Rounding the Cape"', *English in Africa*, 11 (1984), pp. 65–78

Cronje, Johan, *The Griqua of the Northern Cape: Landownership, Identity and Leadership* (Kimberley: The Sol Plaatje Trust, 2006).

Crush, Jonathan, Alan Jeeves and David Yudelman, *South Africa's Labour Empire: A History of Black Migrancy to the Gold Mines* (Boulder, CO: Westview Press, 1991).

Crush, Jonathan and Vincent Williams, 'Labour Migration Trends and Policies in Southern Africa', Southern African Migration Project, Policy Brief No. 23, 2010, http://www.queensu.ca/samp/sampresources/samppublications/policybriefs/brief23.pdf (accessed 31 January 2011).

Cullinan, Patrick, *Robert Jacob Gordon, 1743–1795: The Man and his Travels at the Cape* (Cape Town: Struik, 1992).

Dalrymple, William, 'Proposal for a Settlement on the Caffre Coast' (London: Public Records Office, Chatham Papers, 30/8/128).

D'Arbez (pseud. Johan Fredrik van Oordt), *De Grensbewoners: Een historiese verhaal uit de dagen van de eerste en tweede opstand te Graaff-Reinet in de jaren 1795 en 1799* (Pretoria: J. H. De Bussy, 1920).

De Kiewiet, C. W., *A History of South Africa: Social and Economic* (Oxford: Clarendon, 1941).

De Kock, Victor, *Those in Bondage: An Account of the Life of the Slave at the Cape in the Days of the Dutch East India Company* (Cape Town: Timmins Publishers, 1950).

Dentith, Simon, *Epic and Empire in Nineteenth-Century Britain* (Cambridge: Cambridge University Press, 2006).

Derrida, Jacques, 'La Loi du genre/The Law of Genre', *Glyph Textual Studies* 7 (1980), pp. 176–232.

——, *Of Grammatology*, trans. Gayatri Chakravorty Spivak (Baltimore: Johns Hopkins University Press, [1967] 1976).

Dicey, William, *Borderline* (Cape Town: Kwela, 2004).

Dooling, Wayne, *Slavery, Emancipation and Colonial Rule in South Africa* (Pietermaritzburg: UKZN Press, 2007).

Du Toit, André, 'Experiments with truth and justice in South Africa: Stockenström, Gandhi and the TRC', *Journal of Southern African Studies* 31, 2 (2005), pp. 419–48.

——, 'No chosen people: the myth of the Calvinist origins of Afrikaner nationalism and racial ideology', *The American Historical Review* 88, 4 (1983), pp. 920–52.

—— and Hermann Giliomee, *Afrikaner Political Thought: Analysis and Documents, Vol. 1, 1780–1850* (Cape Town: David Philip, 1983).

Du Toit, S. J., *Di geschiedenis van ons land in di taal van ons volk* (Paarl: D. F. du Toit, [1877] 1895).

Dundas, Henry, *Substance of the Speech of the Right Hon. Henry Dundas, in the House of Commons on the British Government and Trade in the East Indies, 23 April 1793* (London: Black, Parry and Co., 1813).

Duyker, Edward, *Citizen Labillardière* (Melbourne: Melbourne University Press, 2003).

Edgar, Robert and Christopher Saunders, 'A. A. S. le Fleur and the Griqua trek of 1917: segregation, self-help and ethnic identity', *The International Journal of African Historical Studies* 15, 2 (1982), pp. 201–20.

'Editorial', *The South African Commercial Advertiser*, 22 September 1830, p. 2.

Edwards, Isobel, *Towards Emancipation: A Study of South African Slavery* (Cardiff: University of Wales Press, 1942).

Elbourne, Elizabeth, *Blood Ground: Colonialism, Missions, and the Contest for Christianity in the Cape Colony and Britain, 1799–1853* (Montreal: McGill-Queen's University Press, 2008).

Ellis, J. J., *Passionate Sage: The Character and Legacy of John Adams* (New York: W. W. Norton, 1993).

Elphick, Richard, *Kraal and Castle: Khoikhoi and the Founding of White South Africa* (New Haven, CT and London: Yale University Press, 1977).

—— and Hermann Giliomee (eds), *The Shaping of South African Society, 1652–1840* (Cape Town: Maskew Miller Longman, 1989).

—— and V. C. Malherbe, 'The Khoisan to 1828', in Richard Elphick and Hermann Giliomee (eds), *The Shaping of South African Society, 1652–1840* (Cape Town: Maskew Miller Longman, 1989), pp. 3–65.

Faccarello, Gilbert, 'Galiani, Necker and Turgot: A debate on economic reform in eighteenth-century France', in Gilbert Faccarello (ed.), *Studies in the History of French Political Economy: From Bodin to Walras* (London and New York: Routledge, 1998), pp. 120–95.

Fanon, Frantz, *The Wretched of the Earth*, trans. Constance Farrington (Harmondsworth: Penguin, [1961] 1967).

Farwell, Byron, *Queen Victoria's Little Wars* (London: Allen Lane, 1973).

Faulkner, William, *As I Lay Dying* (Harmondsworth: Penguin, [1930] 1963).

Ferguson, Adam, *An Essay on the History of Civil Society*, ed. Fania Oz-Salzberger (Cambridge: Cambridge University Press, [1767] 1995).

Ferreira, O. J. O., 'Adamastor, Gees van die Stormkaap', *Tydskrif vir Volkskunde en Volkstaal* 49, 1 (1993), pp. 20–47.

Festa, Lynn, *Sentimental Figures of Empire in Eighteenth-Century Britain and France* (Baltimore: Johns Hopkins University Press, 2006).

—— and Daniel Carey, 'Introduction: some answers to the question: "What is postcolonial Enlightenment?"', in Daniel Carey and Lynn Festa (eds), *The Postcolonial Enlightenment: Eighteenth-Century Colonialism and Postcolonial Theory* (New York: Oxford University Press, 2009), pp. 1–33.

Figueiredo, Fidelino, 'Camões as an epic poet', *Romantic Review* 17 (1926), pp. 217–29.

Fitzroy, V. M., *When the Slave Bell Tolled* (Cape Town: Howard Timmins, 1970).

Foster, William, 'John Bruce, historiographer, 1745–1826', *Scottish Historical Review*, 9 (1912): 366–75.

Foucault, Michel, *The Foucault Effect: Studies in Governmentality*, ed. Graham Burchell, Colin Gordon and Peter Miller (London: Harvester Wheatsheaf, 1991).

——, *'Society Must Be Defended': Lectures at the Collège de France 1975–1976*, trans. David Macey (New York: Picador, 2003).

Fox-Genovese, Elizabeth, *The Origins of Physiocracy: Economic Revolution and Social Order in Eighteenth-Century France* (Ithaca, NY and London: Cornell University Press, 1976).

Freund, W. M. 'The Cape under transitional governments, 1795–1814', in Richard Elphick and Hermann Giliomee (eds), *The Shaping of South African Society, 1652–1840* (Cape Town: Maskew Miller Longman, 1989), pp. 324–57.

Fry, Michael, 'Bruce, John (1744–1826)', *Oxford Dictionary of National Biography* (Oxford: Oxford University Press, 2004), http://www.oxforddnb.com/view/article/3739 (accessed 25 May 2007).

Fulford, Tim, 'Heroic voyagers and superstitious natives: Southey's imperialist ideology', *Studies in Travel Writing* 2 (1998), pp. 46–65.

Furber, Holden, *Henry Dundas: First Viscount Melville 1742–1811* (Oxford: Oxford University Press, 1931).

Gevisser, Mark, *The Dream Deferred: Thabo Mbeki* (Johannesburg: Jonathan Ball, 2007).

Giliomee, Hermann, *The Afrikaners: Biography of a People* (London: Hurst, 2003).

——, 'Democracy and the frontier. A comparative study of Bacon's Rebellion (1676) and the Graaff-Reinet Rebellion (1795–6)', *South African Historical Journal* 6 (1974), pp. 30–51.

——, 'The Eastern Frontier, 1770–1812', in Richard Elphick and Hermann Giliomee (eds), *The Shaping of South African Society, 1652–1840* (Cape Town: Maskew Miller Longman, 1989), pp. 421–71.

——, 'Herontdekking en herverbeelding van die Afrikaners in 'n Nuwe Suid-Afrika. Outobiografiese aantekeninge oor die skryf van 'n ongewone biografie', *Fragmente* 14/15 (2005), pp. 9–47.

——, *Die Kaap Tydens die Eerste Britse Bewind 1795–1803* (Cape Town: HAUM, 1975).

Góis, Damião de, *Chronicle of the Most Fortunate King Dom Emanuel of Glorious Memory* (1566), in G. M. Theal (trans. and ed.), *Records of South-Eastern Africa*, Vol. 3 (Cape Town: Struik, [1899] 1964), pp. 134–40.

Gqola, Pumla, '"Slaves don't have opinions": inscriptions of slave bodies and the denial of agency in Rayda Jacobs's *The Slave Book*', in Zimitri Erasmus (ed.), *Coloured by History, Shaped by Place: New Perspectives on Coloured Identities in Cape Town* (Cape Town: Kwela Books, 2002), pp. 45–63.

Grant, Charles, *Observations Respecting Commerce of the Cape of Good Hope* (London, 1796).

Gray, Stephen, *Camoens and the Poetry of South Africa* (Johannesburg: Witwatersrand University, 1980).

Great Britain, House of Commons, *Report of Select Committee on Aborigines (British Settlements)* (Cape Town: C. Struik, 1966 [1837]).

Greene, James, 'Camões' birthday', in Malvern Van Wyk Smith (ed.), *Shades of Adamastor: African and the Portuguese Connection: An Anthology of Poetry* (Grahamstown: NELM, 1988), p. 199.

Greenfeld, Liah, *Nationalism: Five Roads to Modernity* (Cambridge, MA: Harvard University Press, 1992).

——, *The Spirit of Capitalism: Nationalism and Economic Growth* (Cambridge, MA: Harvard University Press, 2001).

Griqua National Conference, *Statement by the Griqua National Conference to the United Nations Working Group on Indigenous Populations*, in John Kitching and Johan Meiring (eds), *A Conceptual Report on Griqua History, Griqua Interest Groups and Leadership* (Pretoria: The Constitutional Assembly, 1997), Appendix E.

Grove, Richard, *Green Imperialism: Colonial Expansion, Tropical Island Edens and the Origins of Environmentalism, 1600–1860* (Cambridge: Cambridge University Press, 1995).

Grunebaum, Heidi, 'Unburying the dead in the "Mother City": urban topographies of erasure', *PMLA* (2007), pp. 210–19.

Gumede, William, *Thabo Mbeki and the Soul of the ANC* (Cape Town: Zebra Press, 2005).

Hamilton, Alexander, *New Account of the East Indies*, 2 vols (Edinburgh: J. Mosman, 1727).

Hamilton, Elizabeth, *Memoirs of Modern Philosophers*, ed. Claire Grogan (Peterborough, Canada: Broadview Press, [1800] 2000).

Hanlon, Joseph, *Peace without Profit: How the IMF Blocks Rebuilding in Mozambique* (Dublin: Irish Mozambique Solidarity and International African Institute with James Currey, 1996).

Harington, T. *Remarkable Account of the Loss of the Ship Ganges, East Indiaman, off the Cape of Good Hope, May 29, 1807: and of the General and Miraculous Preservation of the Crew, Consisting of upwards of Two Hundred Persons, Authenticated by Extracts from the Log Book, by T. Harington, Esq. Commander. Also, The Wreck of the Winterton, East Indiaman* (London: Thomas Tegg, 1808).

Harkin, Maureen, 'Adam Smith's missing history: primitives, progress, and problems of genre', *ELH* 72, 2 (2005), pp. 429–51.

Harries, Patrick, 'Culture and classification: a history of the Mozbieker community at the Cape', *Social Dynamics* 26, 2 (2000), pp. 29–54.

——, 'Slavery, social incorporation and surplus extraction; the nature of free and unfree labour in South-East Africa', *Journal of African History* 22 (1981), pp. 309–30.

——, *Work, Culture and Identity: Migrant Labourers in South Africa and Mozambique, c. 1860–1910* (Portsmouth, NH: Heinemann, 1994).

Hart-Davis, Rupert (ed.), *Thomas Love Peacock: Memoirs of Shelley and Other Reviews* (London: Rupert Hart-Davis, 1970).

Hartley, Guy, 'The Battle of Dithakong and "Mfecane" theory', in Carolyn Hamilton (ed.), *The Mfecane Aftermath: Reconstructive Debates in Southern African History* (Johannesburg: Witwatersrand University Press, 1995), pp. 395–416.

Hartman, Saidiya, *Scenes of Subjection: Terror, Slavery, and Self-Making in Nineteenth-Century America* (New York: Oxford University Press, 1997).

Harvey, David, *The Limits to Capital*, 2nd edn (London: Verso, 2006).

——, *The New Imperialism* (Oxford: Oxford University Press, 2003).

Heese, Hans, *Reg en Onreg: Kaapse regspraak in die agtiende eeu* (Bellville: Institute for Historical Research, University of the Western Cape, 1994).

Hegel, G. W. F., *Hegel's Political Writings*, trans. T. M. Knox (Oxford: Oxford University Press, 1964).

Helgerson, Richard, *Forms of Nationhood: The Elizabethan Writing of England* (Chicago: Chicago University Press, 1992).

Hendricks, Hendrick, 'Oppressions of the Griqua', *South African Commercial Advertiser* (5.344), 29 September 1830, p. 2.

Henshaw, Philip, 'The "Key to South Africa" in the 1890s: Delagoa Bay and the origins of the South African War', *Journal of Southern African Studies* 24, 3 (1998), pp. 527–44.

Herbert, Thomas, *Some Years Travels into Divers Parts of Africa, and Asia the Great* (London: R. Everingham et al., 1677).

Hill, John E., *Democracy, Equality, and Justice: John Adams, Adam Smith, and Political Economy* (Lanham, MD: Lexington Books, 2007).

Hirsch, Elisabeth F., *Damião de Gois: The Life and Thought of a Portuguese Humanist, 1502–1574* (The Hague: Martinus Nijhoff, 1967).

Holmes, Rachel, *The Hottentot Venus. The Life and Death of Saartjie Baartman: born 1789 – buried 2002* (London: Bloomsbury, 2008).

Hudson, Nicholas, '"Hottentots" and the evolution of European racism', *Journal of European Studies* 34, 4 (2004), pp. 308–32.

Huigen, Siegfried, *Knowledge and Colonialism: Eighteenth-century Travellers in South Africa* (Leiden and Boston: Brill, 2009).

——, *De weg naar Monomotapa: Nederlandstalige representaties van geografische, historische en sociale werkelijkheden in Zuid-Afrika* (Utrecht: unpublished PhD thesis, 1995).

Hull, Richard W., *American Enterprise in South Africa* (New York: New York University Press, 1990).

Hulme, Peter, *Colonial Encounters: Europe and the Native Caribbean, 1492–1797* (London: Methuen, 1986)

Humphreys, R. A., *Robert Southey and his 'History of Brazil'* (London: Hispanic and Luso-Brazilian Council, 1978).

Jacobs, Nancy, *Environment, Power, and Injustice: A South African History* (Cambridge: Cambridge University Press, 2003).

Jacobs, Rayda, *The Slave Book* (Cape Town: Kwela, 1998).

Jameson, Fredric, *The Political Unconscious: Narrative as a Socially Symbolic Act* (London: Methuen, 1981).

——, 'Third-world literature in the era of multinational capitalism', *Social Text* 15 (1986), pp. 65–88.

Jasanoff, Maya, *Liberty's Exiles: The Loss of America and the Remaking of the British Empire* (London: Harper Press, 2011).

John, P., 'Die abjekte einde van *Verkenning* van Karel Schoeman en die Afrikaanse rewolusie', *Stilet* 14, 2 (2002), pp. 164–85.

Johnson, David, 'The first rainbow nation? The Griqua in post-apartheid South Africa', in Prem Poddar (ed.), *Translating Nations* (Copenhagen: Aarhus University Press, 1999), pp. 115–28.

——, 'Importing metropolitan post-colonials' *Current Writing* 6, 1 (1994), pp. 73–86.

——, 'Talking about revolution: Lady Anne Barnard in France, Ireland, and the Cape Colony', in Glenn Hooper and Colin Graham (eds), *Irish and Postcolonial Writing: History, Theory, Practice* (Basingstoke: Macmillan/Palgrave, 2002), pp. 157–77.

——, 'Theorizing the loss of land: Griqua land claims, 1874/1998', in David Kazanjian and David Ien (eds), *Loss: The Politics of Mourning* (Berkeley: University of California Press, 2003), pp. 278–99.

Johnson, Walter, 'Slavery, reparations, and the mythic march of freedom', *Raritan* (2007), pp. 41–67.

Johnston, Nicola, 'The Point of No Return: Evaluating the Amnesty for Mozambican Refugees in South Africa', Southern African Migration Project, Migration Policy Brief No. 6, 2001, http://www.queensu.ca/samp/sampresources/samppublications/policybriefs/brief6.pdf (accessed 10 November 2010).

Joseph, Betty, *Reading the East India Company, 1720–1840* (Chicago: University of Chicago Press, 2004).

Karasch, Mary C., *Slave Life in Rio de Janeiro, 1808–1850* (Princeton: Princeton University Press, 1987).

Kasrils, Ronnie, 'Speech by the Minister of Water Affairs and Forestry, Ronnie Kasrils, MP, during the Anglo-Boer War Debate, Parliament, 16 December 1999', http://www.info.gov.za/speeches/1999/991203122p1003.htm (accessed 18 September 2010).

Kaul, Suvir, 'Coda. How to write postcolonial histories of empire?', in Daniel Carey and Lynn Festa (eds), *The Postcolonial Enlightenment: Eighteenth-Century Colonialism and Postcolonial Theory* (New York: Oxford University Press, 2009), pp. 305–27.

Kazanjian, David, *The Colonizing Trick: National Culture and Imperial Citizenship in Early America* (Minneapolis: University of Minnesota Press, 2003).

Keegan, Timothy, *Colonial South African and the Origins of the Racial Order* (Cape Town: David Philip, 1996).

Kelsall, Malcolm, *Jefferson and the Iconography of Romanticism: Folk, Land, Culture and the Romantic Nation* (Basingstoke: Macmillan, 1999).

Kendall, Edward Augustus, *The English Boy at the Cape* (London: Whittaker, 1835).

Kindersley, Jemima, *Letters from the Island of Teneriffe, Brazil, the Cape of Good Hope, and the East Indies* (London: J. Nourse, 1777).

Kinsman, Margaret, 'Populists and patriarchs: the transformation of the captaincy at Griqua Town, 1804–1822', in Alan Mabin (ed.), *Organisation and Economic Change* (Johannesburg: Ravan, 1989), pp. 1–20.

Kitching, John and Johan Meiring (eds), *A Conceptual Report on Griqua History, Griqua Interest Groups and Leadership* (Pretoria: The Constitutional Assembly, 1997).

Knight, Brigid, *Walking the Whirlwind* (London: Cassell, 1940).

Kolb, Peter, *The Present State of the Cape of Good Hope*, Vol. 1, trans. W. Innys, ed. Peter W. Carstens (New York and London: Johnson Reprint, [1731] 1968).

Koselleck, Reinhart, *The Practice of Conceptual History: Timing History, Spacing Concepts*, trans. Todd Samuel Presner (Stanford: Stanford University Press, 2002).

Kriegel, Murray and Sanjay Subrahmanyam, 'The unity of opposites: Abraham Zacut, Vasco da Gama and the chronicler Gaspar Correa', in Anthony Disney and Emily Booth (eds), *Vasco da Gama and the Linking of Europe and Asia (Vasco da Gama Quincentenary Conference)* (Oxford: Oxford University Press, 2000), pp. 48–71.

La Caille, Nicolas Louis de, *Travels at the Cape, 1751–53: An Annotated Translation of 'Journal historique du voyage fait au Cap de Bonn-Espérance' into which Has Been Interpolated Relevant Passages from 'Mémoires de l'Académie Royal des Sciences'*, trans. and ed. R. Raven-Hart (Cape Town: A. A. Balkema, 1976).

Labillardière, Jacques-Julien Houtou de, *An Account of a Voyage in Search of La Pérouse, Undertaken by Order of the Constituent Assembly of France, and Performed in the Years 1791, 1792, and 1793, in the Recherche and Espérance, Ships of War, under the Command of Rear-Admiral Bruni D'Entrecasteaux*, Vol. 2 (London: J. Debrett, 1800).

Larsen, Neil, *Determinations: Essays on Theory, Narrative and Nation in the Americas* (London: Verso, 2001).

—— and Robert Krueger, 'Camões' Os Lusiadas and the break-up of epic discourse', *Revista Camoniana* 5 (1984), pp. 69–85.

Latrobe, Christian, *Journal of a Visit to South Africa in 1815 and 1816, with some Account of the Missionary Settlements of the United Brethren, near the Cape of Good Hope* (London: L. B. Seeley and R. Ackerman, 1818).

Lazarus, Neil, *Nationalism and Cultural Practice in the Postcolonial World* (Cambridge: Cambridge University Press, 1999).

Le May, Jean, 'Wee problem for SA motto', *SA Independent on Sunday*, 13 May 2000.

Leask, Nigel, 'Romanticism and the wider world: poetry, travel literature and empire', in James Chandler (ed.), *The Cambridge History of English Romantic Literature* (Cambridge: Cambridge University Press, 2009), pp. 271–92.

——, 'Southey's *Madoc*: reimagining the conquest of America', in Lynda Pratt (ed.), *Robert Southey and the Contexts of English Romanticism* (Aldershot: Ashgate, 2006), pp. 133–50.

Lefeber, Walter, *The American Age: United States Foreign Policy at Home and Abroad*, 2nd edn (New York: W. W. Norton, 1994).

Legassick, Martin, *The Politics of a South African Frontier: The Griqua, the South-Tswana, and the Missionaries, 1780–1840* (Basel: Basler Afrika Bibliographien, 2010).

——, 'Reflections on practising applied history in South Africa, 1994–2002: from skeletons to schools', in Hans Erik Stolten (ed.), *History-making and Present-day Politics: The Meaning of Collective Memory in South Africa* (Uppsala: Nordiska Afrikainstitutet, 2007), pp. 129–47.

Leguat, François, *A New Voyage to the East Indies by Francis Leguat and his Companions. Containing their Adventures in two Desart Islands, and an Account of the most Remarkable Things in Maurice*

Island, Batavia, at the Cape of Good Hope, the Island of St Hélèna, and other Places on their Way to and from the Desart Isles, 2 vols (London: Hakluyt Society, [1708] 1891).

Levaillant, François, New Travels into the Interior Parts of Africa, by way of the Cape of Good Hope in the Years 1783, 84 and 85, 3 vols (London: G. G. and J. Robinson, 1796).

——, Travels from the Cape of Good Hope into the Interior Parts of Africa, Including Many Interesting Anecdotes, Vol. 2, trans. Elizabeth Helme (London: William Lane, 1790).

——, Travels into the Interior of Africa via the Cape of Good Hope, Vol. 1, trans. and ed. Ian Glenn with Catherine Lauga Du Plessis and Ian Farlam (Cape Town: Van Riebeeck Society, 2007).

Lévi-Strauss, Claude, Tristes Tropiques, trans. John and Doreen Weightman (London: Penguin, [1955] 1992).

Lewis-Williams, David and David Pearce, San Spirituality: Roots, Expressions and Social Consequences (Cape Town: Double Storey, 2004).

Leyds, W. J., De eerste annexatie van de Transvaal (Amsterdam: Allert De Lange, 1906).

Leyland, J., 'The story of South Africa', in C. N. Robinson (ed.), A Pictorial History of South Africa and the Transvaal (London: George Newns, 1900), pp. 12–17.

Lichtenstein, Hinrich, Reisen im südlichen Africa in den Jahren 1803, 1804, 1805 und 1806, Vol. 1 (Berlin: Salfeld, 1811).

——, Travels in Southern Africa in the years 1803, 1804, 1805 and 1806, Vol. 1, trans. Anne Plumptre (Cape Town: Van Riebeeck Society, [1812] 1928).

'Lied ter Eere van de Swellendamsche en Diverse andere helden bij de bloedige Actie aan Muisenburg in dato 7 Aug. 1795', Hollandsch Zuid-Afrika (15 August 1920), p. 7.

Lindley, Augustus F., Adamantia: The Truth About the South African Diamond Fields: or, A Vindication of the Right of the Orange Free State to That Territory, and an Analysis of British Diplomacy and Aggression which has Resulted in its Illegal Seizure by the Governor of the Cape of Good Hope (London: W. H. and L. Collingridge, 1873).

Lipking, Lawrence, 'The view from Almada Hill: myths of nationhood in Camões and William Julius Mickle', Portuguese Literary and Cultural Studies 9 (2002), pp. 165–76.

Locke, John, Two Treatises of Government, ed. Mark Goldie (London: J. M. Dent, 1993).

Lukács, Georg, The Historical Novel, trans. Hannah and Stanley Mitchell (Harmondsworth: Penguin, 1981).

Lupi, Luís C., Portugal in Africa: The Significance of the Visit of the President of the Republic to the Overseas Provinces (Lisbon: Agência Geral do Ultramar, 1957).

Lye, William F., 'The emergence of the Griqua culture: an African response to colonialism and Christianity', in David Chanaiwa (ed.), Profile of Self-Determination (Northbridge: California State University Press, 1976), pp. 138–66.

Mabuyakhulu, Michael, 'Address by Kwazulu-Natal MEC for Economic Development and Tourism, Mr Michael Mabuyakhulu during the Kwazulu-Natal Youth Chamber of Commerce and Industry's Annual General Meeting (AGM), 26 Aug 2010', http://www.info.gov.za/speech/DynamicAction?pageid=461&sid=12464&tid=16082 (accessed 10 March 2011).

Macaulay, Rose, They Came to Portugal (Harmondsworth: Penguin, [1946] 1985).

McCombie, Thomas Mcintosh, Governor van Noodt's Revenge, 1727 (Cape Town: Townshend, 1887).

Mackenzie, Norman H., 'Captain Cross and the first English settlement at the Cape', Quarterly Bulletin of the South African Public Library 2 (1947) pp. 3–17, 49–54.

McNally, David, Political Economy and the Rise of Capitalism: A Reinterpretation (Berkeley: University of California Press, 1988).

Majeed, Javed, Ungoverned Imaginings: James Mill's 'The History of British India' and Orientalism (Oxford: Oxford University Press, 1992).

Makanna; or the Land of the Savage (London: Simpkin and Marshall, 1834).

Makgoba, W. M. (ed.), African Renaissance: The New Struggle (Cape Town: Mafube/Tafelberg, 1999).

Mamdani, Mahmood, *Citizen and Subject: Contemporary Africa and the Legacy of Late Colonialism* (Cape Town: David Philip, 1996).

Mandela, Nelson, 'Address by President Nelson Mandela at the Inauguration of the National Council of Traditional Leaders, Cape Town, 18 April 1997', http://www.info.gov.za/speeches/1997/04210x34997.htm (accessed 17 September 2010).

Marais, Hein, *South Africa Pushed to the Limit* (New York: Zed Books, 2011).

Marais, J. S., *Maynier and the First Boer Republic* (Cape Town: Maskew Miller, 1944).

Martin, R. M., *The British Colonies; their History, Extent, Condition, and Resources*, Vol. IV (London: London Printing and Publishing Company, 1851).

Martineau, Harriet, *Illustrations of Political Economy: Demerara. Harriet Martineau's Writings on Empire*, Vol. 1 (London: Pickering & Chatto, [1833] 2005), pp. 65–141.

——, *Illustrations of Political Economy: Life in the Wilds. A Tale. Harriet Martineau's Writings on Empire*, Vol. 1 (London: Pickering and Chatto, [1832] 2005), pp. 1–63.

Marx, Karl, *Capital*, Vol. 1, trans. Ben Fowkes (Harmondsworth: Penguin, 1976).

——, *The Eighteenth Brumaire of Louis Bonaparte* [1852], in D. Fernbach (ed.), *Karl Marx: Surveys from Exile. Political Writings*, Vol. 2 (Harmondsworth: Penguin, 1973).

——, *The Grundrisse: Foundations of the Critique of Political Economy*, trans. Martin Nicolaus (Harmondsworth: Penguin, 1973).

Mbeki, Thabo, 'Address by President Thabo Mbeki at the Unveiling of the Coat of Arms, Kwaggafontein, 27 April 2000', http://www.info.gov.za/speeches/2000/000502438p1001.htm (accessed 17 March 2008).

——, 'Address by the President of South Africa, Mr Thabo Mbeki, to the Assembly of the Republic of Mozambique, Maputo, 2 May 2002', http://www.info.gov.za/speeches/2002/02050309291002.htm (accessed 10 May 2008).

——, 'Address of the President of South Africa, Thabo Mbeki, at the French National Assembly, Paris, 18 March 2003', http://www.info.gov.za/speeches/2003/ (accessed 30 July 2009).

——, *Africa: Define Yourself* (Cape Town: Tafelberg/Mafube, 2002).

——, *Africa: The Time Has Come* (Cape Town: Tafelberg/Mafube, 1998).

——, 'A Farewell to Madiba! Statement of the President of the African National Congress', Cape Town, 26 March 1999, http://www.info.gov.za/speeches/1999/990326530p1001.htm (accessed 10 January 2008).

——, 'Joint Statement by President George W. Bush and President Thabo Mbeki', 26 June 2001, http://www.info.gov.za/speeches/2001/010627945a1009.htm (accessed 12 January 2011).

——, 'Nobody ever chose to be a slave', *ANC Today* 7, 14 (13–19 April 2007), http://www.anc.org.za/ancdocs/anctoday/2007/at14.htm#preslet (accessed 12 December 2009).

——, 'Speech at the Funeral of Sarah Bartmann, Hankey, Eastern Cape, 9 August 2002', http://www.anc.org.za/ancdocs/history/mbeki/2002/ (accessed 30 June 2009).

——, 'Speech of the President of South Africa, Thabo Mbeki, at the Special Official Funeral of Dr C. F. Beyers Naudé, Johannesburg, 18 September 2004', http://www.info.gov.za/speeches/2004/04092008451006.htm (accessed 1 October 2009).

——, 'Statement by Deputy President Thabo Mbeki at the Opening of the Third Session of the SA–USA Bi-National Commission, 17 February 1997', http://www.info.gov.za/speeches/1997/06036797.htm (accessed 12 January 2011).

Meihuizen, Nicholas, *Ordering Empire: The Poetry of Camões, Pringle and Campbell* (Bern: Peter Lang, 2007).

Meiring, Jane, *The Truth in Masquerade: The Adventures of François Le Vaillant* (Cape Town: Juta, 1973).

Meltzer, Lalou, 'Emancipation, commerce and the role of John Fairbairn's *Advertiser*', in Nigel Worden and Clifton Crais (eds), *Breaking the Chains: Slavery and its Legacy in the Nineteenth-Century Cape Colony* (Johannesburg: Witwatersrand University Press, 1994), pp. 169–99.

Mentzel, Otto Frederick, *A Geographical and Topographical Description of the Cape of Good Hope,* trans. G. V. Marais and J. Hoge, 3 vols (Cape Town: Van Riebeeck Society, [1785–7] 1944).

Merians, Linda, *Envisioning the Worst: Representations of 'Hottentots' in Early Modern England* (Newark: University of Delaware Press, 2001).

Meyer, P. J., 'Nasionalisme', in F. A. Van Jaarsveld and G. D. Scholtz (eds), *Die Republiek van Suid Afrika: Agtergrond, Ontstaan, en Toekoms* (Johannesburg: Voortrekkerpers, 1966), pp. 287–307.

Mickle, William Julius, *Almada Hill: An Epistle from Lisbon* (Oxford: W. Jackson, 1781).

——, *A Candid Examination of the Reasons for Depriving the East-India Company of its Charter, contained in 'The History and Management of the East-India Company, from its Commencement to the Present Time'* [1779, by James Macpherson]. *Together with Strictures on some of the Self-contradictions and Historical Errors of Dr. Adam Smith, in his Reasons for the Abolition of Said Company* (London: J. Bew and J. Sewell, 1779).

——, *The Lusiad; or The Discovery of India. An Epic Poem. Translated from the Original Portuguese of Luis de Camoëns* (Oxford: Jackson and Lister, 1776).

Mill, James, *The History of British India*, Vol. 6, 4th edn (London: James Madden, [1818] 1898).

——, 'Publications on the affairs of India', *Edinburgh Review* 16, 31 (April 1810), pp. 127–57.

Millar, John, *The Origin of the Distinction of Ranks*, ed. Aaron Garrett (Indianapolis: The Liberty Fund, [1771] 2006).

Millin, S. G., *The Burning Man* (London: William Heinemann, 1952).

——, *The King of the Bastards* (London: William Heinemann, 1950).

Mitchell, W. J. T., 'Imperial landscapes', in W. J. T. Mitchell (ed.), *Landscape and Power* (Chicago and London: University of Chicago Press, 1994), pp. 5–34.

Moffat, Robert, *Missionary Labours and Scenes in Southern Africa*, 4th edn (London: John Snow, 1842).

Moloka, Eddy and Elizabeth le Roux (eds), *Problematising the African Renaissance* (Pretoria: Africa Institute of South Africa, 2000).

Monteiro, George, *The Presence of Camões: Influence on the Literature of England, America, and Southern Africa* (Lexington: University of Kentucky Press, 1996).

Mooers, Colin, *The Making of Bourgeois Europe: Absolutism, Revolution and the Rise of Capitalism in England, France and Germany* (London: Verso, 1991).

Morrison, Toni, *Beloved* (London: Vintage, [1987] 2007).

Moser, Gerald M., 'What did the Old Man of the Restelo mean?', *Luso-Brazilian Review* 17 (1980), pp. 139–51.

Mostert, Noël, *Frontiers: The Epic of South Africa's Creation and the Tragedy of the Xhosa People* (London: Jonathan Cape, 1992).

Mouton, F. A. (ed.), *History, Historians and Afrikaner Nationalism* (Vanderbijlpark: Kleio, 2007).

Mpahlwa, Mandisi, 'Speech by Mandisi Mpahlwa, Minister of Trade and Industry at the Black Management Forum Annual Achievement Awards, 12 October 2007', http://www.info.gov.za/speeches/2007/07111512451003.htm (accessed 10 March 2011).

Mulemfo, M. M., *Thabo Mbeki and the African Renaissance: The Emergence of a New African Leadership* (Pretoria: Actua Press, 2000).

Müller, André, 'The state and the development of the Cape, 1795–1820', *South African Journal of Economic History* 1, 1 (1986), pp. 58–76.

Muller, C. F. J., *Die Oorsprong van die Groot Trek* (Cape Town: 1974).

Muthu, Sankar, *Enlightenment against Empire* (Princeton: Princeton University Press, 2003).

Nepgen, C. C., *Die Sosiale Gewete van die Afrikaanssprekendes* (Johannesburg: C. S. V. Boekhandel, 1938).

Newitt, Malyn, *A History of Mozambique* (London: Hurst and Company, 1995).

——, *A History of Portuguese Overseas Expansion, 1400–1668* (London and New York: Routledge, 2005).

Newton-King, Susan, *Masters and Servants on the Cape Eastern Frontier 1760–1803* (Cambridge: Cambridge University Press, 1999).

North-Coombe, Alfred, *The Vindication of François Leguat* (Port Louis, Mauritius: Société de l'Histoire de L'Ile Maurice, 1979).

'Obituary: John Bruce', *Gentleman's Magazine* 96, 2 (July 1826), pp. 87–8.

O'Brien, Karen, *Narratives of Enlightenment: Cosmopolitan History from Voltaire to Gibbon* (Cambridge: Cambridge University Press, 1997).

O'Hier de Grandpré, Louis, *Voyage à la Côte Occidentale d'Afrique, fait dans les années 1786 et 1787; contenant la description des moeurs, usages, lois, gouvernement et commerce des États du Congo, fréquentés par les Européens, et un précis de la traite des Noirs, ainsi qu'elle avait lieu avant la Révolution française; Suivi d'un Voyage fait au cap de Bonne-Espérance, contenant la description militaire de cette colonie*, Vol. 2 (Paris: Dentu, 1801).

O'Meara, Dan, *Volkskapitalisme: Class, Capital and Ideology in the Development of Afrikaner Nationalism* (Johannesburg: Ravan, 1983).

Overbeek, Johannes, *Free Trade versus Protectionism: A Source Book of Essays and Readings* (Cheltenham: Edward Elgar, 1999).

Ovington, John, *A Voyage to Surat in the Year 1689*, ed. H. G. Rawlinson (London: Oxford University Press, [1696] 1929).

Pagès, Pierre Marie François, *Travels Round the World, in the Years 1767, 1768, 1769, 1770, 1771*, 2nd edn, 3 vols (London: J. Murray, [1782] 1793).

Pallotti, Arrigo, 'SADC: a development community without a development policy?', *Review of African Political Economy* 31, 101 (2004), pp. 513–31.

Paterson, William, *A Narrative of Four Journeys into the Country of the Hottentots and Caffraria in the Years 1777, 1778, and 1779* (London: J. Johnson, 1789).

Peberdy, Sally, *Selecting Immigrants: National Identity and South Africa's Immigration Policies, 1910–2008* (South Africa: Wits University Press, 2009).

Pemberton, Henry, 'Desirability of establishing a base on the shores of "Croeme Rivier Bay"', in 'Mr. [Henry] Dundas's Miscellaneous Tracts' (No. 4), *Cape of Good Hope Factory Records 1773–1809*, Vol. 1 (London: India Office, G/9/1).

Penn, Nigel, *The Forgotten Frontier: Colonist and Khoisan on the Cape's Northern Frontier in the Eighteenth Century* (Cape Town: Double Storey Books, 2005).

——, 'Labour, land and livestock in the Western Cape during the eighteenth century: the Khoisan and the colonists', in Wilmot G. James and Mary Simons (eds), *The Angry Divide: Social and Economic History of the Western Cape* (Cape Town: David Philip, 1989), pp. 2–19.

——, 'Mapping the Cape: John Barrow and the first British occupation of the Cape Colony, 1795–1803', *Pretexts* 4, 2 (1993), pp. 20–43.

——, *Rogues, Rebels and Runaways: Eighteenth-Century Cape Characters* (Cape Town: David Philip, 1999).

——, 'The voyage out. Peter Kolb and VOC voyages to the Cape', in Emma Christopher, Cassandra Pybus and Marcus Rediker (eds), *Many Middle Passages: Forced Migration and the Making of the Modern World* (Berkeley: University of California Press, 2007), pp. 72–91.

Percival, Robert, *An Account of the Cape of Good Hope* (London: C. and R. Baldwin, 1804).

Perelman, Michael, *The Invention of Capitalism: Classical Political Economy and the Secret History of Primitive Accumulation* (Durham, NC: Duke University Press, 2000).

Petrie, P. (ed.), *Morrell's Narrative of a Voyage to the South and West Coast of Africa* (London: Whittaker, 1844).

'The Philanthropic Society:- a theatre', *The South African Commercial Advertiser* (25 July 1832), p. 1.

Philip, John, *Researches in South Africa; Illustrating the Civil, Moral, and Religious Condition of the Native Tribes*, Vol. 1 (London: James Duncan, 1828).

Pitcher, Anne M., 'Recreating colonialism or reconstructing the state? Privatization and politics in Mozambique', *Journal of Southern African Studies* 22, 1 (1996), pp. 49–75.

Poivre, Pierre, *Travels of a Philosopher; or Observations on the Manners and Arts of Various Nations in Africa and Asia* (Baltimore: N. G. Maxwell, [1770] 1818).

Postone, Moishe, *Time, Labor, and Social Domination: A Reinterpretation of Marx's Critical Theory* (Cambridge: Cambridge University Press, 1993).

Pratt, Mary Louise, *Imperial Eyes: Travel Writing and Transculturation* (London and New York: Routledge, 1992).

Preller, Gustav, *Day-Dawn in South Africa* (Pretoria: Wallachs, [1937] 1938).

Prendergast, Christopher, *The Triangle of Representation* (New York: Columbia University Press, 2000).

Purves, John, 'Camoens and the Epic of Africa, part 1', *The State* 2, 11 (November 1909), pp. 542–55.

——, 'Camoens and the Epic of Africa, part 2', *The State* 2, 12 (December 1909), pp. 734–45.

Quint, David, 'Voices of resistance: the epic curse and Camões's Adamastor', *Representations* 27 (1989), pp. 118–41.

Quinton, J. C. and A. M. L. Robinson, *François le Vaillant, Traveller in South Africa, and his Collection of 165 Water-colour Paintings, 1781–1784* (Cape Town: Library of Parliament, 1973).

Rae, John, *Life of Adam Smith* (Bristol: Thoemmes, [1895] 1990).

Raman, Shankar, *Framing 'India': The Colonial Imaginary in Early Modern Culture* (Stanford: Stanford University Press, 2002).

Rantao, J., '"Let's be partners," says Clinton.' *The Star* 27 March 1998.

Raum, Johannes, W., 'Reflections on rereading Peter Kolb with regard to the cultural heritage of the Khoisan', *Kronos* 24 (1997), pp. 30–40.

Raven-Hart, R. (ed. and trans.), *Before Van Riebeeck: Callers at South Africa from 1488 to 1652* (Cape Town: Struik, 1967).

—— (ed. and trans.), *Cape of Good Hope 1652–1702: The First Fifty Years of Dutch Colonisation as Seen by Callers*, Vol. 2 (Cape Town: A. A. Balkema, 1971).

Renders, L., 'Base en slawe: Ontmoetings tussen Europeane en Afrikane in Afrikaanse historiese romans oor die begin van die Europese kolonisasie van Suider Afrika', *Stilet* 8, 2 (1996), pp. 72–85.

Republic of South Africa, Constitutional Assembly, 'Constitution of the Republic of South Africa', 1996, http://www.info.gov.za/documents/constitution/1996/96preamble.htm (accessed 12 June 2010).

——, Ministry of Welfare and Social Development, 'Mothers and Fathers of the Nation: The Forgotten People – Report of the Ministerial Committee on Abuse, Neglect and Ill-Treatment of Older Persons, 26 February 2001, Volume II: Provincial Reports', http://www.polity.org.za/polity/govdocs/reports/welfare/2001/elderprov.htm (accessed 30 November 2009).

A Resident at the Cape of Good Hope [William Wright], *Remarks on the Demoralizing Influence of Slavery* (London: Bagster and Thomas, 1828).

Robertson, William, *An Historical Disquisition concerning the Knowledge which the Ancients Had of India* (London: A. Strahan and T. Cadell, 1791).

Rogers, Woodes, *A Cruising Voyage around the World: first to the South-Sea, thence to the East-Indies, and homewards to the Cape of Good Hope. Begun in 1708, and Finish'd in 1711*, 2nd edn (London: Andrew Bell and Bernard Lintot, 1718).

Romain, Alain, *Mes ennemis savent que je suis Breton: La vie d'Ohier de Grandpré marin de Saint-Malo (1761–1846)* (Saint Malo: Editions Cristel, 2004).

Romero, Patricia W., 'Encounter at the Cape: French Huguenots, the Khoi and other people of color', *Journal of Colonialism and Colonial History* 5, 1 (Spring 2004), http://muse.jhu.edu/login?uri=/journals/journal_of_colonialism_and_colonial_history/v005/5.1romero.html (accessed 5 June 2006).

Rookmaaker, L. C., P. Mundy, I. E. Glenn and E. C. Spary, *François Levaillant and the Birds of Africa* (Johannesburg: Brenthurst Press, 2004).

Roos, H. 'Die "vaslê en behou van wat eens hier gebeur het": vrouestemme in Karel Schoeman se *Verkenning* en *Dogter van Sion*', *Tydskrif vir Letterkunde* 38, 3–4 (2000), pp. 1–20.

Ross, Ian Simpson, *The Life of Adam Smith* (Oxford: Clarendon, 1995).

Ross, Robert, *Adam Kok's Griquas: A Study in the Development of Stratification in South Africa* (Cambridge: Cambridge University Press, 1976).

——, *Beyond the Pale: Essays on the History of Colonial South Africa* (Johannesburg: Witwatersrand University Press, 1994).

——, *Cape of Torments: Slavery and Resistance in South Africa* (London: Routledge and Kegan Paul, 1983).

——, 'Griqua government', *African Studies* 33, 1 (1974), pp. 25–42.

——, *Status and Respectability in the Cape Colony, 1750–1870: A Tragedy of Manners* (Cambridge: Cambridge University Press, 1999).

Rothschild, Emma, *Economic Sentiments: Adam Smith, Condorcet, and the Enlightenment* (Cambridge, MA: Harvard University Press, 2001).

Rousseau, Jean-Jacques, *Discourse on the Origin of Inequality*, ed. Patrick Coleman, trans. Franklin Philip (Oxford: Oxford Classics, 1994).

Scammell, G. V., *The First Imperial Age: European Overseas Expansion, c. 1400–1715* (London: Unwin Hyman, 1989).

Schapera, Isaac (ed.), *The Early Cape Hottentots* (Cape Town: Van Riebeeck Society, 1933).

Scherr, Arthur, 'Inventing the patriot president: Bache's *Aurora* and John Adams', *The Pennsylvania Magazine of History and Biography* 119, 4 (1995), pp. 369–99.

Schiebinger, Londa, *Nature's Body: Gender in the Making of Modern Science* (London: Beacon Press, 1993).

Schoeman, Karel, *Armosyn van die Kaap: Voorspel tot Vestiging, 1415–1651* (Cape Town: Human and Rousseau, 1999).

——, *The Griqua Captaincy of Philippolis 1826–1861* (Pretoria: Protea Book House, 2002).

—— (ed.), *The Mission at Griquatown, 1801–21: An Anthology* (Griquatown: Griekwastad Toerisme Vereniging, 1997).

Scholtz, A. H. M., *A Place Called Vatmaar*, trans. Chris Van Wyk (Cape Town: Kwela Books, [1995] 2000).

Scholtz, G. D., *Die Ontwikkeling van die Politieke Denke van die Afrikaner* (Johannesburg: Voortrekkerpers, 1967).

Schonhardt-Bailey, Cheryl (ed.), *The Rise of Free Trade: Volume 1. Protectionism and its Critics, 1815–1837* (London and New York: Routledge, 1997).

Schwarz, Roberto, *Misplaced Ideas: Essays on Brazilian Culture*, trans. John Gledson (London: Verso, 1992).

Scott, James C., *Seeing it Like a State: How Certain Schemes to Improve the Human Condition Have Failed* (New Haven, CT: Yale University Press, 1998).

Seekings, Jeremy and Nicoli Nattrass, *Class, Race, and Inequality in South Africa* (Scottsville: University of KwaZulu-Natal Press, 2006).

Semmel, Bernard, *The Liberal Ideal and the Demons of Empire* (Baltimore: Johns Hopkins University Press, 1993).

——, *The Rise of Free Trade Imperialism: Classical Political Economy, the Empire of Free Trade and Imperialism, 1750–1850* (Cambridge: Cambridge University Press, 1970).

Semple, Robert, *Charles Ellis: or, The Friends*, Vol. 2 (London: C. and R. Baldwin, 1806).

——, *Walks and Sketches at the Cape of Good Hope*, Intro. Frank R. Bradlow (Cape Town: Balkema, 1968).

Shell, Robert, *Children of Bondage: A Social History of a Slave Society* (Hanover, NH: Wesleyan University Press, 1994).

——, 'Introduction to S. E. Hudson's "Slaves"', *Kronos* 9 (1984), pp. 44–70.

——, Edward Hudson and Raymond Hudson (eds), *Out of Livery: The Papers of Samuel Eusebius Hudson 1764–1828* (Cape Town: Van Riebeeck Society, forthcoming).

*A Short Conversation on the Present Crisis on the Important Trade with the Indies* (London: Black and Parry, 1813).

Sienaert-van Reenen, Marilet, *Die Franse bydrae to Africana-literatuur 1622–1902* (Cape Town: Human and Rousseau, 1989).

Silva, John de Oliveira, 'Moving the monarch: the rhetoric of persuasion in Camões's *Lusíadas*', *Renaissance Quarterly* 53, 3 (2000), pp. 735–68.

Skotnes, Pippa (ed.), *Miscast: Negotiating the Presence of the Bushmen* (Cape Town: University of Cape Town Press, 1996).

Smith, A. B, 'Different facets of the crystal: early images of the Khoikhoi at the Cape, South Africa', in Martin Hall and Ann Markell (eds), *Historical Archaeology in the Western Cape: The S. A. Archaeological Society Goodwin Series* 7 (1993), pp. 8–20.

Smith, Adam, *The Correspondence of Adam Smith*, ed. E. C. Mossner and I. S. Ross (Oxford: Clarendon, 1987).

——, *The Theory of Moral Sentiments*, 6th edn (Indianapolis: Liberty Fund, [1790] 1984).

——, *The Wealth of Nations. Books IV–V*, ed. A. Skinner (Harmondsworth: Penguin, [1776] 1999).

Smith, Alan K. 'The peoples of Southern Mozambique: an historical survey', *Journal of African History* 14 (1975), pp. 565–80.

Smith, David, 'South African security guards shoot dead at least four illegal miners', *The Guardian*, 12 August 2010, http://www.guardian.co.uk/world/2010/aug/12/south-africa-illegal-miners-killed (accessed 25 August 2010).

Smith, Marleen, 'New chapter in Bushmen's book', *Mail and Guardian*, 20 January 2004.

Smithies, Michael (ed. and trans.), *The Chevalier de Chaumont and the Abbé de Choisy: Aspects of the Embassy to Siam 1685* (Chiang Mai: Silkworm Books, [1686] 1997).

—— (ed.), *A Siamese Embassy Lost in Africa 1686: The Odyssey of Ok-Khun Chamnan* (Chiang Mai: Silkworm Books, 1999).

Sole, Kelwyn, *Land Dreaming* (Scottsville: University of Natal Press, 2006).

——, *Projections in the Past Tense* (Johannesburg: Ravan, 1992).

Somerville, William, *Narrative of his Journeys to the Eastern Cape Frontier and to Lattakoe, 1799–1802*, ed. Edna and Frank Bradlow (Cape Town: Van Riebeeck Society, 1979).

Sonnerat, Pierre, *A Voyage to the East-Indies and China; Performed by Order of Lewis XV. Between the Years 1774 and 1781. Containing a Description of the Manners, Religion, Arts and Sciences, of the Indians, Chinese, Pegouins, and of the Islanders of Madagascar; Also, Observations of the Cape of Good Hope, the Isles of France and Bourbon, the Maldivias, Ceylon, Malacca, the Philippines, and Moluccas*, Vol. 1, trans. Francis Magnus (Calcutta: Stuart and Cooper, 1788).

Southey, Robert, *New Letters of Robert Southey, Vol. 1 1792–1810*, ed. Kenneth Curry (New York and London: Columbia University Press, 1965).

——, 'Observations on Mr. Mickle's *Lusiad*, with the Portuguese criticism on that translation', *The Monthly Magazine and British Register* 2 (November 1796), pp. 787–9.

——, 'On the poetry of Spain and Portugal', *The Monthly Magazine and British Register* 2 (July 1796), pp. 451–3.

——, 'Review of John Barrow's *An Account of Travels into the Interior of Southern Africa*', *The Annual Review and History of Literature for 1804* 3 (1805), pp. 22–33.

——, 'Review of *Memoirs of the Life and Writings of Luis de Camoens* by John Adamson', *The Quarterly Review* 27 (April 1822), pp. 1–39.

——, 'Review of *Poems from the Portuguese of Luis de Camoens* by Lord Viscount Strangford', *Annual Review* 2 (1803), pp. 569–77.

——, 'Review of Robert Percival's *An Account of the Cape of Good Hope*', *The Critical Review; or Annals of Literature* 4 (1805), pp. 375–83.

——, *Selections from the Letters of Robert Southey*, Vol. 1, ed. John Wood Warter (London: Longmans, Brown, Green and Longmans, 1856).

——, '*A Vision of Judgement*' by Robert Southey and '*The Vision of Judgement*' by Lord Byron, ed. R. Ellis Roberts (Harrow Weald: R. A. Maynard and H. W. Bray, 1932).

Special Issue on Camões, *Portuguese Literary and Cultural Studies* 9 (2002).

Special Issue on Slavery, *Kronos. Journal of Cape History* 28 (2002).

Special Issue on Slavery, *South African Historical Journal* 34 (1996).

Speck, W. A., *Robert Southey: Entire Man of Letters* (New Haven, CT and London: Yale University Press, 2006).

Spivak, Gayatri Chakravorty, 'Can the subaltern speak?', in Carey Nelson and Lawrence Greenberg (eds), *Marxism and the Interpretation of Culture* (Basingstoke: Macmillan, 1988), pp. 271–313.

Storey, Mark, *Robert Southey: A Life* (Oxford: Oxford University Press, 1997).

Stout, Benjamin, *The Loss of the Ship 'Hercules', 16 June 1796*, ed. A. Porter (Port Elizabeth: Historical Society of Port Elizabeth, 1975).

——, *Narrative of the Loss of the Ship 'Hercules', Commanded by Captain Benjamin Stout, on the Coast of Caffraria, the 16th of June, 1796; Also a Circumstantial Detail of his Travels through the Southern Deserts of Africa, and the Colonies, to the Cape of Good Hope. With an Introductory Address to the Rt. Honourable John Adams, President of the Continental Congress of America* (London: J. Johnson, 1798).

Strangman, Edward, *Early French Callers at the Cape* (Cape Town: Juta, 1936).

Strother, Z. S., 'Display of the body Hottentot', in Bernth Lindfors (ed.), *Africans on Stage: Studies in Ethnological Show Business* (Bloomington: Indiana University Press), pp. 1–61.

Subrahmanyam, Sanjay, *The Career and Legend of Vasco da Gama* (Cambridge: Cambridge University Press, 1997).

Symson, William, *A New Voyage to the East Indies* (London: A. Bettesworth, 1715).

Szeman, Imre, 'Who's afraid of national allegory? Jameson, literary criticism, globalization', *The South Atlantic Quarterly* 100, 3 (2002), pp. 803–27.

T. C. 'Bruce, John (1745–1826)', in Leslie Stephen (ed.), *Dictionary of National Biography*, Vol. VII (London: Smith and Elder, 1886), pp. 107–8.

Tachard, Guy, *Relation of the Voyage of Siam Performed by Six Jesuits* (London: J. Robinson and A. Churchil, 1688).

Tavernier, Jean Baptiste, *The Six Travels of Jean Baptista Tavernier, Baron of Aubonne, through Turkey and Persia to the Indies during the Space of Forty years. Giving an Account of the Present State of those Countries, viz. of their Religion, Government, Customs, and Commerce. As also the Figures, Weights, and Value of the Money and Coins severally Current therein. The Second Part: Describing India and the Isles Adjacent*, trans. J. P. (London: R. L. and M. P., 1678).

Taylor, George, 'Anti-slave trade drama in England: 1786–1808', *South African Theatre Journal* 13, 1 and 2 (1999), pp. 9–19.

Terry, Edward, *A Voyage to East India* (London: J. Martin and J. Allestrye, 1655).

Thapar, Romila, *Cultural Pasts: Essays in Early Indian History* (New Delhi: Oxford University Press, 2000).

Theal, G. M., *The Portuguese in South Africa* (Cape Town: Juta, 1896).

——, *Records of the Cape Colony: From February 1793 to December 1796*, Vol. 1 (Cape Town: Government of the Cape Colony, 1897).

——, *Records of the Cape Colony: From December 1799 to May 1801*, Vol. 3 (Cape Town: Government of the Cape Colony, 1898).

——, *Records of the Cape Colony: From July 1806 to May 1809*, Vol. 6 (Cape Town: Government of the Cape Colony, 1900), pp. 408–41.

——, *Records of the Cape Colony: From February to April 1825*, Vol. 20 (Cape Town: Government of the Cape Colony, 1904), pp. 188–340.

——, *Records of South-Eastern Africa*, Vol. 8 (Cape Town: Struik, [1902] 1964).

——, *Short History of South Africa (1486–1826) for the Use of Schools* (Cape Town: Darter Brothers, 1890).

Thomaz, Luís Filipe, 'Factions, interests and Messianism: the politics of Portuguese expansionism in the East, 1500–1521', *The Indian Economic and Social History Review* 28, 1 (1991), pp. 97–109.

Thompson, George, *Travels and Adventures in Southern Africa*, ed. Vernon S. Forbes (Cape Town: Van Riebeeck Society, [1827] 1967).

Thompson, Leonard, *The Political Mythology of Apartheid* (New Haven, CT: Yale University Press, 1985).

Tilly, Charles, *Coercion, Capital, and European States, ad 990–1992* (Oxford: Basil Blackwell, 1990).

Tytler, William, *Principles of Translation* (London: T. Cadell and W. Davies, 1797).

Umino, Rumi, 'A backyard (hi)story: doing *geskiedenis* among Griqua people in South Africa', in Kenji Yoshida and John Mack (eds), *Preserving the Cultural Heritage of Africa: Crisis or Renaissance?* (Oxford: James Currey, 2008), pp. 27–42.

Vail, Leroy and Landeg White, *Capitalism and Colonialism in Mozambique: A Study of Quelimane District* (London: Heinemann, 1980).

Vale, Peter and Sipho Maseko, 'Thabo Mbeki, South Africa and the idea of an African Renaissance', in Sean Jacobs and Richard Calland (eds), *Thabo Mbeki's World* (London: Zed Press, 2002), pp. 121–42.

Van der Spuy, Patricia, '"Making himself master": Galant's rebellion revisited', *South African Historical Journal* 34 (1996), pp. 1–28.

Van Duin, Peter and Robert Ross, *The Economy of the Cape Colony in the Eighteenth Century* (Leiden: Centre for the History of European Expansion, 1987).

Van Jaarsveld, F. A., *Van Van Riebeeck tot Vorster, 1652–1974* (Johannesburg: Perskor, 1976).

—— and G. D. Scholtz (eds), *Die Republiek van Suid Afrika: Agtergrond, Ontstaan, en Toekoms* (Johannesburg: Voortrekkerpers, 1966).

Van Oordt, J. W. G., *Slagtersnek: Een bladzijde uit de voorgeschiedenis der Zuid Afrikaansche Republiek* (Amsterdam and Pretoria: J. H. de Bussy, 1897).

Van Pallandt, A., *General Remarks on the Cape of Good Hope* (Cape Town: Trustees of the South African Public Library, 1917 [1803]).

Van Schoor, M. C. E. and J. V. Van Rooyen, *Republieke en Republiekeine* (Cape Town: Nasionale Boekhandel, 1960).

Van Vuuren, H., '"Op die limiete": Karel Schoeman se *Verkenning* (1996)', *Literator* 18, 3 (1997), pp. 57–78.

Van Wyk Smith, Malvern (ed.), '"The most wretched of the human race": The iconography of the Khoikhoin (Hottentots) 1500–1800', *History and Anthropology* 5, 3–4 (1992), pp. 285–320.

——, *Shades of Adamastor: African and the Portuguese Connection: An Anthology of Poetry* (Grahamstown: NELM, 1988).

Verwoerd, H. F., 'Herinneringe', in F. A. Van Jaarsveld and G. D. Scholtz (eds), *Die Republiek van Suid Afrika: Agtergrond, Ontstaan, en Toekoms* (Johannesburg: Voortrekkerpers, 1966), pp. 7–10.

Vicente, Gil, *Three Discovery Plays*, trans. and ed. Anthony Lappin (Warminster: Aris and Phillips, 1997).

Vigne, Randolph (ed.), *Guillaume Chenu de Chalzac, the 'French Boy'* (Cape Town: Van Riebeeck Society, 1993).

Vladislavic, Ivan (ed.), *T'kama-Adamastor: Inventions of Africa in a South African Painting* (Johannesburg: University of Witwatersrand Press, 2000).

Voss, A. E., '"The slaves must be heard:" Thomas Pringle and the dialogue of South African servitude', *English in Africa* 17, 1 (1990), pp. 61–81.

Wahrman, Dror, *The Making of the Modern Self: Identity and Culture in Eighteenth-Century England* (New Haven, CT and London: Yale University Press, 2004).

Waldman, Linda, *The Griqua Conundrum: Political and Socio-cultural Identity in the Northern Cape, South Africa* (Bern: Peter Lang, 2007).

——, 'Klaar gesnap as Kleurling: the attempted making and remaking of the Griqua people', *African Studies* 65, 2 (2006), pp. 175–200.

——, 'The past: who owns it and what should we do about it?', *South African Historical Journal* 35 (1996), pp. 149–54.

Walker, Cheryl, *Land-Marked: Land Claims and Land Restitution in South Africa* (Auckland Park: Jacana, 2008).

Ward, Kerry and Nigel Worden, 'Commemorating, suppressing, and invoking Cape slavery', in Sarah Nuttall and Carli Coetzee (eds), *Negotiating the Past: The Making of Memory in South Africa* (Cape Town: Oxford University Press, 1998), pp. 201–17.

Waswo, Richard, *The Founding Legend of Western Civilization: From Virgil to Vietnam* (Hanover, NH: University Press of New England, 1997).

Waterboer, Andries, *A Short Account of Some of the Most Particular and Important Circumstances Attending the Government of the Griqua People* (London: Council for World Mission Archives, South Africa, Incoming Letters, No. 141, 1827).

Watson, R. L., *The Slave Question: Liberty and Property in South Africa* (Middletown, CT: Wesleyan University Press, 1990).

Weeks, William Earl, 'American nationalism, American imperialism: an interpretation of United States political economy, 1789–1861', *Journal of the Early Republic*, 14, 4 (1994), pp. 485–95.

Weidlich, Brigitte, 'Southern Africa's Bushmen face lifestyle threat', *Mail and Guardian*, 14 October 2007.

Welch, Sidney R., *South Africa Under King Manuel, 1495–1521* (Cape Town: Juta, 1946).

Wheeler, Roxann, *The Complexion of Race: Categories of Difference in Eighteenth-Century British Culture* (Philadelphia: University of Pennsylvania Press, 2000).

White, Hayden, *Metahistory: The Historical Imagination in Nineteenth-Century Europe* (Baltimore: Johns Hopkins University Press, 1973).

Whiteway, R. S., *The Rise of Portuguese Power in India 1497–1550* (Westminster: Archibald Constable, 1899).

Wicomb, Zoë, *David's Story* (Cape Town: Kwela Books, 2000).

Wieringa, P. A. C., *De oudste Boeren-republieken, Graaff-Reinet en Zwellendam van 1775 tot 1806* (s-Gravenhage: Martinus Nijhoff, 1921),

Wilmot, A., *The History of South Africa* (Cape Town: J. C. Juta, 1901).

—— and J. C. Chase, *History of the Colony of the Cape of Good Hope: From its Discovery to the year 1819 by A. Wilmot, Esq. From 1820 to 1868 by The Hon. John Centlivres Chase, M. L. C.* (Cape Town: J. C. Juta, 1869).

Winkler, Harald, 'Land reform strategy: new methods of control', *Review of African Political Economy* 61 (1994), pp. 445–8.

Witz, Lesley, 'Eventless history at the end of apartheid: the making of the 1988 Dias Festival', *Kronos* 32 (2005), pp. 162–91.

Worden, Nigel, '"Armed with ostrich feathers": cultural revolution and the Cape slave uprising of 1808', in Richard Bessel, Nicholas Guyatt and Jane Rendall (eds), *War, Empire and Slavery, 1770–1830* (London: Palgrave, 2010), pp. 121–38.

——, 'The changing politics of slave heritage in the Western Cape, South Africa', *Journal of African History* 50 (2009), pp. 23–40.

——, *Slavery in Dutch South Africa* (Cambridge: Cambridge University Press, 1985).

—— and Clifton Crais (eds), *Breaking the Chains: Slavery and its Legacy in the Nineteenth-Century Cape Colony* (Johannesburg: Witwatersrand University Press, 1994).

—— and Gerald Groenewald (eds), *Trials of Slavery: Selected Documents Concerning Slaves from* the Criminal Records of the Council of Justice at the Cape of Good Hope, 1705–1794 (Cape Town: Van Riebeeck Society, 2005).

York, Anne, 'Travels in India: Jean-Baptiste Tavernier', in Glenn J. Ames and Ronald S. Love (eds), Distant Lands and Diverse Cultures: The French Experience in Asia, 1600–1700 (Westport, CT: Praeger, 2003), pp. 135–46.

Zinn, Howard, A People's History of the United States, 1492– the Present (New York: Harper Collins, 1995).

'Zuma hails Afrikaners, 2 April 2009', http://news.iafrica.com/sa/1377481.htm (accessed 10 November 2009).

# Index